The Lajjāgaurī and Ānandanāyakī

The Lajjāgaurī and Ānandanāyakī

A New Light on the Nature and Worship of the Ādi-Mātā, the Primordial Mother

BY

Rāmacandra Cintāmaṇ Ḍhere

Translated from Marāṭhī
and with an introductory chapter and annotation
by

Jayant Bhālcandra Bāpaṭ

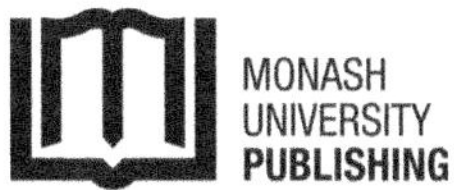

The Lajjāgaurī and Ānandanāyakī: A New Light on the Nature and Worship of the Ādi-Mātā, the Primordial Mother, by Rāmacandra Cintāmaṇ Ḍhere; translated by Jayant Bhālcandra Bāpaṭ

Monash University Publishing
Matheson Library and Information Services Building
40 Exhibition Walk
Monash University
Clayton, Victoria 3800, Australia
www.publishing.monash.edu

Monash University Publishing brings to the world publications which advance the best traditions of humane and enlightened thought.

Monash University Publishing titles pass through a rigorous process of independent peer review.

ISBN: 9781925835243 (paperback)
ISBN: 9781925835250 (pdf)
ISBN: 9781925835267 (epub)

www.publishing.monash.edu/books/la-9781925835243.hmtl

Series: Monash Asia Series
Series Editor: Marika Vicziany

Design: Les Thomas

Cover painting: © Amit Kammar. Used with permission.

A catalogue record for this book is available from the National Library of Australia.

Contents

This translation is dedicated to the primordial mother goddess
who has visited me in many human female forms
and made sure that this book saw the light of the day.

To
Anne Feldhaus
Anuṣā Gavāṇkar
Marika Vicziany
Carol Bolon
Mṛnāl Bhāve
Suhāsinī Agnihotry
Sunandā Bāpaṭ

Jayant Bhālcandra Bāpaṭ
Translator

Acknowledgements

This translation of Ḍhere's most talked about book is a result of over 20 years of intermittent work and has involved different helpers at different times. I am grateful to those who spent their time helping me. The list is long and I am sure I will still miss some names. I only hope they will understand. Listed below are those who must be mentioned.

First and foremost, I must acknowledge a huge debt to three people. Without their help, this translation would not have seen the light of the day. This work contains several Saṃskṛt words, and as a result, includes a very large number of diacritics. It is also very dense in many parts. All of this has meant that the proofreading of it has been a nightmare. Professor Anne Feldhaus and Dr Ian Mabbett, both very close friends, did this unenviable task which literally took them many months. Anne and Ian went through the entire manuscript thoroughly and literally dotted the i's and crossed the t's. Their help, which bordered on stretching the bonds of friendship, has been, for me, a godsend. And Professor Marika Vicziany, who has been a close friend for a number of years, made sure that I continued working on this arduous task. But for her encouragement and support I would have given up this task some years ago. Marika has been a constant source of help for the South Asianists in Austrlia for many years.

Avināś and Suhāsinī Agnihotry spent many a long hour going through the draft several times before I submitted the final manuscript to Monash University Publishing. Avināś also helped me with creating the Index, a difficult task indeed. Professor Mṛṇāl Bhāve offered many thoughtful suggestions. Greg Bailey volunteered to go through the entire completed manuscript and especially the diacritics, and he did all of this within a month.

Our Ph.D. student in India, Anuśā Gavāṇkar, her husband Aniruddha, and their daughter Zuī spared no thought, time or money in order to photograph *Lajjāgaurī* images in Mahārāṣṭra, Karnāṭaka and Gujarāt. Anuśā was also able to get me some very important contacts. I can never repay Anuśā for the enormous amount of work she has done and keeps on doing.

I am thankful to Carol Bolon, who not only provided many images including the large Nāganāthakoḷḷa one, but also sent me her notes on

Lajjāgaurī, written at the time when she produced her important and beautiful art folio on this goddess.

Dr Tejas Garge, Director of Archaeology and Museums, Mahārāṣṭra State, India, took personal interest in my work and offered not only his suggestions but also practical help in acquiring many of the photos of *Lajjāgaurī*. He even organised a special photo shoot of the images at Nāgpūr. I thank Prasād Pawār from Nāgpūr museum for these photos.

The three Ḍhere siblings: Aruṇā Ḍhere, Varśā Gajendragaḍkar and Milind Ḍhere, offered me their help and encouragement when I needed it. Milind provided me with a photo of Aṇṇā included in this book and Varśā promptly answered my queries.

Prof. Mādhavī Narsaḷe, Department of Saṃskṛt, University of Mumbaī, helped with the translation of some difficult Saṃskṛt passages and helped me with some archaic Marāṭhī.

Prof. V.H. Sonāwaṇe made available *Lajjāgaurī* images from around Gujarat. I thank Prof. Ajith Prasād, Head, Department of Archaeology, M.S. University of Baroḍā, for permission to photograph these images.

I must thank Revaṇsiddha Lāmture, Ter, whose knowledge and enthusiasm about *Lajjāgaurī* gave me a lot of help and encouragement. Revaṇsiddha and his late father were custodians of hundreds of *Lajjāgaurī* images before they so kindly handed over the entire collection to the Government of Mahārāṣṭra. Mr Amol Goṭe, Curator, Ter Museum, shared valuable information with me and provided many photographs.

Cetan Rājāpūrkar, coin collector and researcher, provided me with rare images of *Lajjāgaurī* coins and seals and also two *Lajjāgaurī* images in his private collection.

Dr Ravi Korisettar, Karnataka University, has been a source of constant help for me. It was through Ravi that I acquired the excellent painting of *Lajjāgaurī*, drawn by his student Amit Kammar, which adorns the front cover of this book. Dr Ravi and Dr Arjuna Rao provided me with their map of the places where images of *Lajjāgaurī* were discovered.

Anil Ināmdār (American Institute of Indian Studies [AIIS], Puṇe), helped with many Archaeological Survey of India [ASI] contacts.

I am also grateful to the following for their help:

Dr Vandanā Sinhā (AIIS). Sabyasācī Mukherjī (Director General, Chatrapatī Śivājī Mahārāj Vastu Saṅgrahālaya, [CSMVS]), Mumbaī. Aparṇā Bhogal and Pratik Aroskar (CSMVS). Professor G.B. Ḍeglurkar and Professor M.S. Māṭe (Deccan College, Pune). B.S. Gajul (Deccan College Museum), Pune. Dr N.R. Visālātchy (Department of Archaeology and Museums, Government of Telangana). K. Lourdusāmy, Dr Reṣmā Sāwant and Dr Śiv Kumār Bhagat (ASI, Dhārwāḍ Circle). Bhujaṅg Bobaḍe (Museums Heritage). Dr Maya Śahāpūrkar (Solāpūr University) for helpful suggestions. Prof. Arun Pāṭhak, Retired Director, Gazetteers Department, Mahārāṣṭra State.

I thank Amit Kammar for sharing his painting of *Lajjāgaurī* with me and for allowing me to use it for the front cover. Prakāś Pujārī, the priest at Rāmtīrth, shared information about Rāmtīrth. Atindra Kaṭṭī provided with the Kandhār *Lajjāgaurī* Image. Jayaśrī Kulkarṇī (Vyankaṭeś Mahājan College, Osmānābad) helping with contacts in the Osmanabad region.

I thank Les Thomas for his treatment of Amit's painting for the front cover.

Last but not least, Monash University Publishing and in particular, Dr Nathan Hollier and Joanne Mullins deserve many thanks. They have been most understanding, patient and supportive of my requirements. Joanne had to patiently answer every query of mine. She has always been very prompt in her answers and suggestions.

I owe many thanks to my close friend and neighbour, John Harris, for providing the superb line drawings.

Finally, I owe my gratitude to wife Sunandā, who has always shown great patience and understanding in my lonely academic pursuits.

Jayant Bhālcandra Bāpaṭ
Translator

Image Credits

The photographs and Illustrations are subdivided into the following groups. All of the people listed below have given permission to use the photos and illustrations in this translation.

Illustrations by John Harris: Figures 1 to 4; Plate 16.
Photographs taken by Jayant Bāpaṭ: Plates 11, 12, 18, 19, 21.
Photographs taken by Dr Carol Bolon: Plates: 2, 7, 10, 13, 14, 15.
Photographs taken by Ms. Anuśā Gavāṇkar and commissioned by Jayant Bāpaṭ: Plates 17, 20, 22, 23, 24.
Photographs supplied by Dr Tejas Rege. This includes images from Chhatrapatī Śivājī Mahārāj Vastu Saṃgrahālaya (CSMVS), Mumbaī; Nāgpūr Museum and Ter Museum: Plates: 5, 8. The translator is grateful for the assistance given in this regard by Prasad Pawar and Amol Gote.
Photograph supplied by Cetan Rājāpūrkar: Plate 3.
Photographs supplied by Prof. Sonāwaṇe, M.S. University of Baroḍā: Plates 4, 6, 9.
Photograph supplied by Dr Ravi Korisettar and Dr Arjuna Rao: Plate 1.

A Note on Diacritics

This book contains a very large number of Marāṭhī, Saṃskṛt and Kannaḍā words. Although translations into English have been provided where necessary, the translator is of the opinion that the reader, especially the non-Indian one, needs to be able to pronounce words in these languages correctly. This is often not done. Mispronunciation can occasionally result in entirely changing the meaning of the word in Indic languages. It is with this thought in mind that the International Diacritic Convention has been used throughout this book to write Marāṭhī, Saṃskṛt, Hindī and Kannaḍā words, including Indian names. Viz., the name 'Rao' is often pronounced 'Re-o' by non-Indians. I have therefore changed this to *Rāv* to make it clear. Only the non-Indian names (i.e. Kramrisch, Codrington etc.) have been left with their original spellings.

It was felt that. at the risk of being pedantic, this action was necessary to keep uniformity in the pronunciation of words.

I hope that the reader will forgive me for this rather unorthodox approach.

Jayant Bhālcandra Bāpaṭ
Translator

Preface

In 1998 the Metropolitan Museum of Art in New York acquired a miniature sandstone statue of the 'Lotus Headed Fertility Goddess *Lajjāgaurī*' dated to Central India in the 6th century C.E. This exquisite carving of the goddess is rare, for in recent centuries her followers on the Indian subcontinent have diminished as other goddesses have found favour. Despite this relative decline, *Lajjāgaurī* is perhaps one of India's oldest goddesses with images of her found in South Asia dating back to the Indus Civilisation c. 3000 to 1500 B.C.E. According to Max le Martin,[1] her devotees can be traced back even earlier to the Ukraine c. 10,000 B.C.E. In India, new finds continue to expand the geographical spread of *Lajjāgaurī*'s devotees (see Plate 1), most recently to Odiśā.

My good friend and colleague Dr Jayant Bāpaṭ has spent many years translating *Lajjāgaurī*, an important and unique study of the disembodied Indian goddess by the outstanding Marāṭhī cultural specialist Rāmcandra Cintāmaṇ Ḍhere. It is therefore with much pleasure that I can recommend this work to the English-speaking reader. I am aware of only one other English translation of Ḍhere's considerable body of work, that by Anne Feldhaus of *The Rise of a Folk God: Viṭṭhal of Pandharpur* (Oxford University Press, New York, 2011).

As scholarship becomes more inclusive, and less focused on the narrower body of works produced in English, Monash University is pleased to take the lead in publishing translations of important Asian texts to bring world class Indian scholarship to international attention. In the Faculty of Arts at Monash University, we also have a dedicated group of some ten scholars deeply engaged in the study of Indian religions. This has provided the nurturing intellectual environment for Dr Bāpaṭ's translation.

Ḍhere's work on *Lajjāgaurī* is based on tireless pursuits of her image throughout western India. In contrast to the other thousands of Indian goddesses whose images are superabundant, *Lajjāgaurī* has become more reclusive as other deities have risen. Hence, locating *Lajjāgaurī* images has been time-consuming and difficult. Some of the western Indian terrain that Ḍhere spoke about has been visited by Dr Bāpaṭ in his quest to not only appreciate the nature of this 'shameless goddess' who appears to have exposed her genitals to the world, but also to understand the extent of Ḍhere's scholarly work and his ability to bring together the vast array of images with other rare documentary sources and interviews.

The first major study of *Lajjāgaurī* appeared in 1992 when Carol Radcliffe Bolon published *Forms of the Goddess Lajjāgaurī in Indian Art* (College Art Association, USA, Indian Edition by Motilal Banarsidass, 1997). Dr Bolon spent many months working with a Marāṭhī language assistant translating parts of Ḍhere's work, for without access to this important study her own book would have been incomplete. However, the translation was not systematic and whilst informing Dr Bolon's research in important ways, did not lend itself to publication. Dr Bolon's struggles with Ḍhere's original text provide testimony to the importance of the current work by Dr Bāpaṭ.

As Editor of the Monash Asia Series, I would like to take this opportunity to thank Professor Anne Feldhaus for her support to this translation project. The challenging translation work that Monash University has become committed to cannot be successfully completed without the kind of expert advice Professor Feldhaus has given us on numerous occasions.

Marika Vicziany
Director, National Centre for South Asian Studies
Editor, Monash Asia Series, Monash University Publishing

Endnote

1 Le Martin, Max. 2012. *The Goddess Lajja Gauri*. Creative Independent Publishing Platform, Amazon Digital Services LLC – Kdp Print. USA.

Introduction to R.C. Ḍhere and His Works *Lajjāgaurī* and *Ānandanāyakī*

By Jayant B. Bāpaṭ
Translator

Rāmcandra Cintāmaṇ alias Aṇṇā Ḍhere was born in 1930 and spent his early childhood in his maternal grandparents' home at Nigḍe, a small village in Puṇe district. Having lost his parents in his early childhood, he was brought up by his then ninety-year old grandmother and his maternal uncle, who was a bachelor. As a rule, rural Brāhmins in Mahārāṣṭra are used to a spartan existence. However, the abject poverty and the loss of his parents in very early childhood must have made life difficult for Aṇṇā.

The family had virtually no money and suffered severe hardships. In 1944, when he was only 13, Aṇṇā and his little sister were sent to Puṇe to stay with relatives for further education. Within a few years, they lost their grandmother and uncle as well. Aṇṇā used whatever money he could raise from the meagre assets at his family home to support himself and his sister. In addition, he worked during the day to earn his living and went to night-school to complete his education.

As his daughter, Aruṇā, points out,[1] Aṇṇā's early life in the village influenced him deeply. The social and religious world of the village made a lasting impact on him.[2] He was fascinated by village gods and goddesses, folk performances such as Gondhaḷa[3] for the goddess, Tamāśās,[4] Vāghyā-Muraḷī Jāgraṇas for the god Khaṇḍobā,[5] celebrations of the birthdays of various gods and goddesses, the *kīrtanas* performed at temples,[6] and the visitations of Vāsudev, Bhutye and *Potrāj*[7] at the homes of local families. With this deep background in folk culture, Aṇṇā decided to take an unusual step and make his living by researching folk traditions and culture, and presenting these to readers in book form. It was certainly a bold step for a Brāhmin child who had no money. It would have been typical for most Indians in these circumstances to look for a permanent clerical job with the Government, something that Brāhmins coveted. Thankfully, Aṇṇā succeeded in his research and writing, and his publications were well received. They also provided a reasonable income. He produced an enormous amount of substantial research in the form of more than one hundred books and scores of research papers.

Besides making sure that Aṇṇā and their children were properly fed and looked after, Indubālā, his devoted wife, carefully vetted the large number of people who wanted to visit Aṇṇā, assuring that he had the free time to devote himself to his work. Aṇṇā's health was always a problem. He struggled with many health-related issues throughout his life. His quest for knowledge must have been a lonely task too, due perhaps to the physical problems he suffered and the extreme poverty and hopelessness he faced in his early years. That was probably the reason for his special interest in the literature produced by the Marāṭhā Saints.[8]

In order to appreciate Aṇṇā's writing, one needs to understand that Aṇṇā was essentially a poet; an accomplished one at that. Between 1948 and 1960, Aṇṇā wrote, amongst other things, 'Saṅgītikās' (plays with poetry as a major part of them). Much of this was produced for 'All India Radio'. Although his research mind shaped his writing and made him famous, it was his poetic make-up that produced the literary quality and beauty of his writing. The poet within him made sure that his research output was never dry or mundane. It also allowed him to maintain his humanity and embrace logical thought without sacrificing his ardent desire to seek beauty, godliness and the sacred. As a result, Aṇṇā's writing always captured the hearts of the Marāṭhī literati. In addition to enhancing their appetite for fundamental inquiry, sound reasoning and original research, Aṇṇā's lucid and poetic language made sure that he developed a devoted readership. To me, his great success is measured not only by the volume of his work but also the originality of his ideas and the poetic language that he used. Significantly, much of his writing had a strong devotional fervour.

Few people in Mahārāṣṭra, or anywhere in India, have done more to record and analyse the nature of folk culture than Ḍhere. Had Aṇṇā written in English, he would have had no difficulty in occupying the ranks of the other great researchers in folk-culture and mythology, such as D.D. Kosambī, Joseph Campbell, Mircea Eliade and Heinrich Zimmer.

My Interaction with Aṇṇā Ḍhere

It is not uncommon for retired Indian scholars to enter into the study of Hinduism, irrespective of their earlier fields and pursuits. However, having spent nearly 30 years in teaching and research in Chemistry by the late 1970s, Hinduism and Indological research were far from my mind. A very sad event in the life of one of my close friends got me involved in performing a Hindu funeral for his wife in 1978, and that changed my outlook completely. The near absence of Hindu priests in the Australia of the time persuaded me that this was an essential community service that I needed to get myself involved in. I started learning Hindu rituals in a hurry. Collecting of books, manuscripts etc., soon followed. My knowledge of Saṃskṛt came in handy. It was at this time that I decided to investigate the possibility of taking up academic research into Hinduism and Indology. I approached La Trobe University in the early 90s. They allowed me to enrol in a Master's degree by research and soon this was converted into a doctorate. My thesis topic was 'The Gurav Temple Priests of Mahārāṣṭra'. The Guravs, despite being regarded as low caste Śūdras and hence non-Brāhmins, were priests in the majority of Śiva and Goddess temples in Mahārāṣṭra. I decided to focus on this anomaly in my doctoral work.

No one in Australia knew about the Guravs. I went to India to find specialists and everyone pointed me in the direction of Ḍhere. Known popularly as Aṇṇā, I met Ḍhere for the first time in late 1978. Despite the family's reputation for being selective in choosing their visitors, I was welcomed into his home. That was the first of many visits in December each year when I undertook field work and saw Aṇṇā more than a few times a week. By the end of each session with him, I would have filled more than a dozen pages in my notepad. He spoke non-stop about the places I needed to visit, the diaries I needed to keep, the people I should interview and the nuances and inner meanings I should look for. By the time we ended our 1 to 2-hour sessions, I used to be overwhelmed by the amount of information he had provided. It was Aṇṇā who told me that history was not just dates and happenings, but that it was a chronicle of human endeavour and activity and culture. It was he who introduced me to *Sthalapurāṇas* and *Jātipurāṇas.* With his guidance, I published my first paper on the 'Gurav Jātipurāṇas'. He was happy with the result and announced it at a meeting held in his honour in Puṇe. He said words to the effect that scholars in India had ignored an important historical source, the *Jātipurāṇas*, but a foreign scholar, Jayant Bāpaṭ, had taken up the task successfully.

I studied most of Aṇṇā's books carefully, but his book '*Lajjāgaurī*' captured my heart. *Lajjāgaurī* is the name of a nude goddess who was, and still is, worshipped by women who are unable to have children. Her images show her in the form of a nude female torso with large breasts and a prominent vagina. The head, hands and feet may or may not be present. It is her striking iconography that made her 'risqué' in the eyes of Brāhmins. She was called obscene and the places of her worship became secret, kept well away from mainstream Hindu temples. Ḍhere was convinced that these images of *Lajjāgaurī* represented the mother earth in the process of giving birth.

His book *Lajjāgaurī* was so powerful, so moving and so profound that I read it many times. I then decided that it needed to be translated into English and introduced to an international readership. With his permission, I embarked on the task of translation that proved a lot more difficult than I thought.

Firstly, in his own words, Aṇṇā was a devout person. He worshipped village gods and goddesses with fervent devotion. The poet within him came alive when he described village festivals that celebrated the special days for gods and goddesses, the devotees, the folk dances, the loud drums and cymbals, and the atmosphere filled with ardent devotion accompanied by chants. It was this devotion that seeped through his writing. While it read beautifully in Marāṭhī, proper translation of it was another matter. Aṇṇā's poetic base made the translation even more difficult.

Secondly, the way he wrote Marāṭhī was at times archaic and difficult to follow. Thirdly, he often quoted very old Marāṭhī verses and quite a lot of Saṃskṛt poetry. Because of all of this, I often found it impossible to translate many of his nuances into English. Having spent many frustrating hours at this task, I became a firm believer in the Sapir-Whorf hypothesis, which states that there are certain thoughts of an individual in one language that simply cannot be understood by those who live in another language. The controversial hypothesis also states that the way people think is strongly affected by their native languages. I discovered that I was not alone in this feeling of frustration. Anne Feldhaus, who has beautifully translated another great work of Ḍhere's, namely *Śrī Viṭṭhala, Eka Mahāsamanvaya*[9] (*Lit. Śrī Viṭṭhala – A Great Synthesis*), has commented on how hard she found it to convey the true meaning of Ḍhere's work.

I will now comment on some key aspects of Ḍhere's work so that it is easier for the reader to understand his exposition of the goddess *Lajjāgaurī.*

Mother Earth

The worship of mother earth in human form seems to be ancient. Small figurines of female deities, thought to represent the earth as a mother, have been found all over the world. Such terracotta figurines dating back to 3000 B.C.E.[10] have also been found at the excavation sites of the Indus Valley Civilization. Early humans marvelled at the infinite capacity of mother earth to transform a seed into a fully blossoming plant. They were also fully aware of the cycles of life: birth, death and regeneration. Therefore, the earliest primordial images of the Earth Mother glorified a female fecundating principle that held the secret of life and death within itself.[11] The deified mother earth thus came to be looked upon as the symbol of fertility, generation and sustenance.[12] In Hindu thought, she was called Śakti, the creative force emanating from the gods, and was raised to the rank of the divine mother 'Pṛthivī' (*Lit*: the earth, the broad one), who produces and sustains the entire universe. The evidence of Śakti worship in the Indian subcontinent may go as far back as 10,000 years.[13] In conceiving an image for the earth mother, it was natural for early humans to think of the human mother whose functions of ovulation, lactation and parturition were similar. In the words of Eliade:

> ...thus, woman comes to symbolize the irreducibility of the sacred and the divine, the inapprehensible essence of the ultimate reality. Woman incarnates both the mystery of creation and the mystery of Being, of everything that *is*, that incomprehensibly *becomes* and *dies*, and is *reborn*.[14]

Around 1000 B.C.E., with the eventual mix of the Aryans, the local tribes and others, an intermingling of ideas and beliefs, the 'Atharva Veda' was born.[15] One of the Atharvan hymns, addressed to the mother goddess, expresses the anguish of a sage when it discusses creation and destruction. It says:

> What of these [plants] I dig out, let them quickly grow over, let me not hit thy vitals or thy heart.[16]

This feeling of reverence towards the mother earth is still very much prevalent in Hindu thought, both in Brāhminic and folk Hinduism. Thus, one of the daily Hindu prayers worships the earth and seeks forgiveness for walking on her.[17] Also, Hindus perform an elaborate ritual called 'Vāstuśānti' to bless a newly built house. The mother earth (dharādevī/dharaṇīdevī) is worshipped at the end of this ritual and a prayer is chanted to propitiate her and to beg her forgiveness. It says:

> In the construction of this home, I am sure to have destroyed grass seed and roots of various plants. I also removed trees. I have hurt you Mother Earth, by striking you with sharp instruments … Please forgive me for this transgression and bless me.[18]

Previous Work on Goddess *Lajjāgaurī*

Because of her striking imagery, *Lajjāgaurī* has attracted the attention of archaeologists, art historians and historians. However, only two books contain a detailed study of her. Jagdīś Nārāyāṇ Tiwārī's doctoral thesis (published as a book in 1985) included a chapter on *Lajjāgaurī*. Tiwārī agreed with Sāṅkaliā (quoted below) that the origin of *Lajjāgaurī* was foreign. To both of them, her probable precursor was Baubo, the Greek Goddess.

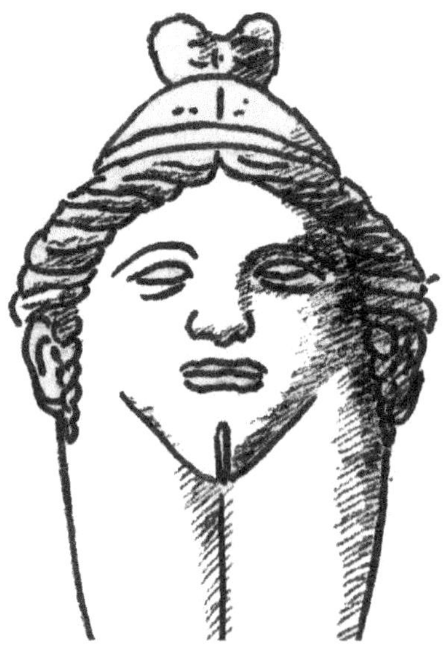

Figure 1: Line Drawing of Bobo
Courtesy John Harris

Ḍhere refuted this; he was convinced that the origin of *Lajjāgaurī* was unquestionably in India.

The second book was the first art-historical study of *Lajjāgaurī* by Carol Radcliffe Bolon in 1997.[19] In a beautifully produced volume entitled 'Forms of the goddess Lajjā Gaurī in Indian Art', Bolon has discussed in detail the origin and iconography of the goddess *Lajjāgaurī*. Her work contains several excellent photographs of the goddess as well. Bolon believes that the image of *Lajjāgaurī* evolved in four stages, from an Uttānapāda (*Lit*: raised legs) pot form to a fully anthropomorphic form. Although I have fundamental problems with this classification,[20] there is no doubt that Bolon's is probably the major and exhaustive study of this goddess. A stylised line drawing of Goddess *Lajjāgaurī* is shown below.

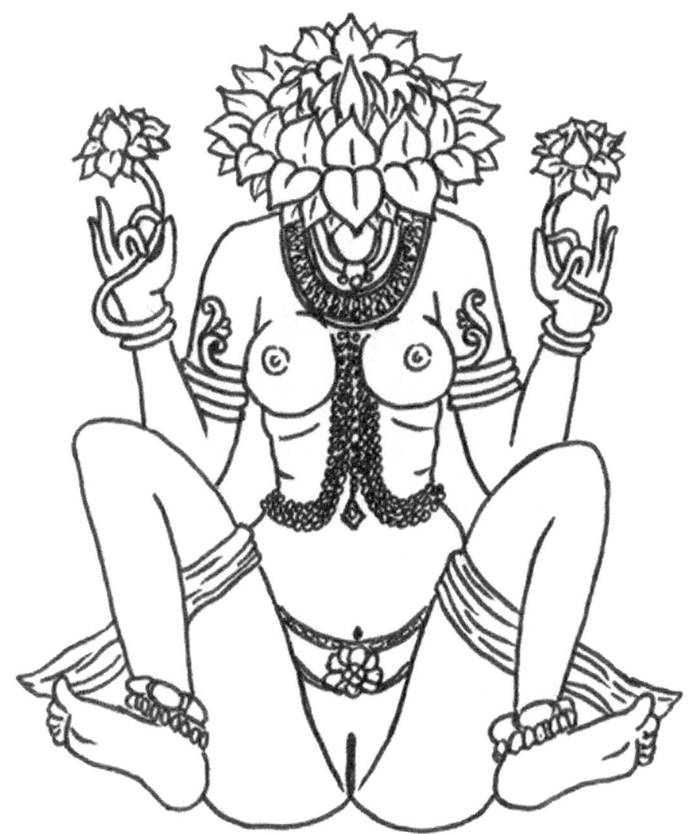

Figure 2: A stylised line drawing of *Lajjāgaurī*
Courtesy John Harris

Apart from these two works, important research papers were written by Campbell (1884),[21] Marshall (1915),[22] Hunter (1933),[23] Codrington (1935),[24] Kramrisch (1956 and 1975),[25] Sāṅkaliā (1960),[26] Dhavaḷīkar (1979–80),[27] Sonāwaṇe (1988),[28] Janssen (1991),[29] Parāśar-Sen (2001),[30] Nassim Khān (2002),[31] Jāmkheḍkar (2004),[32] and Miśrā and Mohanty (2002–2003).[33] I find Nassim Khān's paper about *Lajjāgaurī* seals found in a cave in the present day Afgānistān particularly interesting (See Fig. 3 below). It goes to show the prevalence of *Lajjāgaurī* worship all over India since ancient times. It also ties in well with *Lajjāgaurī* images, seals and coins found in many parts of India.

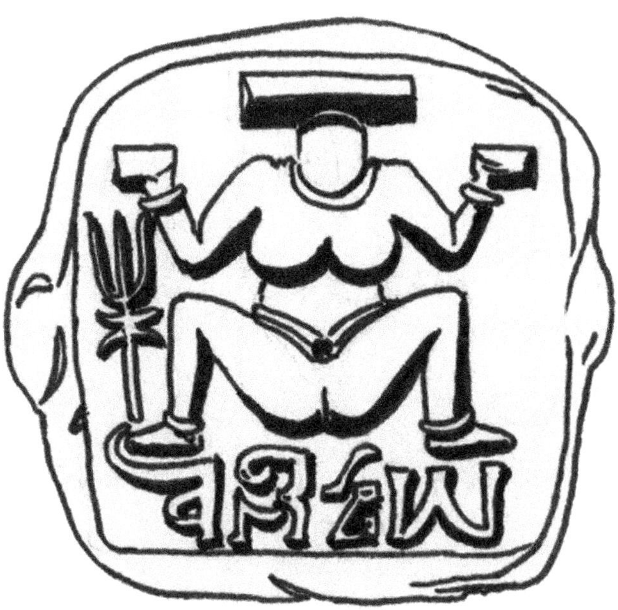

Figure 3: Line drawing of a seal found in a cave in Afgānistān
Courtesy John Harris

My interest in the manner in which this goddess was projected and in the translation of Ḍhere's book led me to examine a number of *Lajjāgaurī* images throughout India. This research culminated in the publication of a chapter on *Lajjāgaurī* in a volume on Indian goddesses in 2008.[34] In that chapter, I have discussed the work of the above-named scholars. The reader is asked to refer to it for background on the previous work on this goddess.

Finally, it is most interesting to know that *Lajjāgaurī* images, seals and what appear to be coins have also been found in many places in western and central India and in particular, places such as Ter in Mahārāṣṭra (see Plates 2–16 and 18).

A collector and researcher in ancient coins and seals, Cetan Rājāpūrkar from Nāsīk in India, has in his collection a number of such coins that have the *Lajjāgaurī* image on one side and images of bulls, elephants, mountains and rivers on the other side.[35] These coins are thought to go back at least to the pre-Sātavāhana period (1st century B.C.E. to 2nd century C.E.). Rājāpūrkar believes that they date back to 400–300 B.C.E. The coins have been found in Mahārāṣṭra, Āndhra Prades̀ and Madhya Prades̀. In Rājāpūrkar's opinion, the reason for inclusion of *Lajjāgaurī* images on coins was probably to do with showing the importance of creation in humans and in nature. This view is supported by the fact animals and nature were portrayed on the other side of the coin. Unfortunately, none of the coins have any script or numbers that would identify the dynasty or the time of their production. The very large number of finds at Ter are particularly interesting because almost all of them are very small in size, varying between 3 and 5 centimetres. One of the broken seals in this collection clearly shows a picture of a Nandī bull (see Plate 16). This strongly suggests that when this seal was made, goddess *Lajjāgaurī* was a part of Śiva's pantheon. Also, the very large number of coins and seals found at Ter indicate that Ter was probably a place where the goddess image was produced in commercial quantities.

The Uniqueness of Ḍhere's Work *Lajjāgaurī*

Ḍhere's writing displays four scholarly virtues: 1) his intimate knowledge of the folk culture of Mahārāṣṭra, 2) his great capacity to connect seemingly diverse data to generate new insights into the patterns of Indian culture, 3) his poetic style of writing, which makes his work so pleasurable to read, and 4) his academic honesty in reconciling his devout Hinduism with the needs of scholarship. He was not a puritanical Hindu.

Ḍhere's writing was directed only to fellow Mahārāṣṭrians and his readership was fundamentally limited to the Marāṭhī literati. Paradoxically, within Marāṭhī literary circles he was an outsider, because he brought folk culture into Marāṭhī academia. Ḍhere pointed out the difference between the classical Hinduism of the *Purāṇas* and how this diverged from the folk culture expressed in *Jātis* (castes). Also, Ḍhere was not a typical scholar according to the Western traditions of scholarship – for example, he did not engage in any reviews of existing literature or theories. Nor did he think of himself purely as a historian. Rather, as a student of cultural history, Ḍhere always looked beyond history. To him, history was much more than a catalogue of chronological dates. He thought of himself as a specialist in Indian mythology, and gave himself the task of prising out the inner meaning of Indian legends. By sound reasoning, he was often able to place the myth within a cultural milieu and thereby arrive at the historical time and date for it. He frequently went against the accepted wisdom of the time. Given his commitment to logical reasoning, he happily faced his critics but refused to change his arguments. Despite disagreements, he was always civil and never resorted to any personal vendettas against any of them. Three of his works, *Cakrapāṇī, Śrī Viṭṭhala* and *Lajjāgaurī,* faced a lot of criticism when they were published, especially from conservative Hindus. Ḍhere's response was to say:

> People always confuse the search for God and the search for human thinking about God. These two must be kept separate. The first one is concerned with a person's looking inwards in search of the truth. The second on the other hand deals with societal beliefs and norms. If one researches the latter in relation to the circumstances of the time and the structure of the society at the time, there is no need to upset personal beliefs about the divine'.[36] (Translation mine)

When the critics were eventually silenced, what remained was praise, accolades and honours – not that he cared much for any of this.

Ḍhere's writing has provided the academic world in India and beyond with an enormous amount of information about Hindu sects, traditions, folk culture and religion, and the history of Mahārāṣṭra in the middle ages. As Ghāre has said, 'the pathway towards tracing the beginnings of culture goes invariably through the difficult terrain of folk literature'.[37] Ḍhere's writing is a living testimony to this dictum. His work on *Lajjāgaurī* provides a powerful example of the nature of his contributions to Indian cultural understandings. I turn now to comment on that work next.

There are a number of factors that make Ḍhere's *Lajjāgaurī* unique. Firstly, Ḍhere chose a topic of great sensitivity for the Indian public in the late 1970's. It was not easy to write an entire book about a nude image that had been denounced as shocking, erotic, obscene, self-displaying and immoral. Ḍhere turned around these common perceptions into an understanding for their essentially 'sacred and divine' nature. Although he did face some criticism because of the controversial nature of the topic, his work was never called erotic or obscene.

Secondly, Ḍhere had a unique interpretation of the mother figure of *Lajjāgaurī*. There are many books on the concept of the divine 'mother'. The topic is very broad and has been explored by environmentalists, feminists, fiction writers, art-historians, psychologists and mythologists. But Ḍhere's mother, as *Lajjāgaurī*, procreates and sustains. For the act of procreation, she needs a male partner. To follow nature's cycles of generation, death and regeneration, mother earth herself goes through the cycles of being a virgin expecting to be united with a male principle, procreating, and then being a virgin again. This is why in her iconography, the *Lajjāgaurī* shows no indication of pregnancy. Although the legs are spread, there is only a hint of the generative organ: a vertical line denoting the pudendum. Naturally her partner does not have to be the same every time. In fact, she is never seen as a consort deity like Lakṣmī and Pārvatī, who depend on their consorts and who do not display a separate existence.[38] Mother-earth, on the other hand, is both transcendent and immanent; her functions involve the creation, preservation and destruction of the universe.[39] Unlike the consort goddesses, who do not seem to have children, mother earth is a true mother.[40]

Ḍhere notes that *Lajjāgaurī* is aptly called the 'perpetual virgin'. In his book, he has shown her taking four such forms, well-known in folk culture and literature: *Lajjāgaurī*, Joguḷāmbā, Mātaṅgī and Aditi. But she is the same earth-mother. Among others, Jotibā and Subrahmaṇya are two of her partners. The work *Lajjāgaurī* is probably the first instance where a detailed treatment of the male consort is rendered. In doing so, Ḍhere looked at many folk gods such as Khaṇḍobā, Jotibā, Hanumān, Subrahmaṇya and Viṭṭhal, in village India. He had already written on many of these folk gods before.[41] However, I believe that when he wrote *Lajjāgaurī*, the eternal and fundamental truth must have dawned on him. That truth was that the various folk goddesses were none other than the earth-mother, whereas the male gods represented the male consort she chose to take at certain times. That to me represents the great synthesis of Ḍhere's ideas about the procreative principles.

Ḍhere, as I have pointed out earlier, was a highly devout individual who saw divinity in every aspect of life. To him, *Lajjāgaurī* was the mother-earth incarnate and she had to be worshipped as such. As she was his mother, he also felt awkward in approaching her naked figure and discussing her anatomy. He sought her forgiveness for doing so and said that he had approached her as her child and she should take him in her lap and forgive his transgression.

Lajjāgaurī to *Ānandanāyakī*: A Natural Progression

In thinking and writing about *Lajjāgaurī*, Ḍhere assumed the role of a devout child. He saw her as the mother who gave birth to nature and to mankind. He was the child who wanted to fathom the greatness and universality of the mother, and he approached her in that spirit. It was *Lajjāgaurī*'s womb that had produced him and her breasts that had sustained him. To further study the procreatrix in her natural form of a womb was the next progression in Ḍhere's thought processes. This is when he saw her as *Ānandanāyakī*, the goddess in her womb form.[42] When he stood at the entrance of the cave that was the shrine of this goddess, he was filled with a sense of awe, mystery and divine presence (see Plate 17).[43] He perceived that he was a foetus in the womb of this goddess. In his words:

> In the inner recesses of my mind, I felt that the cave in which this sculpture of the goddess has been placed is in itself the original form of goddess *Ānandanāyakī*. That is her real form. As soon as I felt that, my physical body simply dissolved into nothingness. In its place, I felt that a lustrous foetus, which was aware of this transformation, had occupied the womb of the great mother. I got goose-pimples all over...For a while I thought that I was the foetus in the golden egg of the universe.[44] (Translation mine)

Ḍhere left this world on the 1st of July 2016. I have no doubt that mother earth took this child in her lap and he will be reborn again in the golden womb (*Hiraṇyagarbha*) of the *Ānandanāyakī*.

Endnotes

1 Ḍhere, Aruṇā. 2000. Prastāvanā (*Lit*: Introduction). In *Lokasaṃskṛtīce Prātibha Darśana* (*Lit*: An Inspired Look at Folk Culture). Edited by Aruṇā Ḍhere and Varṣā Gajendragaḍkar, Puṇe, India: Padmagandhā Prakāśan. (This introductory chapter has no page numbers.) This exhaustive work was produced on Ḍhere's 70th birthday by his daughters. It contains articles by eminent writers and critics on Ḍhere's unique achievements and also contains an overview of his writing.

2 Translator's note: As Ḍhere himself says, 'The inspiration for every writer comes from his upbringing, the environment in his childhood and his heritage. Call it his 'baggage' if you like, that is what shapes his future personality which in turn produces his writing style. My special interests in folk culture and literature, and in the writings of Marāṭha saints have their seeds in my childhood environment and experiences. Ḍhere, R.C. 1998. *Santa, Loka āṇi Abhijana*. Puṇe, Padmagandhā Prakāśan. Introductory chapter entitled, '*mājhyā preraṇā*' (*Lit*. My inspirations). (In Marāṭhī.)

3 Translator's note: A 'Gondhaḷa' is a song and dance performance staged by men of the Gondhaḷī caste in honor of goddesses Reṇukā, Bhavānī and Ambābāī. It constitutes a secular component of an important rite of passage such as a marriage or threading ceremonies amongst the Maraṭhas and some Brāhmin sub-castes. The tradition dates back over a thousand years.

4 Translator's note: The 'Tamāśā' is a specific type of folk theatre in Mahārāṣṭra. Traditionally, the performance begins with a devotional song to Lord Gaṇeśa followed by a *Gauḷaṇ*, a farce that details the escapades of the god Kṛṣṇa as a child.

5 Translator's note: Vāghyā and Muraḷī are traditional devotees of the folk god Khaṇḍobā in Mahārāṣṭra. Vāghyā is a male child and Muraḷī is a female child offered to Khaṇḍobā for life. Their all-night performances are called the Jāgraṇa and consist of dancing and singing praises of the god.

6 Translator's note: A '*kīrtana*' is a temple performance and is a part of the *Bhaktī* tradition. The performer is known as a *kīrtnakāra*, *kathekarī* or *haridāsa*. He usually tells purāṇic stories and instructs people about moral and spiritual conduct and observation of social norms.

7 Translator's note: The 'Vāsudev' is a member of a nomadic caste that seeks alms by visiting people's homes in villages and entertaining them by singing about the deeds of god Kṛṣṇa. He wears a dress made up of peacock feathers. A '*Bhutyā*' (plural Bhutye) is a member of another nomadic caste in Mahārāṣṭra who is a traditional worshipper of the goddesses Bhavānī or Reṇukā. Bhutye dance and sing songs about these goddesses. A '*Potrāj*' is another such nomad who visits people's homes singing songs about goddess Mariāī. Traditionally the males wear female dresses and the accompanying females carry the image of the goddess in the basket that they carry on their heads. The *Potrāj* carries a long leather whip and flagellates himself while he calls the goddess aloud.

8 Translator's note: In addition to several research papers about them, Ḍhere wrote over twenty-five books on the Saints and their literature. Indian Saints almost invariably suffered in the hands of the society, who mercilessly persecuted them.

9 Feldhaus, Anne. 2011. *The Rise of a Folk God: Viṭṭhal of Pandharpur.* New York: Oxford University Press.
10 Preston, James J. 1980. *Cult of the Goddess.* New Delhi: Vikās Publishing House: 10.
11 Jayakar, Pupul. 1989. *The Earth Mother.* New Delhi: Penguin Books. Foreword.
12 Translator's note: While singing her praises, the Atharva Veda devotes an entire hymn (The Atharva Veda, Hymn 12.1.1) to Goddess Earth. It is called *Pṛthivī Pālupada Sūkta.*
13 Clark, J. Desmond and Williams, Martin. 1986. Paleoenvironments and Prehistory in North Central India: A Preliminary Report. In: Jerome Jacobson, ed., *Studies in the Archeology of India and Pakistan*, New Delhi: Oxford and IBH publishing: 39.
14 Eliade, Mircea. 1969. *Yoga: Immortality and Freedom.* Second Edition. New Jersey: Princeton University Press: 203.
15 Translator's note: It is not my intention to enter into a debate about the highly controversial theory of Aryan migration at this juncture. The fact remains that during Vedic times, there were people who called themselves Aryans, spoke the Saṃskṛt language and by the time the *Atharvaveda* was composed, had mixed with local Indian tribes and others. The Aryan migration theory however seems to be on firmer grounds at present with the latest research suggesting that such migration did take place. See: https://bmcevolbiol.biomedcentral.com/articles/10.1186/s12862-017-0936-9, Accessed 27th June 2017.
16 Jayakar, *op.cit*, p. 58.
17 Translator's note: *samudravasane devī parvatastanamaṇḍale* । *viṣṇupatnī namastubhyam pādasparṣam kṣamasva me* ।
Lit: Oh Goddess (Earth), the waters of the sea are your clothes. The mountains are your breasts. You are the wife of Lord Viṣṇu. Please forgive me for stepping on you.
18 *Pūjito 'si mayā vasto homādyaiḥ racanaiḥ śubhaiḥ* ॥
prasīda pāhi viśveśa dehi me gṛhajaṃ sukham ॥1॥
vāsudeva namaste 'stu bhūśayyābhrata prabho ।
madgṛhaṃ dhanadhanyādi samṛdhaṃ kuru sarvadā ॥ 2 ॥
prārthayāmītyahaṃ deva śālāyāḥ adhipastu yaḥ ।
prāyascittaprasaṅgena gṛhārthe yanmayā kṛtam ॥ 3 ॥
mūlachedaṃ tṛnachhedaṃ kṛmikīṭaṃ nipātanam ।
hananaṃ jalabījānaṃ bhūmau śastreṇa ghātanam ॥ 4 ॥
anṛtaṃ bhāṣitaṃ yacca kiṃcit vṛkṣyasya pātanam ।
etatsarvaṃ kṣamasvaino yanmayā duṣkṛtaṃ kṛtam ॥ 5 ॥
gṛhārthe yatkṛthaṃ deva gṛhaśālāṃ śubhāṃ kuru ।
tatsarvaṃ kṣymyatāṃ deva gṛhaśālāṃ śubhāṃ kuru ॥ 6 ॥
19 Radcliffe Bolon, Carol. 1997. *Forms of the Goddess Lajjā Gauri in Indian Art.* First Indian Edition. New Delhi: Motilal Banarsidass Publishers. Originally published in 1992 by College Art Association, USA.
20 Translator's note: I have spelt out this issue in detail in Note 421.
21 Campbell, James McNabb. 1884. Bombay: *Gazetteer of the Bombay Presidency.* Vol.XXXIII, Bijāpūr.

22 Marshall, John. 1915. Excavations at Bhītā. Calcuṭṭā: *Annual Reports of the Archaelogical Survey of India,* 1911–12.
23 Hunter, G.A.P. 1933. Antiquities from Mahūrzarī. In Y.K. Deśpaṇḍe (ed.), Yeotmāl: *Śāradāśrama Vārśik*: 30–35.
24 Codrington, Kenneth de Burgh. 1935. Iconography: Classical and Indian. *Man*, 35, No. 70: 65–66.
25 Kramrisch, Stella. 1956. An Image of Aditi Uttānapād. *Artibus Asiae*, Nos 3–4. Pp. 259–270. See also, Kramrisch, Stella. 1975. The Indian Great Goddess. *Journal of the History of Religion*, 14, No. 4, May: 235–265.
26 Sāṅkaliā, H.D. 1960. The Nude Goddess or Shameless Woman in Western Asia, India and South Eastern Asia. *Artibus Asiae*, 23, No. 2: 111–23.
27 Ḍhavḷīkar, M.K., 1979–80. *Lajjāgaurī. Bulletin of Deccan College Research Institute*, 40: 30–35.
28 Sonāwaṇe, V.H., 1986. Some Remarkable Sculptures of Lajjā Gaurī from Gujarat. *Lalit Kala*, 23: 27–35.
29 Jānssen, H.P.M., 1991. On the Origin and Development of the So-Called Lajjā Gaurī. In: A.J Gail and G.J.R. Mevissen, eds., *South Asian Archaeology*, 34: 458–472.
30 Parāśar-Sen, Aloka. 2000. Squatting Goddesses or Lajjā Gaurīs of the Deccan. In: C.P. Sinha and U.C. Dwivedi, ed., *Proceedings of the 9th Session of the Indian Art History Congress*, Guwāhāṭī: Sandīp Prakāśan: 201–208.
31 Nassim Khān, M. 2002. *Lajjāgaurī* Seals and related antiquities from Kāśmīr Smāst-Gandhāra. *Journal of the Society for South Indian Studies*, 18 (8).
32 Jamkheḍkar, A.P. 2004. Symbols, Images and Rituals of the Mother in Vakāṭaka Period. *Lalit Kalā*, 30: 23–39.
33 Miśrā, Bābā and Mohanty, Pradīp. 2002–2003. Headless Contour in the Art Tradition of Orissa, Eastern India. In: *Bulletin of the Deccan College Post Graduate and Research Institute*, vol. 62–63: 311–321.
34 Bāpaṭ, Jayant Bhālcandra. 2008. The *Lajjāgaurī*: mother, wife or yoginī, In: Jayant Bhālcandra Bāpaṭ and Ian Mabbett, eds., *The Iconic Female: Goddesses of India, Nepal and Tibet*, Clayton: Monash University Press: 79–111.
35 Personal communications with Cetan Rājāpūrkar. I am most grateful to Cetan for sharing photos of some of these seals with me.
36 Naik, Subhāṣ. 2000. Abhiṣṭacintana: *Dr. R.C. Ḍhere Sahitya Sūcī,* Year 21, Issue No. 6. July: 9–16. (In Marāṭhī.)
37 Ghāre, Dīpak. 2000. Lokasāhitya: Śodha āṇi Samīkṣā (Lit: Folk Literature: Search and Examination). In Aruna Ḍhere and Varṣā Gajendragaḍkar, Ed., *Lokasaṃskṛtīce Prātibha Darśan*, Puṇe: Padmagandha Prakāśan: 317. (In Marāṭhī)
38 Erndl, Kathleen. 1993. *Victory to the Mother.* New York: Oxford University Press: 4.
39 Translator's note: It is most remarkable that such sentiments about the genetrix have been expressed in every culture and civilization. For example, Marijā Gimbuṭās, in discussing the goddesses of old Europe, says: 'The female goddesses were the creative principle. The waters of heaven and earth are under their control. The Great Goddess emerges miraculously out of death, out of the sacrificial bull, and in her body the new life begins.

She is not the earth, but a female human, capable of transforming herself into many living shapes…' See Gimbutas, Marija. 1982. *The Goddesses and Gods of Old Europe*. New updated edition. Berkeley and Los Angeles: University of California Press: 236.

40 Erndl, *op.cit*., p. 6.

41 Translator's note: For Ḍhere's exposition of the various folk gods and goddesses, See the following: For Khaṇḍobā, See 2002. *Dakśiṇecā lokadev Śrīkhaṇḍobā*. Puṇe, Padmagandhā Prakāśan. For Lakṣmī, See 1990. *Lokasāhitya: Śodh āṇi Samīkṣā*. Puṇe, Śrī Vidyā Prakāśan, Ch. 7. On Marāṭhī folkculture, See 1996. *Lokasamskṛtīce Upāsak*, Puṇe: Padmagandhā Prakāśan. Ch. 13. (All In Marāṭhī).

42 Translator's note: The idea of a cave representing a womb or the vagina is not new. There are many similarities between a cave and the human vagina. To start with, many caves are similarly shaped, most caves are dark inside and many of them are either moist inside or have water in them. The similarity did not go unnoticed in ancient times. Thus, several ancient caves have been found in Bulgaria which are vagina shaped and some have been further sculpted to exactly resemble the vagina. The most famous one, known as the 'Womb Cave' is near the village of Nenkovo and was discovered in 2001. It is actually a temple, shaped like the opening of the vagina. It is 22 metres deep and 2.5 metres wide. Water seeps constantly through the walls. At the deep end, there is a carved altar which symbolises the womb. At midday, sunlight seeps into the cave through an opening in the ceiling and projects a phallus shaped beam on the floor. The phallus grows longer as the sun progresses further, eventually reaching out to the womb of the Great Mother Goddess. For the ancient Thracians, this was the symbolic fertilizing of the Goddess' womb. See http://visit.guide-bulgaria.com/a/259/the_womb_cave.htm. Accessed 24th February 2017.

43 Translator's note: The shrine of goddess Ānandanāyakī is part of a temple complex at Rāmatīrtha, 35 kilometres from the town of Athṇī (Dist: Belgāv), in Karnāṭaka state.

44 Ḍhere, R.C., 2002. *Śrī Ānandanāyakī*. Puṇe: Padmagandhā Prakāśan: 45. (In Marāṭhī).

At the Entrance to the Supreme Sacred Womb

Introduction

By Dr R.C. Ḍhere

Lajjāgaurī is the mother goddess, the great mother. Right from Vedic times, she was worshipped all over India as the goddess responsible for the creation of the universe. Even today, this practice continues in some parts of India in a small way. Although the prevalence of this form of worship may have diminished today, the importance and greatness of the mother principle continues unabated. Further, human desire to understand and fathom the reasoning behind the diverse naming of this principle is also everlasting. The present work, *Lajjāgaurī*, is a modest attempt on my part to fathom the secrets behind the various names given to this primordial mother principle.

Since *Lajjāgaurī* is worshipped in the form of the female generative organ, her image, by definition, represents the womb for the procreation of the universe. I am only too conscious of the fact that standing in front of this sacred womb in order to fathom the secrets of this mother-principle is awkward, bordering on an obscene and even sinful activity. However, supporting me in my endeavour is the ardent adoration of those worshippers who imagined her, produced her images and worshipped her in that form. I stand in front of her as her infant son. I know that she, as the very essence of forgiveness, will forgive me and bless me.

My book, *Lokasaṃskṛtīcī Kṣitije*, was published on the 9th of August 1971. Incorporated in it was an essay titled *Bālagrahāñcī Upāsanā* (worship of the young planets). In this essay, I criticised H.D. Sāṅkaliā's thesis about the headless image found in the excavations at Ināmgāv in the State of Mahārāṣṭra. After reading my essay, my friend M.S. Māṭe drew my attention to another headless image of a goddess.

Some well-known archeologists and art critics of international repute have put forward their views about this image. The arguments of Stella Kramrisch, H.D. Sāṅkaliā, and Jagdīś Nārāyaṇ Tiwārī are especially important in this regard. I have never been satisfied by the explanations given by these scholars. With my experience in this field over a decade, I have formed a firm belief that, in the absence of devotion, no amount of effort can unfold the secrets of the object of devotion. I therefore started my search into the origin of this strange goddess from the standpoint of studying the tradition of devotion to her. As I researched her in this fashion day and night in the inner sanctum of my mind, she finally revealed her deepest secrets to me by the end of 1971. After that, I studied the very large number of available references and literature. In this new light, her form became more and more visible and ever clearer to me. I had many discussions on this topic with my friend Professor Narahar Kurundkar, and his encouragement and support strengthened my convictions. Whatever I experienced and understood was bounding out from within me to assume the form of the written word. Unfortunately, however, since I earn my living only by writing, other more urgent writing took precedence and I was unable to attend the calls from within, to continue working on *Lajjāgaurī*. I did however produce a lengthy research article on the images of this goddess at Mahākūṭa and Ālampūr and passed it on to my friend Arvind Maṅgḷūrkar for comment. In spite of acute time constraints, he read it and expressed his profound delight. However, since I wanted to publish my research only in the form of a book, I did not rush to publish my essay. In April 1973, Paṇḍit S.G. Jośī collected it from me for publication in *The Marāṭhawāḍa Research Annual*. Tarkatīrtha Lakśmaṇśāstrī Jośī read it for him and was most impressed. The eminent historian and researcher Dr V.B. Kolate also read my essay and talked about it enthusiastically. He also informed me that another image of the strange goddess had been discovered at Mahūrzarī.

Unfortunately, the publication of the above Annual was put off time and time again and I was forced to publish my essay as a booklet on October 25, 1973. It was entitled *Śaktipīṭhañcā Śodha* (*Lit.*: 'The search for the seats of the *Śakti*'). In this publication, I also included a section on Mahūrzarī as a *Śaktipīṭha*. Besides this article, I also published other articles on this important topic in popular magazines such as *Navabhārat*, *Pratiṣṭhān*, and *Santakṛpā,* and in the newspaper *Kesarī*.

Many knowledgeable people were kind enough to congratulate me personally. Bhāusāheb Māḍkholkar (Taruṇ Bhārat, 21st April 1974) and Professor Narahar Kurundkar (Kesarī, 13th January 1974) wrote detailed newspaper reviews of my booklet *ŚaktiPīṭhañcā Śodha*. Researchers including Drs. M.S. Māṭe, M.K. Dhavḷīkar, V.J. Vākaṇkar and Bālkṛṣṇa Dābhāḍe sent me detailed letters.

Professor Dābhāḍe has carefully examined the ancient Mahūrzarī artifacts several times. He has photographed the *Lajjāgaurī* image found there and has personally examined another *Lajjāgaurī* image found at Mansar, currently housed in the Nāgpūr museum. With this background, Professor Dābhāḍe wrote to me that:

> Dr. Kolate has been able to read the copper plate found at Mahūrzarī. He has been unable to place Pṛthivipūra and Pṛthivisamudra... Your interpretation of it shows your genius. It is also noteworthy that you have been able to do it while sitting at Puṇe. Anyone who has travelled extensively around Mahūrzarī will be duly impressed by this new interpretation. The relationship between Pṛthivisena, Pṛthivipūra and Pṛthivisamudra is certainly very important and will arouse avid interest... There is a large tank at Mahūrzarī and experts date it to the pre-Christian era. In the town itself and around the tank, there are stone circles – probably burial sites. Dr. S. B. Dev thinks that they belong to the period between the 6th and 8th centuries B.C. It is likely that the tank at Mahūrzarī was known at that time as Pṛthivisamudra.[1]

Along with his letter, Professor Dābhāḍe has also sent me a rough map of Mahūrzarī. In it, he shows the Samudra (tank) to the north of the present village, the stream (*Skt.*: *jharī*), also to the north of the village, the exact places where the images of the earth mother and other mother goddesses were found, and the placement of the old and new villages. With the information and map that he sent, my literature-based research has been strengthened. I am indebted to him for his steadfast co-operation.

Two great scholars, Dr Vāsudevaśaraṇ Agrawāl and Dr D.D. Kośāmbi, have forever been my inspiration. These thinkers act as the sources of valuable monographs with every single statement they have made. Their books and research papers have been guiding beacons for me in this venture as well. I am forever indebted to these scholars, and I offer them my filial respect. I also thank my many friends.

Although I have made use of disciplinary insight in attempting to unfold the mystery of *Lajjāgaurī*, I have not allowed that – or logic, for that matter – to distract me from aesthetics. Moreover, I sincerely believe that my learned readers will find this exposition not only informative but also analytical.

One learns to appreciate the beauties of nature by developing a thousand eyes. Similarly, the mystery of the emotions, beliefs and aspirations that emanate from within the human mind must be enjoyed with a thousand eyes made up of knowledge and intellect. It is otherwise impossible to enjoy that beauty fully. It would be a great pity if we confined ourselves to a narrow scientific focus. That will certainly limit our view and we will become short sighted. I beseech my readers to warn me in time if they believe me to be guilty of this sin.

Rāmacandra Cintāmaṇ Ḍhere

Endnote

1 Ḍhere discusses this in detail in Chapter 2, *Joguḷāmbā*.

Foreword

By Dr R.C. Ḍhere

'Oh Mother of the World!'

The many splendoured universe and human life, coloured with many desires and uncertainties, have both emanated from your womb. Having recognized your enormous power to conceive and create life forms, the Vedas called you *uttānā mahī*, the extended, spread out, earth mother. Oh divine mother! Your Vedic name *Aditi* has occurred time and time again in the Purāṇas.

It is you who appeared in the guise of Reṇukā and initiated the worship all over South India of your generative organ in the form of the anthill made out of soft *reṇūs*, i.e., specks of sand. It is from this anthill form that your representation as *Yonimūrtī*, the image of the female generative organ, has evolved. Oh Kamalā! The lotus (*kamala*) is also the symbol of your all encompassing generative power. As a partner in this celebration of regeneration, you embraced the male principle variously as the bull, the horse, the serpent and the cloud in the shape of the elephant.

Oh great earth mother! Please forgive me for walking on you.

Rāmcandra Cintāmaṇ Ḍhere

Chapter 1

The *Lajjāgaurī*

The history of Śakti worship is as old as the history of humankind itself. Humans seem to have imagined and worshipped god first of all in the form of the female principle, a goddess who possessed the secret of the complex and mysterious act of creation. The mother goddess is the primordial power in the cultural history of humankind. Humans gave her the highest prominence, saw her as a many-splendoured being, addressed her with myriad names and worshipped her in a variety of ways. The researcher who attempts the study of the history of Śakti worship from every possible angle comes across many different and unexpected turns and bends in the flow of human life. In that process, he unravels the inner secrets of the human mind.

The worship of the female principle has pervaded the cultural history of India in a very major way. Śākta worship is not confined only to the Tāntrics. It has, until recently, influenced the daily religious activities of many Indians. One hears of the greatness of Śakti worship in the literary wellsprings from the Aditi of the *Ṛgveda* to the Bhavānī/Reṇukā sung to in the songs of the Bhutyes and Gondhaḷīs, the village bards who come to one's doorsteps from time to time. The continuity in the worship of the mother goddess can be seen from the three-thousand-year-old images found on the banks of the Sindhu river to the still-active shrines of Grāmadevatās found in villages in every nook and corner of India.

The iconization of the mother goddess is as amazingly diverse as her description in literature. While she exhibits her primitive form in the shape of the un-sculpted stone covered with red-lead, she also expresses herself in her full-fledged form with many hands adorned with weapons. All these forms of her represent to us the way she manifests herself to her devotees. Unless one carefully attempts to unravel the many loose threads that have been woven in this complex pattern, one would not be able to comprehend the peculiarities and complexities of her iconic forms.

The Goddess with the Strange Form

In the excavations performed at Tagarpūr in Marāṭhawādā (Currently 'Ter' in Osmānābād district of Mahārāṣṭra State), some very strange images of a goddess have been discovered. These images are made of fired clay. In these images, the female form is totally nude and consists only of the area below the navel. In addition, both legs are shown folded at the knees and spread sideways so as to accentuate the shape of the vulva. Lotuses adorn all four corners of the image.

Similar images have been discovered at excavations elsewhere. By themselves, none of these excavated images can tell us anything about the mystery of their creation. To shed light on that, one must search for the devotees of this strange goddess form. It is the imagery in the minds of devotees that gives rise to particular iconographic forms of deities. Fortunately, even today, there are places where the worship of images such as those found at Ter is still very much alive and prevalent. The present work details my investigations into some of these places.

In the present Badāmī district of Karnāṭaka, the village of Nandikeśvara is only three miles away from Badāmī, the capital of the early Cālukyas. From Badāmī, the path leading to Nandikeśvara consists entirely of paved stone steps. Strewn around in the vicinity of this village are many ancient artifacts and sites. In particular, the group of temples called Mahākūṭa are considered important in terms of their architecture and iconography. Badāmī itself is a place of pilgrimage (*kṣetra*) considered particularly important because of the shrine of the goddess Śākambharī or Banaśankarī. It also has an ancient temple of the goddess Ellammā.

The temples of Mahākūṭa are enclosed in a large precinct protected by well-constructed stone walls. Although they display a variety of temple architectural styles, it is the Cālukyan style of architecture that is most prevalent here. The main temple in this precinct is that of Śiva, known as Mahākūṭeśvara. In the midst of the group of these temples, there is a tank called 'Viṣṇu-puṣkariṇī'. It is said to have been built by the mythical sage Agastya. In the middle of the tank there is a *maṇḍapa* which houses a beautiful four-headed image of Brahmā. According to the *Śākambharī Māhātmya*, which I describe later on, the attendants (*dvārapālas*) in front of the enclosure are the demons Vātāpī and Ilvala.

There are six inscriptions on the pillars of the Mahākūṭeśvara temple. One of them is from the reign of the Cālukya king Vijayāditya (696–733 C.E.) and records a grant given by a courtesan. The second is dated 934

C.E., and mentions a grant given by one Bappuvarasa, while the third records the grant of the pillar itself. The other three inscriptions are not important for our purposes here.

The *kṣetra*, known by the two names Nandikeśvara and Mahākūṭa, is replete not only with architectural but also natural beauty. The composer of the *Kṣetra Māhātmya* (*Lit.* importance of the place) extols the sacredness of this place by calling it the Vārāṇasi[1] of the South (Dakṣiṇa-kāśī).[2]

The Importance of Mahākūṭa as Described in the *Śākambharī – Māhātmya*

Both Śiva and Śakti are said to be found at Mahākūṭa Kṣetra. There are so many Śivaliṅgas in the place that it would not be an exaggeration to call it *Śivamaya* (engulfed entirely by Śiva). According to the *Śākambharī – Māhātmya (ŚM)*, there are crores of Śivaliṅgas here. The *ŚM* is a work that describes the greatness of the goddess Śākambharī or Banaśaṅkarī at Badāmī.[3] Claimed to be a part of the *Skandapurāṇa*, the *ŚM* mentions Mahākūṭa several times. The following verses which describe the surrounding woods, the *tīrtha*, the main Śiva temples, and the goddess are particularly noteworthy.

> *taṭe malāpahāriṇyāḥ santi liṅgāni koṭiśaḥ* |
> *tāni sarvāṇi gaditum nālaṃ varṣaśatānyapi* ||
> *bilvarājīvanaṃ cātra vidyate sumanoharam* |
> *śivayā sahitaḥ śambhurviśrāmyati sukhaṃ tviha* ||
> *viṣṇupuṣkariṇītīre mallikārjunasannidhau* |
> *pātāleśaṃ pinākīśaṃ lajjāgauryāhvyayaṃ tathā* ||
> *koṭiliṅgaṃ vaiṣṇaveśaṃ vīrabhadreśvaraṃ tathā* |
> *nārasiṅhaṃ vāmanākhyaṃ śṛgāleśvarameva ca* ||
> *etāni navaliṅgāni duritaghnāni tāpasāḥ* |
> *parvate koṭiliṅgāni bilvacandanarājite* ||
>
> (*Śākaṃbharīmāhātmyam*, 8.19–23)[4]

Thus, according to this passage in the *ŚM*, there are crores of liṅgas on the banks of the Malaprabhā river. A hundred years will not suffice to adequately describe their greatness. There are beautiful and dense forests of *Bilva* trees here and it is among these that Śiva resides happily with Śakti. At the Viṣṇupuṣkariṇī tīrtha, there are nine shrines of Śiva that cleanse us of our sins. These include Mallikārjuna, Pātaleśvara, Lajjāgaurīśvara, Koṭiliṅgeśvara, Vaiṣṇaveśvara, Vīrabhadreśvara, Nārasiṃheśvara, Vāmaneśvara and Śṛgāleśvara. This mountain, adorned with *Bilva*[5] and Sandalwood trees, houses a crore of Śivaliṅgas.

Of these nine liṅgas, Lajjāgaurīśvara (*Lajjāgaurī* + Iśvara) is none other than Śakti along with Śiva (śivayā sahitaḥ śambhuḥ). Śiva is also called Mahākūṭeśvara here. This means that the presiding goddess here is *Lajjāgaurī*. The presence of *Lajjāgaurī* among nine Śivaliṅgas must be significant, because, even at Ālampūr, she is among the nine liṅgas known as Navaliṅgeśvara (Iśvara with nine Liṅgas) or Navabrahmeśvara. One must therefore assume that the number nine is significant here. It is a common number associated with Devī, such as Navadurgā, Navarātrī, Navapatrikā etc., and needs to be further investigated.

Lajjāgaurī's Unusual Image

Lajjāgaurī is a strange name for a goddess. It is not found in the main body of literature that deals with goddesses. The image of the goddess at Mahākūṭa that bears this strange name is even stranger. Towards the end of the 20th century, Gaṇeśaśāstrī Lele Tryambakkar accompanied Sardār Raghunātharāv Vincūrkar on a pilgrimage to Mahākūṭa. He described this pilgrimage in his work called 'Tīrthayātrā Prabandha.' His description included the image of *Lajjāgaurī*:

> The *Lajjāgaurī* shrine is close to the shrine of Mahākūṭeśvara. The image of this goddess is very peculiar and strange. It is totally naked and is shown lying on her back in a position that a woman assumes during sexual intercourse. All her limbs are exquisitely sculpted and show meticulous detail. The image however has no head, only the torso below the head is shown. I have not heard of such an image elsewhere.[6]

Discovery of Similar Images

Ninety years ago, Leleśāstrī had not heard of similar images elsewhere. Now however, the existence of many such images has been recorded by researchers. The places where clay images of this goddess have been found during excavations include: Ālampūr (Tāluk: Ālampūr, District: Mehabūbnagar, Āndhra Pradesh), Nāgārjunakoṇḍā (Āndhra Pradeś), Siddhankoṭṭe (North Karnāṭaka), Saṅgameśvar (Taluk: Nandīkoṭkūr, Karnāṭaka), Vyāghreśvarī (Near Hospeṭ, Karnāṭaka), Vaḍagāv (Dist: Sātārā, Mahārāṣṭra), Ter (Dist: Osmānābād, Mahārāṣṭra), Māhūrzarī (Dist:

Nagpur, Mahārāṣṭra), Bhokardan (Dist: Aurangābad, Mahārāṣṭra), Bhītā (Uttar Pradeś) and Kauśāmbī (Uttar Pradeś).[7]

All of these images have some things in common. The figure is mostly represented as lying on her back. The legs are spread out and bent at the knees in order to accentuate the pudenda. Some of the images cover the area below the navel only, whereas others go from the shoulders down. In almost all of them, the head has been deliberately left out. The images that start from the shoulders downwards are shown with the hands folded away from the body to accentuate the breasts. The relief images at Ālampūr, Mahākūṭa and Bhītā show a lotus flower in place of the head. All three of them also hold lotuses or lotus buds in the hands. The earthen image found at Ter also contains four lotuses in the four corners of the slab. The Vaḍgāv image portrays a bull nearby.

Clearly, these images of the goddess deliberately accentuate the breasts and the vagina; i.e. the organs associated with motherhood. This explains the absence of the head, because only those organs that are associated with motherhood are to be portrayed. The images have a close connection with the lotus flower and also the bull. Among these known images, the image in the cave at Siddhankoṭṭe and the image at Mahākūṭa are both known as *Lajjāgaurī*.[8]

The Reasons for Worship

Women worship the *Lajjāgaurī* images at Siddhankoṭṭe and Mahākūṭa in order to conceive children. The composers of the *Devīkośa*[9] say that women who are unable to conceive make a vow to the *Lajjāgaurī* at Mahākūṭa. Women are said to worship the *Lajjāgaurī* at Siddhankoṭṭe for the same purpose by applying butter and red oxide of lead (*sindūr*) to the image's breasts and vagina and then offer verbal prayers.[10]

A similar goddess is housed in a small niche within the compound of the Navaliṅgeśvara temple at Ālampūr,[11] and yet another one is found at Saṅgameśvara in Nandikoṭkur district. Both of these images are also worshipped by women seeking children.[12]

The marble image of a similar goddess at Nāgārjunakoṇḍā carries an inscription underneath. This inscription in Brāhmī records that the image was created for queen Khaṇḍuvulā, the wife of king Ehavala Śantamūla of the Ikṣvāku dynasty.[13] The queen is described as Jīvatputrā (one whose sons are alive) and Avidhavā (never a widow). It is obvious that the two adjectives are used specifically to indicate the abundance of children and a long, married life.

It should be amply clear from this discussion that the goddess known as *Lajjāgaurī* at Mahākūṭa and at Siddhankoṭṭe was worshipped everywhere as a goddess who gave and protected progeny.

Previous Literature on the Subject

Although such strange images have been located at many sites in India, they have hardly been studied in any detail. Marshall has touched on the image found at Bhīṭā in the course of his discussion of the many images of mother earth found at Harappā.[14] These images include ones with a head, some in yogic postures such as the upside-down śīrṣāsana, some giving birth to plants (*vanaspatiprasū*[15]) and some nudes. In an article in *Artibus Asiae*, Stella Kramrisch[16] has sought to unravel the symbolic meaning of the image kept in the museum at Ālampūr. Kramrisch was struck by the similarity of this 'uttānapāda' (spread-eagled) image with the description of the 'uttānapāda Aditi', the mother of the universe in the Vedas. She therefore concluded that the Ālampūr image was that of Aditi. Kramrisch has also lucidly explained the relationship of the symbolism of the lotus with the act of procreation.[17]

The well-known archeologist H.D. Sāṅkaliā, however, did not agree with Kramrisch's interpretation. Writing in the same journal,[18] Sāṅkaliā put forward the hypothesis that this strange goddess must have originated in Egypt as Baubo and was probably brought into India during Roman times around the 1st or 2nd century C.E. (See figure 1. page XXIV)

Sāṅkaliā believed that Baubo's Indianization took place almost immediately after her arrival in India. He bases his opposition to Kramrisch's hypothesis on the grounds that all the images found in India belong to the post-Christian era and there is no conclusive evidence of their existence in the pre-Christian era. Sāṅkaliā, greatly influenced by Codrington and Murray,[19] could not accept the similarity between *Lajjāgaurī* and Aditi.

Quite recently (June 1971), Dr Jagdiś Nārāyaṇ Tiwārī submitted a Ph.D. thesis at the Australian National University on goddess worship in North India.[20] In two exhaustive appendices to this thesis, Tiwārī has examined in detail the nude goddess of our discussion and also another nude goddess called Koṭavī. Tiwārī agrees with Kramrisch about the symbolism of the lotus and says that the relationship between the lotus and the image is a beautiful and telling example of Indianization. He does not however agree with Kramrisch on the connection between *Lajjāgaurī* and Aditi. He supports Sāṅkaliā's view that *Lajjāgaurī* is the Indianised Baubo.

Marshall, Kramrisch, Sāṅkaliā and Tiwārī are the only four researchers who have discussed this strange and peculiar goddess image. While the attempts to discuss the possible relationship between the earth-mother Aditi and Baubo reflect on the great scholarship of these scholars, most surprisingly, they have totally ignored the worship of this goddess in the present day, her worshippers, their beliefs, and the myths and legends they have produced.

I strongly believe that no god or goddess can be adequately studied without the study of their worshippers. One must always remember the dictum, 'gods and demons have both been created by man'. One must always keep in mind that 'the concept of god is whatever worshippers make it to be'. It is impossible to understand the making of a god without the knowledge of the background.

We have seen that the goddess under discussion was identified as *Lajjāgaurī* at Mahākūṭa and at Siddhankoṭṭe. What was her name at the other places where she was worshipped? And if the names were different, what was the reason for that? What was the traditional explanation for this variety of names? How have the worshippers constructed the biography of this goddess, who has the same peculiar form but a variety of different names? How ancient is this goddess? Was she worshipped in some other iconic form before this unusual form became established? What is the reason for her torso being headless? Are there local myths and cults associated with this goddess who is found all over India? Do these myths have anything in common?

All kinds of questions such as these have challenged researchers for a long time. It would therefore not be proper to study her without coming up with answers to these questions. Only when this challenge is accepted, would one be able to decide whether Kramrisch and Marshall were correct in their hypothesis or whether Sāṅkaliā and Tiwārī's interpretation is more appropriate.

The Importance of the Image at Mahākūṭa

Since Mahākūṭa was one of the traditional centres for the worship of this goddess, it is important to see whether the study of past traditions at Mahākūṭa would help us unravel the mystery behind her image.

Although Stella Kramrisch mentioned the images found at Bhītā and Kośāmbī, the main focus of her study was the image at Ālampūr. In a detailed study, she compared the Ālampūr and Mahākūṭa images. However, because her studies were mainly concerned with comparing the sculptural and aesthetic qualities of the two images, she did not examine the tradition of worship in either place. The photograph of the Mahākūṭa image that she accompanies in her article shows that the image is badly disfigured and broken. Kramrisch ruefully mentioned that the image was lying sadly unattended in one corner of the temple precinct at Mahākūṭa (See Plate 18).

On the other hand, one can see from Leleśāstrī's description quoted earlier that, when he saw it some ninety years ago, it was intact. Dr Sāṅkaliā, on the other hand, fails altogether to mention the image.

I believe that as a centre for the traditional worship for this goddess, Mahākūṭa is particularly important. Also, after deliberating about it for a long time, I have come to the conclusion that a detailed investigation of Mahākūṭa will unravel the mystery behind the goddess's strange name.

Lañjikeśvara, Not Nandikeśvara

We have already noted that the holy place Mahākūṭa has another name, Nandikeśvara. Further, the presiding deity at this place, Śiva, is also known by two names: Lajjāgaurīśvara and Mahākūṭeśvara. One can be forgiven if one deduces from this that the two names of the *kṣetra*, Nandikeśvara and Mahākūṭa, must be closely associated with the presiding deity, Lajjāgaurīśvara and Mahākūṭeśvara. One must of course see if any historical evidence is available in support of this view. Fortunately, such evidence does exist.

In the cave temples at Badāmī, cave No. 3, called Viṣṇugṛha (Viṣṇu's abode) was commissioned by Maṅgaleśa of the Badāmī Cālukya dynasty, in the reign of his elder brother Kīrtivarmanl. Maṅgaleśa also installed an image of Viṣṇu there. A pillar in this cave contains an inscription dated Śaka 500 (578 C.E.) which states that Maṅgaleśa donated a town called Lañjīśvara for a Nārāyaṇabalī[21] and for regularly feeding sixteen Brāhmins at the place. To the left side of this inscription, there is another one by Maṅgaleśa in the Kannaḍā language. It states that a part of the income from the town is assigned to the maintenance and worship of the god.[22]

Experts in Indian inscriptions agree[23] that the town known to Maṅgaleśa by the names Lañjīśvara or Lañjigeśvara is the same as the present day Nandikeśvara. It is thus clear that Nandikeśvara is a Saṃskṛtised and phonetically similar version of the original name Lañjigeśvara or Lañjikeśvara.

Lañjikā and *Lajjāgaurī*

The *Śākambharī Māhātmya* has told us that Śiva resides at Mahākūṭa in association with Śakti. Further, to indicate his union with Śakti at this place, he has taken the name Lajjāgaurīśvara. Also, as I have just mentioned, of the two names of towns in Maṅgaleśa's inscriptions, the name Nandikeśvara is a Saṃskṛtization of the original name Lañjikeśvara. *Lajjāgaurī*, the name of the goddess, is of course a constituent part of Śiva's name, Lajjāgaurīśvara (*Lajjāgaurī* and Iśvara). It follows that in the original inscription, in the name that denotes Śiva, i.e. Lañjikeśvara, Lañjikā must be the name of the goddess. *Lajjāgaurī* is thus a Saṃskṛtized version of the name Lañjā or Lañjikā.

What then is the meaning of these words, Lañjā and Lañjikā? In this connection, I sought help form Tirumalai Tātācārya, the well-known historian and scholar of the Tamil, Telugu and Kannaḍā languages and especially of Haḷḷe-Kannaḍā. He wrote back to me saying that Lañjikā meant either a prostitute or a temple dancer (Devadasī). Kittel's Kannaḍā English dictionary[24] states that the word Lañje means an adulteress, and notes that the word is derived from Saṃskṛt. [Many] feminine words ending with 'ā' in Saṃskṛt end with an 'e' in Kannaḍā. For example, Reṇukā becomes Reṇuke. This means that the word Lañje in Kannaḍā would be equivalent to the Saṃskṛt word Lañjā. In his Kannaḍā-Marāṭhī dictionary,[25] Puṇḍalīkjī Kātagaḍe lists both Lañje and Lañjā as meaning an adulteress (vyābhicāriṇī) or an amoral woman (*durvartinī*). On the other hand, Monier-Williams, in his Sanskṛit-English dictionary, gives two meanings for the word Lañjā; Lakṣmī or a prostitute. Finally, Āpṭe's Saṃskṛt-English dictionary[26] lists Lañjā as meaning an adulteress and Lañjikā as meaning a prostitute or harlot.

This etymological discussion makes it amply clear that the original name Lañjikā for the goddess at Mahākūṭa is indicative of her nudity and shamelessness, and that *Lajjāgaurī* is a Saṃskṛtized version of the same name. Dr Sāṅkaliā's thesis that *Lajjāgaurī* is a name used euphemistically to denote a shameless woman is correct, but in a different way. It may be noted that one meaning of the word Lajjā in the Kannaḍā language is 'the private part of the female.'[27] This may be what is expressed in the name *Lajjāgaurī*.

It must be remembered that the mention of Nandikeśvara as either Lañjiśvara or Lañjigeśvara occurs in inscriptions from the 6th century. While these names refer to the town itself, it is clear that the name of the town was derived from its presiding deity. This demonstrates the antiquity of the Śiva shrine of Lañjikeśvara. The important conclusion that can be drawn from this discussion is that Lañjikā, the goddess whose name is incorporated in Śiva's name Lañjikeśvara, coalesced completely with Śiva as his Śakti, and was present at this place even before the 6th century C.E.

Lankecī Pārvatī

While deliberating upon the names Lajjā, Lañjikā and *Lajjāgaurī*, I suddenly came upon the inner meaning of the Marāṭhī phrase *Laṅkecī Pārvatī* (lit. Pārvatī from Śrī Laṅkā). This derogatory term is used to denote a woman who is dressed very plainly and is not wearing any jewellery. Marāṭhī women usually use this phrase for referring with disdain and sarcasm to a woman who does not have a single ornament on her. (They usually say, *phuṭkā maṇī suddhā nāhī aṅgāvar*, which literally means that the woman is not wearing even a broken precious stone.) To them, a woman and her womanhood are not complete without some kind of jewellery; her natural grace and inner beauty are not enough!

I do not particularly want to dwell on the excessive importance Indian women place on jewellery and ornaments. Neither do I wish to comment upon the appropriateness or otherwise of women's disdain for one who is deprived of these. The real question before me is, 'What does *Laṅkecī Pārvatī* mean? When did Pārvatī go to Śrī Laṅkā? And in Śrī Laṅkā, why did she remain without ornaments?'

To start with, Pārvati is the wife of a simple yogī. She deliberately discarded all her father's wealth and vehemently practised penance in order to marry Śiva, whose only abode is a cemetery. Thus, as Śiva's wife alone, she is the perfect example of a woman without ornaments; she does not have to have any connection with Laṅkā at all! There is no need for her to go to Laṅkā so as to remain uninterested in ornaments. The phrase *Lankecī Pārvatī* in Marāṭhī is not used for a woman who has substantial wealth, but for one who prefers not to wear jewellery. Then what exactly is the meaning of this derogatory phrase? The question is simple but perplexing.

It is well known from the Rāmāyaṇa story that Rāvaṇa, the king of Laṅkā, went to Kailāsa. However, I am not aware of any Purāṇic tale which mentions Pārvatī going to Laṅkā, and that too without jewellery. Laṅkā originally belonged to Kubera and became Rāvaṇa's kingdom later on. However, neither Kubera nor Rāvaṇa could ignore Pārvatī, because

Kubera was Śiva's close companion, whereas Rāvaṇa was Śiva's special devotee. It is inconceivable that either of the two could treat Pārvatī in a derogatory manner. Even if Pārvatī went to Laṅkā, would either Kubera or Rāvaṇa shower her with jewellery and precious stones? Certainly not! Pārvatī had chosen to be without ornaments.

Then why do we call a woman *Laṅkecī Pārvatī*? I feel that the paradox has been created by taking for granted a particular meaning for the word 'Laṅkā'. If we wish to follow this line of thought, one can say that we are either using the wrong word or that the correct meaning of the word has been lost over the years. Since Pārvatī is the wife of the great yogi Śiva who resides in the cemetery, it would be quite normal for her not to wear any ornaments. Therefore, it would be appropriate to use her name for a woman without ornaments. Hence what we should think seriously about is the mystery behind the name Laṅkā.

While Laṅkā is the name of Rāvaṇa's capital, its other dictionary meaning is 'a naked woman' or 'a prostitute'. If we take this latter meaning, then *Laṅkecī Pārvatī* would mean naked Pārvatī, unclothed mother of the world, or naked Devī. This meaning, although not literal, would fit well with our intended meaning. I obviously remembered *Laṅkecī Pārvatī* because of the similarity in its meaning with the goddess named *Lajjāgaurī*. The prefix Lajjā in *Lajjāgaurī* has been derived from the original word, Lañjā, a naked woman or a prostitute. It is quite natural for a goddess whose main function is creation to be given the name Lañjā, a name that spells out her function. The mother of the world is traditionally considered to be a virgin (Kumārī); the appearance of the male in her life is but subordinate. Therefore, there is no need for us to be concerned about her being described by a word which signifies prostitution. Since the life of a prostitute does not involve widowhood, it is customary in many parts of India for a prostitute to tie around a bride's neck the Maṅgala-sūtra, the necklace signifying married status. The great saint-poet Jñāneśvara has called a prostitute *aheva*, i.e. a woman residing on the border of the town, who is never widowed. While his reference is not complimentary and is obviously sarcastic, there is no doubt whatsoever, that a prostitute is forever not a widow.

The mother goddess has been worshipped as the presiding deity of creation since antiquity. Although her image as the Ādi-Śakti, the primordial female principle, evolved later on in many different ways, her original form is still to be seen in folk culture and religion. Many bards have sung her story through their songs. It was however understood that her name

Lañjā, which signified her original form, is but another name for Gaurī. The name *Lajjāgaurī* or Lañjāgaurī must have been coined to give her an air of respectability. Once we understand that both words Lañjā and Laṅkā have the same meaning and that both Gaurī and Pārvatī are names for the one wife of Śiva, we understand the mystery of *Laṅkecī Pārvatī.*

We invariably clothe the images of our gods and adorn them with ornaments according to our likes and dislikes. The image of *Lajjāgaurī* or Laṅkā Pārvatī, on the other hand, is in its natural form, and it has been deliberately left that way. As a matter of fact, clothing her image or decorating it in any form would be contrary to her name and the very purpose behind her name. Indian folk culture must have been very aware of this fact.

We can now understand clearly that because Laṅkā Pārvatī is a goddess without any clothes or ornaments, a woman without ornaments is compared to her. Unfortunately, the word Laṅkā was mistakenly interpreted as meaning the city of Rāvaṇa. Also, with the passage of time, the meaning of the word Laṅkā as a 'naked woman' was lost. Hence, people mistakenly interpreted Laṅkā-Pārvatī as Pārvatī from Laṅkā, and this wrong meaning eventually became common.

The Myth behind the Name *Lajjāgaurī*

We know through inscriptional evidence that the name Lañjikā given to the Mahākūṭa goddess denotes nakedness. We have also seen that the name *Lajjāgaurī* for this goddess is a Saṃskṛtization of the name Lañjikā. Folk culture, on the other hand, by its very nature, invents myths and constructs new myths which substantiate the older myths. There are several myths which explain the nakedness and headlessness of *Lajjāgaurī.* The composers of the *Devīkośa*[28] have reproduced one such myth about the image at Mahākūṭa.

> Once Śiva and Pārvatī were sporting together in a lake when a devotee happened to come there to pay homage to Śiva. Both Śiva and Pārvatī felt highly embarrassed. Śiva ran to the temple and coalesced with the *liṅga,* whereas the abashed Pārvatī assumed an invisible form and disappeared into the lake itself. The highly embarrassed and naked Pārvatī, therefore, acquired the name *Lajjāgaurī.*

The author of the *Tīrthayātrā-prabandha*, Leleśāstrī, on his pilgrimage to Mahākūṭa, made inquiries about the origin of the name *Lajjāgaurī*. The people at Mahākūṭa told him the following story:

> Once Śiva felt like testing Pārvatī's devotion and gave her a woollen quilt to look after. He then assumed the form of a rat and made a hole in it. When Pārvatī saw the hole, she was petrified because she feared Śiva's anger. In the meantime, Śiva returned in the guise of a tailor and when Pārvatī asked him to repair the hole, he agreed to do it only if Pārvatī had intercourse with him in return. Fearing Śiva's anger, Pārvatī reluctantly agreed. While they were having intercourse, Śiva discarded the guise of the tailor and reappeared as himself. This embarrassed Pārvatī in the extreme. As a result, her head fell off and the rest of her torso remained in the position of a woman having intercourse.

The first of the tales explains the nudity and etymology of the name *Lajjāgaurī*, while the second attempts to explain the headlessness of the image.

Mākoṭe Mukuṭeśvarī

There is ample evidence to believe that the goddess at Mahākūṭa had not only attained deification on the local scene but was well-known all over India. With good reason, I believe that in the various lists of the 108 seats (Śakti-pīṭhas) of the goddess,[29] the following account is that of our Mahākūṭa goddess.

kuraṇḍale trisandhyā syāt mākoṭe mukuṭeśvarī |
maṇḍaleśe śāṇḍakī syāt kālī kālañjare punaḥ ||

(Devī-Bhāgavata, 7.38.29)

(The goddess Trisandhyā (will be) is at Kuraṇḍala, the goddess Mukuṭeśvarī is at Mākoṭe. At Maṇḍaleśa there is the goddess Śāndakī and at Kālañjara there is the goddess Kālī.)

rudrakoṭyām tu kalyāṇī kālī kālañjare tathā |
mahāliṅge tu kapilā mākoṭe mukuṭeśvarī ||

(*Skandapurāṇa*, Avantī-Revā Khaṇḍa, 198.70)

(There are the goddesses Kalyāṇī at Rudrakoṭī and Kālī at Kālañjara. The goddess Kapilā is at Mahāliṅga, and the goddess Mukuṭeśvarī is at Mākoṭa.)

mahāliṅge tu kapilā markoṭe mukuṭeśvarī |
Śālilgrāme mahādevī Śivaliṅge jalapriyā ||

(*Matsyapurāṇa*, 13–33)

(Kapila is the goddess at Mahāliṅga, and Mukuṭeśvarī is the goddess of Mākoṭa. Mahādevī is the goddess at Śāligrāma and Jalapriyā is the goddess at Śivaliṅga.)

mākoṭākhye mahākoṭaḥ śivā ca muṇḍakeśvarī |
maṇḍaleśvarapīṭhe ca śaṅkaraḥ khāṇḍavī śivā ||[30]

(*Bṛhannīlatantra* and *Prāṇatoṣaṇītantra*)

(The goddess called Muṇḍakeśvarī and the (Bhairava) called Mahākoṭa reside at Mākoṭa. At the seat of Maṇḍaleśvara, Śiva resides with the goddess Khāṇḍavī.)

A careful perusal of these verses shows that although the name of the seat and the name of the goddess may vary somewhat, the most common name for the seat is Mākoṭa and the most common name of the goddess there is Mukuṭeśvarī. Alternative names that have been used for Mākoṭa are: Markoṭa, Karkoṭa and Sākoṭa. Mukuṭeśvarī has also been referred to as Muṇḍakeśvarī and Maṅgaleśvarī. The use of the name Muṇḍakeśvarī in the *Bṛhannīlatantra* and *Prāṇatoṣaṇī tantra* seems to me to be inappropriate; the word Mukuṭeśvarī would have been better in terms of observing prosodic rules. In view of the fact that the name of the seat is Mākoṭa and the name of Bhairava is Mahākoṭa, the word these tantras meant to use must have been Mukuṭeśvarī.

The name Mukuṭeśvarī can also be found in places other than the list of 108 Śakti-pīṭhas. For instance, the *Skandapurāṇa* mentions a Mukuṭeśvarī as one of the gotra-mātṛkās (gotra-mothers) or kula-devatā (clan-goddesses) established by the gods in order to protect the people in the Dharmāraṇya forest.

rakṣaṇārthaṃ hi viprāṇāṃ lokānaṃ hitakāmyayā |
gotrān prati tathaikekā sthāpitā yoginī tathā ||

yasya gotrasya yā śaktir rakṣaṇe pālane kṣamā |
sā tasya kuladevīti sākṣāt tatra babhūva ha ||

mātaṅgī ca mahādevī vāṇī ca mukuṭeśvarī |
bhadrī caiva mahāśaktiḥ saṃhārī ca mahābalā ||

cāmuṇḍā ca mahādevī ityetā gotramātarāḥ |
brahmāviṣṇumaheśādyaiḥ sthāpitāstatra rakṣaṇe ||

(*Skandapurāṇa*, *Brahmakhaṇḍa*, *Dharmāraṇyamāhātmya*, 10.106–107, 110–111)

(For the protection of vipras [*brāhmins*] and for the well-being of people, a Yoginī has been established for each gotra. Such a Yoginī (Śakti) then becomes the Kuladevatā of that Gotra and is capable of protecting and preserving it. Mātaṅgī, Mahādevī, Vāṇī, Mukuṭeśvarī, Bhadrī, Mahāśakti, Saṃhārī, Mahābālā and Cāmuṇḍā are the gotra mothers (*gotra-matṛkāḥ*). They have been established by Brahmā, Viṣṇu and Maheśa.)

Similarly, in the Caṇḍīkavaca, Devī mentions the name Mukuṭeśvarī when she advises devotees about the protection of the different parts of their body.

antrāṇi kālarātriśca pittaṃ ca mukuṭeśvarī /
padmāvatī padmakośe kaphe cūḍāmaṇīs tathā //

Caṇḍīkavaca, 32

(Let Kālarātri protect my intestines. Let Mukuṭesvarī protect my phlegm, Let the cavities within my body be protected by Padmāvatī and let Cūḍāmaṇi protect my bile duct.)

All these references help us ascertain the exact location of the goddess called Mukuṭeśvarī. The information above, obtained from the one hundred and eight names of the Śaktipīṭhas, reveals that the Śakti named Mukuṭeśvarī resides at a seat called Mākoṭa and a Bhairava called Mahākoṭa resides there along with her.

Mahākoṭa is Mākoṭa

We have now established that the present place names Nandikeśvara and Mahākūṭa are derived from the name of the well-known Śiva shrine known as Lañjikeśvara or Mahākūṭeśvara. This would mean that the current place-name Mahākūṭa is closely associated with the Śiva shrine of Mahākūṭeśvara. The word Mahākūṭeśvara has been shortened to Mahākūṭa. The name Mahākoṭa listed in the one hundred and eight names mentioned above must then mean Mahākūṭa, the letter 'o' having been altered to 'u' by a phonetic transformation. It then follows that the name of the seat, Mākoṭa, must have come from the name of the Bhairava, Mahākūṭa. This transformation of Mahā to Mā is fairly common in Kannaḍā, as can be seen from the following Saṃskṛt words and their Kannaḍā equivalents.

Mahākālī > Mākāḷi
Mahālakṣmī > Mālakumi
Mahājāla > Mājāla
Mahāsarasvatī > Māsarasati
Mahāphala > Māpaḷa
Mahāheya > Māheya
Mahāpuruṣa > Māpuruṣa
Mahāsatī > Māsati, Māsti

Any number of such examples can be found in the treasury of Kannaḍā literature where the conversion of Saṃskṛt *mahā* to Kannaḍā *mā* has taken place. It is therefore not unreasonable to say that the seat (*pīṭha*) name Mākoṭa is the same as the current seat name Mahākoṭa, which itself is the same as Mahākūṭa.

Mukuṭeśvarī = Mahākoṭeśvarī

Let us now consider the Śakti name Mukuṭeśvarī. I believe that this is a variation of the name Mahākoṭeśvarī or Mahākūṭeśvarī. I must explain why I think so. We have seen that one of Maṅgaleśa's inscriptions at Badāmī mentions Śiva as Lañjigeśvara. In another of his inscriptions at Mahākūṭa itself, Śiva, the Mahākūṭeśvara, is also described as Makuṭeśvaranātha, as follows:

makuteśvaranāthasyāsmākaṃ pitrā jyeṣṭhena copadattam[31]...

Maṅgaleśa's elder brother's wife, Durlabhādevī (wife of Kīrtivarman I) had this inscription recorded on the 12th of April 602. It describes a donation from the Kalacurīs of ten villages and of the income obtained from these villages to Makuṭeśvaranātha. In the Maṅgaleśa inscription described above, Śiva is called Lañjigeśvara (= Lañjikeśvara) and Makuṭeśvara (= Mahākūṭeśvara, Mahākoṭeśvara). Just as Lañjikā is the Śakti incorporated in the name Lañjikeśvara, Makuṭeśvarī is the Śakti in the name Makuṭeśvara. Being unaware of the proper meaning of Makuṭeśvarī, the writer of the manuscript would have found it difficult not to convert Makuṭa to Mukuṭa, the latter meaning a coronet, a word that also fits aptly in this context. The Saṃskṛt word Makuṭa also has the same meaning as the word Mukuṭa, both meaning a coronet. Therefore, it would have been logical for the writer to change Makuṭeśvarī to Mukuṭeśvarī.

This rather lengthy exposition yields us three important truths: 1) The seat of Śakti described in literature as Mākoṭa is today's Mahākūṭa (Mahākoṭa). 2) The presiding deity here is Mukuṭeśvarī, who is also known as Lañjikā, *Lajjāgaurī* and Mahākoteśvarī. Iconographically, she is portrayed as lying naked on her back with her legs spread apart and folded at the knees. She is also headless. 3) The Śiva at this seat is known by three names; Lañjikeśvara, Lajjāgaurīśvara and Mahākūṭeśvara. He is the Mahākoṭa Bhairava at this shrine.

The Mystery of the Name Mahākoṭeśvarī

Finally, we need to answer a few more questions. Why is one town known by two different names, namely, Nandikeśvara and Mahākūṭa? Why does the same god bear two names, Lañjikeśvara and Mahākūṭeśvara/ Mahākoṭeśvara? Why is the same goddess known by two different names: Lañjikā and Mahākoteśvarī? It should be clear that all three of these questions are really about the same thing. The name of the god has been derived from the name of the goddess, and the name of the town from the name of the god. Therefore, if we are able to answer the question regarding the two names for the same goddess, we are able to solve the mystery of the two names for the god as well as the town.

We already know what Lañjikā means. Lañjikā or Lañjā means a naked woman, a shameless woman. The question that now begs an answer is the meaning of the name Mahākoṭeśvarī. Can this also mean the same as Lañjikā? An affirmative answer would make our task easy. On the other hand, if the meaning is different, one will have to delve deeper into the reasoning behind it. If we remove the adjective prefix *mahā* and the suffix *īsvarī* from the name Mahākoṭeśvarī, the remnant is *koṭa*. I believe that this word is the clue to the mystery.

In this connection, I am reminded of a goddess named Koṭavī. She is also known as Koṭarī, Koṭarā, Koṭṭakiriyā, Koṭṭamahikā and Koṭamāī. All of these names have the basic element *koṭṭa* or *koṭa* in common. Although it is Saṃskṛtised, I believe that this element must have originally belonged to a South Indian language. Saṃskṛt dictionaries list the word *koṭavi,* giving its meaning as a 'naked woman'. The words *koṭa* and *koṭṭe* remind me of the current Marāṭhī word *koḍgā.* The word appears as *koṭagā* in Dāsopant's *Grantharāja* and as *koṭigā* in Moropant's *Kekāvalī.*[32] We know that the meaning of this word in Marāṭhī is a 'shameless person'.[33] Similar to the Marāṭhī word *lahānagā*, where 'gā' is a suffix attached to the word *lahāna*, 'gā' is a suffix attached to the word *koṭ.* Thus, one can consider the word *kotgā* as having been made of *koṭ* and *gā.* Removal of the suffix gā leaves only the base *koṭ* (or *koṭī* for feminine) meaning 'shameless'. The *Mahārāṣṭra Śabdakośa* lists the word *koṭa* as meaning 'shameless' and notes that it came from the Kannaḍā word '*koṭṭi*'.

It should now be clear that the two names Lañjikā and Mahākoṭeśvarī for the goddess Mahākūṭa both mean the same thing. Both words mean 'naked or shameless'. Mahākoṭeśvarī is the great naked goddess, while Mahākoṭeśvara is the great naked god. She is the personification of the great *Yonī* whereas he is the personification of the great *Liṅga.*

Mahāyonī and Mahāliṅga

Lañjikā-Mahākoṭeśvarī is the great yonī that creates the whole universe. She is the beginning of it all. She begets all the living and non-living things. It is the milk from her breasts that keeps all living things going. The sole purpose for her creation by primitive man has been to portray her as the organ of generation and of sustenance. First of all, she is the goddess of the creation of the world. It follows therefore that she is also the goddess of its sustenance. Her Yonī signifies creation and her breasts signify sustenance. It is no wonder, then, that only these two organs require prominence in her iconography.

The lotus, associated closely with her image, is itself a symbol of generation. As a matter of fact, it has obtained a special place in the Indian tradition as an enchanting symbol of the Yonī. The odd occasion where her image is associated with the bull is also noteworthy. In Indian mythology, the bull has always been looked upon as a symbol of powerful virility responsible for generation and manhood, and hence fatherhood. The bull Nandi's close association with Śiva is strongly suggestive of all these attributes. Lañjikā, who has coalesced with Śakti, is the Mahāyonī, the great generative female organ. Śiva on the other hand is the Mahāliṅga – the magnificent male organ. No wonder they have been called the 'parents of the world' (*jagataḥ pitarau*). Śiva is always represented as the phallic symbol; there is no need for any other part of the body in that representation. One must look upon this mother of the world in the same way. Her representation can only be the Yonī and nothing else. It would be wrong to call her headless. It would be more appropriate to say that of her available images, some are only in the form of Yonī whereas others consist of the Yonī and the breasts.

Rise and Neglect

So far, our attempt to investigate the nature of this goddess of generation represented in the form of Yonī has been confined to the context of her worship at Mahākūṭa. Because of this constraint, we have had to deliberately overlook many questions that naturally arise. For instance, at how many of the various places where her image has been discovered, is her worship still prevalent? Has she been elevated to the status of Śakti in all her places of worship? If the answer is in the affirmative, then has the process by which this has happened been similar to the process that took place at Mahākūṭa? However, if the process was different, why was this so? Since all of her images described above are from the post-Christian era, does this mean that she has a non-Indian origin?[34]

Was the goddess known long before her images were made and worshipped? If she was known, what kind of worship was in practice? All such questions await answers.

One point must however be noted. After she attained the status of Śakti, the goddess's original folk image slowly became neglected. At Mahākūṭa, she lies partially broken, out in the open, in one corner of the temple courtyard. Śiva the Lajjāgaurīśvara or Śiva, the Mahākoṭeśvara has incorporated her name within himself, and she herself has coalesced with Pārvatī. The same situation exists at Ālampūr, and at many other places. This is, of course, in line with the way people perceive gods and goddesses. The moment a deity becomes popular, religious leaders identify the deity with one who is already well established. They elevate the deity's position, give him or her a new name and develop a myth that suits the new image. While they do this, they carefully preserve aspects of the deity's original history and myth. In doing so, they are of course careful to relate this new history and the elevated image with the previous one in such a way that the former remains subordinate. The folk image does however get a minor place in the new worship regime. In the case of Lañjikā, all of these things have happened in this same way.

In attempting to decipher the mystery of Lañjikā, it occurred to me once again, this time ever more strongly, that deities never reveal their inner secrets to us if we look at them in display cases in museums or examine photographs of them on our desks in the luxury of our homes. To unravel what is in the minds of the folk deities, one has to examine all the avenues and the media available to the researcher. This is because it is these deities who occupy the minds of people. Researchers must always bear this adage in mind.

Endnotes

1 *Gazetteer of India: Mysore State-Bijāpūr District*, 1966, pp. 513–514; Aṇṇigerī, A.M. 1966, *A Guide to Badāmī*, Dhārwār, India: Cālukya Prakāśan, p. 3.

2 Translator's note: This form of nomenclature is a tribute to the site. It is not taken to be literally true, although at times, legends are built around such places which link them to the holy city of Banaras on the banks of the Gaṅgā river.

3 Mallār Banambhaṭṭā Pujār (Publisher). 1937. Badāmī, India. *Śakambharīmāhātmyam*.

4 Translator's note: I have not given a literal translation here, because Ḍhere's paragraph below the verses is very much a literal translation.

5 Translator's note: *Bilva* (Bel, *Aegle marmelos*) is an Indian tree whose leaves are thought to be very dear to Śiva.

6 Ganeśa Śāstrī Lele-Tryambakkar, 1964. *Tīrthayātrāprabandha*, Pune, India: Deśmukh Prakāśan, 2nd Edition, p. 166. (In Marāṭhī).

7 *Prabuddha Karnāṭaka*: 1943. *University of Mysore Journal*, Dīpavalī Issue, No. 96, pp. 25–30.

(Ḍhere's note: This contains Dr Pāndurangrāv Desai's article in Kannaḍā. It mentions the image found at Saṅgameśwara as well).

Ḍhere adds the following references and short notes as well, under this reference:

Śāradāśram Varshik (Annual), Puṇe. Śaka 1855. (1923 CE). (Contains the photograph of the image found at Māhūrzarī, in the Article by Dr G.A.P. Hunter entitled, 'The Antiquities of Māhurzari'.

Artibus Asiae, Vol. XIX, pp. 259–270, article by Stella Kramrisch entitled, 'An Image of Aditi-Uttānapād.' This article includes photographs of the images found at Ālampūr and Mahākūta. She also mentions the images from Bhītā and Kauśāmbī).

Artibus Asiae, Vol. XXIII, pp. 111–123. Article by Dr H.D. Sāṅkaliā, entitled, 'The Nude Goddess or Shameless Woman'. This article contains photographs from Ter, Osmānābad, Vaḍagāv, Ālampūr, Bhītā, Nāgārjunakoṇḍā and Siddhankoṭṭe.

Dr J. N. Tiwārī, *Studies in Goddess Cults in Northern India*: Unpublished thesis, Deccan College Library. (This thesis was later published as a book,

See Ref. 14.) This contains photographs of the images from Nāgārjunakoṇḍā and the ones mentioned above.

S.B. Deo and R.S.Gupte, *Excavations at Bhokardan*:, Nāgpur, 1974, p. 212.

8 *Artibus Asiae*, 1968. Vol. XXIII, p. 121. (According to the information given to Dr Sāṅkaliā by one Mr. Chapgar).

9 P. K. Prabhudesāī (Ed), 1968. *Adiśaktīce Viśvarūpa* (Devīkośa), Vol. 3, Pune: Tilak Mahārāṣṭra Vidyāpīth, p. 499. (In Marāṭhī).

10 *Artibus Asiae, op. cit.,* Vol. XXIII, p. 121.

11 Translator's note: This image now rests in the Archaeological museum at Ālampūr.

12 *Prabuddha Karnāṭaka*, 25.2, pp. 25–30.

13 Tiwārī, J.N., *Studies in Goddess Cults in Northern India*, 2014. Australian National University, Ph.D. Thesis, Open Access Theses, p. 281. Translator's note: Tiwārī's thesis was published in book form with the same title in 1985, by Sandīp Prakāśan, Delhi.

14 Marshall, J.M. 1931. *Mohenjodaro and the Indus Civilization*. London: Vol. 1, p. 62.

15 Translator's note: The term literally means 'giving birth to vegetation'. There is indeed a relief image of a female portrayed upside down, legs wide apart, with a plant emanating from her vagina.

16 *Artibus Asiae*, Vol.XIX, pp. 259–270.

17 Translator's note: In a poetic mode, Kramrisch says, 'India's foremost sacred plant is the lotus. It flowers on and above the surface of the water, rising from the mud under the water. The flower opens to the sun and closes in the evening… With its root in the mud, its stalk traversing the entire depth of the waters on which it rests its leaves, its flower open to the light of heaven, the lotus belongs to this world and those below and above, to light, earth and water… The opening and closing of the petals fans into ripeness the seed in the pericarp. It is seed pod, womb and ground of new plants, and on its high level of perfected beauty it holds the mystery of the lotus. This wondrous plant, having its being in earth, water and light, enacts their transmutation from earth to light, from mud to scent, through water to gleaming colour in the regularity of its movement…The earth below, the mud, is but the intermediate ground …productivity and generation above, are one continuous process within the lotus flower. When the lotus flower is supported not by its stalk in nature, but on the female body in art, a place of productivity and generation is also that of consciousness…' See Kramrisch *ibid*., pp. 264–265.

18 *Artibus Asiae*, Vol. XXIII, pp. 259–270, *op.cit.*

19 *Man*, XXXV, 1935, No. 70: 65 (Codrington's article entitled 'Iconography, Classical and Indian'. See also *Journal of the Royal Anthropological Institute of Great Britain and Ireland*, Vol. XIV, 1934, pp. 93–100 (Ms. M.A. Murray's article entitled, 'Female Fertility Figures').

20 Tiwārī, *op.cit*., pp. 269–337.

21 Translator's note: This is a ritual consisting of worshipping and making offerings to the god Viṣṇu.

22 *A Guide to Badāmī, op cit*., pp. 53–54. The second reference Ḍhere quotes here is a personal letter he received from Tirumalāi Tātācārya Śarmā. No details of the contents of it are available.

23 *Ibid.*, p. 54.
24 Rev. F. Kittel, 1894. *A Kannaḍā-English Dictionary*, Mangalore.
25 Puṇḍalīkjī Kātgaḍe (Ed), 1969. *Kannaḍā-Marāṭhī Śabdakośa*, Mahārāṣṭra Rājya Sāhitya Saṃskṛti Maṇḍal.
26 V.S.Āpṭe, 1963. *The Student's Sanskrit-English Dictionary*, Delhi.
27 See the word 'Lajjā' in *Kannaḍā-Marāṭhī Śabdakośa, op.cit.*
28 See *Adiśaktīce Viśvarūpa (Devīkośa), op.cit.*
29 D.C.Sarkār, *The Śākta Pithas*. (Quoted from the reprint of an article from the Journal of the Royal Asiatic Society of Bengal, Vol.XVI, No. 1, 1948: 32.)
30 The word 'Śivā' also means 'an auspicious female'. Therefore, an alternative translation of this verse will be, "Śiva with the name Mahākoṭaḥ and the auspicious goddess Muṇḍakeśvarī are at Mākoṭa. At the seat of Maṇḍaleśvara, Śiva resides with the auspicious goddess Khāṇḍavī".
31 S.Srikāntha Sāstri (Ed). 1940, *Sources of Karnataka History*, Vol. 1. Mysore, pp. 36–37.
32 '*Sabaḷaprati jo kotagā* (*Grantharāja*, 3–107), and '*Svayam hi kathito, nase tīḷahī lāja, mī kotigā*, Moropanta's *Kekāvalī*, Verse 17.

Translator's note: Dasopant (1551–1615) was a Marāṭhī writer belonging to the Datta sect. His work Grantharāja is considered to be the precursor to Rāmdās Swāmī's well-known work, *Dāsbodh*.

The second reference is that of a well-known work in Marāṭhī by the Seventeenth century Marāṭhī poet, Moropant, alias Moreśwar Rāmjī Parāḍkar (1729–1794). Kekāvalī (Peacock's screams) is his last work which he completed in the early 1790's.

33 Translator's note: The suffix gā is often used in Marāṭhī to construct a diminutive; viz. *lahān* to *lahānagā* (*Lit.* small to smallish).
34 Translator's note: Ḍhere recalls here Sāṅkaliā's identification of the goddess as Baubo.

Chapter 2

Jogulāmbā

As I mentioned before in Chapter One, in addition to Mahākūṭa, another important centre for the worship of the naked goddess is Ālampūr. Ālampūr is located in Nandikoṭkur tāluk, a tāluk that was in Rāicūr district in the old Hyderābād state and is now included in Mehbūbnagar district in the new state of Āndhra Prādeś. Ālampūr lies on the west bank of the Tuṅgabhadrā river, near the confluence of the rivers Kṛṣṇā and Tuṅgabhadrā and on the border of Mehbūbnagar district, close to Kurnūl district. On the Hyderabād-Bangalore railway line, there is a station called Ālampūr Road. The town is only six miles from the station. Ālampūr is of great importance to devotees, art historians and archaeologists alike. It is considered to be the western entrance to Śrī Śailam, and it claims to be the Kāśī of the South. As the Sthalapurāṇa of Ālampūr says:

> *brahmeśo'yam sa viśveśaḥ, sā kāśī hemalāpurī* |
> *sā gaṅgā tungabhadreti satyametanna samśayaḥ* || [1]
>
> (Hemalāpurī is the Kāśī wherein god Brahmeśvara is [Kaśī] Viśveśvara. The river Tuṅgabhadrā here is the same as Gaṅgā. Without a doubt this is so.)

Ālampūr has several ancient temples with exquisite carvings. They contain beautiful images of deities. There are also inscriptions that speak for an otherwise silent history. The temples here cluster in two groups: the Navabrahmeśvara group and the Pāpanātha group. The latter is a mile away from the town, in a densely wooded area on the banks of the Tuṅgabhadrā River. However, the Pāpanātha temples do not have much to do with Ālampūr as a *kṣetra*. Also, in terms of architectural beauty, they do not compare well with the Navabrahmeśvara group. One more temple, that of Saṅgameśvara, stands at the confluence of the Kṛṣṇā and Tuṅgabhadrā rivers, in the present-day town of Saṅgameśvara in Nandikoṭkur tāluk of Kurnool district. It must be included as part of the rich heritage of Ālampūr.

In terms of religious and architectural importance, the Navabrahmeśvara temples, also called Navaliṅgeśvara, are noteworthy. These are nine temples of Śiva that stand as one large complex on a hillock. The main temple, which stands in the middle, is called Bālabrahmeśvara or just Brahmeśvara. The other eight are known as Kumārabrahma, Arkabrahma, Vīrbrahma, Viśvabrahma, Tārakabrahma, Garuḍabrahma, Svargabrahma and Padmabrahma. Because of these Śiva temples, Ālampūr has come to be known as Brahmeśvara-Kṣetra or Navabrahmālaya-Kṣetra (*Lit*: the nine abodes of Brahmā).

Next to the Bālabrahmeśvara temple, there is a shrine of the goddess Joguḷāmbā, who is said to be the consort of Bālabrahmeśvara. She is also known by her Saṃskṛt name, Yoginī, and her icon has a fierce expression.[2] There are several beautiful images of the goddess Mahiśāsuramardinī at this shrine as well.[3]

The Images of the Naked Goddess

At one stage, in a small niche in the precinct of the Navaliṅgeśvara temples, there was an image of *Lajjāgaurī* similar to, but larger and more beautiful than, the Mahākūṭa image. Presumably that is the same image which is now housed in the local museum at Ālampūr. In an article entitled 'An Image of Aditi Uttanapāda', Stella Kramrisch discusses this image at the Ālampūr museum. Some thirty years ago, Dr Pāṇḍuraṅg Desāī had tried to interest researchers in the artifacts at Ālampūr, including especially the *Lajjāgaurī* image. After a field trip to Ālampūr in 1943, he published a brief but important note (in *Prabuddha Karnāṭaka*, the journal of Mysore University) in Kannaḍā. Desāī had seen the image at the temple site. He describes the image thus:[4]

> Female lying on her back, ample (*sthūla*) body, headless, naked. Women wishing to beget children worship her. The locals say that this image is that of Reṇukā. They believe that her head is at Saundatti in Beḷgāv district in the form of the goddess Ellammā.[5]

Dr Desāī saw a similar image in the nearby town of Saṅgameśvar (Tāluk Nandikoṭkur, Dist. Kurnūl) in the temple of Saṅgameśvara. He described that image thus:

> Also naked, legs folded in such a way as to accentuate the vagina. Headless. In place of the head, there is a wheel similar

to a bullock-cart wheel. The locals call her Bhūdevī and say that women worship her in order to beget children.[6]

The image, described beautifully by Stella Kramrisch in her article mentioned above,[7] has a lotus in place of the head. The hands carry lotus buds. (See Plate 11).

The Myth from the Sthala-māhātmya

The Saṃskṛt work 'Sthala-māhātmya of Ālampūr' includes a myth about this headless goddess. It consists of five chapters and is thought to be a part of the Skandapurāṇa. The work describes in great detail the various gods, goddesses and holy places at Ālampūr, including the Navabrahmeśvara temples, Papavināśatīrtha, Gaṇikāsiddheśvaratīrtha and Rājarājeśvaratīrtha.

The myth about the naked goddess included in this work is narrated below. It is quite revealing.[8]

> Reṇukā was the devoted wife of the seer Jamadagni. Every day, she fetched water required for her husband's rituals from the Tuṅgabhadrā river, bringing it each time in a freshly made unfired clay pot. Her daily routine thus consisted of going to the river, making a fresh clay pot from mud, filling it with water and taking it back to the āśrama. Because of the heat of her devotion to her husband, the unfired clay pot would stay intact without disintegrating. However, one day this heat proved to be inadequate. On that occasion, she saw a king dallying amorously with his young and beautiful queen in the waters of the Tuṅgabhadrā. Thereupon, Reṇukā was momentarily stirred by desire. Even this small transgression resulted in the loss of her ascetic heat, so that she was unable to keep the clay pot in one piece. Despondent, she returned to the āśrama without water. Due to the powers of his ascetic heat, her husband Jamadagni found out what had transpired. He was incensed, and, illustrating the short temper that he was known for, ordered each one of his sons in turn to behead her instantly. The first three sons refused to perform this dreadful deed.
>
> Paraśurāma, the youngest son, by contrast, obeyed his father. Pleased with his obedience, Jamadagni asked Paraśurāma to choose a boon. Upon this, Paraśurāma asked his father to bring his mother back to life. Jamadagni, however, replied that it was

impossible for Reṇukā to come back to life in her erstwhile form because her head had fallen into a pot of water in a cobbler's shop and had thereby become impure. It was therefore improper to attach it to the torso. Hence, Jamadagni granted that Reṇukā's head would be worshipped as Ellammā and the torso would be known as the 'mother goddess earth'. Thus, the head of Reṇukā at Ālampūr became known as Ellammā and the torso came to be worshippd as Bhūdevī, the mother goddess earth. Ellammā is the *grāmadevatā* of Ālampūr.

Ellammā, Reṇukā and Bhūdevī

Scholars now agree that the southern Indian goddess Ellammā has coalesced with the goddess Reṇukā. Along with the author of the Sthalapurāṇa, locals at Ālampūr and at Saṅgameśvara call the naked headless images Bhūdevī, mother earth. The locals also believe that the headless torso is that of Reṇukā.

When one sets aside the elements of mystique and wonder infused in the myth in its folk version, the real meaning of the myth becomes apparent. The goddess who was worshipped in the form of an un-sculpted stone was the same one whose images were made in the form of the Yonī, the female generative organ. Her Prākṛt name was Ellammā, whereas her Saṃskṛt name was Reṇukā. However, irrespective of her name, people firmly believed that she was 'mother earth'. Women worshipped her in order to obtain children. Ellammā, Reṇukā and Bhūdevī were three names for the same goddess. It is clear that the myth about Reṇukā losing her head was fashioned to explain the headlessness of the image.

The Mystery behind the Name Ālampūr

The place called Ālampūr or Ālamapūr (the present day Ālampūr) appears to have had several names. In the Jharikā copperplate of the Raṣṭrakūṭa king Govinda III (Śaka 725),[9] it has been called Alampūr.[10] In the Sañjāna copperplate (Śaka 793)[11] of Govinda's son Amoghavarṣa, it has been described as Helāpur.[12] In his Ālampūr inscription (Śaka 1225),[13] the Kākatīya king Pratāparudra calls it Ālampūrī.[14] S.P. Srinivasachar has read the beginning of this inscription as *hataṃpuravarapratītamahodayam*. In my opinion, *Hatampur* should be read as *HĀlampūr*. The beginning of the inscription should therefore be read as *hĀlampūravarapratītamahodayam*. It is likely that the scribe has carved it wrongly as

Hatampura in place of *HĀlampūra*. Dr Pāṇḍurangrāv Desāī has also suggested HĀlampūra in place of Hatampura.[15]

We have already noted that the Sthalapurāṇa calls Ālampūr 'Hemalāpurī'. Finally, the name has also been Saṃskṛtised to Alakāpurī or Alakāpur. A careful perusal of these alternative names suggests that the letter *h* in Halaṃpūra, Helāpura and Hemalāpurī is indicative of a particular style of pronunciation. Originally, these names must have been Ālampūr, Elāpur and Elamāpurī. In phonetic terms, a shift (*varṇaviparyaya*) from E to He has taken place: Elamāpurī has become Hemalāpurī. It is also easy to comprehend Alakāpur as the Saṃskṛtized version. In this regard, we already know that the Āḷandī of Jñāneśvara and the Āḷanda of Rāghava-Caitanya have been Saṃskṛtized as Alakā or Alakāvatī. It would therefore seem quite logical that Ālampūr, which sounds a little like Āḷanda and Āḷandī, would become Alakāpur in the Saṃskṛtised version.

We have thus three alternative choices for the same place name: Alampur, Elāpur or Elamāpur. All of these names have been derived from Ellammā, the presiding deity of Ālampūr. One can deduce that these names must be more easily pronounceable transformations of the original name Ellammāpura.

Ālāpure Yugalā Devī[16]

Although the name Ālampūr is associated with the goddess (Śakti) Ellammā, who is traditionally the presiding deity of the place, when listing Ālampūra as one of the Śaktipīṭhas, scholars in this field seem not to have included Ellammā as one of the names of Śakti. The first scholar who showed that Ālampūr was one of the Śaktipīṭhas was Dr Pāṇḍuraṅgrāv. He has unequivocally shown this in the above-mentioned article and also in another article, entitled "Tantric Cults in Epigraphs".[17] There is also a short work in Saṃskṛt, the *aṣṭādaśapīṭham*, which, although attributed to the Ādi-Śaṅkarācārya, was obviously written much later.[18] This work mentions Ālampūra as a Śaktipīṭha in the following verse:

> *ālāpure yugalā devī śrīśaile bhramarāmbikā /*
> *ujjayinyām mahākālī māhūre ekavīrakā //*
>
> (The goddess Yugalā is at Ālampūra, Bhramarāmbikā is at Śriśailam. Mahākālī is at Ujjain, and Ekavīrā is at Māhūr.)

Dr Dineś Candra Sarkār carried out important research on the number of Śaktipīṭhas and their exact locations.[19] However, he failed to include

Mahākūṭa and Ālampūr among the pīṭhas he discussed. Mahākūṭa especially seems to have been totally ignored in this regard by all researchers. Although Dr Pāṇḍuraṅg Desāī recorded it as a Śaktipīṭha even before Dr Sarkār wrote his article, Dr Desāī's article remained totally ignored, probably due to its being written in Kannaḍā. Dr Desāī has poignantly shown that the Ālāpura included in the list of the eighteen Śaktipīṭhas is the Ālampūr of today. He has also shown that the Śakti by the name Yugulā at Ālāpura is the same as Joguḷāmbā, the consort of Brahmeśvara. It is obvious that similar to the word Yoginī, which is a Saṃskṛtization of the word Joguḷāmbā, Yugulā is also a Saṃskṛtization of the same name.

The importance of Ālampūr as a *kṣetra* can be seen from the fact that the *Matsyapurāṇa* includes Ālāpura among the places suitable for performing Śrāddha rites, as described below:

> *puṇyaṃ rameśvaraṃ tadvat elāpuramalampuram* ।
>
> (*Matsyapurāṇam*, 22, 50)
>
> (Elāpura-Ālampūra is as auspicious [for Śrāḍḍhas] as is Rameśvaram.)

Ellammā, Reṇukā and Joguḷāmbā

Ellammā and Reṇukā are two names of the same goddess. Or, one can say more appropriately, that Reṇukā is the Ellammā of the higher tradition. In the *Reṇukā-Sahasranāma* (the hymn of the thousand names of Reṇukā), Reṇukā is given several names associated with the town of Māhūr. Some of these are: Mahāpuranivasinī and Mahāpurādrinilayā (one who resides in the great city of Māhūr), Mahāpurakṛtasthitiḥ and Mahāpurasukhāsīnā (one who resides happily in the great city of Māhūr) and Mahāpuramahādevī (the great goddess from the great city of Māhūr).[20] She has also been called Alakāpūrasaṃsthānā (one who resides in Alakāpura), thus referring to Ālampūr as one of her seats.[21] This same hymn calls Reṇukā by names such as Ekavīrā, Yamāmbā (Yamāī), and Ekāmbā (Ellammā).[22] With this in mind, the question that begs an answer, is: If Ellammā is the presiding deity of Ālampūr, i.e. if Ālampūr is the original Ellammāpura, then why is it that the Śakti at the place is called Yugalā-Joguḷāmbā?

Reṇukā is Identical with Joguḷāmbā

The answer to this question is to be found in the folklore of Āndhra. In Āndhra Prades there is a caste of leatherworkers known as the Mādigā. Within this caste is a group of folk singers called Bavanīḍas who are worshippers of Joguḷāmbā. Bavanīḍa men and women sing the praises of this goddess, and their songs incorporate many of her myths. Their singing and story-telling is accompanied by a drum called Javanikā or Jamaḍikā. The Bavanīḍas actually call these performances 'the story of Ellammā' or 'the story of Reṇukā'. Incorporated in these songs are many of the myths associated with Reṇukā. Bavanīḍa folk performances are especially prevalent in Mehabūbnagar district, the district in which Ālampūr, the seat of Joguḷāmbā, is located. Playing their Jamaḍikā, which makes a sound like *jyuke jum, jyuke jum*, these Bavanīḍa singers unfold the stories of Reṇukā in a vigorous manner. A Telugu work entitled *Krīḍābhirāmamu*, written during the Kākatīya period, paints a wonderful picture of Bavanīḍa performances.[23]

Another work in Telugu, the *Śukasaptati*, composed during the Vijayanagara period, describes how the *jogurāḷūs*, the female worshippers of Joguḷāmbā belonging to the Mādigā caste, wander all over the countryside begging alms in the name of the goddess.[24] The *Sukasaptati* says:

> Adorned with a necklace of leather in the shape of the goddess's feet, another long necklace of cowrie shells, and a darśanamālā, a large mark of tumeric on their forehead and a fistful of the goddess's tumeric in their left hand, a staff of Nāgphaṇī (cobra-headed wooden staff) in their right hand, adorned in a sarī, and singing songs of Paraśurāma, the Joguḷāmbā goes begging.

Obviously, the connection between Paraśurāma and Joguḷāmbā depicted in this song is indicative of the identity of Joguḷāmbā and Reṇukā. As we shall see later, the cobra-headed staff in the hands of the female devotee of Joguḷāmbā is very important for worshippers of Ellammā-Reṇukā as well.

The *Krīḍābhirāmamu* at one place describes a day-long pilgrimage to Waraṅgaḷa undertaken by two friends, a Brahmin and a Vaiśya. The work portrays a scene wherein these two friends arrive at the temple of Ekavīrā at Wāraṅgaḷa. With this scene as the background, the writer of the *Krīḍābhirāmamu* provides quite a bit of information about Ekavīrā.[25] He calls her Reṇukā, the mother of Paraśurāma. Since Māhūr is the most important seat for Reṇukā, he calls her Māhūrāmmā (the mother from Māhūr) as well. He also makes a note of one more of her names, Kākatammā, the clan-deity of the Kākatīya kings. Most importantly, he mentions that she is naked. His Telugu words are, 'krīḍāśūnya kaṭīra-maṇḍaḷamu devī śambhaḷīvrātamum'. The adjective 'śambhaḷī' in this sentence is clearly indicative of the nakedness of Ekavīrā. It is also synonymous with the other names that we have come across so far, namely, Lañjā, Lañjikā and Mahākoṭeśvarī.

From their mentions quoted in the two works described above, namely the *Krīḍābhirāmamu* and *Śukasaptati*, it should now be amply clear to us that all three of the names, Ellammā, Reṇukā and Joguḷāmbā, are three different names for one and the same goddess. This same goddess is still worshipped by the Māḍigā tribe in the state of Āndhra Pradeś. The priestesses belonging to this tribe are called 'Jogurāḷu. They beg for alms in the name of goddess Joguḷāmbā and hold a wooden staff in the shape of a cobra-hood in their hands. The folk singers who belong to the Māḍigā caste are known as 'bavanīḍa'. These singers roam the countryside singing the mythical tales of this goddess. These mythical songs are called 'Ellammā-kathā' or Reṇukā-kathā. During the reign of the Kākatiyas, there used to be a shrine devoted to this goddess at Warangaḷa. At this shrine, she was worshipped in her nude form.

Joguḷāmbā is the Mother Goddess Who Gives Children

We have already seen that the goddess who was worshipped as Lañjikā, *Lajjāgaurī* or Mahākūṭeśvarī in the form of a Yonī at Mahākūṭa and who was called Bhūdevī (mother earth) at Ālampūr, is the one who grants children to her devotees.

From the traditions at Mahākūṭa, Siddhanakoṭṭe, Ālampūr and Saṅgameśvara, we already know that barren women worship her for this purpose. With good evidence, we have now shown that this same goddess is also called Joguḷāmbā. As a matter of fact, the word Joguḷāmbā means a goddess who grants children to the devotees. Yoginī and Yugulā are similar sounding names, obviously created deliberately during the process of Saṃskṛtisation. If one removes the suffixes *ammā* or *ambā* which both signify motherhood, one is left with the root 'Joguḷ'. This word is the answer to the mystery of the goddess's name. 'Joguḷ' in South Indian languages means a lullaby.[26] Obviously Joguḷāmbā is the mother goddess who makes the singing of lullabies and the rocking of the cradle possible at home. While the names Lañjikā, *Lajjāgaurī* and Mahākūṭeśvarī signify the nature of her form, the name Joguḷāmbā is indicative of her function.

I have, in my collection, an incomplete manuscript with the title, "*Śrīskānde siṅhyādrikhaṇḍe uttarārdhe svayāmbhuve... rāmakṣetra-varṇanam*". This is obviously the description of the holy land of Rāma (Rāmakṣetra) contained in the Sahyādrikhaṇḍa of the *Skandapurāṇa*. It describes the religious importance of the land of the Konkaṇ and Goa created by Paraśurāma. In typical Purāṇic style, the eleventh chapter of this manuscript describes how the various seats of Reṇukā came into existence in the land created by Paraśurāma. According to it, Reṇukā, intensely desirous of seeing her son Bhārgavarāma (another name for Paraśurāma), came from Ambālaya (Māhūr) with her attendant Yoginīs to the land that had been created by her son. Paraśurāma praised her in the highest possible terms and expressed a wish that in the land created by him, Reṇukā should be present in many places. He also expressed a wish that she should become the clan-deity of the Brāhmins that he had settled on the land. He told these Brāhmins that they should worship his mother for the growth and well-being of their clan. In describing this occasion, the work uses transparent adjectives such as Yogāmbā, Yogāmbikā and Ambujayonīmātṛkā for Reṇukā. These names are quite obviously Saṃskṛtised versions of Joguḷāmbā. Ambujayonīmatṛkā[27] (the mother with a Yonī like a lotus) is an adjective that most appropriately describes both the icon of Reṇukā in the form of a female generative organ and the close connection between the lotus and such an icon. It is especially meaningful in our context to know that Reṇukā has been described as Ambujayonīmātṛkā and by Saṃskṛtising the name Joguḷāmbā. It is also important to know that the goddess who is Paraśurāma's mother and whose main seat is at Mahūr is the same one who became the protector of the Brāhmin clans of Konkaṇ and Goa.

Jogalādevī in Mahārāṣṭra

There is evidence to show that in addition to Joguḷāmbā, the goddess Jogalā was also worshipped in Mahārāṣṭra. The *Līḷācaritra* mentions that a disciple of Cakradharasvāmī, Ausā, had a brass image of Jogalādevī among her belongings.[28] Ausā was born into a good Brāhmin family and had belonged to the Nāth sect beforehand. After joining that sect, she traveled extensively, came in contact with Cakradharasvāmī and, as a result, became his disciple. The Swāmī was totally antagonistic to idol-worship. When he himself opened Ausā's bundle of belongings, various idols fell out. A brass image of Jogalādevī was among them. A Kṛṣṇa image from Titariya Mahuva (?)[29] was also there. The Swāmī wanted to throw these images away, but Ausā said to him, 'You can throw away the image of Jogulā but please do not throw away the Kṛṣṇa image. He is the one who has shown me the way'. This clearly goes to show that Ausā used to worship Jogulā regularly in the form of a brass image and that she carried it with her on her travels.

Jogalādevī is the name of a small town in Mahārāṣṭra. It is situated on the northern bank of the Godāvarī river, three miles west of Rāmdāsgav in the district of Aurangābād. Mahānubhāva literature mentions that Cakradharaswāmī visited this place and that, while he was there, he was worshipped in the morning at the local temple.[30]

Viśṛṅkhalā Devī

The well-known Śakti worshipper and tantric, Bhāskararāya alias Bhāsurānanda,[31] knew about Ālampūr and the image of the nude goddess at the place. He mentions this explicitly in his commentary on the *Lalitāsahasranāma* called '*Saubhāgyabhāskara*'. After explaining the meaning of 'Viśṛṅkhalā' as 'someone who has shed the shackles of mundane obligatory duties and the demands of socially imposed morality,' Bhāskararāya comments further:

> *nagneti va* |
> *Ālampūrādipīṭheṣu tādṛśadevīmūrtidarśanāt 'svayonidarśanānmuhyatpaśuvargāmanusmare'diti tiraskāriṇīdhyānadarśanācca, javanikāyā javanikāntarānapekṣatvena tādṛśadhyānasya yuktatvācca* |*'sṛṅkhalā syātkatīvastrabandhe 'pi nigaḍe 'pi ce'ti viṣvah* ||
>
> (Or thus 'nude' [Thus we begin with the explanation of the word, 'nude']. Such an image of the goddess is seen in the seats (religious pedestals) of Ālampūr etc., She should be remembered as one, who, by displaying her own vagina, confuses animal categories. Thus, she is slighted in meditation and in divine vision, and it is appropriate to meditate upon her by expecting to behold her through a curtain via other curtains. Viśva says, 'śṛṅkhalā should mean a loin cloth covering the waist, also chain or fetters'.)[32]

In this commentary, Bhāskararāya gives 'naked' as another meaning of the word Viśṛṅkhalā and mentions similar goddesses such as the one at Ālampūr to support his view. Bhāskararāya was a well-known left-handed devotee of Śakti,[33] a great commentator on Śākta-tantra, a resurrector of the Śaktipīṭhas, and a regular traveller to religious places within India from the Himalayas to the South. For him to specifically mention Ālampūr as a seat of Śakti, and to explain the meaning of Viśṛṅkhalā as 'naked', goes to show that these naked images and the places where they were found were important seats of Śakti.

An Important *Kṣetra* for the Śākta Tāntrics

In the list of the important seats for Śakti, the inclusion of Mahākūṭa and Ālampūr is obviously not there simply as an honorific mention. There is a great deal of evidence to suggest that the Śākta tāntrics played a major part in the development of these places as illustrious examples of Śakti worship.

We have already seen that in the 'Reṇukāsahasranāma', Reṇukā has been called 'Alakāpurasaṃsthānā' (one who resides in Alakāpura). Also, for the tāntric worship of Reṇukā, a work called 'Reṇukātantra' has been composed. This text deals mainly with her worship in the form of her yonī. In this context, it is worthwhile noting the information provided by Dr Pāṇḍuraṅg Desāī in relation to the Ālampūr image, which is also in the form of the yonī.[34] Dr Desāī mentions that in the home of a Brāhmin family of Sardārs who are Reṇukā worshippers, the worship is conducted regularly on two idols of Reṇukā in the shape of the yonī: one made of gold and the other of silver.

In thinking about the influence of Śākta worshippers, I am specifically reminded of the nine Śivaliṅgas near the goddess, both at Mahākūṭa and at Ālampūr. In chapter 1, we have already noted that the *Śākambharīmāhātmya* mentions the Śivaliṅgas at Mahākūṭa collectively as *navaliṅgas* (nine *liṅgas*). Similarly, the Ālampūr Śiva temples are known as Navabrahmeśvara or Navaliṅgeśvara. In the latter place, the word *brahma* has been used as an alternative for the word *liṅga*.

What is the significance of nine of these liṅgas at both these places? Of the nine liṅgas at each place, one is obviously prominent and must somehow have a close connection with the Śakti. This arrangement must also have a particular devotional significance. While pondering this, I was reminded of the following verse from the '*Saundaryalaharī*':

Śarīraṃtvaṃ śambhoḥ śaśimihiravakṣoruhayugam |
tavātmanaṃ manye bhagavati navātmanamanagham |
ataḥ śeṣaḥ śeṣītyayamubhayasādharaṇatayā |
sthitaḥ sambandho vā samarasaparānandaparayoḥ || 35 ||[35]

(Oh Bhagavatī with nine souls! Your beautiful body with the sun and the moon as your breasts appears like the body of Śiva himself. Therefore, the oneness of you and Śiva is like the unity of Śeṣa and Śeṣī. Neither is dominant, neither is subordinate.)

Bhagavatī has been called Navātmā here. People have explained the meaning of this adjective in several different ways. However, one explanation is particularly relevant in relation to the seats of Śakti at Mahākūṭa and Ālampūr.[36] Śiva is normally considered Aṣṭamūrtī (one with eight images); Kālidāsa has offered prayers to Aṣṭamūrtī Śiva in the Nāndī (invocatory prayer at the beginning of a play) of his play, *Śākuntalā*. The Śakti is also considered Aṣṭadhā (of eight types). They thus each have eight faces. However, Śiva is only complete if he is with Śakti, otherwise he is considered inactive. Similarly, Śakti can only function if she is with Śiva. This united form of the two is the ninth form of the Śakti, the Navātmā. The eight forms of Śiva are represented by the eight Śivaliṅgas. Combined with the ninth *liṅga*, representing the unity of the two, must be the Navātmā-Bhagavatī, the one that the *Śākambharimāhātmya* terms Śiva with Śakti (Śivayā sahitaḥ Śambhuḥ). I am convinced that this is the significance of the Navaliṅgeśvara in the minds of the Śākta tantrics at Mahākūṭa and at Ālampūr.

The Bhūdevī Images at Māhūrajharī

Some forty years ago, Dr G.A.P. Hunter found a headless image of a naked goddess in the Uttānapāda posture at Māhūrajharī in the state of Vidarbha. In the article that he published in the *Śāradāśrama Annual* in 1933, which dealt with the ancient artifacts from Māhūrajharī, Dr Hunter included a photograph of this image. Māhūrajharī is a town in Nāgpur taluk (District Nāgpur), and lies on the Nāgpur-Kaṭol railway line only seven miles away from Nāgpur. In this small town, with a population of only about 500, a large number of ancient artifacts have been found. These include burial stones in the shape of concentric circles, many semi-precious stones, bricks belonging to the Vākāṭaka period, coins of the Kṣatrapas and some clay seals. In spite of Dr Hunter's efforts, no one had paid much attention to Māhūrajharī until 1971 when the archeology department of the University of Nāgpur excavated the stone circles. About the same time, Dr V.B. Kolate deciphered a copper plate belonging to the Vākāṭaka period found at this site.[37]

Dr Hunter postulated that the headless goddess image found at Māhūrajharī was a pre-Dravidian Earth-Mother goddess.[38] At this stage,[39] we do not know the whereabouts of this image that he found forty years ago. However, quite recently, Dr Bāḷakṛṣṇa Dābhāḍe has found two more images at Māhūrajharī.

The fact that more than a few images of the naked goddess were found at Māhūrajharī means that it must have been a place of worship for this goddess. The suffix *Jharī* in this name is obviously there to differentiate it from the other well-known town, Māhūr. This means that both of these places, the abovementioned Māhūr near the Jharī and the present-day Māhūr, the famous seat of Reṇukā on the banks of the Praṇitā river, were called Māhūr or Mātāpūra, literally, the town of the mother. Both were obviously important because they were seats for the mother goddess.

Māhūr and Māhūrajharī

To recapitulate, we have now seen that the kind of image that has been found at Māhūrajharī has been called Bhūdevī (earth mother) in the Sthalapurāṇa of Ālampūr. Although her name in the folk culture is Joguḷāmbā (= child giving), she is also known as Reṇukā. The Telugu work *Krīḍābhirāmamu* tells us that the image of Ekavīrā in the Ekavīrā temple at Fort Wāraṅgaḷ also looks very similar. The fact that headless and naked images of the goddess in the Uttānapāda position are called Bhūdevī, Reṇukā and Ekavīrā, is helpful in trying to attribute a name to the Māhūrajharī image. The finding of a specific type of naked image, and the knowledge that Māhūr is the place of the find, suggest that the name of the goddess at Māhūrajharī could well be Reṇukā, Ekavīrā or Bhūdevī.

Before we embark on a search for the mother goddess at Māhūrajharī, it is important to investigate the nature of the image of Reṇukā at Māhūr and the various names that have been given to her. This is because the names of the two seats are nearly identical, suggesting strongly that there is also a similarity between the forms of the image and between the names given to these forms.

The Headless Naked Image of the Māhūr Goddess

As we know, the most important shrine for Reṇukā is at Māhūr in Nānded district, Mahārāṣṭra. The image at this shrine, as it stands, is in the form of an un-sculpted stone (Swayaṃbhu in Saṃskṛt). Although the present-day devotees believe that this image represents the face of Reṇukā, religious literature states unequivocally that the image is that of *Pṛthivī*, mother earth, and that she is in the headless and naked *uttānapāda* posture.

A work called *Kedāravijaya* that sings the praises of the god Jyotibā[40] is in print. It was composed in the form of couplets by the poet Harī Aṅgāpūrkar.[41] There is a famous shrine of Jyotibā on a hillock known as Vāḍī-Ratnāgirī near Kolhapur. There, Jyotibā is the husband of Yamāī and the wedding of Jyotibā and Yamāi is celebrated at this shrine each year. Among the devotees, it is a common belief that Yamāī is identical with Reṇukā. The other name that has been used for Yamāī is *Pṛthivī*, mother earth.

In accordance with the myth elaborated in the story of Jamadagni, Reṇukā and their son Paraśurāma that we have seen earlier, *Kedāravijaya* describes the beheading of Reṇukā by Paraśurāma at the order of his father. Pleased by his son's obedience, Jamadagni asks his son to choose a boon. Seeing his father in this good mood, Paraśurāma reminds him that with the demise of Reṇukā, the world has become devoid of Śakti, the female power (*viśva jāhale hi śaktihīna*). He then begs his father to forgive all the transgressions of his mother and bring her back to life (*ātāṃ sarva aparādha karāvā kṣamā | māyesī uṭhavona dīje kṣemā ||*). Jamadagni agrees and asks Paraśurāma to offer Reṇukā's headless body to the sacrificial fire so that she can be reborn with a lustrous body and meet Paraśurāma on the Ratnāgirī mountain. Paraśurāma does as his father told him to:

> *jāṇona puḍhīla bhaviṣyāsī | hoṃīṃ ghātaleṃ reṇukesī |*
> *taiṃ bhavānī vade anādiveṣīṃ | paraśarāmāteṃ ādareṃ ||*
> *mhaṇe putrā aika goṣṭī | tūṃ cāla mī yeteṃ tuze pāṭhīṃ |*
> *māteṃ pāhasī phirona viṣamadṛṣṭīṃ | tarī mī tuzī bhetī na gheī ||*
> *aisī vadona jvālāmukhāṃ | nābhīparyanta bāhira Reṇukā |*
> *nighālī, na dharona manīṃ śaṅkā | taiṃ dharona āśaṅkā rāmeṃ pāhilī ||*
> *rāmeṃ phirona pāhatāṃ māgeṃ | Reṇukā rāhilī teheṃ ci rāgeṃ |*
> *yetāṃ maja na ye nagna aṅgeṃ | mātāpūra Māhūr yālāgīṃ mhaṇatī ||*
>
> (*Kedāravijaya*, 27. 144–147)[42]

(Assured of the future, Paraśurāma put Reṇukā's body into the sacrificial fire. Mother Bhavānī then said to Paraśurāma with affection, 'Son! You start walking and I will follow you. However, if you turn around to look at me, I will cease to do so'. Having said thus, and without doubting that her son would do as he was told, Reṇukā came out of the fire up to her navel. Paraśurāma however did not believe her and turned around to see if she was following him. Because of this, Reṇukā was angry with him and remained right there. She said that, being naked, she would not be able to follow him anymore. [The place where this happened] is therefore called Mātāpūra [city of the mother] or Māhūr.)

The above verses clearly mention Reṇukā's naked body only up to her navel. It is therefore clear that the myth has been formulated to accord with the peculiarity of the image. Thus, as it happened, the body of Reṇukā was slowly appearing out of the sacrificial fire. However, Paraśurāma, doubtful of the efficacy of the boon, turned backwards to look before the full body appeared and so only part of the body came out. The poet says that Reṇukā refused to go to Ratnāgirī and decided to stay permanently at Māhūr. From the words '*yetāṃ na ye maja nagna aṅge*' ('I cannot come with a naked torso'), it is to be understood that the image is from the feet to the navel and not from the head to the navel.[43]

These kinds of explanatory tales always leave some windows of inconsistencies in them and the researcher can grasp the inner truth and its meaning by examining these.

From the myth in the *Kedāravijaya*, we are able to ascertain that the Reṇukā at Māhūr is headless, naked and in the *uttānapāda* posture, similar to the goddesses at Ālampūr and Māhūrajharī. In the large number of hymns addressed to Jyotibā, he has been called Ekavīrāpatī (the husband of Ekavīrā) and Reṇukānātha (the husband of Reṇukā), both names essentially meaning the same thing. Similarly, he has also been called Medinīpatī (the husband of the earth). This goes to show that while Jyotibā is *kṣetrapāla* or *ksetrapatī* (the keeper of the field), Reṇukā is the field, the goddess earth.

Reṇukā is the Earth

Substantial evidence is available from which to infer that Reṇukā is primarily mother earth, as her very name suggests. However, citing it all in order to shed light on her true form as a deity is a task that would involve writing a major volume.[44] For obvious reasons, I wish to refrain from undertaking that task. The only evidence I wish to draw the reader's attention to here is the fact that a well-known family whose clan-deity (Kula-daivatā) is Reṇukā understands her to be the mother earth. The Bhālerāv family in Hyderābād, known by their title of 'Rāje Rāyarāyāṃ Bahādūr', are worshippers of Reṇukā, and the Reṇukā at Māhūr is their clan-deity. Until recently, it was a common custom to name family members after the deity to whom one is devoted. In accordance with this tradition, women in Bhālerāv family were given names such as Bhavānībāī, Ambābāī, Tuljābāī and Durgābāī, whereas the men in the family were called Bhavānīrāv, Bhavānīśaṅkararāv, Reṇukādāsa and Ambādāsa. One of the current male members in this family is called 'Pṛthivirāja'. The suffix Rāja in this name, like Rāya, is an honorific title. Therefore, similar to Tukojī, Ambājī and Tuḷojī, Pṛthvirāja is named after the goddess Pṛthvī, adapted for a man. In the hymn of the one thousand names of Reṇukā (*Reṇukāsahasranāma*), verse sixteen also calls her Pṛthivī.

In view of the above discussion, it should now be clear that the Reṇukā on the banks of the Praṇītā river was a headless and naked goddess in the *uttānapāda* posture, and that she was also called Pṛthivī, a name that connotes her original form. With this background, it would now be worth our while to think about the naked and headless goddess at Māhūrajharī. We can in fact deduce that the two goddesses in these two places with very similar names must bear the same name. Māhūr is Mātāpūra (the town of the mother), a name that suggests Reṇukā's motherhood of the world. Māhūrajharī, the Māhūr near the Jharī, is also indicative of the goddess's motherhood. It is therefore likely that it may well be Pṛthivīpūra.

Where is Pṛthivīpūra?

A copperplate inscribed during the reign of the Vākāṭaka king Pṛthivīseṇa was found at Māhūrajharī in June 1971. Dr V.B. Kolate published an edited version of this copperplate in the *Vidarbha Samśodhan Maṇḍaḷ Annual* in the same year.[45] The copperplate records the donation of a place called Jamalakheṭak to two Brāhmins, Viṣṇudatta and Bhavadatta, who lived at a place called Pṛthivīsamudra.

Dr Kolate did not discuss the exact locations of Pṛthivīsamudra or Pṛthivīpūra. He wrote:

> It is not possible to ascertain the exact location of the place called Pṛthivīsamudra where this copperplate was inscribed. One must

> ignore the first part, pṛthivī, which is a prefix indicating kingdom, and look for the place by concentrating on the latter part of the word; i.e. Samudra, which is often a place name. The main branch of the Vākāṭaka dynasty ruled over eastern Vidarbha and it is therefore likely that Pṛthivīsamudra would be somewhere around there. With this in mind, three places appear to be likely candidates: the town of Samudrī in the Sāvaner taluk of Nāgpur district, the town of Kṣīrasamudra in Vardhā taluk of Vardhā district and Samudrapūr in Hiṅgaṇghāṭ taluk. The Vakaṭakas moved their capital westwards, and it is therefore unlikely that they would have moved it again from Pravarapūr (the present day Pavanār) to the east. The town of Samudrī must therefore be discounted. The town of Kṣīrasamudra is in the southwest of Pavanār, only six miles away. If a capital had to be moved, it seems inconceivable that it would have been moved so close from Pravarapūr. The Samudrapūr mentioned above is about twenty kilometers southeast of the present day Pavanār (Pravarapūr). Therefore, it seems likely that Pṛthivīsamudra is the present day Samudrapūr. It is also possible that Kṣīrasamudra is Pṛthivīpūr. It is difficult to locate the Pṛthivīpūr from where the Brāhmins who were given the donation came.[46]

Dr Kolate's arguments can be summarised as follows: Pṛthivīsamudra is the name of a town. It must be the name of the capital of king Pṛthivīṣeṇa. The Vākāṭakas moved their capital from the east to the west, and hence Pṛthivīsamudra must be to the west of Pavanār (Pravarapūr), the earlier capital. Therefore, Pṛthivīsamudra must be either Samudrapūr (Tāluk: Hiṅgaṇghāṭ, District Vardhā) or Kṣīrasamudra (Tāluk and District Vardhā). Finally, Pṛthivīpūr must be a different place from Pṛthivīsamudra. However, it is not possible to locate it.

Māhūrajharī is Pṛithivīpūra

I think that confusion arose because Dr Kolate believed Pṛthivīsamudra to be the name of a town, and hence he separated Pṛthivīsamudra from Pṛthivīpūra. However, it is possible to put together a logical alternative, and to argue as follows:

1) I believe that Pṛthivīsamudra is not a place name but the name of a *tīrtha*. The word Samudra in the name denotes a tank.[47]

2) A tank called Pṛthivīsamudra must be located at the town of Pṛthivīpūra.
3) It has been a longstanding custom to offer '*dāna*' (religious donations) on the banks of a sacred stream or tank. It would therefore have been quite natural for Pṛthivīṣeṇa to give a donation on the site of the tank Pṛthivīsamudra.
4) The copperplate registering this donation was found at Māhūrajharī. Archeologists have found a large number of bricks, seals and other artifacts belonging to the Vākāṭaka dynasty at Māhūrajharī, showing that the town was a strong centre of Vākāṭaka culture.
5) Māhūrajharī (Māhūr = Mātāpūra) and Pṛthivīpūra are town-names with essentially the same meaning. Therefore, Māhūrajharī, the place where this copperplate was obtained, must be the same as Pṛthivīpūra.
6) The Vākāṭakas called themselves *hārītīputras*[48] (sons of *hārītī*, the earth). Hārītī is also a mother goddess.
7) Just as the first element in the names Hariṣeṇa, and Damodarasena stand for the names of deities, the first element, Pṛthivī, in the name Pṛthivīṣeṇa is indicative of a goddess's name. It points to the original form of the mother goddess at Māhūrajharī.
8) It would be quite appropriate for Pṛthivīṣeṇa, who belonged to a dynasty of kings who called themselves sons of the earth, to name Māhūrajharī, 'Pṛthivīpūra'. The name would signify 'the place of the mother. It would also be a memorial to his own name.

This train of logic suggests that during the reign of the Vākāṭakas, the place called Māhūrajharī was also known by two other names, Matṛpūra and Pṛthivīpūra. It was an important centre for the worship of Pṛthivī, mother earth, synonymous with Reṇukā. It was thus very appropriate that Dr Hunter described the image found at this place as an 'Earth Mother Goddess'.

Having perused the one thousand-five–hundred-year history of the goddess with the strange form at Mahākūṭa, Ālampūr and Māhūrajharī, one thing is quite clear to us. Although later on she became one with Śakti and united with Śiva, she is basically Bhūdevī or Pṛthivī, mother earth. At Ālampūr, she acquired the guise of Reṇukā. As a matter of fact, it is her association with Reṇukā that has made it possible to fully unravel the mystery of her iconography. Thus:

1) Reṇukā literally means Bhūdevī, mother earth. (Reṇu = fine particle, Reṇu+kā = made of particles = earth).
2) Made out of soft particles of sand, the ant's nest is a natural symbol used in the worship of Reṇukā. It is the symbol of the *yonī* of the earth, the womb of the earth. The South Indian word Poṭṭu in Tamil (*poṭa* = womb) signifies both the womb and the ant's nest.
3) The goddesses Mātaṅgī and Sānterī, who are worshipped in the form of an ants' nest, are analogous, if not identical, to Reṇukā. Mātaṅgī's mythology is of course closely associated with that of Reṇukā. On the other hand, Sānterī, who is well known in the southern Konkaṇ and Goa, is believed to have been established by Paraśurāma, the son of Reṇukā.
4) The work *Reṇukāmāhātmya* considers Reṇukā to be an incarnation of Aditi. It is a well-known fact that the Vedic seers considered Aditi to be mother earth.
5) Pṛthivī, who holds the world as a foetus in her womb, has been called *uttānā mahī* (mother earth – the great nude), by Vedic seers. This description is most appropriate in every possible way for the image of the Bhūdevī found at Mahākūṭa and at other places.
6) The worship of the ants' nest as a symbol of the female generative organ has been in vogue, at least in southern India, from ancient times. However, as the real nest is itself so very delicate, there is some evidence to show that sculpted stones in the form of ant hills were occasionally worshipped. The next stage of development in sculpture was the making of *yonī* images from the feet to the navel. Finally, in addition to giving birth, motherhood is also characterized by providing sustenance. Therefore, images from the feet to the shoulders were then created, which, in addition to the *yonī*, gave prominence to the breasts as well. It is possible, with adequate evidence, to trace the development of the iconography of Bhūdevī, mother earth, from the ants' nest to the image with the *yonī* and breasts.
7) Because of his close association with this field goddess who carries his seed in her womb, one is able to fathom the mythology of the equivalent male principle, the *kṣetrapāla*, who has also been worshipped in a variety of forms and carries a myriad of names.

8) It is important to note that *Lajjāgaurī*, the goddess with the strange form, has no connection whatsoever with any goddess in the western world. Such imagery, portraying either just the vagina or the vagina and the breasts, but decidedly without a head, has not been found elsewhere in the world. If there are some small similarities between *Lajjāgaurī* and any western goddess, it is only due to the fact that primitive people everywhere would have had similar ideas regarding the form of the goddess responsible for generation.
9) The worship of this deity seems to have bridged the divide between Āryan and Dravidian as well. Her worship has transcended this postulated divide and has done so for at least three thousand years.

The small window comprising of the biography of Reṇukā and the nature of the devotion to her, unfolds for us the history and the wonder of the worship of the female generative organ for over three thousand years.

The Temple and the Museum

The devotion that made this possible is in itself so strange that although it elevated this goddess to great heights, her original form has become nearly forgotten. In that original form, she is lying, out in the open, in one corner of the temple precinct at Mahākūṭa, subjected to the cruel ravages of time and weather. At Ālampūr, on the other hand, she dwells in a glass box in the museum, having been displaced from the niche that was her seat at the temple.

However strange the path of human devotion may seem, many examples can be cited in the historiography of gods and goddesses to theorize about how it progresses. One has to keep this thought in mind when one carries out research on the deities that have been created by human devotion.

Endnotes

1 Saṃskṛt to Marāṭhī translation by Ḍhere. Marāṭhī to English translation by Jayant Bāpaṭ.
2 *Prabuddha Karnāṭaka*. 1943. 25.2, No. 96. Dīpāvalī Issue: 25–30. See also, Ramesan, N. 1962. *Temples and Legends of Andhra Pradesh*. Bombay: Bhāratīya Vidyā Bhavan: 32–38.
3 Indian History Congress: *Proceedings of the Twenty-first Session*. 1958. Trivāndrum: xxx: 129–136.
4 Kannaḍā to Marāṭhī translation by Ḍhere. Marāṭhī to English translation by Jayant Bāpaṭ.
5 *Prabuddha Karnāṭaka*. *op.cit.*
6 *Ibid.*
7 Stella Kramrisch, *Artibus Asiae*, Vol.XIX, pp. 259–270.
8 Ramesan, N. *op.cit.*
9 C.E. 793.
10 *Vidharbha Samśodhan Mandaḷ Annual*, 1958, p. 115.
11 C.E. 861.
12 *Epigraphica Indica*, Vol.XVIII, p. 235.
13 C.E. 1303.
14 *Hyderābād Archeological Series*, No. 13, pp. 167–168.
15 *Vidharbha Samśodhan Mandaḷ Annual*, 1958, Note on p. 104.
16 *Lit*: The Yugalā Devī at Ālāpura.
17 *Journal of Oriental Research*, Madrās, Vol.XIX, p. 287.
18 Sarkār, Dr R.C. 1998. *The Śākta Pīṭhas*, Delhi: Motilal Banarassidāss: 19.
19 *Ibid.*
20 The *Reṇukāsahasranāma*, Hymns 101, 103.
21 *Ibid.* Hymn 126.
22 *Ibid.* Hymns 105, 106.
23 Reḍḍy, Suvārām Pratāp. 1959. *Āndhrakā Sāmājikā Itihāsa*. New Delhi: Sāhitya Academy, pp. 59 and 201 (in Hindi).
24 *Ibid.*, p. 314.
25 *Ibid.*, p. 58. See also Rama Rāv, Dr M. 1966. *Select Kakatiya Temples*. Tirupati: Śrī Veṅkaṭeśvara University: 27–28.
26 Kātagaḍe, Puṇḍalīkjī. *Kannaḍa Marāṭhī Śabdakośa*, *op.cit*, p. 264.
27 Ambuja = born in water – i.e., a lotus.
28 Tuḷpuḷe, Dr S. G. 1966. *Līḷācaritra*. Part 1. Nāgpur and Puṇe: Suvicār Prakāśan Maṇḍal, p. 87.
29 Translator's note: This question mark was written by Ḍhere himself. Anne Feldhaus thinks that the words mean a piece of bent rosewood. (Private Communication with Anne Feldhaus.)
30 Kolate, Dr V. B. ed., *Sthānapothī*. Malkāpūr: Arun Prakāśan, pp. 50 and 104 (Year of publication unavailable).
31 Translator's note: He was also known as Bhaskarācārya.
32 Translator's note: I am grateful to Professor Mādhavī Narasale, Department of Saṃskṛt, Mumbai University, for providing the translation of this difficult passage. Although syntax-wise the passage is not altogether clear, it does suggest that the goddess was looked upon as inferior to Brāhminic goddesses at that time as well.

33 Translator's note: Tāntrism has two main branches: the right-handed path (dakṣiṇamārga) and the left-handed path (vāmamārga).
34 *Prabuddha Karnāṭaka*. 25.2. Notes at the end of pages 25–30.
35 Saṃskṛt to Marāṭhī translation by Ḍhere. Marāṭhī to English translation by Jayant Bāpaṭ.
36 Bhiḍe, Prof. H.B. and Bhiḍe, Mrs. Māyāvatī. (1969). eds. *Saundaryalaharī*, Ahmedābād: pp. 81–84. See also Swāmī Dhanapati and Paṇḍit N.N. (1946). *Saundaryalaharī*, Mysore: University of Mysore, pp. 111–117.
37 Deśpaṇḍe, G. T. ed. *Vidharbha Samśodhan Mandaḷ Annual*, 1952 and 1971. (Articles by Dr V.B. Kolate, Dr S. B. Dev and Dr Ajayamitra Śāstrī). The University of Nāgpūr has recently published a detailed report on the archeological excavations at Māhūrzarī. (Translator's note: this would be closer to 1978, when the first edition of *Lajjāgaurī* was published).
38 Deshpande, Y.K. *Śāradāśrama Annual* (Śaka 1855, 1933 C.E.), Śāradāśrama, Yavatmāḷ. Note on p. 34.
39 At the time of the second edition of *Lajjāgaurī* in 1972.
40 Translator's note: Ḍhere seems to use the words Jyotibā and Jotibā interchangeably.
41 Sāvant, Śivājirāv Ābājirāv. (1965). *Śrikedāravijaya*, Beḷgāv: 1965, Śrirāmatatvaprakāśa, p. 324.
42 Saṃskṛt to Marāṭhī translation by Ḍhere. Marāṭhī to English translation by Jayant Bāpaṭ.
43 Translator's note: This explanation is somewhat puzzling to the translator. If the goddess appears from the sacrificial fire, her head and upper torso must come out first. As to how her lower parts up to the navel can come out before the rest of the body does, is very puzzling. Ḍhere, however, seems to be happy with this explanation.
44 Translator's note: There seem to be two sets of identifiable myths about Reṇukā. The first one explains how she came to be a goddess. The other myth makes no mention of her goddess-hood. See Desāī, Raśmī. 2008. When Reṇukā was not a goddess. In: Jayant Bhālcandra Bāpat and Ian Mabbett, ed., *The Iconic Female: Goddesses of India, Nepal and Tibet*, Clayton: Monash University Press, pp. 65–78.
45 *Vidharbha Samśodhan Maṇḍaḷ Annual*. 1971, pp. 53–77.
46 *Ibid*., pp. 71–72.
47 Translator's note: Traditionally, a reservoir of water in a temple precinct has been called a 'tank' (tīrtha) in India.
48 Mirāśī, V.V. 1957. *Vākāṭaka nṛpati āṇi tyāncā kāḷa*, Nāgpur: University of Nāgpūr, pp. 24, 72 and 329. (In Marāṭhī).

Chapter 3

Mātaṅgī

In the previous two chapters, we have seen that some elements of the worship of mother earth in the form of the female generative organ have been a common feature in the region that covers the present-day states of Āndhra, Mahārāṣṭra and Karnāṭaka. In this general region, this goddess has existed since ancient times under the name of Mātaṅgī, similar to, or at times identical with Reṇukā. An investigation into the mode of devotion and of the devotees of Mātaṅgī will help us in unravelling the mystery of the shy *Lajjāgaurī*.

Sons of the Earth

The Mahārs, who live all over Mahārāṣṭra, have called themselves 'sons of earth' since ancient times. There are fifty-three sub-groups of Mahārs; Gopāḷa is one of them.[1] This agrees with the statement, recorded in Mahānubhāva literature, that 'the devotees of Mātaṅgī call themselves Gopāḷa'. Mariāī, the main goddess of the Mahārs, is one of the ancient mother goddesses of the South. The firm belief in folk Hinduism is that she is responsible for both creation and destruction. The Tamil word Mārī signifies rain. One can therefore say that Mārī is someone who makes *Parjanya-deva*, the god of rain, produce rain.[2] It therefore follows that Mariāī, the tutelary deity of the Mahārs, is none other than mother earth. Generally, at all the places where she is known as Mātaṅgī, it is the Mahārs who are her priests. Occasionally, however, it seems, a Māṅg[3] performs this function. In this context, it is worth remembering that, when fields are being sown, women from farming castes traditionally make a ritual offering of coconut and a piece of cloth to a married Māṅg woman.[4]

The seats of Mātaṅgī are at Māhūr and Tuljāpūr in Mahārāṣṭra and at Soundattī in Karnāṭaka. The temple priests at these temples are Mahārs or Māṅgs. Māhūr is a *kṣetra* place and is often mentioned as the main seat of this goddess. Although it is in Mahārāṣṭra at present, Māhūr is very close to the border between Mahārāṣṭra and Āndhra Pradeś. For the purpose of our inquiry, it is necessary to investigate the strata of the society in these adjoining states where the worship of Mātaṅgī is prevalent. Such an investigation tells us that it is the Mādigā and Parihā, two particular castes in these southern states, who are devotees of this goddess. In socio-economic function and status, the Parihās are similar to the Mahārs and Cāmbhārs of Mahārāṣṭra, whereas the Mādigās are identical to the Māṅgs in Mahārāṣṭra. In both of these castes, there is a prevalence of myths surrounding the goddess Mātaṅgī. They also refer to her by two other names, Ellammā and Reṇukā.

The Mādigā caste is also known as Mātaṅga; it is spread throughout Āndhra Prades̀ and Karnāṭaka. Mādigās believe that their ancestor was a Ṛṣi called Jambū Ṛṣi. A certain Jambū Māḷī (Jambū, the gardener) is often mentioned in the songs of the Ḍhago-Megho sect in Mahārāṣṭra. The Mādigās eat beef, lamb and buffalo meat and also consume Toddi liquor freely. Sweeping is one of their major professions. The goddess they are devoted to is variously called Māramma, Māsanamma, Mātaṅgī and Mahālakṣmī.[5] These alternative names confirm that the goddess Marīāī, who has often been addressed by the laudatory name Mahālakṣmī in Mahārāṣṭra, is none other than Mātaṅgī.

We have seen previously (p. 29) that folk singers of the Mādigā caste called Bavanīḍas are worshippers of Joguḷāmbā. Joguḷāmbā is of course Mātaṅgī. This is clear from the fact that the Mātaṅgī devī at Soundatti is also called 'Juguḷubāī'. It should be amply clear from the discussion above that the goddess Reṇukā who is the presiding deity at Māhūr is the same as goddess Mātaṅgī. However, we will not rely simply on these suggestive pieces of evidence. We will research the stories and myths associated with Reṇukā and find out if they contain any evidence of the identical nature of the goddesses Reṇukā and Mātaṅgī.

Reṇukā and Mātaṅgī

A myth dealing with the relationship of Reṇukā and Mātaṅgī is to be found in the songs of the Gondhaḷīs,[6] the traditional worshippers of Reṇukā.[7]

> The sage Jamadagni, who had a very hot temper, had an aśrama on a hilltop at Māhūr. His wife was very devoted to him. Every day, instead of a pot, she would bring water from the river in a hollow made by her in her scarf. Because of the heat generated by her devotion to her husband (pātivratya), not a drop of it would leak out. One day, while she went to the river to fetch water, she

saw some Gandharva[8] couples who had entered the river water. Seeing their beautiful bodies and their uninhibited sporting and dallying filled Reṇukā with desire just for a moment and she forgot all about filling the scarf with water that she needed to take home. But in the next instant she came back to her senses and realised that she was late returning home.[9] Hurriedly she filled the scarf with river water. However, this little indiscretion on her part was enough to destroy her ascetic power, and some of the water leaked from the scarf, drenching her from head to foot. The moment she entered the āśrama, Jamadagni saw her in this state and was incensed. He ordered his son Paraśurāma to behead her straight away. Being the obedient son that he was, Paraśurāma did this summarily. Pleased with his obedience, Jamadagni asked his son to ask for a boon, so Paraśurāma asked that his father bring his mother back to life. Jamadagni agreed and told his son to look for the head and put it back on the torso. He told him that this action would bring Reṇukā back to life. Paraśurāma looked all over for his mother's head but was unable to locate it. Disappointed, on his way home he saw a Māṅg woman who looked somewhat similar to his mother. In desperation, he beheaded the woman with the intention of attaching her head to his mother's torso. However, Jamadagni stopped him from doing so. Instead, with his ascetic powers, he brought his wife's head back and restored her to life.

Although his mother came back to life, Paraśurāma was sad that a poor Māṅg woman had lost her life because of him. With the same respect that he showed for his mother, he installed the head of the Māṅg woman on the hillock at Māhūr and promised her that 'the devotees of Reṇukā will take your darśana and offer you naivedya[10] before they do so at the shrine of Reṇukā'. This is the same goddess Mātaṅgī who has the right of the first pūjā on the hillock at Māhūr.

Paṇḍit Mahādevśāstrī Jośī has this story in his collection. He heard it from a Gondhaḷī,[11] Mārutī Anājī Pācaṅge from Pune. As a tale which throws important light on the close connection between Reṇukā and Mātaṅgī, it is certainly very important.

Thus, it goes to show that in raising the status of Mātaṅgī by renaming her Reṇukā and thereby giving her a new identity, those responsible sought to preserve her original character at least to a small extent. This they did by allowing a niche, albeit a small one, for the worship of the original form of Mātaṅgī, along with the right to her first worship in the ritual worship of Reṇukā.

Several variations of this myth are available. One claims that there was an inadvertent exchange of the heads of Reṇukā and Mātaṅgī, whereas another one claims that the swapping of the heads was between a woman of the Parihā caste[12] and Ellammā. The Parihās also have a myth similar to the one above. In their version, Mariammā has been called the mother of Paraśurāma. The myth says that Mariammā was created by taking the torso of a Parihā woman and the head of the wife of a sage. Ellammā was born from the Parihā woman's head and the torso of the wife of the sage.[13]

Among songs that the Jogatī and Jogatīṇ worshippers[14] of Ellammā at Soundatti frequently sing, there is one which says:

> Wearing a Pītāmbara,[15] Reṇukā stands in water.
> Paraśurāma stands by her side and Mātaṅgī stands in front.

While both women are mentioned separately in here, the same song continues:

> The head belongs to Ellammā while the torso belongs to Mātaṅgī.
> The first bow is therefore for Mātaṅgī.[16]

These songs once again show the identity of Mātaṅgī and Reṇukā.

In the literature of the Mahānubhāvas, Mātaṅgī has been called Mesko-Māyarāṇī. It is this relationship that I now wish to examine.

Mātaṅgī and Mesko-Māyarāṇī

Mesko and Māyarāṇī are two goddess names which frequently occur along with Mātaṅgī in the literature of the Marāṭhī saints. These saints have included the three in the list of the names of the subordinate goddesses and have routinely spoken against the worship of these deities, as seen below:

1) *vāsanā māṅgīṇa mātaṅginī* |
kāmanā jaḷī Māyarāṇī |
abhāva bhāṅgaḍa bhūta joginī |
tyānsī nagna pūjitī kīṃ ||

(*Ekanātha Gāthā*, No. 3892)

2) *śimagā phālguna hoḷīce dinīṃ* |
nagna houna pūjitī māyarāṇī |
tī doḷe davaḍī avalakṣaṇī |
jo pāhūṃ jāya tyāce ||

3) *khaṇḍerāva ase nāpika houna* |
tarāḷī jagadambā vāhe pāṇī |
darabāra zāḍī mesko māyarāṇī |
bhairava gastī karitase ||

(Shekh Mahammad: *Yogasaṅgrāma*, 12.49, 82)

4) *tukāīi nā naraso māyarāṇī* |
vasatī smaśānīṃ |
bhogeṃ ghālitī gondhaḷa ||

(Shekh Mahammad: *Kavitāsaṃgraha*, p. 109)

5) *jākhamātā māyarāṇī* |*bāḷā baguḷā mānaviṇī* |
pūjā māṅgiṇī jogiṇī |
kuladharme karāvī ||

(Rāmdās' *Dāsabodha*, 4,5.16)

6) *navhe jākhāī jokhāī* |
māyarāṇī mesābāī ||

(*Tukārāmagāthā*, No. 2384)

7) *maiḷī mukī māyarāṇī* |
apulāliyā parivāragaṇīṃ |
uṭhāvalyā samaraṅgaṇīṃ |
nagna yakṣiṇī dhāṃvatī ||

(*Harivaradā*, 55.178)

(Translations:[17]

1) Mātaṅginī, the goddess of the Maṅg women, is greedy, and seeks worldly pleasures. Goddess Māyarāṇī (grants boons) in waters. Such godlings, who are in the class of ghosts and goblins, are worshipped in the nude.

2) On the day of the *hoḷī* festival in the month of *Phālguna*, Māyarāṇī is worshipped in the nude. On the other hand, she, the ill-omened one, turns those who look at her blind.

3) (The god) Khaṇḍerāya has become impotent. Jagadambā (the great goddess) has become the night watchman and is now carrying water. Mesko-Māyarāṇī is sweeping the floors of the Darbār and Bhairava is patrolling.[18]

4) Goddesses Tukāī, Naraso and Māyarāṇī occupy the cremation grounds and create havoc there.

5) If the worship of Jākhamātā, Māyarāṇī, Bālā, Bagulā, Mānavinī, Joginī and Maṅginī is part of a tradition in your family, then it should be performed as well.

6) No, it is not Jākhāi and Jokhāi, neither is it Māyarāṇī and Mesābāī.[19]

7) The dirty and inauspicious Māyarāṇī lives amongst her entourage. In the battlefield, she is accompanied by naked Yakṣiṇis.)

The first two of these references suggest that on the full-moon day in the month of Phalguna (Phālgunī Paurṇimā),[20] the goddess Māyarāṇī was worshipped by people in the nude. Ācārya K.V. Kālgāvkar has described the traditional worship of Māyarāṇī in some Brāhmin families in Mahārāṣṭra. At the time of this worship, it is customary to invite a shaven-headed widow (vikeśā)[21] as an auspicious guest[22] and feed her.[23]

In some of the above references, Māyarāṇī and Mesko are listed as separate goddesses. However, in others, they are one single entity. In this regard, the following information given by Bābā Padmanjī in his work 'Hindudharmāce Svarūpa' is noteworthy.[24]

> These deities are normally common among the Mahārs. They are worshipped mostly in the month of Bhādrapada on the day called Bhādavī.[25] It is thought that the Mahār goddess Mesko-Māyarāṇī is responsible for Smallpox and similar things. Therefore, villagers and Townsfolk invite the Mahārs on this day and offer them donations of grain, goat, sheep etc. as items of worship to appease Mesāī.[26]

The day of Bhādavā mentioned as the special day of worship for Mesko by Bābā Padmanjī is also known as 'Māhūr-Bhādavī'.[27] This is an obvious indication of the identical nature of Mesko, Mātaṅgī and Reṇukā.

Mātaṅgī Dīkṣā[28]

As I have stated, there is a caste in Āndhra and Karnāṭaka called the Mādigā who worship the goddess Mātaṅgī. Similar to Muraḷī, Bhāvīṇ and Jogtīṇ women, Mādigā virgins get initiated into the worship of Mātaṅgī.[29] Such initiated virgins are, in fact, called 'Mātaṅgī'. This is because of the firm belief of Mādigās and other related castes that a virgin initiated in such a manner is an incarnation of Mātaṅgī herself. It is worth our while to examine the procedure used to select such a girl.

In a village that wishes to select a virgin to represent Mātaṅgī, the villagers bring together all the unmarried girls and make them stand in front of the Mātaṅgī temple. They then beat the ḍhol (barrel) drums loudly, sing the goddess's songs and pray her to manifest herself in one of the virgins arrayed in front of her. A short time after this invocation, one of the girls starts acting as if she is possessed, and the villagers are convinced that the goddess has chosen her medium. This chosen maiden must however undergo further arduous tests to prove her suitability. She is made to sit upon a maṇḍala drawn on the floor with powdered sandstone (rāṇgoḷī, also known as muggu). Five pots of yoghurt are placed around her, in close proximity to her. A rope is then tied around each pot and the pots are suspended from the ceiling. If, in spite of her constant and feverish movements due to possession, she manages to avoid touching the yoghurt pots accidentally, she is considered to have passed the test for initiation as a Mātaṅgī. The girl is next given a cane basket, a stem of *nāgaphaṇī*[30] a bouquet of twigs from a neem tree and a string of cowrie shells, all of which are considered to be the distinctive marks of Mātaṅgī. These marks bestow a special status on the young woman, such that, as far the Mādigās are concerned, she is more than a representative of the goddess, she is the goddess herself. People start addressing her as *devī* from then on.

In addition to the procedure described above, there are other means that are occasionally used for the initiation of a virgin as Mātaṅgī. At unscheduled times, a young unmarried girl unexpectedly may start acting as if she has been possessed by the goddess. On such occasions, the villagers, even without a pre-planned initiation ceremony, subject her to various tests. If she successfully completes these tests, the villagers bestow upon her the marks of a Mātaṅgī.

At a place called Ceṇḍulūra, an entirely different procedure is followed. Here, people search for an anthill for the ceremony. They then dig into the anthill, and the girl wishing to undergo Mātaṅgī initiation is asked to sit inside it. Her head is covered with a cane basket. With the help of their drums and other instruments, the Bavanīḍu singers then start singing the praises of Mātaṅgī, her well-known devotees and their deeds. While the singing continues, the maiden sitting inside the anthill becomes suddenly possessed by the goddess. She forcefully throws away the cane basket and rushes out of the anthill. The Madigās accept this sudden movement by the maiden as a sign of her deification, and they offer her the special marks of Mātaṅgī such as the *nāgaphaṇī* staff. Since the anthill is the original symbol of Mātaṅgī, this particular form of initiation must be considered highly significant.

There is one more ceremony that would appear to be the ultimate endorsement of the initiation of a maiden as Mātaṅgī. The village of Malinathapaḍu near Kumbam in the Kurnūl district of Āndhra Pradeś is well known as a seat of Mātaṅgī-Ellammā. Mātaṅgī female initiates come here from many different places at considerable financial expense to themselves. Upon their arrival, they are asked to sit in a row in front of the goddess. A Brāhmin then paints the same marks on their faces as are found on the image of Mātaṅgī. A male buffalo is then sacrificed in front of the goddess. The ritual lasts for five days. At the end of this period, the devotees believe that all of the young women have acquired the life-essence of the goddess. Each of these Mātaṅgīs is then married to a tree. After this symbolic marriage, the Mātaṅgī is free to cohabit with any man of her choice; such an act is not considered to make her immoral.

The Secret behind the Appearance of the Mātaṅgī from the Ant-hill

The ant-hill is the original symbol of Mātaṅgī. It is in this symbol that Reṇukā-Ellammā-Mātaṅgī is worshipped in many parts of the South. In Gomāntaka (Goa) and in southern Konkaṇ, she is worshipped as Sānterī in this ant-hill form. The worship of both Reṇukā and Sānterī is thought to have been started by Paraśurāma himself. The ant-hill, which is made out of the soft, mysterious and sensuous particles of soil, is the representation of the Yonī of the earth and the serpent that inhabits it is supposed to represent the male principle. The goddess name Reṇukā itself means 'the earth' (Reṇu + kā = made out of Reṇus, particles, i.e. pṛthivī, the earth). This is also why she is called *Korī Bhūmikā* (virgin earth). Sānterī is also known as *Bhūmikā* in Goa. Since the goddess that dwells in the field (*kṣetradevatā*) is worshipped in the form of an anthill in this way, it is but natural that Murugan, Subrahmaṇya, Khaṇḍobā, Jyotibā, Ravaḷnāth, and Bhairava, who are the corresponding male gods that dwell in fields (*kṣetrapāḷa*), are thought to exist in the form of a serpent as well. As a matter of fact, as we shall see in a later chapter, even today, Subrahmaṇya is worshipped in the form of a serpent residing in an anthill. In particular, the Maṇmailāra at Bellārī in Karnāṭaka and the Ādimailāra on the banks of the Karhā river at Jejurī are both thought to be represented as serpents in ant-hills. It should now be quite apparent as to why, iconographically, the goddess Sānterī at Goa is shown holding serpents in her hands and why the devotees of Mātaṅgī hold a staff in the shape of a serpent (*nāga-kāṣṭha*) in their hands. The reason must lie in the portrayal of the serpent as the god and protector of the field (*kṣetrapāḷa*).

In the collection of myths associated with Reṇukā, there is one that actually portrays her as *ādiśakti* herself who appeared out of an ant-hill and was raised as a princess.[31] In the initiation into the Mātaṅgī cult, the devotee experiences this myth over and over again. As early as the composition of the Brāhmaṇas, the ant-hill had acquired inordinate importance in the worship of the earth. There is good evidence to suggest that in many of the rituals described in the Brāhmaṇas, the earth from an ant-hill is utilised as being symbolically highly fertile.

Virgin Reṇukā and Fatherless Paraśurāma

We now know that the Reṇukā worshipped as a virgin is none other than the earth mother, the virgin earth. Although she bears the foetus of creation in her womb all year around, and in every season, she is a virgin forever. A firm belief that consistently runs through the devotional tradition of the cult of the mother goddess is that, although she embraces the male seed in a variety of ways, her virginity is never compromised. The devotional songs in the cult of Ellammā-Reṇukā at Saundattī repeatedly mention her unblemished virginity. In these songs, Paraśurāma is constantly taunted by his peers for being a fatherless child. He therefore goes to his mother Reṇukā and asks her to take him to his father straightaway. Reṇukā replies:

Saṃbhācyā lekī kheḷāy gelyā hotyā |
sahā jaṇīnī gaṇa detānā |
tulā bin bāpācā māgūna ghetalā |
malā nāhī pati, tulā nāhī bāpa |
kuṭhalā davūm aśā yeḷalā ||

> (Sambhā's daughters had gone to play. Six of them were giving gaṇa.[32] That time I asked for you, a son, without a father. I don't have a husband; you do not have a father. How can I show you a father at this time?)

Mataṅga and Mātaṅgī

The worship of mother earth as Mātaṅgī and that of water as Ḍhago-Megho[33] reminds me of Gajalakṣmī. Gajalakṣmī, also known as Lakṣmī-Padmā, Padmajā and Padmahastā-Lakṣmī, is considered to be identical with the earth. Gaja, the elephant, on the other hand, symbolizes the cloud that drenches her, and is thus the representation of *dyaus*, the sky. The Gajalakṣmī sculpture which resoundingly exhibits the auspicious union of the sky and the earth spells out the secret behind the entire creation. The symbolism behind this sculpture must be one of the most fundamental ideas in the development of human thought and can therefore lay claim to archetypicality.

Those who claim that the Gajalakṣmī motif first evolved as a symbol of the Buddha's nativity and that it was first sculpted at the Sāñci-Bharhūt *stūpas*, have obviously not considered the antiquity and the basic nature of the idea. Even today, the worship of Gajalakṣmī based on this ancient symbolism is prevalent in the folk culture of Mahārāṣṭra. At Sātārā, Solāpūr, Kolhāpūr and some other places nearby, Gajalakṣmī is worshipped as a folk goddess (*grāmadevatā*). She has several shrines in the vicinity of Kolhāpūr and at these places she is variously called Bhāveśvarī, Bhāvakā and Bhāvakāī. At many of these places, female devotees worship her in order to have an easy childbirth. Since she is fundamentally the goddess of auspicious conception, it is but natural that she be worshipped for an easy childbirth.

In the idea behind Gajalakṣmī, the gaja (elephant) is a symbol for a cloud. It is no mere coincidence that the poet Kālīdāsa equated the cloud with an elephant in his epic poem Meghadūta. Traditionally, Indians have always accepted that a cloud and an elephant are one and the same.[34] Airāvata, the legendary vehicle for Indra, the god of rain, is also a cloud. Irā means water and hence Airāvata means a cloud full of water. In this connection, one remembers Mātaṅga, an alternative name for an elephant.[35] Mātaṅga is the male principle in the form of an elephant, whereas Mātaṅgī is the female principle in the form of earth.

The Importance of the Cowrie Shell in the Worship of Goddesses

The cowrie shell carries enormous importance in the cults of the southern goddesses Reṇukā, Ellammā, Mātaṅgī, Mariāī, Bhavānī and Mahālakṣmī. The Gondhaḷī, Bhutye, *Potrāj*, Mātaṅgī, Jogtī and Jogtiṇī, who are totally diverse worshippers of these deities, adorn themselves with various ornaments made out of cowrie shells. The Gondhaḷī, Bhutye and Mātaṅgī-Jogtiṇī have cowrie necklaces; the conch-shell-shaped hats of the Bhutye are covered with cowrie shells on the outside; the *jagā*[36]of the Jogtiṇī have cowrie shells woven on them; the bags of Bhandāra[37] that devotees carry have cowrie shells attached to them, and the flower baskets that Mātaṅgī women carry are decorated with cowrie shells. The Gondhaḷī, Bhutye, *Potrāj*, Mātaṅgī, Jogtī and Jogtiṇī all wear around their necks a thick band of cloth which holds images of the goddess embossed on a metal plaque. This cloth is also decorated with cowrie shells.

Folk songs about the goddess suggest time and again that she also likes to put on cowrie shells when she does her make up.[38]

> A yellow silk garment (pītāmbara) for Ambā to wear |
> A silk garment (pītāmbara) for the Devi to wear ||
> ambā has adorned herself with cowrie shells |
> devi has done so ||

The garland and the flower basket made out of bamboo strips are the main distinguishing marks of devotees of the goddess. Both of these are adorned with cowrie shells. With pride, these devotees often say:

> *māḷa paraḍī āliyā mazyā naśibālā*
>
> (the garland and the basket are my lot in life.)

The Potrāja also mentions these marks in his chant:

> *māḷa paraḍī āhe tyālā* |
> *udo bolalī jogavyālā* ||
>
> (the one who has the garland and the cowrie shell basket, she (the goddess) allowed him to ask for *jogvā*.)

When the Jogatīṇa describes goddess Ellammā, she says with great devotion:

yallū maṅgalavārā diśīṃ |
yallū śukravārā diśīṃ |
ālī ḍoṅgara utaruniyāṃ |
bhaṇḍāra ibhutīcā maḷavaṭa bharatī ||
vara kukavācā tiḷā letī |
māḷa paraḍī śikkā maga ghetī |
yallu jogavā māgatī ||

> (On Mondays and Fridays, goddess Yallammā comes down the hill. She smears her forehead with tumeric and then puts the red kumkum on top. Holding in her hand her marks of the garland and the flower basket, she goes begging for alms.)

In this song, the Jogtiṇ says that Goddess Yallammā herself is seeking alms (*jogvā*). She holds the Māḷa and Paraḍī as her ornaments. The garland of cowrie shells which adorns the goddess' neck, is full of Bhaṇḍārā (turmeric) and is a representation of her generative powers. In the stories and myths of the Jogtiṇs, an innocent devotee removed the Bhaṇḍārā from the cowrie shells that he was wearing. Because of this, he suffered a burning sensation over his whole body.

kavaḍicyā māḷetalā bhaṇḍārā kāḍhilā |
tyācyā aṅgāvaratī jhokalā |
āgin jaḍalī tyācyā aṅgālā ||

Cowrie Shell: A Symbol of the Vagina

The inordinate importance of the cowrie shell in the worship of the goddess is due of course to its shape, which resembles a vagina. All over the world, the cowrie shell is considered to be a symbol of the vagina. Briffault spells out this aspect of the cowrie shell unequivocally when he says:

> Cowrie shells are often worn, usually as charms against sterility. Like all fertility charms, the cowrie shell and other shells have come to acquire magic protective virtues against all evils. The Japanese, if a cowrie shell happens to be unavailable, use a pornographic picture representing the female genitals as a substitute.[39]

Since the cowrie shell is accepted this way as a symbol of the vagina, it is but natural that it be considered the favourite of the deities associated with reproduction and that it has gained great importance in the cult of such deities.

The Importance of the Cowrie Shell in the Marriage Rite

The importance of the cowrie shell as a symbol of female generativity in the form of the physical organ led to its recognition in folk culture as an emblem of fertility. As a result, it has gained importance in the rites associated with fertility. The most important of such rites is of course the wedding. It is marriage that gives social recognition through ritual to the sexual relationship between a man and a woman, which is responsible for the continuation of life. For this reason, the rite of marriage is closely connected with many fertility charms.[40]

Certain communities who have the custom of offering *dej* (bride-price) to the bride consider the cowrie shell an essential part of it. In Āndhra Prades̀, the Erukal community makes an offering of *dej* to the father of the bride. An essential part of this presentation is some cowrie shells. In Punjab, a spinning wheel is among the items given to a bride, and this wheel is decorated with cowrie shells. In many parts of India, when a bride leaves her parental home, she is given a cane basket full of things essential for day-to-day living. In Orissā, this basket is called *Jagathī Peḍī,* whereas in Āndhra it is called *Kaviḍa Peṭṭe*. A few cowrie shells are invariably included in this basket. In some areas of Āssām, it is customary for the bridegroom to present the bride with a cowrie shell. The bride carefully preserves this gift obtained at the time of the wedding in a container of kumkum (vermilion) powder and uses the kumkum from this container only on special occasions. In Rājasthān, certain articles are tied in a piece of red cloth and are hung over the head of the bride and groom in the wedding canopy. These articles include a cowrie shell. In most marriage ceremonies, a red cotton thread is tied around the wrists of the bride and the groom. As a rule, a betel nut also forms a part of this bracelet. However, in some parts of India, a cowrie shell replaces the betel nut. While in Mahārāṣṭra the bride and groom play a game of releasing the betel nut from this thread, in Orissā a cowrie shell is released in a similar way. In both cases, the bride tightly holds the betel nut or the cowrie shell in her fist and the groom tries to open her fist with one hand and collect the prize.

The cowrie shell has long been considered to give life, to give children and to bestow a long married life. Symbolically, presenting the bride with a cowrie shell at the time of her wedding is thought to give her progeny. In Āssām, people believe that the mother goddess resides in the cowrie shell. Elders of the Ahoma community in Āssām hold cowrie shells in their fists and shake the fists close to the ears of the bride and groom at the time of the *Cakalāṅga* (wedding) ceremony, making the characteristic sound of a rattle. It is their firm belief that hearing this sound brings wealth and progeny to the couple. In the Mīnā community of Rājasthān, when the bride goes to the bed chamber on her first night, her garment is decorated with cowrie shells.

I need not repeat that it is the vagina-like shape of the cowrie shell that has resulted in its being given such importance in marriage rituals. There are many other games similar to the 'opening the fist' described above that are played by brides and grooms. In Bengāl, the future success of the couple's married life is predicted by their casting cowrie shells. If an even number of shells that they have thrown fall face up, it is considered auspicious for the couple. On the other hand, an odd number falling face up spells misfortune.

The games mentioned above have been designed with one purpose in mind: the newly-weds should get to know each other, achieve a meeting of minds and develop mutual attraction. The cowrie shell plays an important part in such games. When they are engrossed in playing such games on the chess-like board, giving cowrie shells to each other, their eagerness for physical union is automatically enhanced. The game of chess between the father and the mother of the world, Śiva and Pārvatī, has been the subject of many folk and purāṇic tales. Among the sculptures of Ellorā, this game of chess between Śiva and Pārvatī is beautifully portrayed. This play of life is portrayed by the cowrie shell; that is the greatness of it!

Endnotes

1 Kālelkar, G.M. 1928. *Mumbai Ilākhyātīla Jātī*, Barodā: 202–208. (In Marāṭhī).
2 Mahālingam, T. V., The Cult of Śakti in Tamilnad, in D.C.Sarkār ed. 1967. *Śakti Cult and Tārā*, Calcuṭṭā: University of Calcuṭṭā Press: 33. Mahalingam says, 'It is also thought that Mariamman is a goddess of rain, the Tamil term *Mari* meaning a 'shower'.
3 Translator's note: The Maṅgs are another caste who were classified as untouchables before the caste system was abolished.
4 Translator's note: The custom called *oṭī bharaṇe* [lit. to fill the lap (of a married woman with rice, fruit, tumeric, betel nut, and especially a coconut)] is common all over India. Symbolically, it signifies fertility.
5 Jośī, Paṇḍit Mahādevaśāstrī. 1972. Ed., *Bhāratīya Saṃskṛtikośa*, Bhāratīya Saṃskṛtikośa Maṇḍaḷa, Pune: Vol. 7: 309–312. This reference describes the Mādigā caste in detail. (In Marāṭhī). Ḍhere quotes the original reference as follows: Iyer, Nanjundayya. 1931. *The Mysore Tribes and Castes*, Mysore, University of Mysore.
6 Translator's note: A different version of the same myth appears in the previous chapter.
7 Jośī, Paṇḍit Mahādevaśāstrī. 1962. *Lokakathākunja*, Pune: 21–24. (article with the title: *māṅgiṇīce śīra* = The head of the Māṅg woman). (In Marāṭhī).
8 Translator's note: Gandharvas are celestial singers whose women are called Apsarasas.
9 Translator's note: Fresh water is essential for ritual worship and Reṇukā would have been taking it home for her husband's ritual oblations etc.
10 *Naivedya* is a food offering.
11 See Ref. 3.
12 Translator's note: Parihā (Pariah) is another name for the untouchables (now called Dalit) spread all over India. See, Viśwanāth, Rūpā. 2014. *The Pariah Problm: Caste, Religion, and the Social in Modern India*, Columbia University Press.
13 Whitehead, H. 1921. *The Village Gods of South India*, Calcuṭṭā: p. 116. See also Elmore, W.T. 1925. *Dravidian Gods in Modern Hinduism*, Madrās: 98–106.
14 Translator's note: These are the traditional worshippers of Ellammā.
15 Translator's note: A Pitāmbara is a traditional silk garment worn by men at the time of performing rituals.
16 Bābar, Sarojinī. 1964. ed. *Eka Hotā Rājā*, Bombay: 93–94. (The songs of goddess Ellammā).
17 Translator's note: Ḍhere has not provided detailed translations of the verses quoted here by him. Instead, he has chosen to give a generalised summary in a few lines. The verses are from the writings of various saint-poets. In spite of considerable efforts, and consultation with experts who are well-versed in archaic Marāṭhī in Mahārāṣṭra, I have been unable to get satisfactory translations of some of these verses. Translations of only some verses have been provided here. I am indebted to Professor Mādhavī Narsaḷe for help with some of these translations.
18 Translator's Note: The poet is probably describing the untoward and abnormal happenings in the Kali Yuga.

19 Translator's note: The complete verse here is:
navhe jākhāī jokhāī | *māyarāṇī mesābāī* | *baḷiyā mājhā pandharīrao* | *jo yā devancāhī deva* ||
(These minor godlings such as *jākhāī, jokhāī, māyarāṇī* and *mesābāī* [should not be worshipped]. My God Paṇḍharināth [Viṭṭhala] is most powerful. He is the god of all gods.)
Source: *Sārtha tukārāmācī gāthā*, Gopālrāv Govind Benāre (Ed.), Saraswatī Granth Bhāṇḍār, Śake 1923 (C.E. 2001).

20 Translator's note: Falgunī Paurṇimā occurs at the end of March or in the 1st week in April.

21 Translator's note: Until about the 1940's, it was common, especially among Brāhmin families, to completely shave the hair of a woman immediately upon the death of her husband. Such women were considered to be inauspicious and were forced to live only within the confines of the house. It is most interesting that in this case, such a woman is being considered auspicious. This is an example where, similar to Tantra, societal norms are deliberately transgressed.

22 Translator's note: There is an interesting role inversion here. Traditionally, widows are considered inauspicious and certainly those whose hair has been (deliberately) removed are most certainly so. In this case however, perhaps because the goddess is worshipped by the polluted untouchable castes, the inauspicious becomes auspicious.

23 Bhārat Itihās Samśodhak Maṇḍaḷ, Quarterly. Ḍhere gives no date.

24 Padmanjī, Bābā. 1901. *Hindudharamāce Svarūpa*, Part 2, p. 261.

25 Translator's note: Bhādrapada is usually the month of September in the English calendar.

26 Mesāī = mother Mesā, another name for Mesko-Māyarāṇī.

27 Roberson, A. 1938. *The Mahār Folk*, Calcuṭṭā: 71.

28 Initiation into the Mātaṅgī cult.

29 Elmore, *op.cit.* pp. 22–26.

30 Translator's note: Nāgaphaṇī or Nāga-kāṣṭha is a kind of wood often used by holy men and ascetics to make their staffs. Its branches are often somewhat coiled, giving the appearance of a cobra. Hence the name, *nāgaphaṇī* (a cobra's hood) or Nāga-kāṣṭha (cobra-wood).

31 Elmore, *op.cit.* pp. 98–106.

32 Translator's note: The exact meaning of this verse is unclear. Ḍhere himself is not sure what the word *gaṇa* means here.

33 Translator's note: The Dhago Megho sect is covered in the chapter, *Mātaṅgīpaṭṭa*.

34 Translator's note: It is not an uncommon theme in Indian iconography to show an elephant having intercourse with a woman. In here, the monsoon clouds are represented by an elephant who fertilizes the feminine earth. See Rawson, Philip. 1981. *Oriental Erotic Art*, New York, Gallery Books: p. 20.

35 A work called *Mātaṅgalīlā* dealing with elephants and written by one Nīlakaṇṭha is available.

36 Translator's note: A *jaga* is a cane basket containing an image of the goddess. It is traditionally carried by the Jogtīṇa on her head.

37 Translator's note: *Bhaṇḍāra* is powdered turmeric, which is a favourite of god Khaṇḍobā. It is sprinkled liberally on him and on his devotees with the chants of 'yelkoṭ, yelkoṭ' at Khaṇḍobā temples.

38 Bābar, Sarojinī. 1964. ed. *op.cit.* pp. 11, 90, 94.

39 Briffault, R. 1959. *The Mothers*, London: 390.

40 Bhavan's *Journal*, XVIII, 23, 11th June 1972: 51–53.

Chapter 4

The Mataṅgīpaṭṭa

The Mātaṅgīpaṭṭa is a devotional cult that has received little scholarly attention in Mahārāṣṭra. It has remained so because of its prevalence mainly among the lowest strata of the society. The word literally means, 'the seat of the goddess Mātaṅgī'. It should be clear from this name that it is goddess Mātaṅgī who is the presiding deity of this cult. For the past four or five centuries, people in Mahārāṣṭra have assumed that this cult and the much-discussed Mahānubhāva sect[1] are one and the same thing. This has led to severe and unwarranted criticism of the Mahānubhāvas by Mahārāṣṭrian society. Incensed by this, in the distant past the Mahānubhāvas made counter attacks, albeit feeble, against this treatment. Lately, they have also filed complaints against such treatment in the courts. However, for one reason or another, such attempts by the Mahānubhāvas have proved fruitless. As a result, every so often, it has been claimed that the myths about the origins of the Mahānubhāva sect and the Mātaṅgīpaṭṭa are identical.

It is with this background of age-old conflicts, attacks and counter-attacks that we have to examine the origin of the Mātaṅgīpaṭṭa. In order to ascertain the exact direction of our research, we must at first seek answers to the following questions:

1) Are the Mahānubhāva and Mātaṅgīpaṭṭa cults different or are they a single cult called by two different names?
2) If they are two different cults, what was the reason for their being mistaken as a single cult? Is there some commonality between the two?
3) If the Mātaṅgīpaṭṭa is different from the Mahānubhāva sect, when did the former originate? How and where in Mahārāṣṭra did it spread? Is it still practised today? Finally, what is or was its exact nature?

Antiquity of the Kṛṣṇaṃbhaṭa Myth

Over the past four centuries, a rumour about the origin of the Mahānubhāva sect has periodically surfaced. It states that this sect, which worships five aspects of Kṛṣṇa (pañca-kṛṣṇopāsaka) has as its founders five men who were born to a low-caste Māng woman from an adulterous Brāhmin called Kṛṣṇaṃbhaṭa. The rumour explains that these five Māng bhāvas (brothers) started the cult which later became known as Mānabhāva or Mahānubhāva. Two works, Nagesh's *Mahātmākathānaka* in Saṃskṛt[2] and *Mānabhāvotpattikathā* in Marāṭhī[3] elaborate upon this origin of the Mahānubhāva sect. The exact timing of publication of these works is unknown. However, after an examination of the paper and the style of its writing, Candorkar, who edited the Saṃskṛt work in the early 20th century, thought that it must have been written no earlier than 200 to 250 years ago. The Marāṭhī work appears to be based on the Saṃskṛt *pothi*. The well-known composer of (Marāṭhī) lexicons in the previous century, Raghunāthśāstrī Goḍbole, has included the Kṛṣṇaṃbhaṭa myth as the origin of the Mahānubhāva sect in his lexicon, *Bhārata Khaṇḍācā Arvācīna Kośa* (*Lit*: Modern Encyclopaedia of the Indian Subcontinent).[4] The Pharsi work *Tārikhe Amajadī* was produced around the same time, in 1870 C.E. This work also mentions that the opponents of the Mahānubhāvas trace the origin of the sect to an illicit union between a Brahmin, Kṛṣṇaṃbhaṭa, and a low caste Māng woman.[5]

The Mahānubhāva poet Kṛṣṇamunī Ḍimbh (second half of the 17th century), in his unpublished work called *Phalṭaṇ Māhātmya* (*Lit*: The Importance of the town of Phalṭaṇ) wrote about the Jain opponents of the Mahānubhāvas in the following manner:

> *yerīkaḍe nimbanātha jaineṃ* |
> *mātāṅgmūḷeṃ kelīṃ sarva darśaneṃ* |
> *to grantha vācilā teṇeṃ* |
> *singaṇāpratī* || (8.44)
>
> (In this manner, Nimbanāth Jain described all of the darśanas including that of mātaṅgī. He then read this work in front of [King] Singhaṇa.)

Although Kṛṣṇamunī mentions "all the darśanas", in actual fact he is suggesting that the Jains equate Jain 'mundī darśana' with that of Mātaṅgī.[6] On the other hand, he himself is highly critical of the worship of Mātaṅgī devī. Thus, he says:

jeṃ daivat jayāciyā manā |
to tayācī karī upāsanā |
sāṇḍoni kaivalyarāṇā |
pūjitī mātaṅginītem || (1.42)

(People worship only those deities that they are fond of. Thus, instead of worshipping Kaivalyarāṇā [Kṛṣṇa], they worship Mātaṅginī.)

Kṛṣṇamunī thus thinks that it is highly improper for people to give up worshipping great gods such as the Kaivalyarāṇā (Kṛṣṇa) and instead worship petty and worthless godlings such as Mātaṅginī.

A contemporary of Kṛṣṇamunī, Śekh Mohammadabābā Śrīgondekar who took Samādhī probably around 1675 C.E., is a strong critic of the Mahānubhāvas as well. In his work called *Niṣkalaṅka Prabodha*, he specifically mentions the Kṛṣṇaṃbhaṭa myth in order to denigrate the Mahānubhāvas. He declares:

upharāṭā mārga thāṭalā kṛṣṇambhaṭeṃ |
tyāce śiśya cāṭe teṃca ācaritī ||

(Kṛṣṇaṃbhaṭa established the reverse path.[7] His disciples follow the same.)

The foregoing discussion conclusively proves that the Kṛṣṇaṃbhaṭa myth was regarded as the story of the origin of the Mahānubhāvas as early as the middle of the 17th century. Naturally, the events that probably led to such beliefs getting a firm foothold must have taken place well before this time.

Although the opponents of the Mahānubhāvas use the Kṛṣṇaṃbhaṭa myth to malign them, writers belonging to the Mahānubhāva sect have always insisted that the Kṛṣṇaṃbhaṭa sect is a totally separate cult known as 'Mātaṅgīpaṭṭa or Māṅginīpaṭṭa'. They have also expressed over and over again their strong dislike of it. I wish to cite two Mahānubhāva works in particular: the *Dinakaranibandha* in Saṃskṛt and the *Gajakesarī* in both prose and verse forms in Marāṭhī. These two unpublished works give a detailed account of many extant sects. They compare them with Mahānubhāva teachings and have, on that background, sought to denigrate them, thereby attempting to show the superiority of the Mahānubhāvas. The Mātaṅgīpaṭṭa and the Kṛṣṇaṃbhaṭa myth are among those that these works denigrate. Although these two works are no more than between one hundred and one hundred and fifty years old,[8] I feel it is necessary to examine them in the context of the information they provide about our current interest, the Mātaṅgīpaṭṭa. Rather than analyse the arguments advanced by the opponents of the Mahānubhāvas (about the latter being the same as the Mātaṅgīpaṭṭa sect), I have chosen to analyse these Mahānubhāva works to see how truthful the information given by them is with respect to the Mātaṅgīpaṭṭa. If their information proves to be correct, the opponents of the Mahānubhāvas would be shown to be wrong. This would give us an additional direction in our search for the reasons behind the maligning of the Mahānubhāvas by their opponents.

Description of the Mātaṅgīpaṭṭa in the *Dinakaranibandha*

The *Dinakaranibandha* describes the Mātaṅgīpaṭṭa in the following manner.

> *kanthaḍīnāthaśiṣyo 'sau kṛṣṇabhaṭṭo 'tha māntrikaḥ* |
> *mātāpure nyavāsīt sa śābarāgamatatparaḥ* || 83 ||
> *tenāgamarahasyena mātaṅgī devatā kila* |
> *prārthitā mānyatāyai ca jātā sā varadāyinī* || 84 ||
> *mātaṅgyai devatāyai ca dattā mataṅgakanyakā* |
> *balistām jīvayitvā ca dadau tasyātha devatā* || 85 ||
> *jātā sā varadā tasya yatheṣṭaṃ tena tattathā* |
> *tasyā mātaṅgakayāyāscakre pāṇigrahaṃ svayam* || 86 ||
> *kṛṣṇabhaṭācca tasyāṃ vai jātāḥ pañcakumārakāḥ* |
> *datto ḍhagastathā megho guṇḍaścāṅgaśca pañcamaḥ* || 87 ||
> *putraiśca pañcabhiḥ kṛṣṇabhaṭṭastriśatavatsarān* |
> *jīvito 'bhūnmahārāṣṭre ekavīrā prasādataḥ* || 88 ||
> *te vai pañcakumārāsca jātā vai māntrikāḥ kila* |
> *ātmānaṃ pañcakṛṣṇaṃ ca rāvaḷaṃ kathayanti hi* || 89 ||
> *cāṅgo 'tha mantravādī ca tatprasannā tvabhūt kila* |
> *ekavīrā mahādevī dadau bhūtiṃ salāghavām* || 90 ||

Kanthaḍīnātha, who is mentioned here, belonged to the Nāth cult. However, in śloka 82 of the *Dinakaranibandha*, the author calls his teachings, 'a fallen, degenerated path of the *Mudrīmārga*', i.e. the Nāth cult.

Ślokas 83 to 90 can be summarised as follows: Kṛṣṇaṃbhaṭa, who lived at Mātāpūr, was a disciple of Kanthaḍīnātha. He was a māntrika (a performer of black magic) and an expert in the *Śābarāgama*.[9] He was well aware of his lack of status in the society of the time, and therefore worshipped the goddess Mātaṅgī at Mātāpūr. He hoped that by doing so, he would acquire a boon to achieve high status. To this end, he also performed a human sacrifice of a Māṅg (an untouchable caste, also called Mātaṅga) girl. Because of this, the goddess was pleased with him, brought the girl back to life and asked Kṛṣṇaṃbhaṭa to marry her. Kṛṣṇaṃbhaṭa did so and the couple had five sons out of this marriage: Datto, Ḍhago, Megho, Guṇḍo and Cāṅgo.

Because of the boons he received from goddess Ekavīrā (another name for Goddess Mātaṅgī of Mātāpūr), Kṛṣṇaṃbhaṭa lived with his five sons in Mahārāṣṭra for 300 years. All three of his sons became Māntrikas as well. They called themselves Rāvaḷa. The five of them together were also called Pañcakṛṣṇas. One of them, Cāṅgo, worshipped goddess Ekavīrā fervently and, as a result, obtained a special power (*Siddhī*) from her.

Ślokas 91 to 106 of the *Dinakaranibandha* continue the story of Cāṅgo. They describe how, on the strength of this power, Cāṅgo created havoc in the town of Paiṭhaṇ.[10] He was however defeated by the Mahānubhāvas. In particular, after he was joined by a Mahānubhāva called Munirāja Navagrahī, he was deeply influenced by Mahānubhāva philosophy, and his behaviour and entire life changed.

The author of the *Dinakaranibandha* then describes the fate of the other four sons of Kṛṣṇaṃbhaṭa as follows:

> *Dattādyāścaiva catvāraḥ kṛṣṇambhāṭṭātmajāśca ye* |
> *taiscaturbhiḥ samākhyātaṃ dharaṇī-vāri-daivatam* || 107 ||
> *kāyaprakṣāḷamātmānaṃ gopālaṃ kathayanti hi* |
> *te vai mātaṅgaguravo mātaṅgāste tadānugāḥ* || 108 ||
> *datto jāṭhavaḍe grāme mṛto yātrāsthalam tvabhūt* |
> *Ḍhago 'sya bābulgrāme mṛtavān bālaparvate* || 109 ||
> *ḍombegrāme mṛto megho gunḍo nimbapure mṛtaḥ* |
> *teṣām dhūtādibhedāśca bahavo vāsanāvaśāḥ* || 110 ||

All the above information in the work *Dinakaranibandha* can now be summarised as follows:

The tutelary deity of Kṛṣṇaṃbhaṭa was goddess Ekavirā, alias Mātaṅgī, of Māhūr. From the Māṅg maiden that he had sacrificed for the goddess (and who was later revived by her), Kṛṣṇaṃbhaṭa had five sons. Apart from Cāṅgo, the other four, i.e. Datto, Ḍhago, Megho and Guṇḍo, initiated and advocated the worship of mother earth (dharaṇī) and water (pāṇī). They called themselves Kāyaprakṣāḷa (those who had discarded their bodies) and Gopāḷa (cowherds). They became the gurus of the Māṅgas (Mātaṅgas). Datto passed away at Jāṭhavaḍā, Ḍhago at a place called Babhuḷagāva near Bālāghāṭa, Megho at Ḍombegrāma and Guṇḍo at Nimbapūra. These places where they died became places of pilgrimage for their devotees, the Māṅgs. Kāyaprakṣāḷa and Gopāḷa were the marks of merit in the followers of their devotional sects. Later on, due to some differences within, these sects underwent further divisions such as the 'dhūtas'.

The information provided by the *Dinakaranibandha* is in accord with that provided by the *Gajakesarī* in describing the Mātaṅgīpaṭṭa-Māṅgiṇīpaṭṭa.

Description of the Ḍhago-Megho Sect in the the *Jākhadevabā Pāṭha*

I came across another *pothi* entitled *Jākhdevabā Pāṭha*, compiled by the Mahānubhāvas and written in cryptic language It describes five sub-divisions within the Mātaṅgīpaṭṭa, such as the *Navagraha* sect created by Cāṅgo and his disciple Mhāyā Ācārya. The work briefly describes the Ḍhago-Megho sect as well. I think the information is important in the present context and I therefore quote it here verbatim.

> Ḍhago-megho mārgakathana: kṛṇabhaṭṭāce pāñca putra.: te āpaṇayāte pañcarāūḷa, pañcakṛṣṇa mhaṇavitī: eka datto. to jāṭhavaḍāṃ sāmāvalā: Ḍhago to bāḷeghāṭī bābhūḷagāvī sāmāvalā: megho to ḍomegrāmī sāmāvalā: gunḍo to bhaṭṭācāṃ nimbā sāmāvalā: te tayāncī tīrthe jālī: tayān caughāncā eka saṃpradāya: dharaṇī pānī devata: mātaṅgāsī mantradīkṣā: āpaṇayā kāyāpākhī mhaṇavitī: gopāḷa mhaṇavitī: kavaṇī ekī vāsanā: āpaṇayāte avadhūta mhaṇe ||
>
> (Now [I] describe the path of Ḍhago and Megho. Kṛṇabhaṭṭa had five sons. They called themselves 'Five Kings' as well as 'Five Kṛṣṇas'. The first one was Datto. He died at Jāṭhavaḍā. Ḍhago died at a place called Babhuḷagāv in the Bāḷeghāṭa area. Megho passed away at Ḍomegrām. Guṇḍo passed away at Bhaṭṭāce Niṃbagāv. These became their pilgrimage places. All four started a cult which regarded earth and water as deities. They gave mantra initiation to (the low) caste Māṅgs. The brothers called themselves Kāyāpākhī and Gopaḷa. Kavaṇī ekī vāsanā.[11] They also called themselves avadhūta[12].)

Description of the Mātaṅgīpaṭṭa in the *Gajakesarī*[13]

There is a work in prose called *Gajakesarī*, which seems to have had another version in verse as well. In attempting to denigrate the followers of the Mātaṅgīpaṭṭa and to distance themselves from the same, the religious leaders of the Mahānubhāvas have published a booklet in the beginning of the 20th century.[14] It contains excerpts from the verse version of the *Gajakesarī*, quoted below.

> *kṛṣṇabhaṭa mātāpurīcā* | *kanthaḍīnātha guru tayācā* |
> *sakalārtha jāṇe āgamiñcā* | *vastī toraṇamāḷī* || 36 ||
> *jāraṇa māraṇa mohana* | *vīryastambhana uccāṭana* ||
> *teṇem kṛṣṇabhaṭā kele nirūpaṇa* | *mātaṅgī mantra upadeśilā* || 37 ||
> *mātaṅgakanyā kṛṣṇabhaṭī* | *pāhilī sulakṣaṇa gomaṭī* |
> *meḷavilī āhutīsāṭhī* | *devatecyā* || 38 ||

> (Kṛṣṇabhaṭa came from Mātāpura. His Guru was Kanthaḍīnātha. The latter knew the Āgamas and Tantras well and lived at Toraṇamāḷa. Thus, he knew black magic, incantations and charms that would cause destruction and death, and the yogic technique of withholding seminal discharge. He gave all this knowledge to Kṛṣṇabhaṭa and gave him the mantra for the propitiation of goddess Mātaṅgī. Kṛṣṇabhaṭa saw a beautiful girl belonging to the Mātaṅga caste and acquired her in order to offer her to goddess Mātaṅgī.)

(Ḍhere does not quote verses 39 to 42 but translates them as follows:)

The young daughter of the Mātaṅga who was sacrificed, was brought back to life by the goddess and handed over to Kṛṣṇabhaṭa. He married her and the couple had five sons. He then continues with the next verses:

> *prathama datto dujā ḍhago* | *guṇḍo tijā cauthā megho* |
> *pāñcavā jhālā cāṅgo* | *battīsalakṣṇī* ||43||
> *datto jāṭavāḍā nimālā* | *ḍhago bābhuḷagāvīṃ melā* |
> *ḍomegrāmī megho sāmāvalā* | *guṇḍo nimbyāsī* || 44 ||
> *cāṅga phāra vyābhicāra karī* | *he māta phākalī rājadvārī* |
> *śirachheda kelā devagirī* | *cāmbhāraṭekiye* || 45 ||

> (The first one was Datto and the second one was Ḍhago. The third one was Guṇḍo and the fourth Megho. The fifth one, Cāṅgo was endowed with thirty-two virtues.[15] Datto passed away at Jāṭawād, Ḍhago at Babhuḷagāv, Megho at Ḍomegrāma and Guṇḍo at Nimbā. A rumour circulated at the King's court that Cāṅgo was

committing adultery in a major way. He was therefore executed by the king at Devagiri. His head was cut off.)

Description of the Mātaṅgīpaṭṭa in the Prose Version of the *Gajakesarī*

The prose version of the *Gajakesarī* has also elaborated the Mātaṅgīpaṭṭa myth in some detail. I feel it is necessary to examine it as well. The myth in the prose version reads as follows:

> ātā Māṅgiṇīpaṭṭa ‖ mātāpurī kṛṣṇambhaṭa hotā: tayācā guru kanṭhaḍīnātha to agamika: sakaḷa mantratantra upadesile: maga bhaṭe mātaṅgīcī kanyā salakṣaṇika pāhunī mātāṅgī devatesī baḷī didhalī: mātāṅgī mhaṇaje meśako: te prasanna jālī: bhaṭāsī vara didhalā: āṇi mātāgīcī kanyā amṛta simponī uṭhavilī: aṇi devatā prateksa hoūna mhaṇitale: he kanyā tuvā varāvī: icā ṭhāī tuja pāñca putra hotīla: āṇi vādī vivādī jaya pāvasīla: dhanadhānya hoīla: rājā prajā vaśa hotīla; yaisā varu deuna devatā adṛṣa jālī: maga kṛṣṇabhaṭe tiye kanyece pāṇigrahaṇa kele. tiyepāsūna pāñca putra jāle ‖ teci datto: ḍhago: megho: guṇḍo: cāṅgo: teṇeṃ pāñca mārga nirmāṇa kele: cāṅgocā śiśa mhāyā to ācāryā: yeka navagre mārga meśakocā ḍāū pūjitī ‖ śāhālamaprabhu mārga ‖ sidhavoḷī mārga ‖ brahmajñānī mārga ‖ pāñcavā upariyā mārga | yaise mārga teṇe pratiṣṭhile: āṇi: caughī miḷonī Ḍhago megho mārga nirmilā ‖ dharaṇī pāṇī devatā: mātāṅgāsī mantradīkṣā: te kāyāpāṣī mhaṇavitī: gopaḷa mhaṇavitī: yaisā mārga prateṣṭhūnī caughe sāmāvale ‖ datto jāṭhavaḍā sāmāvalā: ḍhago bābuḷagāmvī sāmāvalā: megho ḍombegrāmī sāmāvalā: guṇḍo nimbā sāmāvalā: tī tayāncī tīrthe jālī: yaisī māṅgiṇīpaṭācī ādi ase:
>
> "te lokīṃ mānya karūni darūpaṇīṃ bhajetī: teṇe adhapātā jātī: kāṃ pāṃ: meśako he kṣudra devata: hīnayonīce karmacāṇḍāḷa tyāsī mānya: para brāhmaṇa-veda-śrotriyānsī āṇi brahmavidānsī atemta viṭāḷa: āṇi pramāṇagranthī bolile nāhī ‖ kaṃ: te jīvakṛta: ateta ṣoteṃ: teṇe jīvāceṃ dukkha na cuke ‖ tathā ca ‖
>
> *ye yathà māṃ prapadyante tāṃstathaiva bhajāmyaham* |
> *mama vartmānuvartante manuṣyàḥ pārtha sarvaśaḥ* ‖ (Gītā, 4.11)

mhaṇije: je prāṇī jayā kṣūdradevātatem̥ bhajetī: te tayācem̥ phaḷa pāvatī: āṇi: jaṇonī parameśvarāsī bhajetī: te acyutapadāsī pāvetī II yakṣiṇī ityādi kṣudradevatādī karunī visvapariyem̥ta adhogatī ase: tethem̥ meśako māyārāṇī koṭhem̥ lāge || 34 ||

After analysing the above description of the *Māṅgiṇīpaṭṭa* in the *Gajakesarī*, one can put it into summary form as follows:

1) The founder of the *Māṅgiṇīpaṭṭa* was a Brāhmin called Kṛṣṇam̥bhaṭa.[16]
2) He was a disciple of one Kanthaḍīnātha, who was an expert in the Āgamas and in Tāntrism. Kṛṣṇam̥bhaṭa had acquired the knowledge of these from his guru.
3) Kṛṣṇam̥bhaṭa used to live at a place called Mātāpura.
4) He was a devotee of goddess Mātaṅgī at this place.
5) This goddess was also known by two other names: Meśako and Māyarāṇī.
6) Kṛṣṇam̥bhaṭa found a beautiful girl belonging to the Mātaṅga caste and sacrificed her to the goddess Mātaṅgī.
7) Pleased with this offering, the goddess sprinkled the dead body of the girl with ambrosia and brought her back to life. She ordered Kṛṣṇam̥bhaṭa to marry the girl.
8) The goddess gave Kṛṣṇam̥bhaṭa several boons. She told him that he and his wife would have five sons. He would always win debates and discussions, the family would have plenty of money and food, and finally, he will exert control over the king and his subjects.
9) As per the goddess' orders, Kṛṣṇam̥bhaṭa married the Mātaṅgī girl and the couple had five sons: Daṭṭo, Ḍhago, Megho, Guṇḍo and Cāṅgo.
10) Cāṅgo had a disciple called Mhāyā who was a religious preceptor in his own right (ācārya). Cāṅgo established five sects: Navagrahamārga, Śahālamaprabhu mārga, Siddha oḷī mārga, Brahmajñāna mārga and Upariyā mārga. He gave Mhāyā the responsibility of spreading them.
11) The other four sons established the Ḍhago-Megho sect. This sect had the earth and the sky as their objects of worship. The sect used to give māntric initiations to people of the Mātaṅga caste.

The followers of the sect addressed themselves as Kāyāpākhī, Gopāḷa and Dhūta.

12) After establishing the Ḍhago-Megho sect and gaining recognition for it, the four brothers eventually passed away. Datto died at Jāṭhavaḍā, Ḍhago at Bābhuḷagāva, Megho at Ḍombegrāma and Guṇḍo at Nimbā.
13) The followers of the *Māṅgiṇīpaṭṭa* suffered eventual degradation. This is because their goddess Meśako is a goddess of the people belonging to the lowest order (*hīnayonī*). The latter are classed as untouchables due to their *karma*.[17] Their very touch is polluting to Brāhmins and those who are well versed in the Vedas. It is said that the worship of even the Yakṣas and their entourage leads to degradation. It therefore follows that the worshippers of Meśako-Māyarāṇī would suffer a fate much worse than that.

After summing up the above discussion, one starts to discern a rough picture of *Māṅgiṇīpaṭṭa*. Obviously, this sect consists of the devotees of the Devī at Mātāpūra, which is the present day Māhūr. This Devī is none other than the goddess Reṇukā at Māhur. Her other names are Mātaṅgī, Meśako (Meśko) and Māyarāṇī. Her special worshippers are the Māṅgs or Mātaṅgas who are considered untouchables by the higher castes due to their performing unclean and polluting tasks. Daughters of Māṅgs devote their entire life to the worship of the Devī and are free to have sexual relations with other Devī worshippers. This sect is also known as the Ḍhago-Megho sect and its followers consider the earth and water as their two major deities. Members of the sect are also known as Kāyāpākhī, Dhūta and Gopāla. The Navagrahamārga, Śahālamaprabhū mārga, Siddhavoḷī màrga and Upariya mārga are four other sects established by the other four sons of the Mātaṅgī. They have nothing whatsoever to do with the *Māṅgiṇīpaṭṭa*, also known as the Ḍhago-Megho Mārga.

After an analysis of the descriptions given by the Mahānubhāvas about the nature of the *Māṅgiṇīpaṭṭa,* we have with us an outline of what the sect stood for. To check the validity of these descriptions, we need to ask ourselves five questions:

1) Does the presiding deity of the holy city of Māhūr, goddess Reṇukā, have other names, namely, Mātaṅgī, Mesako and Māyarāṇī?

2) Do the people in the lower rungs of Mahārāṣṭrian society, such as the untouchable Māṅgs, have a special place in the worship regimen of this goddess?
3) Among those who have been ordained in the worship of Reṇukā, does one come across young unmarried girls of the Māṅg community who have open sexual relationships with other devotees?
4) Is there a sect called Ḍhago-Megho sect among the worshippers of Reṇukā? If the answer is in the affirmative, does this sect worship the earth and water?
5) Are the members of this sect also known as Kāyāpākhī, Dhūta and Gopāla?

If the answers to these questions are in the affirmative, one can then say that the description of the *Māṅgiṇīpaṭṭa* in the literature of the Mahānubhāvas is correct and that there is no relationship whatsoever between the followers of the *Māṅgiṇīpaṭṭa* and the Mahānubhāvas. We have already seen in the previous chapters that the answers to most of the above questions are in the affirmative. At this juncture, I am deliberately avoiding a discussion of the Navagraha Mārga, Śahālamaprabhu Mārga, Siddha-oḷī Mārga, Brahmajñānī Mārga and the Upariyā Mārga. Their relationship with one another, and with the Mahānubhāva sect and their place in the religio-cultural history of Mahārāṣṭra, has little to do with our discussion of the *Māṅgiṇīpaṭṭa.* My research into these five sects is still at a very early stage and it would therefore be wrong of me to elaborate any further at this juncture.

The Places of Ḍhago-Megho Worship

The Mahānubhāva work *Gajakesarī* tells us about the places where the five sons of Kṛṣṇaṃbhaṭa passed away. Of these, Bābhuḷagāv is said to be at Bāleghāṭa and Nimbā has been termed 'Bhaṭṭāce Nimbā' (lit. Belonging to a person called Bhaṭṭa). It is quite clear that *Bhaṭṭāce Nimbā* is the same as the Nimbā of Nāgadevācārya. Ḍomegrām is known to be a place where Cakradharaswāmī, the founder of the Mahānubhāva sect, once stayed. Details of the elaborate worship of the Swami at Ḍomegrām three times a day is the very subject of the work *pūjāvasara* by Bāī Devabāsa. This means that two of the four places of pilgrimage important for the followers of the Ḍhago-Megho Mārga (sect), are also important for the Mahānubhāvas. Ḍomegrām has been sanctified by the residence in it by

Cakradharaswāmī and the same goes for Nimbā, which became sacred for the Mahānubhāvas due to the residence there of Nāgadevācārya, the well-known disciple of Cakradharaswāmī.[18] Since Ḍomegrām and Nimbā were important pilgrimage sites for the followers of both the Mahānubhāva and the Ḍhago-Megho sects, it is not at all surprising that many people of the time suspected that the two sects were identical.

In order to ascertain whether the above places were important sites for the followers of the Ḍhago-Megho sect, I made preliminary inquiries at Jāṭhavaḍā, Bābhuḷagāv, Ḍomegrāma, and Nimbā through people who knew these places well. Our inquiries led to the findings that there are currently no places of worship belonging to the Ḍhago-Megho sect at Babhuḷagāv and Nimbā.[19] However, they do exist even to this day at Jāṭhavaḍā and at Ḍomegrāma.

Because Ḍomegrāma is a sacred place both for the Mahānubhāvas and the followers of the Ḍhago-Megho sect, I had a special interest in visiting it. I visited this place on the 15th of January 1972. At the present time, it is known as Kamālapūr and is situated 13 miles from Śrirāmpūr in Nagar District. There is a separate Mahānubhāva shrine at this place and it has no connection with the place of worship of the Ḍhago-Megho sect. The latter is situated on one side of the village and is considerably elevated from the street level. The shrine is enclosed with a stone wall on all four sides. The area within measures 112 ft by 81 feet. The main door faces east and there is also a small door on the south side. Outside the brick wall opposite the main door, there is a stone square, seven feet high on which a stone image of the bull Nandī is situated. Out of special respect for this image, followers of the sect call it 'sāheb'.

When one climbs the steps leading to the main door, one comes across a stone quadrangular terrace, fifty-five feet in length, nineteen feet wide and three and a quarter feet high. It has a north-south aspect. On the south of this structure, there are five small terraces in a row, these being the shrines devoted to the five deities of this sect including Ḍhago and Megho. Mahārs from this as well as the nearby villages worship these deities. A Mahār called Gopāḷā Pirājī Ambhore is currently the pujārī at this shrine. I was unable to meet him during my visit. However, a Māṅg called Viśvanāth provided me with information about this and many similar shrines belonging to this sect in Ḍomegrām area. He also told me that Māṅgs in the district worship at this place as well. In the books of the municipality (grāmapañcāyata) of Kamālpur, this place has been recorded as *Ḍhegū Meghūce deūḷ* (*Lit.*: The Temple of Ḍhago and

Megho) and the record describes it as 'a common place of worship for the untouchables'.

There are some other places of worship belonging to this sect at Ḍomegrām. In close proximity to the open Ḍhago-Megho temple, there is a memorial stone housing the remains of one Siddhanāth or Somanāth. There is yet another place not far from here called Biradāvana or Korī Bhūmī (uncultivated earth). Close to that is an area of the Godāvarī river where the riverbed is very deep. This is called *Jaman Ḍoha*. It is customary among the devotees of this sect to collect stones from this riverbed and include them in their daily worship. The annual pilgrimage (yātrā) for the followers of the Ḍhago-Megho sect takes place on the 9th, 11th and the 10th days of the month of Vaiśākha (around May in the Gregorian Calendar). In the past, some two to three hundred Mahār devotees used to attend this pilgrimage. However, of late, since the Mahārs converted to Buddhism en-masse, only about twenty or thirty devotees attend. A fire sacrifice is performed at the time of the Yātra and a goat is sacrificed at that time. The songs of the pujāris of the sect often mention the names Somanāth and Somājī. Viśwanāth Māṅg informed me that some of the deeds (*līḷās*)[20] performed by Somājī are connected with *Jamanā Ḍoha*.

Mahānubhāva works such as the *Gajakesarī* mention Jāṭhavadā as the place where Datto died. This place is near the town of Harsul in Aurangabad district and is only six miles northwest of the Delhī Gate at Aurangābād. I visited the place on the 16th of January 1972 and found that the information in the Mahānubhāva sources was correct. Even to this date, at the bottom of the hill behind the village of Jāṭhavadā, there is a place called *Pāṇadeva* (*Lit*: god of water) or *Ḍhago-Megho*. This place consists of a 15ft by 15ft raised square on which is placed another two and half feet by two and half feet raised square. The Mahārs have been the traditional priests in this place. Kisan Koṇḍājī Vāghmāre, a Mahār from Varhād, is the present pujārī at this place. The annual Yatrā festival of this shrine takes place on the ninth day of the first quarter of the month of Vaiśākha. The piece of land donated to this shrine by the town of Jāṭhavadā is known as Meghavan.

On this research trip, I was accompanied by one of my researcher friends from Deccan College and also some ascetics from the Mahānubhāva sect. Kisan Vāghmāre was most unhappy about the presence of the Mahānubhāvas with us. He openly criticised the sect many times. He was also partially drunk and was often unable to give straightforward answers to my questions to him. He was often abusive as well. In spite of this, I was trying to keep him on an even keel and get maximum information out of him. Once he got really irate and told me that:

> The secrets of (the connections between) our Pāṇadeva, the mother earth and our gods are not to be found in your Brāhmanic Purāṇas and Pothis, they are situated in our mothers' arses and our fathers' cocks.[21]

My colleagues were most upset by this outburst of his and tried to persuade me to let go of the rude man and return to Aurangābād. On the other hand, I was most pleased by his outburst. In that rude outburst of his, Vāghmāre had revealed the inner essence of the Ḍhago-Megho Sect and of the Mātaṅgīpaṭṭa in a very simple, straightforward fashion. I knew that the devotees of this sect who worship the earth and water, worship the male and female principles in their most fundamental form. His outburst was a confirmation of my intrinsic belief.

Kisan Koṇḍājī also sang many songs for me; some complete, some incomplete. He gave me information about many Ḍhago-Megho shrines. In singing the praises of the Mother Earth and Pāṇadeva, his song went:[22]

> Oh Paṇḍit! Let me tell you about the fame of the mother and the father.
> Who is the mother who looks after this entire world?
> This is the one who does it.
> She feeds all according to what they want.

In his songs, there was regular repetition of the words, 'sat bolā' (speak the truth).[23]

> Speak the truth, follow the path of truth, and look for truth within yourself.
> The secret of longevity is to seek the test of truth.
> Jaṭhoḍā town is so far away but how can I describe its greatness?
> The Jatrā of the people belonging to the Soma clan happens there.
> Ḍhagojī and Meghojī are the gods of the Mahārs.
> Pleased with them, the gods bless the devotees.

The songs that Kisan Koṇḍājī sang contained many tales and myths about his cult. However, since he did not sing any of the songs completely, it was impossible for me to make much sense out of them.

During my researches at Ḍomegrām and Jāṭhavaḍā, I discovered the whereabouts of many other places where the Ḍhago-Megho cult was practised. Koṅkankhedā or Konkaṇgāv (Talukā: Saṅgamner, Dist.: Nagar); Paratūr near Aurangābād; Mehuṇbārā (Talukā: Kannaḍ, Dist.: Aurangābād); Akolā Khurd (Talukā: Jaḷgāv-Jāmod, Dist.: Buldhāṇā); Pimpaḷḍol Talāv at Songav (Talukā: Jaḷgāv, Dist.: Buldhāṇa), Deśmukhāce Limbā (Talukā: Pāthri, Dist.: Parbhaṇī); and Sāvangā (Talukā: Cāndūr, Dist.: Amarāvatī) are some of the places where Ḍhago-Megho or Pāṇadeva shrines exist. Āratis of mother earth and Pāṇadeva are sung at all these places. At the time of the annual Yātrā, they have a Bhajan programme during which they sing a variety of folk songs. These songs consist of a mixture of the philosophy of the Ḍhago-Megho sect about the origin of life on the planet, and the miracles performed by the Siddhas belonging to the sect. Devakīrām Sāḷve, a knowledgeable member of the Ḍhago-Megho sect, has a large collection of the songs of this sect.

When one writes in Marāṭhī, one starts a new document or letter with the words 'Śrī'[24]or 'Śrī Rāma Samartha' on top. On the other hand, the Ḍhago-Megho sect people begin their documents with 'Meghaśyāma Samartha'. Needless to say, this signifies Ḍhago-Megho (the *megh* coming from Megho). Megh (*Lit*: cloud) is also associated with rain and hence Pāṇadeva (the god of water). I quote below one of their devotional songs without changing a single word.[25] This will show the style of their written Marāṭhī and also their religious philosophy.

Meghaśyāma Samartha

When talking of the One, think of and recognize the Brahman which controls.
When talking of two, think of Śiva and Śakti. But is there really any duality in them?
Three means three, the three guṇas. Three is their sign.
Recognize the three as Brahma, Viṣṇu and Maheśa at all times.
Four means the four Vedas which were sung.
Five are of course the five elements/principles of the body.
From the five great elements, twenty-five were formed.
Six means the darśana of the six liṅgas.
Where do you think the six Śāstras and eighteen Purāṇas came from?
Seven means the seven elements that the body is made of.
Tell me where the seven days of the week came from?

Eight means the eight petals that got burnt.
The eight Bhairavas came from eight, just listen to me.
Nine is the sign of the nine doors.
From the senior Ṛṣis, you find the way to salvation.
Ten is the tenth door, the sign of Satguru.
The one who has experienced Guru will know about it.

Such a song could easily form a part of the repertoire of the *ḍaf*[26] singers. Its use of numbers to impart to the audience some 'knowledge' and the tendency to surprise them by spelling out the background of such knowledge is akin to the methods used by the Kalgi-turā[27] singers. In studying the Kalgi-turā tradition, it would be worthwhile examining the above songs based on folk religion.

A song with the title, "Pāṇadevācī Āratī" describes the greatness of Ḍomegrām.

The town of Ḍombegir is sacred and is a place of puṇya.
Lord Bāpasāheb stays there. One should trust him.
The town of Deulgāv is on this side, Ḍombesar is on the other side.
In between the two, the pure river flows.
Śiva says to the Guru, 'Tell me about the greatness of Ḍombesar.'
While describing the greatness of the place, I forgot the gods and dharma.

The name that the devotee uses for Pāṇadeva in this song is 'Bāpasāheb'. The devotee and his sect firmly believe that the earth is their mother and water (Pāṇadeva: Ḍhago-Megho) is their father. In another song that extols the greatness of Ḍomegrām, the use of the cryptic phrase, 'tirakoṭī-cyā varate savā hātācī golāṭ' shows the desire to use mystical yogic terms such as trikūṭa and golhāṭa. However, the pursuit of truth is the foremost message in all of the Ḍhago-Megho religious writing, as seen from their oft repeated message:

satte bolā satte cālā hā dharma kharā |
satnāmālā visaru nakā bābā sāngūna gelā ||

(Always speak the truth and behave truthfully. This is the true Dharma. Do not forget the name of the god. This is what Baba has told us to do.)

Ḍhagojī Meghojī during the Peshwa Rule

Documents from the Peshwa period reveal the existence of the Ḍhago-Megho sect during this time. In the diaries of Śāhū Mahārāj (1682–1749), the following entry, which deals with the management of the memorial for Sambhājī Rāje at Vaḍū, can be found.[28]

> The Vṛndāvana[29]for his Highness the King, is situated at Vaḍū, tarf Pābal, Dist. Junnar. A person called Govind Gopāḷ Ḍhagojī Meghojī cleans the area around the Vṛndāvana and maintains it. For this service, a five bighā[30] piece of barren land situated at Mauje Vaḍu, tarf Pābal, has been donated to him.

This entry is dated 1732–33 CE (Salās salāsīn mayā va alaf sābān 24).

Mahāmahopadhyāya Datto Vāman Potdār has written a special note about it. He says:[31]

> A thought arose in my mind about the name Govind Gopāḷ Ḍhagojī Meghojī. I have never heard a surname called Ḍhagojī Meghojī. However, the English version of Kolhāpūr District Gazetteer (p. 114) mentions that the name Ḍhagojī Meghojī appears in the Guru (religious preceptor) clan of the Mahārs and Māṅgs. According to this Gazetteer, these Guru clans have three seats (gādī) of lineage: the first one from Kolhāpūr, the second one from Ḍombiṇgāv on the river Godāvarī and the third one from Vāśī. With this as the background, my deduction runs as follows: Since the king (Sambhājī) has donated a lot of land (inām) at Vaḍū, and since this land is near the Vṛndāvana of the King, and since Govind Gopāḷ has been called Ḍhagojī Meghojī, is it therefore possible that this person belongs to the Guru clan of the Mahārs? Since he is a cleaner around the area of Vṛndāvana, my argument is certainly not illogical. The Mahārs do have names such as Govind Gopāḷ and it is possible that members of their Guru clans, especially those who sing their devotional songs, will carry these names as well.

This deduction by the Mahāmahopadhyāya should now be considered to be the truth. We already know that in their writing, writers of the Mahānubhāva sect have made a mention of the Mahār and Māṅg community, using adjectives such as 'Gopāḷ' to describe their religious leaders (mahants). It looks as though the suffix Ḍhago Megho has traditionally remained with this sect in the same way. A note in the diary of Savāi Mādhavrāv Peśwā conclusively supports this view.[32] Apparently two gentlemen at Pauḍkhore, Raghunāth Tryṃbak and Kriśṇa Dāmodar Jyotiśī had lodged a complaint with the Peśwā. Traditionally, priesthood, allied religious duties and horoscope reading ran in the families of these two people. However, the Kamāvisdār[33] of the area was forcing them to conduct marriages within the Mahār community. Objecting to this, the duo maintained that they did not conduct marriages for the Mahārs, that was not part of their brief (within Hindu Society). The only thing they did for the Mahārs was to look up auspicious times (muhūrta) for their weddings. The Mahār weddings were conducted by their own priests called Meṭhe Mahārs. In support of their petition, the duo produced a statement by Vedamūrtī Raṅga Jośī Junnarkar. The latter had written:

> Around Junnar, there are over seventy-five villages and five forts. In these areas and at Junnar itself, he has traditionally practised composing and reading of horoscopes (in addition to his priestly duties). However, he does not perform marriages for the *ati-śudras* (the untouchables). In the castes of these *ati-śūdras*, there are Ḍhago Meghos. They are the ones who perform marriages for them.

It is clear from this statement that the priests who perform marriages and other rituals for the Mahārs are called Ḍhago Megho or Ḍhagojī Meghojī. It is possible that this term is still used for them. Since this term is closely associated with their being the 'Gurus' for these low castes, it is also indicative of the presence of a 'sect' that carries this name. Since there are even stronger signs of their presence in Mahārāṣṭra today, there is no need to depend upon indirect means to prove their existence in the past.

It is worth noting that a work called Darśanaprakāśa, which lists many religious sects and sub-sects, has, in a small chapter, included the Ḍhago Megho sect, as a part of the Mahānubhāva tradition. They have been mentioned along with Wāghye, Bharāḍī, Vāsudeva, Śaṅkhāsura, Danḍī, Ṭāḷadhara, Pahāṭagāṇa and others.[34]

Korī Bhūmī

We have already noted that Dharaṇī (the earth) and Pāṇī (water) are the deities of this (Ḍhago Megho) sect. Members of the sect call Dharaṇī, '*Korī Bhumī*' (virgin earth). She is worshipped under this name at a specified site at Ḍomegrām. This place is mentioned in one of the songs sung by Kisan Konḍājī.

> *Ḍomegrāmāmadhīṃ korī bhūmakā homācī jāgā* |
> *tyā homāṃtuna soma nighālā meghaśyāma vartā* |
> *pṛthvīsāṭhīṃ avatāra dharalā meghaśyāma dūtā* |
> *cārhī ratneṃ hṛdayīṃ suṭalīṃ satanām vartā* ||

> (The virgin earth at Ḍomegrām is a place for performing a Homa, the fire sacrifice. Out of that Homa came Soma, the Meghaśyāma. For the sake of the earth, Meghaśyāma, the grey cloud, took an avatāra. All of the four gems became free in the heart. Always speak the truth.)

It is obvious that the virgin earth (*Korī Bhūmī /Korī Bhūmakā*) and the grey cloud (*meghaśyāma*) signify the earth and water respectively. In the place called Akolā Khurd, the singer Devakīrām also mentions the virgin earth in his songs when he says

> *Korī bhūmakācaṃ makāna āhe ḍombegirāṃta* |

> (The home of virgin earth is at Ḍombegīra)

It is noteworthy and surprising that the Gondhaḷīs, devotees of goddess Reṇukā at Māhūr, also mention the 'virgin earth' (*korī bhūmakā*) when they sing praises of Reṇukā:[35] They say, 'Māhurgaḍ has virgin earth, and Reṇukā resides there'. Finally, the *korī bhūmakā* appears in the songs of the Bhutyes as well. One of their songs declares:[36]

> *māhurgaḍa savvāī savāse korī bhūmakā* |
> *parasarāmācī mātā titham nānde reṇukā* ||

> (Māhūrgaḍ has a large amount of virgin earth. Reṇukā, the mother of Paraśurāma, happily lives there.)

The Main Devotees of Goddess Mātaṅgī

The Mahānubhāv works, *Dinakaraprabandha* and *Gajakesarī*, both state that the majority of the devotees of Mātaṅgī come from very low (hīnayonīya) castes. We have already seen that the places considered holy (*tīrthakṣetras*) by the followers of Ḍhago Megho sect or Mātaṅgāpaṭṭa are frequented even to this day by Mahārs and a small number of Māṅgs.

The presiding deity of this Mahār-Māṅg sect is known variously as Mātaṅgī, Dharaṇī and Korī Bhūmakā.[37] We have also seen that the male principle that is associated with this goddess has been known either as Pāṇī, Pāṇadeva or Ḍhago Megho. We have experienced this through the devotional regime of the devotees and through written works. Quite obviously, both of these deities (mother earth and water) are ancient in the folk religious tradition. They are closely connected with the traditional religion of the Mahār and Māṅg communities.

Logical Meaning of the Kṛṣṇaṃbhaṭa Myth

When one considers three things in their entirety: goddess Mātaṅgī, the caste groups that worship her, and the fact that a woman of these castes is chosen as her representative, one is able to glean the hidden meaning behind the Kṛṣṇaṃbhaṭa Myth. A woman who had taken initiation in the cult of Mātaṅgī was free to cohabit with any male devotee of Mātaṅgī. It was therefore quite possible for her to have had a sexual relationship with Kṛṣṇaṃbhaṭa. In all probabilities, Kṛṣṇaṃbhaṭa's clan deity would have been Goddess Reṇukā of Māhūr or Goddess Mātaṅgī. The myth mentions that Kṛṣṇaṃbhaṭa was an āgamic and hence a tāntric. It is well known that left-handed tāntrics deliberately used women of untouchable castes such as Ḍombinī, Mātaṅginī and Rajakinī in their spiritual practices (sādhanā) where women were prominent. Kṛṣṇaṃbhaṭa, a Brāhmin, developed a sexual relationship with a woman of the Mātaṅgī caste, herself a devotee of goddess Mātaṅgī. It was but natural that, having been excluded by Brāhmins because of this misdeed, Kṛṣṇaṃbhaṭa and his five children would keep using their traditional Brāhminic knowledge in developing the devotional regime of goddess Mātaṅgī.

This would mean that the sect Mātaṅgīpaṭṭa is a true representation of the ancient folk tradition and the fact that Kṛṣṇaṃbhaṭa and his children accepted this path is a minor incident in the history of this cult. Mātaṅgīpaṭṭa alias the Ḍhago Megho Mārg is an ancient sect that worships folk deities and it certainly predates the Kṛṣṇaṃbhaṭa myth. Apart from Cāṅgo, the other four sons of Kṛṣṇaṃbhaṭa did accept this ancient faith. Cāṅgo on the other hand propagated his own sects such as Śahālam, Śiddhaboḷī, Brahmajñānī and Upariyā. The history of these four sects that originated from Cāṅgo is totally unknown. Also unknown is the fact as to whether the above sects had any relationship with the Mahānubhāva sect or the Mātaṅgīpaṭṭa. The answers to these questions will have to be found in separate research. Also, one does not know why the Mahānubhāva sect was equated with the Mātaṅgīpaṭṭa time and time again for three to four centuries, and what effect this had on the former. Because of the lack of positive proofs, it is very hard to answer these questions.

Endnotes

1 Translator's note: The Mahānubhāva sect was a Bhakti cult devoted to Lord Kṛṣṇa and was propagated by its founder, Cakradhar Swāmi in 1267. It rejected the caste system and the ritualistic Hindu religion. Cakradhar Swāmi's biography called 'Līḷācaritra' was written by his disciple Mhaimbhaṭ and is the earliest written work in Marāṭhī literature. The sect still has a large following in India today.

2 Report of the Bhārat Itihās Samśodhan Maṇḍaḷ, 5th Congress, Śaka 1839 (1917 CE): 35–53.

3 Annual report of the Bhārat Itihās Samśodhan Maṇḍaḷ, Śaka 1835 (1913 C.E.): 150–157.

4 Goḍbole, Raghunāthaśāstrī. 1881. *Bhāratakhaṇḍācā Arvācīna Koṣa*: 101–104. (In Marāṭhī).

5 Kolate, V.B. 1962. Malkāpur: Mahānubhāva Samśodhan: 146, 159.

6 Translator's note: Although he says so, the verse (1.42) quoted by Ḍhere does not mention that the Jains equate 'mundi darśana' with that of Mātaṅgī. I think Ḍhere is erroneously alluding to another verse, not quoted here.

7 Translator's note: Śrīgondekar is probably alluding to 'left-handed tantrism' when he says, 'upharāṭā mārga', the reverse path.

8 Translator's note: Ḍhere first published *Lajjāgaurī* in 1978. Therefore, the two works he quotes will now be 200 to 250 years old.

9 Translator's note: *Śābarāgama* is not listed in the list of the 28 Śaivagamās. It is probably the same as the Śābaratantra of the Śāktas. Śābara was one of the well-known ancient Siddhas.

10 Translator's note: Ḍhere does not describe the nature of this havoc. One can perhaps surmise that this would have been in the nature of performing black magic on people with a view to gaining undue advantage over them.

11 Translator's note: According to Prof. Anne Feldhaus, an expert on Mahānubhāva literature, the phrase 'kavaṇī ekī vāsanā' is used to introduce a variant version of the text. It is not clear to the translator what that would be in connection with this paragraph.

12 Translator's note: In Marāṭhī, the word *avadhūta* has three meanings: 1) an incarnation of god Dattātreya, 2) one who does not observe caste distinctions and 3) a naked person. There is no mention anywhere of these brothers going naked. The first two meanings can however be equally applicable to them. It is conceivable that they called themselves an incarnation of Dattātreya, a deity who was particularly popular in Mahārāṣtra of the time. However, in view of the fact that these brothers gave initiation to the low castes, the second meaning seems to be particularly appropriate.

13 Translator's note: Since both the words *māṅgiṇī* and *mātaṅgī* have the same meaning, the authors of these works seem to have used them interchangeably.

14 Translator's note: Ḍhere published *Lajjāgaurī* in 1978. Now, nearly 40 years later, this would of course change to 'last century'.

15 Translator's note: The Marāṭhī word *Battīsalakṣaṇī* (Lit: one who shows 32 good signs) is used to describe someone who has every possible virtue, i.e. he is handsome, brave, clever etc.

16 Translator's note: These authors have used the names Kṛṣṇambhaṭa and Kṛṣṇabhaṭa interchangeably.

17 Translator's note: The Māṅgs and the Mahārs are two untouchable castes in Mahārāṣṭra who, in the past, traditionally stayed on the outskirts of the village and were involved, amongst other things, in the processing of carrion and cleaning of toilets etc. for the upper castes. As a result, their very shadow was anathema to the upper castes, especially the Brāhmins.

18 Translator's note: Professor Anne Feldhaus does not agree with this statement. To her, Nimbā is not a sacred place for the Mahānubhāvas. With Ḍhere's demise in 2016, it is difficult to know where he got his information from.

19 Mr. Puruśottama Nāgpure, a young researcher who belongs to the Mahānubhāva sect, believes that places of worship of the Dhago-Megho sect at Nimbā (Limbā) and Babhuḷagāva do exist but they are in a dilapidated state.

20 A *līḷā* is a very common Mahānubhāva term which describes miraculous deeds performed by the founder of the sect, Cakradharaswāmī.

21 Kisan's exact Marāṭhi words, as quoted by Ḍhere are: "*āmcyā devaṃca-dharaṇīcaṃ an pāṇdevācaṃ-guhya tumcyā devaṃcyā sārkhaṃ pothyāpurāṇāt nāhī, tar te āmcyā āīcyā gāṇḍit an bāpacyā boṇḍit āhe*".

22 *aika paṇḍitā, tulā sāṅgato āībāpāṅcī kīrtī* |
yā duniyeceṃ pālana kele tī mātā hāye koṇatī |
yā duniyece pālana kele hyāca āīnam |
sarva janānā bhojana dete ichheparamāṇam || (In Marāṭhī).

23 *satya bolā satya cālā śodhā antarīm* |
sat nāmācī lāvā kasoṭī, hi aukṣācī dorī |
jaṭhodā gāva dūravar, nāva kitī varṇū vāni |
somavanśāci varhādajatrā yete cālūnī |
are Dhagojī Meghojī deva āhe maharance pīr |
bhaktajanāna prasanna jhāle deva avatāra || (In Marāṭhī).

24 Translator's note: When writing in Marāṭhī, it is customary to start any writing with a 'Śrī' on top of the document. This is the shortened version of Śrī Gaṇeśāya Namaḥ. (Lit: we bow to Gaṇeśa, the remover of obstacles).

25 Ḍhere quoted this and the other songs quoted below in Marāṭhī. The translation is by Jayant Bāpaṭ.

26 Translator's note: The *ḍaf* is a percussion instrument made out of leather and used by village singers and in particular the Kalgī-Turā singers (see endnote below).

27 Translators note: The popular folk dance-drama of Mahārāṣṭra in called *tamāśā*. There are two branches of *tamāśā* performers: the Kalgī group and

the Turā group. The Kalgī are worshippers of Śaktī whereas the Turā are Śiva worshippers. When a *tamāśā* is staged, the two groups stand opposite each other and fire questions at each other. The questions and the answers are both required to be in verse form. These cryptic questions are to be answered straightaway, putting the skills of the answering group to test. The questions and answers continue throughout the night and the winning team then forcefully takes the loser's *ḍaf* and flag away.

28 Vād, G.C. and Pārasnis, D.B. (eds): *Śāhumahārāja yāncī rojaniśī*, Pune: p. 36.

29 Translator's note: The Saṃskṛt word *vṛndāvana*, comes from the groves of *vṛndā*, Tulasi (Holy Basil) plant (*Ocimum tenuiflorum*), with the word *vana* meaning a forest. In Mahārāśṭra, the word is used to denote a square enclosure built of bricks, usually in the backyard of the home. In the middle of this enclosure, there is a hole which is filled with soil and a Tulsi plant is planted in it. This plant is worshipped daily mainly by the women of the house and certainly on special days, by making circumambulations around the square.

30 Translator's note: A measure of land area in South Asia varying locally from 1/3 to 1 acre (1/8 to 2/5 hectare).

31 Potdār, D.V. 1938. *Bhārat Itihās Maṇḍaḷ Quarterly*. October, 19.2: 61. (Dhagojī Meghojī).

32 Vād, G.C. and Marāṭhe, K.B. eds., 1911. *Savāī Madhavrao Peśwe yāncī rojaniśī*, Mumbai: 279–281. (In Marāṭhī).

33 Translator's note: A government official.

34 Paṭhāṇ, Dr Y. M. October 1967. *Marāṭhī Samśodhana Patrikā*, 15.1, pp. 7–12. (article on *Mahānubhāva Darśanaprakāśa*).

35 *māhuragaḍacī korī bhūmakā* |
tithe nānde reṇukā || (In Marāṭhī).

36 Ḍhere, R.C. 1964. *Marāṭhī Lokasaṃskṛtīce Upāsaka*, Pune: 44. (In Marāṭhī).

37 Both of the words, Bhūmikā and Bhūmakā, seem to be used by the Mahārs and Māṅgs interchangeably.

Chapter 5

Ambuvācī

The earth is our primordial mother. In the previous chapters we have looked at some length at a folk religion that celebrates her motherhood. The earth mother, who, since ancient times, has held in her womb plant life resplendent with a variety of forms, colours, fragrances and tastes, has often been compared with a woman. In her womb, the universal woman carries foetuses which will produce humanity in various forms, shapes and thinking patterns. The mode of fertilization of a human female is often talked about in terms of the fertilization of the earth. Similarly, the fertilization process of the earth is often described in terms of the changes that take place in a pregnant woman's body. Further, iconographically, the earth is often portrayed as a woman and worshipped as such.

It is hardly necessary to reiterate here that terms such as coming of age, beginning of the menstrual cycle and fertility are applicable both to a woman and to the earth. From the very beginning of human life on earth, the changes in a woman's body that eventually lead to her motherhood have been linked to similar changes in the earth. Just as a woman cannot conceive a child without having started her menstruation, it is commonly thought that the earth must also menstruate before new life can be produced.

Ambuvācī: A Peasant Festival

Ambuvācī is a peasant festival associated with the celebration of the start of the earth's menstruation. Ambuvācī literally means the beginning of menstruation. The Āssāmese scholar Jogeś Dās has given the etymology of the word as follows:[1]

> In Saṃskṛt the word ambu means water. The word 'bācī'[2] denotes expression or blossoming. Water has always been equated with the ability of the female to reproduce. These procreative waters of the earth are called *ambu* here.

The procreative capability of waters, which is equivalent to the menstruation of the earth, is expressed by the term Ambuvācī. The capability of the earth to sustain the foetus i.e. the food, in her womb becomes possible only after the festival of Ambuvācī. The festival is therefore an important part of the peasants' calendar. It is not only in the folk milieu that the importance of Ambuvācī is recognized, but the literature associated with agriculture also reserves a special place for the signs associated with Ambuvācī.[3]

> *dyauḥ pumān dharaṇī nārī bījambho divaścyutam* ।
> *dyu-dhātrī-bīja-saṃyogād dhānyādīnaṃ tu sambhavaḥ* ॥
> *annaṃ hi jagadādhāraṃ sarvamanne pratiṣṭhitam* ।
> *mūlamāpo hi annasya tasmādāpo hi jīvanam* ॥[4]
>
> (The sky is the male; the earth is the female. The rains that fall out of the sky are the 'seed.'[5] The union of the sky and the earth via the rains – the seed – produces plant life and grain. Food is the sustenance of life, and every living thing lives because of it. Since water is the source of this food, it is called *jīvana* [life-giving].)

All agriculture depends upon rain. So do all life forms. Ancient works dealing with agriculture propound this same message. Take the following aphorism:

> *vṛṣṭimūlā kṛṣiḥ sarvā vṛṣṭimūlam ca jīvanam* ।[6]
>
> (The root of all agriculture is rain, and the root of rain ["life" or "subsistence"] is water.)

The meaning of this aphorism has always been taken as a basis of all of the writing related to agriculture, and that is why astronomical knowledge about rainfall and predictions about it have acquired inordinate importance in such writing. In view of the above discussion, it is but natural to think that when the earth gets moist at the beginning of the monsoon, she is taken to be menstruating. It is only after she gets soaked with the torrential rains during the appearance of the *Mṛga* constellation that she gets wet enough and can then carry the foetus of new growth. It is this 'wetness' of the earth at the time of plant growth that is denoted by the term Ambuvācī. The work *Kṛṣiparāśara,* written between the 6th and 8th centuries C.E., discusses in detail the period of the menstruation of the earth and the allowed and disallowed agricultural processes during this period:[7]

jyeṣṭhānte tridinaṃ sārdhamāṣādhādau tathaiva ca |
vapanaṃ sarvasasyānāṃ phalārthīṃ kṛṣakastyajet || 174 ||
vṛṣānte mithunādau ca trīṇyahāni rajasvalā |
bījaṃ na vāpayet tatra janaḥ pāpād vinaśyati || 175 ||

and:

mṛgaśirasi nivṛtte raudrapāde 'mbuvācī |
bhavati ṛtumatī kṣhmā varjayet trīṇyahāni ||
yadi vapati kṛṣāṇaḥ kṣetramāsādya bījam |
na bhavati phalabhāgī dāruṇaścātra kālaḥ || 176 ||[8]

(The farmer who wishes to get good crops should avoid sowing the seed during the three and half days at the end of the month of Caitra and the beginning of the month of Āṣādha. The earth menstruates during this time and hence no seed should be sown. One who ignores this dictum is destroyed by his sinful behaviour. The earth menstruates for three days between the end of the Mṛga and the beginning of the Ārdrā constellation. This state of the earth is called *Ambuvācī*. Sowing must not be done on these three days. If a farmer does sow, he will not get a good crop.)

This prohibition is easily understood if one keeps in mind the similarity between a woman and the earth. Just as intercourse with a woman is prohibited while she menstruates, so is the touch of the plough for the earth during the three days of Ambuvācī.

Ambuvācī Celebration at the Kāmākhyā Pīṭha[9]

The Kāmākhyā pīṭha in Kāmarūpa (Āssām) is one of the well-known Śaktipīṭhas (seats of Śakti) in India. Legend has it that it was here that Satī's vagina (*yonī*) fell. The goddess here has the form of a *yonī*. The Ambuvācī festival is celebrated here with great enthusiasm. Naturally, to the populace, Kāmākhyā is none other than mother earth, Bhūdevī. Every year, between the fourth phase of the constellation Mṛga and the first phase of the constellation Ārdrā, when the skies open and the earth is inundated with rains in Āssām, Goddess Kāmākhyā is believed to menstruate. This period comes between the sixth and the eleventh days of the waxing fortnight of the month of Āṣādha and generally lasts for eighty-four hours. Since it is forbidden to take the darśan of the goddess while she is menstruating, the doors of the temple are completely closed.

They are opened on the fourth day and it is only after the goddess has been bathed and worshipped that the devotees are allowed to take her darśan. When they do this, each of the devotees is given a piece of red cloth as *prasād*. This red cloth is considered to be a part of the goddess' menstrual-blood-soaked attire. Devotees firmly believe that this special *prasād* gives them good luck and also fulfils their wishes.[10] The seventh paṭala (section) of the Kubjikā Tantra describes the importance of this cloth as follows:[11]

> *kāmākhyāvastramādāya jap-pūjāṃ samācaret* |
> *pūrṇakāmo labhed devīṃ satyaṃ satyaṃ na saṃśayaḥ* ||[12]
>
> (If one fetches Kāmākhyā's *vastra* [a piece of cloth worn by Kāmākhyā], and worships it while chanting her name, his every wish will be fulfilled and he will obtain favours from the goddess. Without doubt this is true.)

During the Ambuvācī festival at the Kāmākhyā pīṭha, thousands of pilgrims flock to the temple and its surroundings. The entire atmosphere is charged with the sounds of percussion instruments. A large number of mangoes are imported from Bengāl and Bihār. Thousands of garlands are made ready for the devotees. Maidens wander around seeking *jogvā*[13] from devotees. The majority of the pilgrims are from Bengāl.

In the district of Kāmarūpa, the festival of Ambuvācī is known as 'Amatī'. On the other hand, people from the eastern parts call it 'Sāt'. Jogeś Dās thinks that Amatī is a corruption of the word Ambuvācī and that, since the festival of Ambuvācī usually starts on Āṣādha Śukla Saptamī (the seventh day of the waxing-moon fortnight of the month of Āṣādha), that must be why it is called 'Sāt'.[14] There is a ritual called 'Sāt' in Mahārāṣṭra which is performed before sowing rice. It is obvious that this is a ritual designed for the performance of a 'śānt' (*śāntī*).[15] In some parts of Āssām, sprouting grain is placed in water in earthenware pots during the time of Ambuvācī. When this period is over, the entire pot containing the grains is released into river water.[16]

The well-known scholar Baṇīkānt Kākatī has also said that although the festival of the Goddess's menstruation is celebrated annually, devotees believe that she menstruates monthly like human women.[17] It is important to note that, although the celebration of Ambuvācī is associated closely with the worship of the goddess Kāmākhyā, its original basis is still recognized as an agricultural festival.

The Rājñīsnāpana in Kaśmīr

A *vrata*[18] called Rājñīsnāpana is observed in the land of Kāśmīr. The word Rājñīsnāpana means the 'coming of age [i.e. the start of menstruation] of the queen.' The queen in question is the wife of the Sun, i.e. the earth. In Mahārāṣṭra, Māḷvā and Gujarāt, she is also known as Rāṇūbāī, Ranūbai, and Rāṇḍaldevī.[19] Citing the *Brahmapurāṇa*, the work *Kṛtyaratnākara* states that the period for the performance of this *vrata* is four days, from the fifth to the eighth day of the waning-moon fortnight of the month of Caitra.[20] During this *vrata*, it is believed that the land menstruates for the first three days and is pure on the fourth. The *Nīlamatapurāṇa*, which describes in detail the cultural traditions of the land of Kāśmīr, describes this *vrata* in detail.[21] However, it gives a different timing for the performance of the *vrata*: from the fifth to the eighth day of the waning moon fortnight of the month of Phālguna.

> *tasyāmeva tu pañcamyāṃ kaśmīrā tu rajaswalā* |
> *yasmād bhavati kartavyā tasyāḥ pūjā tato dvija* || 549 ||
> *ramyā śailamayī kāryā kaśmīrā tāṃ ca pūjayet* |
> *abhyaṅgavastradānena naivedyaṃ ca nivedayet* || 550 ||
> *puṣpadhūpādyalaṅkārāṃ na dātavyāṃ dinatrayam* |
> *naivedye gorasāṃ sarvāṃ varjanīyāṃ dvijottama* || 551 ||
> *strībhistu pūjā kartavyā mānuṣairna kathāṃcana* |
> *snāpyā strībhirbhaved devī kṛṣṇapakṣāṣṭamīm tu tām* || 552 ||
> *anantarāṃ dvijaiḥ snāpya sarvauṣadhiyutaiḥ ghaṭaiḥ* |
> *tato gandhaistato bījaiḥ tato ratnaistatasphalaiḥ* || 553 ||
> *snāpayitvā ca taṃ devīṃ gandhairmālyaiśca pūjayet* |
> *vastrālaṅkaraṇaiścānnairviśeṣairgorasodbhavaiḥ* || 554 || …
>
> *bhojanaṃ prekṣaṇīyaṃ ca tathā mitragṛhe dvija* |
> *tantrīvādyaṃ sumadhuraṃ śrotavyaṃ svāśitaiḥ sukham* || 558 ||
> *tataḥ prabhṛti kaśmīrā ṛtusnātā dvijottama* |
> *garbhaṃ gṛhṇātyataḥ kāryaṃ kṛṣyārambhaṃ tataḥ param* || 559||[22]

(Oh Dvija, the land of Kāśmīr menstruates from the fifth day of Phālguna and hence it is necessary to worship her. One should make a stone image of the Kaśmīra bhūmi, bathe the image, clothe her and offer *naivedya-prasād*. This pūjā is to be performed by women only on the eighth day of Phālguna. During the first three days, the Devī should not be bathed and should not be adorned with flowers or ornaments. Neither should she

> be offered food (*naivedya*), *gorasadān*[23] etc. These things are totally prohibited during these first three days. On the eighth day, married women should bathe her and perform her pūjā. It is only after this that Brāhmins should bathe her with water containing aromatic herbs and perform her pūjā with sandalwood, garlands of flowers, grains, fruit, clothing, ornaments and precious stones. She should be offered foods containing milk, curds and buttermilk. The *prasād* should be sent to the houses of neighbours and close friends. After the meal, melodious instruments should be played. Oh Brāhmin, the land of Kaśmīr, who has thus come of age, is now able to hold offspring in her womb. Therefore, from then on, agricultural activities such as sowing should be started.)

We have noticed that the *Rājñīsnāpana vrata* of Kaśmīr considers the earth as the wife of the Sun. In this ritual, one can clearly see the implied belief in the primordial union of the sun and the earth.

The *Trippukharaṭaṭu* and *Uchāral* in Keraḷa

Briffault, in his well-known work, *The Mothers*, has written about the taboos concerned with menstruation. In that context, he mentions the celebration of menstruation in India. He writes:[24]

> It is not unlikely that on her 'evil day' the goddess was thought to be actually menstruating. The notion that goddesses are subject to the infirmities of mortal women is common in India today. Thus, in Bengal it is believed that at the first burst of rain, Mother Earth prepares herself for being fertilized by menstruating. During that time, there is an entire cessation from all ploughing, sowing and other farm work. The menstruation of the Earth Goddess is thus observed by Bengalis as Sabbath. In Travancore there is an important ceremony known as 'trippukharaṭaṭu' or purification ceremony, in connection with the menstruation of the goddess, which is believed to take place about eight or ten times a year, in which a cloth wrapped around the metal image of the goddess is found to be discoloured with red spots and is subsequently in demand as a holy relic. Another menstruating goddess is found at Chunganur.[25]

The similarities between the bodily functions and resultant reproductive capabilities of a woman and that of the earth are expressed in the festival of Ambuvācī, and that is what Briffault is hinting at in the above passage. He has said further that a similar custom is observed in Keraḷā as well. Particularly important is the information he gives about the 'trippukharaṭaṭu' festival in Keraḷa. In both of these places, it is the blood-stained menstrual cloth of the goddess that is considered auspicious and is accepted by devotees as *prasād*. In his volume on the history of Keraḷa, Padmanābha Menon[26] offers the following information about the festival of Uchāral. He says that In Keralā, the festival of Uchāral is celebrated in the month of Makaraṃ (January-February), at the end of the harvest period. It is considered to be the start of the menstruation of goddess Bhagavatī. On the first day, all of the godowns and warehouses that store food are closed; the door-latches are closed using thorny plant stems and brooms. They remain closed for three days. During these three days, no grain is sold in the shops; houses, including their front-yards and gardens, are neither mopped nor cleaned by spraying of water. The use of farm implements is totally tabooed. On the fourth day, only after goddess Bhagavatī has been ritually purified, are the godowns opened. A bagful of leaves is then taken to the farm and mixed with fertilizer and spread. The field is then burnt according to the annual practice.[27] The festival is particularly prevalent in the areas of Cerrappāśśerī and Śornūr in the district of Valluvanāḍ.

Menstrual Fluid (*rajodravya*) and Snake Bite

In many early civilizations, people sought to establish a relationship between the snake and menstruation. They also connected the moon with menstruation. Many societies also believed that a snake was responsible for the start of menstruation. According to Pāpuan belief, which they record on their totem poles, a snake bite on the vagina starts menstruation in a female. Briffault[28] has reviewed many such myths about the relationship of the snake and menstruation, and has postulated that, 'This notion has been thought to derive from the phallic shape of the animal, and the idea is undoubtedly present in those worldwide beliefs.'

In the Ambuvācī festival in Bengāl, there is a totally different interpretation of the relationship between menstruation and the snake. During the period of Ambuvācī, people in Bengāl consume a drink made out of a mixture of mango juice and milk. They firmly believe that by imbibing this drink, they will not be bitten by a snake for the entire year.[29] The question naturally arises as to the relationship between the period of Ambuvācī, drinking of the mixture of mango juice and milk and freedom from snake bite for the entire year. The answer to this question is to be found in the shape of the animal. A serpent, especially the cobra, is akin to the shape of the male human organ of generation, the phallus. It is a symbol of masculinity. This is what Briffault meant in the quote above. Sexual contact between a man and a menstruating or pregnant woman has been strongly tabooed. There is an omnipresent myth throughout India that if a snake has eye contact with a pregnant woman even for a very short time, he loses his eyesight due to such an act being totally tabooed. It is also said that once the woman delivers, touching the waters in her bathroom after she has bathed restores his eyesight.[30] Once one sees the similarity between a human male organ and a snake, and the earth and a woman, it is not difficult to see that the menstrual fluid of the earth in the form of a woman's menstrual blood has the ability to repel contact with a snake representing the human male. The idea of drinking mango juice with milk simulates the drinking of the menstrual fluid. If one compares this with drinking yoghurt during the ritual of impregnation (*garbhādhāna*), one is able to understand the logic behind these beliefs. Because he represents the male, a snake has to avoid eye contact with a woman who is producing menstrual fluid. It is therefore easy to understand the reasoning behind the belief that drinking that fluid, albeit symbolically, as a mixture of mango juice and milk, will protect one from snake bites.

The Celebration of Menstruation in Orissā

Similar to the Ambuvācī festival in Āssām and Bengāl, the state of Orissā also celebrates the menstruation of the goddess. The festival is one of the most popular ones in Orissā.[31] It is held between the last day of the month of Jyeṣṭha and the first two to three days of the month of Āṣādha. This period is considered to be the menstruation period for the earth.

> *vṛṣānte mithunasyādau tad dvitīye dinatrayam* |
> *rajasvalā syāt pṛthivī kṛṣikarma vigarhitam* ||[32]

> (On the last day of the month of vṛṣa [Jyeṣṭha] and the first two days of the month of mithuna [Āṣādha], the earth menstruates. During this time, agriculture is inappropriate)

In the Oḍissī language, this first day is called 'pahali raj', the second is, 'bhuī na-aṇa' and the third is called 'thakurāṇī gāḍhuon'. During these three days, people of the land of Utkala (Orissā) consider holding the plough, sowing any seed, digging the earth or pounding grain completely forbidden.

> *Halānāṃ vāhanaṃ caiva bījānāṃ vapanaṃ tathā* |
> *tāvadeva na kurvanti yāvat pṛthvī rajasvalā* ||
> *pṛthvī rajasvalā yāvat khananaṃ chedanam tyajet* |[33]
>
> (While the earth menstruates, the use of a plough and sowing of seed is not done. Also, during this period, digging and cutting of trees etc. is not undertaken.)

During this period, there are public holidays in Orissā. People get ready for the festival before it begins. Dancers get their groups ready for the performances. The entire land is filled with the melodious sounds emanating from instruments such as mṛdaṅga, karatāla, tablā, pakhavāj, bāsarī and bugle. Many folk plays are staged as well. People forget the hard life of the year gone by and enjoy themselves with these festivities. Young girls and newly married women bathe on the first day (pahali raj) and wear wooden clogs or other footwear. They do not perform household chores. During these three days, they are not allowed to touch the earth with their bare feet. They fast during these three days and eat only fruit. They do not bathe. Women in adjoining neighbourhoods get together, sit on mats that are not to be removed for the three days, and sing and chat. They may use swings as well. Neither the mats nor the swings are to be cleaned for three days. If they have to move, they have to use their clogs and not walk barefoot.

During the festival, newly married women receive 'bhār' (presents) from their parents' home. These include sarees, sindūr and bangles. Unmarried girls who live at home are also given such presents by their parents. This celebration of the menstruation of the goddess is one of the most popular festivals in Orissā.

The Importance of Menstrual Fluid for the Tāntrics

Because of its direct relationship with reproduction, menstrual fluid has achieved enormous importance in folk religion, especially in tantric practices which require a woman to be the main vehicle. For left-handed tāntrics, the worship of a menstruating vagina is of prime importance. The '*Bhagamālinīrajasvalāstotram*' (*Lit*: the hymn of the menstruating and flowering vagina) sings with great devotion high praises of a yonī coloured with menstrual blood:[34]

ṛtuvatyā bhagaṃ paśyan japate yadi sādhakaḥ |
kevalaṃ guptabhāvena sa tu vidyānidhirbhavet || 7 ||
rajasvalāmukham dṛṣṭvā sarvapāpaiḥ pramucyate |
sambhāṣanam ca kurute rājasūyādhikaṃ phalam || 9 ||
tasyāḥ smaraṇamātreṇa labhenmuktiṃ caturvidhām |
tasyā lokanamātreṇa trailokyoccāṭane kṣamaḥ ||10 ||
śraddhayā pūjayet tasyā bhagaṃ ca rajasānvitam |
snānasaṃdhyāviśuddhātmā nyāsadhyānaparāyaṇaḥ || 11 ||[35]

(If a Sādhaka stares at the vagina of a menstruating woman and meditates on it in secret, he becomes the very sea of knowledge. If he looks at the face of a menstruating woman, he becomes free of all sins. If he converses with such a woman, he achieves merit which is even higher than performing a Rājasūya sacrifice. Even if he thinks of her, he obtains fourfold mukti. If he meets her in person, he acquires the strength to conquer the three worlds. Therefore, a Sādhaka should bathe, perform the Sandhyā prayers, purify himself with *nyāsa* and meditation, and then perform a pūjā of the vagina of a menstruating woman.)

This extraordinary praise of menstrual fluid as sung by tāntrics can also be observed in the well-known 'Tripurasundarī' hymn by none other than the Ādi-Śaṅkarācārya (Original Śaṅkarācārya). The Ācārya invokes Tripurasundarī with the following hymn:

smaret tripurasundarīṃ rudhirabindunīlāmbarām |

(one should meditate upon the Tripurasundarī whose loin cloth has assumed a bluish red colour due to menstrual blood.)

Coming from the great ascetic Ādi-Śaṅkarācārya, such a description is somewhat unexpected. However, in connection with our current theme, it is worth making a note of it. While it is true that left-handed tāntrics have sung praises of menstrual fluid in this fashion, it is also worth noting that even the *Devībhāgavata*, the earlier *Śrīsūkta*, and the much earlier *Asyavāmīyasukta* from the *Ṛgveda*, all praise menstrual fluid in a very healthy and forthright manner and in a way that seeks harmony with the secrets of nature.

The *Ratikalā* Image of the Earth[36]

In the *Devībhāgavata Purāṇa*, Ambuvācī is mentioned in the "Pṛthivyupākhyāna" section in Skanda 9, Adhyāyas 9–10. The passage says that in the Vārāhakalpa, Viṣṇu in his incarnation as Varāha (the boar) killed Hirāṅyākṣa, dragged the earth out of the depths of hell and established her in water like a lotus leaf in a lake. Lord Brahmā then created the beautiful universe around her. The moment she gazed at the Varāha who had rescued her from the depths of hell, the earth became sexually attracted to him and sought union with him. Having seen her in such a state, Hari, whose lustre was like a crore of Suns, became enamoured of her and himself became lustful towards her. He created a *ratikalā* image of her and had repeated intercourse with her for one divine year.[37]

dṛṣṭvā tadadhidevīṃ ca sakāmāṃ kāmuko hariḥ |
varāharūpī bhagavān koṭisūryasamaprabhaḥ ||
kṛtvā ratikalān sarvān mūrtiṃ ca sumanoharām |
kriḍāṃ cakāra rahasi divyavarṣamaharniśam ||

(*Devībhāgavata*, 9.9.29–30)

(Having seen the highly aroused goddess (looking at him in a lustful way), Hari, [in the form of a boar], whose lustre was like a crore of Suns, also became aroused. He created a beautiful image of her. She was accomplished in the arts of love. Hari performed repeated intercourse with her in secret for one divine year.)

The *ratikalā* image of the earth mentioned in this passage is of course none other than her image in the form of a vagina, ever ready to make love.[38] She is *Lajjāgaurī*, whom we have seen described as the "nude squatting earth goddess". The composer of the purāṇa must have seen such an image of *Lajjāgaurī* being worshipped, and it is likely that he constructed this myth about the intercourse between the earth and the Varāha to account for the unusual image.

After performing prolonged intercourse with the earth in her *ratikalā* image, the tired but satiated Hari mentally concentrated on her image and worshipped her. He then joyously said to her:

sarvādhārā bhava śubhe sarvaiḥ sampūjitā sukham |
munibhirmanubhirdevaiḥ siddhaśca dānavādibhiḥ ||
ambuvācītyāgadine gṛhāraṃbhe praveśane |
vāpītaḍāgāraṃbhe ca gṛhe ca kṛṣikarmaṇi ||

tava pūjāṃkariṣyanti madvareṇa surādayaḥ |
mūḍhā ye na kariṣyanti yāsyanti narakaṃ ca te ||

(*Devībhāgavata*: 9.9. 35–37)[39]

(Oh auspicious one! May you be a support for all. May the seers, gods, demons, and Manu himself offer worship to you. As a result of my boon to you, gods and people alike will worship you on occasions such as the end of the period of Ambuvācī, before beginning the construction of a house, before constructing a well or a water reservoir, on auspicious occasions at home and at the time of farming. The fools who do not worship you this way will end up in hell.)

After Hari in the form of a boar bestowed this boon on the earth, he himself, Brahmā and all other gods worshipped her and praised her with a hymn narrated in the Kaṇvaśākhā of the Veda. In this hymn, the earth is addressed with the following adjectives, all of which are concerned with grain and food: *sarvasasyālayā* (*Lit*: the store of all of the grains), *sarvasasyādhyā* (*Lit*: one who is proud of possessing all the grains), *sarvasasyadā* (*Lit*: the giver of all food and grains), *sarvasasyaharā* (*Lit*: one who takes away all the grain) and *sarvasasyātmikā* (lit. one who has all the grain within her).

In the next chapter (adhyāya 9.10), there is a discussion concerning donation of land and other topics related to land. In the course of their discussion, the sage Nārada asks Lord Viṣṇū:

aṁbuvācyāṃ bhūkhanane vīryasya tyāga eva ca |
dīpādisthāpanātpāpaṃ śrotumicchāmi yatnataḥ ||

(*Devībhāgavata*, 9.10.2)[40]

(Sage Nārada asks of Lord Viṣṇu what sins result from digging the earth, placing a lamp on the floor and discharging and dropping semen on the floor while the earth is menstruating.)

Lord Viṣṇu gave the following answer to Nārada's question:

ambuvācyāṃ bhūkaraṇaṃ yaḥ karoti ca mānavaḥ |
sa yāti kṛmidaṃṣam ca sthitistatra caturyugam ||

(*Devībhāgavata*, 9.10.14)[41]

(During the period of Ambuvācī, when the earth is menstruating, the person who practices digging and other similar actions goes to a hell by the name of 'Kṛmidaṃśa' and suffers for four yugas.)

The mention of the *ratikalā* image of the earth, her worship, and the actions forbidden during the period of Ambuvācī are very important for our discussion. The composer of the purāṇa has specifically mentioned an image of the earth which is eager for love-play (*sarvā ratikalā mūrtī*). This goes to show that he was aware of the fact that such images existed and were used for worship. People still use them for this purpose. It is but natural that the composer of the purāṇa, which is especially important for the Śaktas, should see a relationship between these images and the observance of Ambuvācī.

The 'Wet' Goddess Śrī in the *Śrīsūkta*

In folk religion, the image of the menstruating earth seems to have existed since the hoary past. Her reflection distinctly appears even in the Vedic *Śrīsūkta*. The 13th and 14th ṛcās (verses) of this *sūkta* describe the earth with the adjective *ārdrā* (the wet one).

ārdrām puṣkariṇīṃ puṣṭiṃ piṅgalāṃ padmamālinīm |
candrāṃ hiraṇmayīṃ lakṣmīṃ jātavedo ma āvaha ||
ārdrāṃ yaṣkariṇīṃ yaṣṭiṃ suvarṇāṃ hemamālinīm |
sūryāṃ hiraṇmayīṃ lakṣmīṃ jātavedo ma āvaha ||

(Oh Agni [Jātaveda], Invoke for me that Lakṣmī who is moist like the moisture in a pond, who is nourishing, who is red-brown in colour, who wears a garland of lotuses, who is like a moon with a golden aura, who is slim and slender, who is lustrous like the sun and who wears golden ornaments.)

If one peruses the *Śrīsūkta* even casually, one cannot fail to see that the Śrī described in this sūkta is the one who celebrates the rapture of recreation through the ever-recurring seasons on earth. Jan Gonda[42] has described her most appropriately as a guardian deity of the farmer. Unless the earth is *ārdrā*, she cannot become a mother. It is for this reason that the *ṛcās* above declare that it is through *kardama* (mud) and *ciklīta* (moisture), that Śrī conceives and becomes a mother. It is in this 'khila sūkta' of the *Ṛgveda* that Śrī has been described as padmasthitā (one who is seated on a lotus), padmavarṇā (one who has the complexion of a lotus), padminī (lotus) and padmamālinī (one who wears a garland of lotuses). This close connection with the lotus shows her intimate relationship with *kardama* (mud) and *ciklīta* (moisture). It gives special importance to her *ārdratā* (wetness for sexual union). In this respect, it is important to note the connection of Ambuvācī with the constellation of *Ārdra*.

The *Bībhatsu* and *Garbharasā* Mother in the *Asyavāmīya Sūkta*

The Asyavāmīya Sūkta from the *Ṛgveda* describes the motherhood of the earth in telling words. The following Ṛcā from this sūkta (1,164, 8) is well worth examining in this regard:

> *mātā pitaramṛta ā babhāja dhītyagre manasā saṃ hi jagme* |
> *sā bībhatsurgarbharasā nividdhā namaswanta idupavākamīyuḥ* ||

The deeper meaning of this verse can be deduced from Dr Vāsudevaśaraṇ Agrawāl's commentary on the Sūkta, quoted below.[43]

1) The male and female principles separated on the level of Ṛta.
2) In line with her wishes and using her intellect, the mother chose an appropriate husband.
3) In order to be able to bear a child, the mother first produced the required fluids (garbharasa). Because of this, she first became untouchable and then became capable of producing offspring.
4) This mother was none other than 'vāc'. All the gods and goddesses came to pay their respects to her.

Dr Vāsudevaśaraṇ Agrawal has explained the meaning of this Ṛcā of the Asyavāmīya Sūkta in the most appropriate and profound manner. I think it is necessary to look at it in his own words, which I quote below:[44]

> The meaning of the third part of this stanza is a little obscure, but becomes clearer by paying attention to nature's process of 'Motherhood' made manifest in each female. In her period of puberty, some secretions as menstrual flow appear, which make her ready for the babe to come in her womb. That is the first stage signified by 'garbharasa'. The second stage is indicated by the word 'bībhatsu' (abhorrent). As soon as the woman has her first period, she becomes abhorrent, i.e. 'not worthy of being touched or seen'. It is same as 'malavadvāsā' of later

> literature. Waters are spoken of as the Mother, and unless those secretions become turbid, i. e. imbued with the principle of matter, which in later language was said to be the 'rajasvalā' form of the woman, she can neither conceive nor bring forth. The doctrine of the Muddy waters is clearly mentioned in the *Ṛgveda* (*bībhatsūnāṃ apāṃ divyānām*, 10.124.9).

In order to conceive so as to be able to give birth to the universe, the waters that do so have got to become 'muddy,' red with menstrual blood. That is why we say that the river is menstruating when she floods for the first time in the season. This is the secret of the celebration of the festival of Ambuvācī.

Endnotes

1 Jogeś Dās, 1972. *Folklore of Āssām*, New Delhi, p. 90.
2 Translator's note: In Bengālī and Āssāmese languages, the sound va is replaced by ba.
3 Mahārāṣtra Sāhitya Patrikā, 4, Issues 1 and 2. March-June 1931. (Ḍhere mentions here that 'this has been quoted in the beginning of the article by K. V. Vaze entitled, '*Bhāratīya Kṛṣiśāstra: Vṛkśavidyā*'. Vaze has not given the original reference to the quotation').
4 Saṃskṛt to Marāṭhī translation by Ḍhere. Marāṭhī to English translation by Jayant Bāpaṭ.
5 Translator's note: This idea of the rains acting as seed to impregnate the earth is a part of ancient Chinese erotology as well and their yin and yang symbolism. Thus, one of the standard expressions for the consummation of sex is 'the meeting of the clouds and the rain'. See, Philip Rawson, 1981, *Oriental Erotic Art,* Gallery Books, New York: 103; Also, by the same author, 1968, *Erotic Art of the East*, Minerva, USA: 230.
6 Girijaprasād Mujumdār (Ed), *Kṛṣiparāśara*, 1960, Kolkaṭā, Sureścandra Banerji, Śloka 10: 2.
7 *Ibid.*, p. 43.
8 Saṃskṛt to Marāṭhī translation by Ḍhere. Marāṭhī to English translation by Jayant Bāpaṭ.
9 Translator's note: A very good description of Kāmākhyā Pīṭha and its surrounds is to be found in, Vivekananda Kendra Institute of Culture, 2010, *Heritage of Kāmākhyā on the Nīlāchala Hill*, Guwāhāṭī.
10 *Folklore of Āssām*, 1972. National Book Trust, Delhi: 90–92. Also see, Mohan Sharma, 1973, *Kāmākhyā: A Town in Assam*, New Delhi: 58.
11 Dharaṇikānta Dev Śarmā, 1953, *Kāmarūpa Kāmākhyā*: 79.
12 Saṃskṛt to Marāṭhī translation by Ḍhere. Marāṭhī to English translation by Jayant Bāpaṭ.

13 Translator's note: *jogvā* are the alms sought by the Jogṭiṇis-worshippers of the goddess, who smear tumeric on their forehead, wear a necklace of cowrie shells and carry the image of the goddess in a cane basket on their head, seeking alms.
14 *Folklore of Assam*, *op.cit.*, p. 91.
15 Kosāmbī, D.D., 1972, *Myth and Reality*, Bombay: 95. (Ḍhere comments that Dr Kosāmbī has called this ritual 'Gava-Sāī'. In Māvaḷ, it is simply called Sāt).
16 *Folklore of Āssām*, *op cit.*, 91.
17 Baṇīkānt Kākatī, 1948, *Mother Goddess Kāmākhyā*, Guahāti, 45.
18 Translator's note: The word *vrata* means a 'vow or resolve,' and refers to pious observances such as fasting on particular days and going to pilgrimage (Tirtha) during auspicious times.
19 Agrawal, Vāsudevaśaraṇ, 1964, *Prācīn Bhāratīya Lokadharma*, Vārāṇasī, 116.
20 P.V. Kāṇe, *History of Dharmaśāstra*, Vol. V, Part 1, Puṇe, Bhāṇḍarkar Institute, p. 391. (Translator's note): The exact wording of Kaṇe's description is as follows: "On Cai. kṛ. 8; the land of Kāśmīra is deemed to be rajaswalā for three days from Cai. kṛ. 5th; it is washed by women (whose husbands are living) in each home with flowers and sandalwood-paste and then by Brāhmaṇas with water in which sarvauṣadhīs are put; then people should listen to music of lutes; the earth is the queen of the sun; therefore, this *vrata* is so called."
21 Ved Kumari, 1973, *The Nīlamatapurāṅa*, Vol. II (Text with English translation), Śrīnagar: 140–143.
22 Saṃskṛt to Marāṭhī translation by Ḍhere. Marāṭhī to English translation by Jayant Bāpaṭ.
23 Translator's note: Gorasa is milk. During worship, gods are often offered milk as a 'naivedya' (ritual food offering).
24 Briffault, Robert, 1959. *The Mothers*, Macmillan, London: 203.
25 Translator's note: *Chengannur* is a town in the Alāppuzhā district of the state of Keraḷā in South India.
26 Padmanābha Menon, History of Keraḷā, part 1: 99–100.
27 This is supposed to kill weeds and make the land ready for sowing of the new crop.
28 Briffault, Robert, *The Mothers*, *op cit.*, p. 315.
29 Aśutoś Bhattācārya, The Serpent in Folk Belief in Bengal, April 1958, *The Quarterly Journal of the Mythic Society*, Vol. XLIX, No. 1: 4–24.
30 See Chapter Nine, 'Subrahmaṇyam' in this volume.
31 Kānhūcaran Paṇḍā, *Utkalakā Raja Utsav*, 1972–73, *Samanvaya*, Varsha 14, Anka 14, Kendrīya Hindi Samsthān, Āgrā: 110–112.
32 Saṃskṛt to Marāṭhī translation by Ḍhere. Marāṭhī to English translation by Jayant Bāpaṭ.
33 Saṃskṛt to Marāṭhī translation by Ḍhere. Marāṭhī to English translation by Jayant Bāpaṭ.
34 '*Śrī garbhakulārṇavāntargataṃbhagamālinīstotram*'. Hand written manuscript in Dr Ḍhere's possession.
35 Saṃskṛt to Marāṭhī translation by Ḍhere. Marāṭhī to English translation by Jayant Bāpaṭ.

36 Translator's note: *Ratikalā* literally means the art of lovemaking.
37 Translator's note: According to the Purāṇas, the divine time scale is different to that of humans. The Vedas have defined a yuga as a period of four years. The four yugas, Kṛta, Tretā, Dvāpāra, and Kali, together make a Mahāyuga. Each one of these yugas has 4800, 3600, 2400 and 1200 years respectively. Totally, these make 12,000 divine years. One divine year is equivalent to 360 human years. Thus, one Mahāyuga would translate into 4,320,000 human years.
38 Translator's note: Leleśāstrī translated the words '*kṛtvā ratikalām sarvām*" etc. as, "he made love to her and also created a beautiful image of her" (Original Marāṭhī: sarva *ratikalā* kelī va ticī atyanta manohar mūrtīhī nirmāṇ kelī). This is illogical because lovemaking would be impossible without the image.
39 Saṃskṛt to Marāṭhī translation by Ḍhere. Marāṭhī to English translation by Jayant Bāpaṭ.
40 Saṃskṛt to Marāṭhī translation by Ḍhere. Marāṭhī to English translation by Jayant Bāpaṭ.
41 Saṃskṛt to Marāṭhī translation by Ḍhere. Marāṭhī to English translation by Jayant Bāpaṭ.
42 Gonda J., *Aspects of Early Visnuism*, 1954, p. 214.
43 Agrawāl, V. S., 1963, *Visions in Long Darkness*, Pṛthivī Prakaśan, Vārāṇasī: 41.
44 *Ibid.*, p. 43.

Chapter 6

Kumbhapratīka

Pūrṇakumbha
The Iconic Pot Brimming with Water

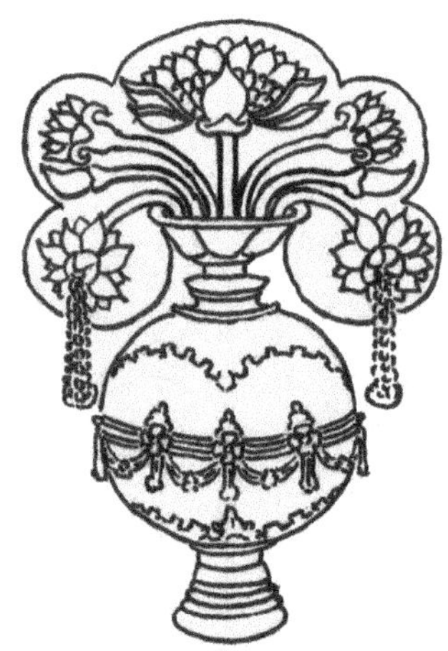

Fig. 4: The Iconic Pot: Symbol of Auspiciousness
Courtesy John Harris

Ever since the beginning of life on this earth, the cycles of birth, death and rebirth have been constantly repeating themselves. The process of the full pot brimming to overflow, becoming empty and getting itself re-filled again goes on forever without stopping. One observes these cycles of life, death and regeneration in the plant world as well. The Ādi-Śaṅkarācārya describes this process aptly in his hymn '*Carpaṭapañjarikā Stotraṃ*' (*Lit*:

hymn of repetitive uttering) as 'being born again, dying again and lying in the mother's womb again'. Even though we constantly experience the continuous movement of this universal wheel of life, we still marvel at its mystery. We find it beyond human understanding. Although we can describe it, we find it impossible to unravel this mystery. For the first humans, the earth, which produced this play of generation, destruction and re-generation was a highly complex, involved and divine power. It is this unusual, exalted and divine status that early humans bestowed upon the earth that has produced the tales and mythologies which explain the background of their beliefs. In fact, the ancient myths and associated lore ascribed to early humans are the only means that can adequately explain the actions that they performed and the resultant vibrations that may have been produced in their minds. Irrespective of how much we excavate and however many archaeological remains we unearth, without such myths it is impossible to re-create and appreciate the workings of the primitive mind.

The Place of the Pot in Last Rites

Of the two highly mysterious processes associated with life – birth and death – one finds a large amount of evidence associated with the latter in the form of human remains through excavations carried out by archaeologists. There is no doubt that this evidence points to the practice of burying the remains of the dead. The form and the process of burial can vary. The two common burial processes adopted in India involved burying the body directly in a pit dug for the purpose or enclosing the body in a burial-urn and then burying this urn in a pit. In both of these processes, the feet are placed toward the south[1] and the head toward the north. In excavations performed all over the world, it has been found that when a child's body is placed in a burial urn, the placement of the body is done in such a way as to simulate the embryonic position of the foetus, i.e. the body crouching in the middle, the hands and feet bent and the knees almost touching the head. Naturally, the urn that holds the body automatically becomes the iconic womb of the mother. In these excavations, another peculiarity has been discovered about the urns that are used to bury children. In place of a single urn, one often finds two tall urns facing each other with their mouths touching. Such dual urns containing the dead bodies of children have been found at Dāyamābād, Cāṇḍolī, Nevāse and Ināmgav in Mahārāṣṭra state. In many cases, these urns were buried under the family's home. In his comments on such burials, the archaeologist Puruṣottam Singh[2] has said that

> The burial in embryonic posture was accorded possibly in the belief that 'as a man came out of his mother's womb, so shall he return whence he came'.

I believe that Singh's thinking is very logical and fitting.

A Pot Full of Water: The Icon of the Mother's Womb

There is plenty of evidence within the cultural heritage of India to deduce that a pot, by its very shape, is an icon of the mother's womb. This iconic symbolism of the pot has been described in the literature and expressed in many of the rituals within Indic religions. The term '*kumbha*' is closely related to the term 'earth' in Saṃskṛt. The terms *ku* or *kum* both mean the earth in Saṃskṛt. This one-syllable word has been used in many compound words in Saṃskṛt to denote the earth. For example, *ku* + *kīl* is *kukīl,* which means a mountain. *Ku* + *bhṛt* is *kubhṛt,* which also means a mountain. *kum* + *kaṇā* becomes *kuṅkaṇā,* which is one of Reṇukā's names. A pot is made out of earth; hence it is called earthenware. In the early days of Indian civilization, it was only women who made pottery.[3] Because of the close similarities in the reproductive cycles of the earth and the human female, early humans must have sensed within their inner selves an innate oneness and a divine relationship between a woman and the earth. While a human female is a single representative of motherhood, the earth represents an all encompassing plurality of the same. It is tempting to think that when early women were making their pots, they had in mind the oneness of such an earthenware pot and the womb in mind. Since the womb as the reproductive organ is the first manifestation of motherhood, it was natural that the *kumbha*, a pot filled with water, became the icon of motherhood and the mother goddess.

The installation of a pot filled with water at the celebration of the festival of nine nights (*navarātrotsava*) is the celebration of the mother goddess in the form of a pot. It is through this pot that the primordial mother celebrates the regeneration of life. It is because of its image as the primordial mother that a pot brimming with water is seen as an icon of regeneration, auspiciousness and plentifulness. The same thinking seems to be behind the installation of the *Kumbha* in the folk festival of 'Karagā' in the state of Karnāṭaka.[4] Similarly, one of the names for a prostitute in

Saṃskṛt is *Kumbhā*. It is clear that this must be due to her lifestyle as a *kumbha*–a receptacle.

In the *Vājasaneyī Saṃhitā* of the *Yajurveda* (19.87), a *kumbha* has been described as the cause of regeneration. The perceptive seer who composed this verse says that it is within the *kumbha* located in the inner recesses of the vagina that the foetus of regeneration resides, and that this *kumbha* has divine powers of regeneration. The *Atharvaveda* (19. 3. 3) goes even further and declares that it is in the womb of time that a *kumbha* full of procreative waters resides. This womb in the form of a *kumbha* that resides within infinite time is what regulates and controls the generation of life in the universe. Wanting to manifest itself, the unmanifest within this procreative *kumbha* surges to its mouth and then expresses itself in the many-splendored iconic form of new branches and young leaves.

The *Asyavāmīya Sūkta* of the *Ṛgveda* (1.164.32) states:

> *sa māturyonā parivīto antarbahuprajā nirṛtirmā viveśa*
>
> (He who resides in the womb of the mother (surrounded by umbilical fluid etc.), has to experience a number of births or gives birth to many. Such a person experiences the pain named Nirṛti.[5])

This is obviously applicable to both birth and death. A human being gets engulfed in the inner recesses of the vagina, is surrounded by amniotic fluid and enters the land of the goddess Nirṛti. Nirṛti is *mahāmātā*, the great mother. Just as she is the goddess of creation, so is she the goddess of destruction. The processes of birth and death are both connected to her womb. The *Śatapatha Brāhmaṇa* (7.2.1.11) declares, '*iyam pṛthvī vai nirṛtiḥ*'. Nirṛti is therefore the sole controller of the miraculous processes of birth and death. When one thinks about the universal motherhood of the earth, one cannot help but realise the great truth behind this Marāṭhī proverb:

> *mātī asaśī mātisa miḷaśī*
>
> (you are [made of] earth; you [will] coalesce with earth.)[6]

To me, there is no more need to delve further into the reasoning for the *kumbha* being equated with the mother's womb. Every living being takes shape in the procreative waters of this divine *kumbha*, experiences life for a certain period and then re-enters the *kumbha* in order to be reborn again. And all of this happens just to experience Śaṅkarācārya's dictum:

punarapi jananaṃ punarapi maraṇaṃ punarapi jananījaṭhare śayanaṃ ।

(being born again, dying again, lying in the mother's womb again.)

Our divine father Prajāpati, the procreator of every life form on this planet, was on his own in the beginning. He had to become 'many' (bahudhā) in order to start the endless cycles of life-and-death-and-life. He is the one who, out of his mind, produced a daughter with a hundred forms, and it was he who impregnated her with the foetus of recreation. Since he was on his own, he became the father of the woman he produced. Because his sole purpose was recreating life, he had to resort to incest with his daughter.[7] The living nature that he created moves in the womb of mother earth between her two forms: giver of life and giver of death. The earth's procreative life is worshipped in her form as Gaurī. Her form as the destroyer of life is venerated as Kālī.

Many of the pots and potsherds found in the excavations at one of the Indus river sites bear a peacock emblem on them. Some of them show a dead body in the womb of the peacock.[8] Such a peacock holding a dead body within its womb is a representation of motherhood, an icon of the *kumbha*. I shall elaborate this further when I deal with the myth of Kalpakāmbā later in this chapter. The Mahābhārata calls the peacock a necrophile.[9] This must be due to its close relationship with the *Kumbha* used to bury the dead.

The Relationship of Potters with Last Rites

Performances of the *Gondhaḷa, Bharāḍ* and *Jāgaraṇa* play an important part during the last rites for many families, depending on the customs and traditions of their clan. Similarly, potters have also held an important role in conducting these rites. Accompanied by an instrument called the *ḍāṅk*, potters tell many stories and myths through their songs. Because of this instrument, the performance itself has been termed *ḍāṅk*.[10]

It is obvious that the importance of the potter at the time of last rites must be related to the burial of the dead in pots. Since the potter makes the *kumbha*, it is appropriate for him to celebrate the burial of the dead in the *kumbha*. Dr Prabhākar Māṇḍe has quoted some lines from a song called '*muñjābāce gāṇe*'[11] (*Lit*: song of the *muñjābā*), which is sung as part of the *ḍāṅk* performance. Among these lines, the following are important for our purpose:

āre to muñjā velhāḷa re, bāḷā muñjā re |
pimpaḷā ṭāngalā ḍolārā re, bāḷā muñjā re ||

kavāṃ rāv, kadhīn kāy jhālaṃ re, bāḷā muñjā re |
maraṇa kasāyānaṃ āla re, bāḷā muñjā re ||

prāṇa gelā hoḍāhoḍīṃ, ātmā ṭākūn gelā koḍī |
karatārācī gat nyārī, tuṭalī sargīcī dorī ||

(The baby *muñjā* was a lovely child. His swing would be hung on the Pipal[12] tree. No one knows how it happened, how his death came about. The soul left the lifeless body, leaving behind some puzzles. Fate is strange, the cord to heaven was broken.)

In the context of our present discussion, it is important to note that the song is closely connected with the death of a child.

Hiraṇyagarbha Mahādāna[13]

The notion of entering the mother's womb as a foetus for the purpose of regeneration after death seems to be behind the ritual of *Hiraṇyagarbha Mahādāna*. We already know that *Hiraṇyagarbha* is one of the names of Brahmā, the creator. However, it is also one of the sixteen great *Mahādānas* (*Lit*: most propitious religious gifts) described in religious texts. These sixteen have been discussed in detail in the *Matsyapurāṇa*, the 'Vratakhaṇḍa' of Hemādrī's *Caturvargacintāmaṇī* and the work *Dānasāgara* by Ballāḷasena. The eminent epigraphist and scholar of ancient Indian history and culture Dineścandra Sarkār has described how these *mahādānas* are mentioned in many stone inscriptions.[14]

Thus, for example, in the Gorantalā inscription, King Attivarman is described as *aprameya-hiraṇyagarbhaprasava* (*Lit*: the inscrutable one who has taken birth from a golden womb). In the Mahākūṭa pillar inscription of the Cālukya king Maṅgaleśa, Pulakeśin 1 has been honoured with the honorific title *hiraṇyagarbhasambhūta* (*Lit*: born out of a golden womb). The adjective *aprameya-hiraṇyagarbhaprasava* also appears in the Maṭṭepāda (Dist: Gunṭur) copperplate inscription of King Dāmodaravarman. In the Ipūr and Polmurū inscriptions of king Mādhavavarman 1 of the Viṣṇukuṇḍin dynasty, the adjective *hiraṇyagarbhaprasūta* is used In discussing this adjective that appears in the inscriptions of many south Indian kings, Fleet states that it describes those who belong to the lineage of the god Brahmā. On the other hand, Hultzsch thinks that the real meaning of the term is "the one who commissioned the *Hiraṇyagarbha Mahādāna.*" Sarkār, however, refutes both of these interpretations and believes that all three versions of this adjective – i.e., *hiraṇyagarbhaprasava, hiraṇyagarbhasambhūta and hiraṇyagarbhaprasūta* – must be taken to mean "one who has been born from a golden womb."

The accuracy of Sarkār's interpretation is easily ascertained when one observes the ritual of *Hiraṇyagarbha Mahādāna.* In this ritual, a two-metre-high golden urn is initially constructed. The king who wishes to perform the ritual bows in front of the pot and then enters it. All of the rituals that follow assume that the golden urn, *Hiraṇyagarbha,* is now pregnant and carries the king's foetus. With this belief, the priest then performs the pre-natal rites of Garbhādhāna, Puṃsavana and Sīmantonnayana. The golden womb then undergoes a delivery and the new-born king steps out. The priests then perform on the king the necessary rites of passage for a newborn. When these rituals are over, the *hiraṇyagarbhasambhūta* king expresses his indebtedness to the golden womb by declaring:

> *mātrā 'ham janitaḥ pūrva martyādharmā surottama* |
> *tvadgarbhasambhavādeṣa divyadeho bhavāmyaham* ||
>
> (*Matsyapurāṇam*, 275.20)
>
> (Oh Lord of Lords, *Hiraṇyagarbha*! In my previous life, I was given birth by my mother and was therefore a mortal. Now however, because I have taken birth in your womb, I have become divine-bodied.)

After the king utters the words of this hymn expressing his indebtedness, the priests once again perform *abhiṣeka* (sprinkling of consecrated water while chanting) on the king and chant the following mantra

> *adyajātasya te 'ṅgāni abhiṣekṣāmahe vayam* |
>
> (*Matsyapurāṇaṃ*, 275.22)
>
> (We offer this consecrated water to your new-born limbs.)

When one analyses the details of this ritual, it becomes abundantly clear that the entire purpose of the ritual is to symbolically do away with the mortal body of the king and replace it with an immortal divine body. *Hiraṇyagarbha Mahādāna* then is the expression of the symbolic death of a person belonging to royalty, the symbolic construction of the primordial womb of mother nature and the divine rebirth of the royal who has entered the womb of mother earth. It should also be clear that the golden urn used in this ritual represents the womb of mother nature. The sequence of events in life experienced by humans – birth, death, entering the mother's womb for re-birth and being reborn again – is what this ritual portrays.

Inside the Womb of Dagobā

Let me now reiterate what we have learned in the previous chapters. In the states of Āndhra Pradeś, Mahārāṣṭra and Goā, and in many adjoining areas in the south, the mother goddess is often worshipped as an anthill, which is considered to be an iconic representation of the womb. Elsewhere, she may be represented as an aniconic stone. In some places, she is represented as the fully iconic Durgā. Finally, she is sometimes worshipped in the form of a headless torso showing only her genitals and breasts, her reproductive and sustaining organs. In all of these places, she is variously called Reṇukā, Joguḷāmbā, Yamāi, Yallammā, Ellammā, Ekavīra and Santeri.[15]

One of the well-known, major shrines for this goddess is the Ekvīrā temple in front of the great *Caitya* cave at Kārle.[16] The Son Koḷīs of the western sea are devotees of this goddess. At this shrine the goddess has the form of a figure carved in relief on the rock face of the hill. When Son Koḷīs come here to worship, they make offerings not only to the goddess but to the *stūpa* at the *Caitya* as well. The circumambulation they need to do for the Goddess is done instead for the *stūpa*.[17] They consider the *stūpa* to be a symbol of the goddess. The alternate name they have for Ekvīrā is *'beherāī'* (the mother from the Vihār). In his well-known and thought-provoking work *Myth and Reality*, the great Indian scholar Dāmodar Dharmānand Kosāmbī looked at the devotional regime at Kārle and compared it with the possible worship of the *Caitya* in the pre-Buddhist period. Kosāmbī was surprised to find that the Son Koḷīs equate the *stūpa* with Yamāī or Ekavīrā. He says:

> It is natural, as has happened in other cases, to take a *stupa* (trimmed suitably if necessary) as Śiva's phallus; but to take it as a mother goddess is extraordinary to say the least.[18]

I look at a *stūpa* differently. A *stūpa* is equated with a *śivaliṅga* only by its external appearance and shape. However, if one examines its interior and the purpose it is designed for, it makes sense for it to be equated with an icon of the mother goddess. The word *dāgobā* that one uses for a *stūpa* clearly shows the close connection of the term with the devotional basis of the Son Koḷīs. Etymologically, the term *dāgobā* derives from the (Saṃskṛt) term *dhātugarbha*. The body that holds within its interior, the *dhātu* (relics of the Buddha) as a foetus, or the body in whose womb the *dhātu* is cared for, is *dhātugarbha*. It is therefore natural for a body holding a foetus to be equated with motherhood rather than with a phallus.

The Mystery of the Joined Pots

We have now established that, symbolically, a pot represents the mother's womb. We have also examined the symbolic meaning behind placing a dead body into such a pot so as to ensure that the person will be reborn. It is however difficult to comprehend why, when burying a child's lifeless body, ancient Indians sometimes used two small pots facing each other. The body was placed in the foetal position surrounded by these two pots. If one pot represents the womb, one cannot see the need for the second pot. One can see the need for a large pot for an adult. But the two pots together have been used only for the burial of children. One must therefore look for some deeper meaning behind this practice.

It may come as a surprise that while the symbolism of the pot representing the womb comes from Vedic literature, the symbolism of the dual pots holding a foetus also comes from the same source. In fact, nothing describes more appropriately the condition of the remains of the skeletons of the young children found in excavations than the following hymn from the *Ṛgveda*:

dyaurme pitā janitā nābhiratra bandhurme mātā pṛthivī mahīyaṃ ‖

(The *Ṛgveda*: 1.164.33a)

uttānayoścamvor 'yonirantaratrā pitā duhiturgarbhamādhāt ‖

(The *Ṛgveda*: 1.164.33c)

This hymn from the *Asyavāmīya Sūkta* aptly elaborates the symbolism of the dual pots. The seer who wrote this hymn states, 'The sky is my father, the creator. I am thus related to him. This great earth is my mother. She is very close to me. Her vagina is situated in between the openings of the two pots facing each other. My father has deposited his seed in the womb of his daughter'.

I have previously discussed the nuances of this father-daughter relationship. In order to become "many", i.e., to procreate, Prajāpati, alias Brahmā the creator, created Śatarūpā,[19] a beautiful maiden out of his mind. Because he created her, she became his daughter, Duhitā (*Lit*: one with a separate existence). However, he deposited his seed into her in order to procreate the living earth. This is the real meaning behind the creator's incest. The all encompassing symbolism of the womb and the vagina is now able to offer a fascinating insight into the practice of burying deceased babies into two pots with their mouths joined together. Dyau (the sky) is the father and the earth is the mother. The above hymn tells us about the common womb formed by the union of these two in the form of two pots facing each other. The words 'inverted bowls forming a common womb' (*uttānayoścamvo 'ryoniḥ*) in the hymn are apposite for the twin burial pots with children's remains found in excavations.

In this regard, I would like to quote the highly original exposition by Vāsudevaśaraṇ Agrawāl. He writes:

> The earth and the Heaven are both described as *'uttānacamū'*... The real purport is that these are the two Bowls turned to each other and therefore forming a single cavity. The one is recumbent against the other, as is exactly the position of the two parents in the act of congress.[20]

I contend that, against this background, there should be no problem calling the two bowls 'inverted'. The heaven and the earth are thus 'inverted' during sexual intercourse. As Agrawāl puts it, if one looks from the top, the mother looks inverted, but if one looks from below, the father looks inverted.[21] Because the earth conceives as a result of intercourse between her and heaven in the characteristic position facing each other, the only image that can give justice to the womb in this position, would be in the form of two pots facing each other. The body of the dead child is placed in the pot with the assumption that it is going to be reborn through this earthly womb of the mother. It is therefore essential that the sky, the father, be present in congress with the earth, the mother.

The Rituals and Their Emotional Purport

In excavations in Mahārāṣṭra at places such as Nevāse, Cāṇḍolī and Dāyamābād, archaeologists have discovered Stone- and Copper-age burial pots facing each other which held the remains of children. From our discussion so far, it is abundantly clear that the symbolism of such burials is fully elaborated by Vedic hymns and by traditional rituals. Such rituals portray a surge of tender emotions displayed by early humans, their acute reaction to the two inevitables of human life – birth and death – and their firm belief in rebirth. This last belief must have led them to bury the dead child back in the mother's womb with the greatest of tender care. We can envision all of this through the agencies of archaeology and ancient scriptures.

Tumultuous Surge of Tender Feelings

The discussion we have had so far would be more than adequate to convince us that the symbolism behind the placement of earthen pots into the grave of a child can be explained by examining Vedic hymns, and by looking at the customs that were followed at such times. These customs point to an explosion of tender feelings that early humans must have experienced when they encountered birth and death. Their intense and serious reaction to these events must have been strengthened by their firm belief in the repetitive processes of birth, death and re-birth, something they observed with mother nature. These firm beliefs must have led them to install the dead infant into the womb (earthen pot) of the mother with the utmost and delicate care.

The Kalpakāmbā of Mayalāpūra (Mylapore)

In the context of the burial of the dead in earthen pots, one must think of one goddess who has a close connection with mother-earth worship. The unfolding of this goddess's origin will be instructive in our present investigation. Researchers have discovered again and again that, just as there are many radical and often strange changes in human life, there are changes in the lives of deities as well. The latter happen at times due to a lapse in the memory of the devotees. They also happen when religious fanatics deliberately attempt to exalt the otherwise worldly status of a particular deity. I recently discovered the truth of this axiom in reading about Śrī Kalpakāmbā of Mayalāpūra (Mylāpore).

Mayalāpūra is at present an important suburb of Cennāī, the capital of Tamilnāḍu.

Most religiously-minded people know Mayalāpūra because of the presence of the well-known Rāmakṛṣṇa Ashram there. However, although it is only a suburb of Cennāī today, Mayalāpūra used to be a famous city on its own in the past. Before the beginning of the Christian Era, it used to be a renowned cultural centre, a thriving port and a major centre for Śaivism. This was the place where the great sage Tiruvalluvar and the Aḷavār saint Periyāḷavār were born. Legend has it that it is in a Śiva temple at Mayalāpūra that the great Śaivite saint Jñānasambandha brought back to life a girl called Pūpāvai who had died of snake bite.

Śrī Kalpakāmbā alias Śrī Kalpakavallī is the presiding deity of Mayalāpūra. Her consort is Śrī Kapālīśvara. The temple devoted to the father and mother of the world, Śrī Kapālīśvara and Śrī Kalpakāmbā, is located right in the middle of Mayalāpūra. Near the temple is a lake. The new temple is not all that old. The old temple used to be on the seashore, where the waves of the sea strove to wash the feet of Lord Śrī Kapalīśvara. That temple was, however, destroyed, and right in the midst of the remnants of the old temple stands the mansion of the bishop of Mayalāpūra. We are not concerned here with the history of either Mayalāpūra or the destruction of the temple. What we will concern ourselves with is the mystery behind the name of the place, i. e. Mayalāpūra, and the presiding deities, Śrī Kalpakāmbā and Śrī Kapālīśvara at this place.

To my knowledge, Tamil historians, or scholars who have worked on the deities of Tamilnāḍu, provide no information about the origin of these names. The only information I have at hand is in a book entitled *The Temples of Tamilnāḍu* written by R.K. Dās and published by Bhāratīya Vidyā Bhavan, Mumbai, in 1964; and in an article published in the 1973 issue of the magazine *Kāmakoṭī Vāṇī*. The article, with the title 'The Kapālīśwara Temple at Mylāpore', was written by someone with the assumed name, 'Yātrik' (*Lit*: traveller). Both of these sources deal with the following story of the appearance on earth of Kalpakāmbā and the establishment of the temple of Kapālīśvara as it appears in the *Sthalapurāṇa* of Mayalāpūra.

Once when Brahmā went to Kailās, the abode of Śiva, he did not pay appropriate respect to Śiva. Śiva became very angry and cut off one of the four heads of Brahmā with his trident. Badly hurt, Brahmā came to Mayalāpūra and started practising penance with the purpose of removing his sins and thereby pleasing Śiva. Pleased with his penance, Śiva appeared there in person. Brahmā established a *śivaliṅga* at the place. The Sthalapurāṇa explains that, because Śiva appeared there holding one of Brahmā's heads in his hand, the place came to be known as Kapālīśvara (*Lit*: Śiva holding a skull). The shrine of Kapālīśvara is ancient and is also highly popular among Śiva devotees. Scholars believe that, in the distant past, this may have been a centre for Kāpālika Śaivism.

The same Sthalapurāṇa also tells the story of how Kalpakāmbā, the presiding goddess of Mayalāpūra, incarnated herself at this place: Once while Śiva and Pārvatī were enjoying a quiet moment, a beautiful peacock, with its colourful feathers spread, appeared and started dancing. Pārvatī was so taken by the beauty of the bird and its enchanting dance that she momentarily ignored Śiva and kept watching the dance. Angry, Śiva cursed her and said that since she was so attracted to the bird and its dance as to ignore him, she would become a peahen. As a result of the curse, Pārvatī instantly became a peahen and came to the forest that is known today as Mayalāpūra. In this forest, she practised penance in order to win back Śiva. As a result of her penance, Śiva's anger was appeased and he came to the forest in the form of a peacock, Mayūra. Since the goddess came here in the form of Mayūrī, a peahen, the place became known as Mayūrapūra. In Tamil, the word for Mayūra is Mayila. The place therefore became Mayilāpūra. This then is the etymology of the word Mayalāpūra. The eminent scholar 'Prativādībhayaṅkara' Śrī Annaṅgaracārī Swāmī has expressed the view that the word Mayalāpūra probably comes from Mahilāpurī (lit. abode of women). However, his etymology does not sit well with the form of the goddess or the Sthalapurāṇa and cannot therefore be accepted.

The information at hand tells us that the name of the place is Mayūrapūra, the presiding deity of the place appeared here in the form of a peahen, and her partner came to visit her in the form of a peacock. Given this background, it seems odd that the present name of the presiding deity of Mayalāpūra is Kalpakāmbā and the name of her partner is Kapālīśvara. I have a strong feeling that these odd names are either deliberate or inadvertent transformations of the original names.

In Saṃskṛt, the word *kalāpa* refers to a peacock's tail. The words *kalāpakā* (peahen) and *kalāpī* (peacock) are obviously derived from the word *kalāpa*. Therefore, the word *kalāpakāmbā* would obviously mean the mother earth in her form as a peahen. Similarly, the word *kalāpīśvara* would denote Śiva in the form of a peacock. It would seem logical that the word *kalāpakāmbā* was transformed into *kalpakāmbā* by the loss of the vowel 'ā'. Similarly, the word *kalāpīśvara* must have become *kapālīśvara*, by a simple transformation of a consonant. *Kapālīśvara* is the present name of Śiva at this place. If one looks at the background of the aforementioned myth in the Sthalapurāṇa, one can readily see the logic of the transformation of the names of Śiva and his consort. Also, once this transformation took place, a new myth must have emerged to explain the origin of the name Kapālīśvara, the name of Śiva at this place.

Although equating mother earth with a peahen may sound somewhat strange, this comparison seems to be common and age-old in Dravidian culture. In his article entitled, "Peacock: The National Bird of India", the researcher P. Thankappan Nāyar clearly states:[22]

> In the eyes of the Dravid culture, a peacock is the representative of mother earth. The peacock cult originated in south India and spread all over the world. The tribals in India always associate the peacock with mother earth. For instance, the Khoṇḍ tribals always worship mother earth in the form of a peacock.

Nāyar believes that the Saṃskṛt word '*mayur*' is a Saṃskṛtization of the word '*mayil*' in Dravidian languages, and his work shows that the peacock has been associated with mother earth for a very long time.[23]

The Peacock and Mother Earth

The oneness of the peacock and mother earth in the minds of early humans points us in another direction. During the excavations that were done at the sites of the Indus river culture, several burial urns have been discovered. Many of these portray drawings of the peacock on them. In addition, the dead have been shown in the wombs of these peacocks. These burial pots, which represent the peacock holding the dead in its womb, inform us in depth about the myth of the Kalpakāmbā at Mayalāpūra.

From the very beginnings of the human race, the human mind has always associated the earth with motherhood. This eternal truth has come to us in the form of many myths, rituals, tantras, folklore and folk traditions. As we saw in the previous chapter, a pot completely full of water has frequently been taken to represent the mother's womb. The idea of enclosing a dead body in a pot before burial has this same thought behind it. The dead person is put to rest in the same place that he or she came from. To echo Śaṅkarācārya's words again, it is 'going back to the mother's womb.'[24] We are now able to understand the symbolism behind picturing the peacock on a burial urn. Since the peacock is the representation of the great mother goddess, picturing the dead sitting in the womb of the peacock would indicate that the great mother Kalpakāmbā has once again taken the baby in her womb and is nursing it forever with tender love. This then is the secret of the symbolism of the peacock on the burial urn. One often associates old myths with idle talk or baseless gossip. However, examples such as the Kalpakāmbā and peacock myths that we have seen above shed important light on the unravelling of the development of historical thought.

During the process of the investigation of the nature of the god and the goddess installed at Mayalāpūra, and by the study of the associated myths, we have been able to get a glimpse of the all encompassing universal forms of these deities. This led us to unravel the symbolism behind the myth of the pot brimming with water. It is through these myths behind the potful of water and the burial urns that we are able to fathom the all encompassing motherhood of the primordial supreme goddess.

Endnotes

1 Translator's Note: South is the direction of the Lord of death, Yama. Hence, the feet of the dead are turned towards this direction.
2 Singh, Puruṣottam. (1970). *Burial Practices in Ancient India*. Varanasi: 174.
3 Kosāmbī, D.D. (1962). *Myth and Reality*. Popular Prakāśan, Bombay: 76.
4 Kosāmbī, D.D. *op.cit.* 72–74.
5 I am grateful to Professor Mādhavī Narasaḷe for this translation.
6 Translator's note: This is of course very similar to the Biblical proverb, 'ashes to ashes, dust to dust'.
7 Agrawāl, V.S. (1963). *Vision in Long Darkness. op cit.* 63–65.
8 Kosāmbī. *op. cit.* 75.
9 *Mahābhārata*, Ādiparva: Adhyāya 85, Śloka 6.
10 Cāphekar, N. G. *Badlāpur*, Puṇe: Śake 1855 (C.E. 1933): 70–85; Mājgavkar, G. V. (1934). *kumbhār jnātibāndhavānce ḍānkecī kathā*. Kolhāpūr: Māṇḍe, Prabhākar. (1975). *Lokasāhityāce Antaḥpravāha*. Puṇe: 24–26 (All in Marāṭhī)
11 Translators Note: In Marāṭhī, a *muñjā* is a young Brāhmaṇ male who has died before his threading ceremony. It is worth noting that a *muñjā* is a child and it was normally a child that used to be buried in pots.
12 '*Ficus religiosa*' tree.
13 Lit: Great Offering of the Golden Foetus.
14 Sarkār, D. C. (1971). *Studies in Religious Life of Ancient and Medieval India*, Delhi: 164–167.

15 See chapter 2, 'Jogulāmbā' in this volume.
16 The world-famous rock-cut caves at Kārlā are near the town of Loṇāvlā, 94 kms east of Mumbai.
17 Translator's note: Because of the fact that the goddess is carved on a hill face, it is physically impossible to circumambulate the shrine.
18 Kosāmbī. *op. cit.*, pp. 96–97.
19 Translator's note: According to Vedic mythology, when Brahmā, also known as Prajāpati, desired to procreate, he produced a female, Śatarūpā, from his mind. Because he produced her, he automatically became her father. However, for procreation, he had to deposit his seed in her and she thus became his wife as well. From this incestuous relationship, Manu, the father of the world, was born.
20 Agrawāl. *op. cit.*, pp. 119–122.
21 Agrawāl. *Ibid.*, pp. 121–122.
22 Folklore Magazine, Kolkaṭā, November 1973.
23 Nāyar, P. Thankappan. (1977). *The Peacock*. Firma KLM, Kolkaṭṭā: 202, 203, 261.
24 *Punarapi jananī jaṭhare śayanaṃ* |.

Chapter 7

The Parental Home of Mother Nature[1]

We have already seen that many of the images of *Lajjāgaurī* are associated with the lotus. Kamala and Kamalā[2] are thus forever linked to each other. When the autumn season,[3] with its golden days and moonlit nights, comes upon us, we become aware of the mystery of this relationship. Around this time, fields are full of fresh crops and lakes are endowed with the beauty of lotus blooms. When *Dhānya-Lakṣmī* (Lakṣmī bringing in the fresh crop), who has been enriched with the annual rain, comes home with her golden feet, the *Kamala-Lakṣmī*, who sways happily on the waters of the lake, is there to welcome her. That is why Saṃskṛt poets have portrayed the autumn season, Śarad, which is profusely endowed with lotuses, with *Kamalā-Lakṣmī*, in her lotus-like form as a beautiful, statuesque young woman. The poet says:[4]

> The season of Śarad is like a beautiful woman whose complexion is akin to ruby-red lotuses, whose eyes are like full-blown blue lotuses and whose smile is enchanting and alluring like a blooming lotus. May that enchanting season enrich your happiness and contentedness.

In Indian society, we use the term 'Lakṣmī' to describe a woman of good character who is happily married and who has mothered children. As she is a mother, we worship her and consider her to be a representative of the great earth mother. In Indian culture, the earth and woman are one and the same; both are mothers. Both are goddess 'Lakṣmī', the living essence of the 'goddess principle'. We worship them in their image form, and we consider the lotus their symbolic representation. This means that in our eyes, mother earth, a woman, and the lotus are identical.

Although he comprehends the reasons behind this inordinate importance given to the lotus, the somewhat envious poet says:[5]

lakṣmī svayaṃ nivasati tvayi lokadhātrī |
mitreṇacāpi vihito 'sti dṛḍho 'nurāgaḥ |
vandīva gāyati guṇānstava cañcarīkaḥ |
kaḥ puṇḍarīka! tava sāmyamurīkaroti? ||[6]

(World-bearer Lakṣmī herself resides within you. The friend of the entire universe, the Sun, has a special place in his heart for you. The roving black bee sings your ballads like a bard. Oh Lotus! Who is going to be courageous enough to compete with your fortunes?)

It is but natural for the lotus, a symbol of mother earth, to hold a special place in the heart of the Sun. The Sun is a representative of the heavens. In fact, he *is* the heavens. He is the male principle in the universal couple, 'heaven and earth'. It is therefore only natural for his fiancée, the earth in the form of the lotus, to fully bloom when she notices the sun rising. It is the universal plan by none other than Brahmā, the creator, that as soon as she is touched by the Sun's rays, the hands of the male principle, every part of the earth's body should respond by blossoming. Finally, through this cosmic union, the foetus of the universe is conceived.

Just like the sun, the moon too is a representative of the heavens. The earth in the form of a lotus therefore responds equally to the rays of the moon. The lotus therefore is the symbol of the regenerative power of the earth and the mother.

The Padmā in the Hymn *Śrīsūkta*

The close and intense relationship between the earth and the lotus is to be found in the *Śrīsūkta*, a hymn that is thought to be a later attachment to the *Ṛgveda*.[7] There is ample evidence within the *Śrīsūkta* itself to suggest that the Śrī in this Sūkta is none other than Bhūdevī, mother earth.[8] She becomes a mother because of *kardama* (Skt: mud). Waters make her soft. This softness makes her 'wet' (Skt: ciklīta) and moisture-bearing.[9] The two adjectives *kardama* and *ciklīta* clearly refer to earth that has become wet either due to the rains or due to the proximity of water and is therefore ready to hold seed for the process of germination. The same meaning is conveyed by verses 13 and 14, where she is referred to as *ārdrā* (Skt: moist). The adjective *hastinādaprabodhinī* in verse 3 reminds us of her form as *Gajalakṣmī*, Lakṣmī flanked by two elephants showering water on her. Since the elephant is being compared here with a cloud, naturally she is the Lakṣmī who blossoms with the sound of the elephant's call. This particular form of mother earth is primarily associated with the growing of rice in paddy fields. In verse 9, the seer uses the adjective *karīṣiṇī* (*Lit*: one who is smeared with dung, which is used as a fertilizer for rice) to describe her. In applying the adjectives *hiraṇyavarṇā* (*Lit*: of golden hue), *jvalantī* (*Lit*: on fire) and *hiraṇyaprākārā* (*Lit*: like gold) to her, the poet-seer wishes to paint a picture of the earth covered completely with a fully-grown rice field. This is the earth that provides us with ample food, wealth and cattle and it is she who has been described by various appropriate adjectives in the *Śrīsūkta*. She is the *Lakṣmī* who destroys *Alakṣmī*.[10] Naturally she is the womb responsible for the birth of every living being, and she is also the cause of wealth and amplitude.

In establishing and elaborating the relationship between Śrī and the lotus, the poet-seer has remained true to the mythology of Ṛgvedic times. We will now investigate the Ṛgvedic version of the myth of the relationship between mother earth and the lotus. The visionary seer who authored the *Śrīsūkta* sees the goddess seated on a lotus seat (*padme sthitā*). To him, her complexion is like a lotus (*padma varṇā*) and she looks just like a lotus vine (*padminī*). He also says that she wears lotus garlands around her neck (*padmamālinī*). This relationship between the earth and the lotus as elaborated in the *Śrīsūkta* becomes even more pronounced in the *Lakṣmīsūkta*, an appendage to the *Śrīsūkta*. In this latter *sūkta*, the transformation of *Śrī* to *Lakṣmī* appears to be complete, as can be seen from the following three verses:

padmānane padma-ūru padmākṣī padmasaṃbhave |
tanme bhajasi padmākṣī, yena saukhyaṃ labhāmyaham || 1 ||

padmānane padmini padmapatre padmapriye padmadalāyatakṣī |
viśvapriye viśvamanonukūle tvatpādapadmaṃ mayi sannidhatsva || 3 ||

sarasijanilaye sarojahaste dhavalatarāṅśukagandha-mālyaśobhe|
bhagavati harivallabhe manojñe tribhuvanabhūtikarī prasīda
mahyam || 7 ||[11]

(Oh lotus faced one! Your thighs are like soft lotuses. Oh lotus-born goddess! Your eyes are like lotuses. Please grant me something that will give me lasting happiness. Oh lotus faced one! You are seated on a lotus leaf. You are very dear to the lotus. Your eyes are like lotuses. You are very dear to the universe. Please rest your feet on me. You reside in the lotus and you wear lotuses

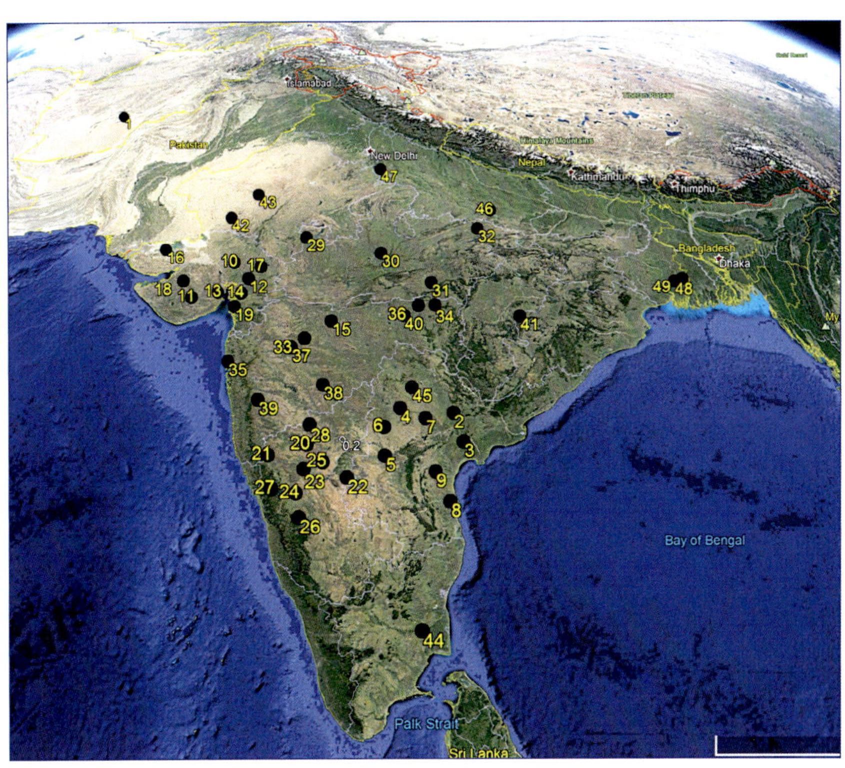

Plate 1: Map showing places where Lajjāgaurī images have been found.
Courtesy Drs. Ravi Korisetṭar and Arjuna Rao

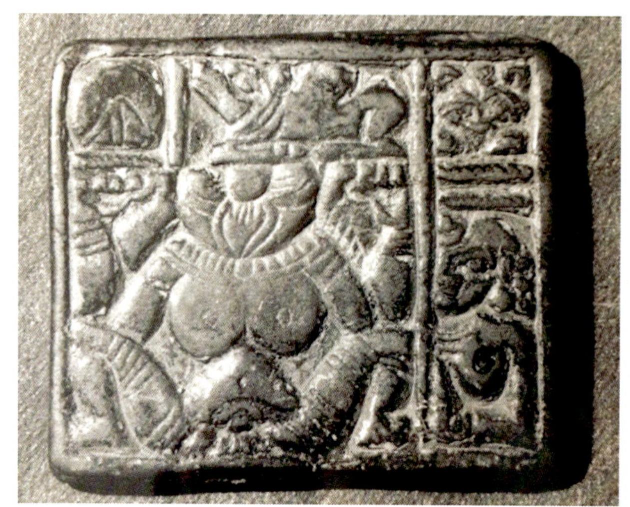

Plate 2: Lajjāgaurī seal, Ter Museum,
Ter, Osmānābād District, Mahārāṣṭra.
Courtesy Carol Bolon

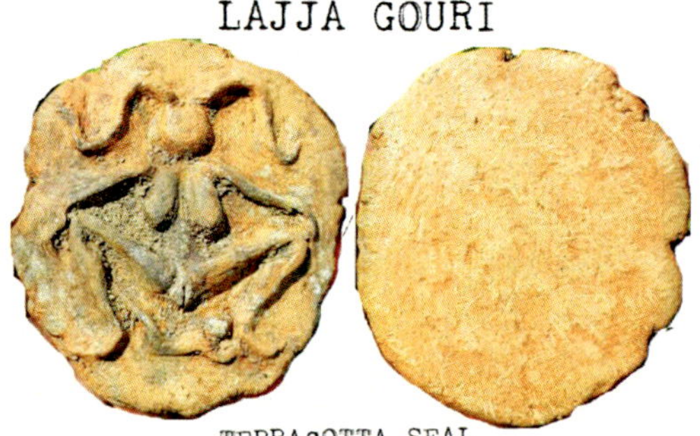

Plate 3: Lajjāgaurī coin,
Cetan Rājāpūrkar Private Collection.
Courtesy Cetan Rājāpūrkar

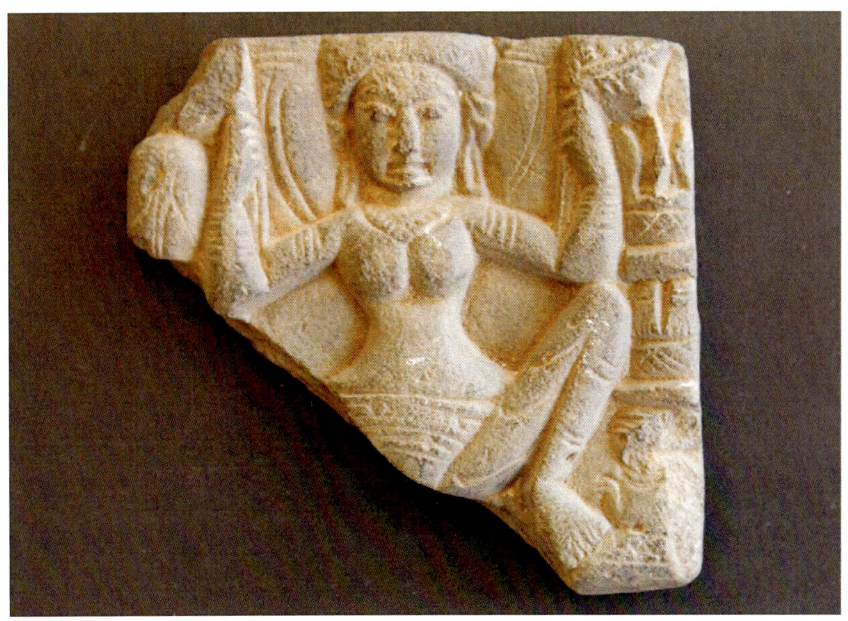

Plate 4: Lajjāgaurī image from the Department of Archaeology Collection, M.S. University of Baroḍā.
Courtesy Professor V.H. Sonāvaṇe

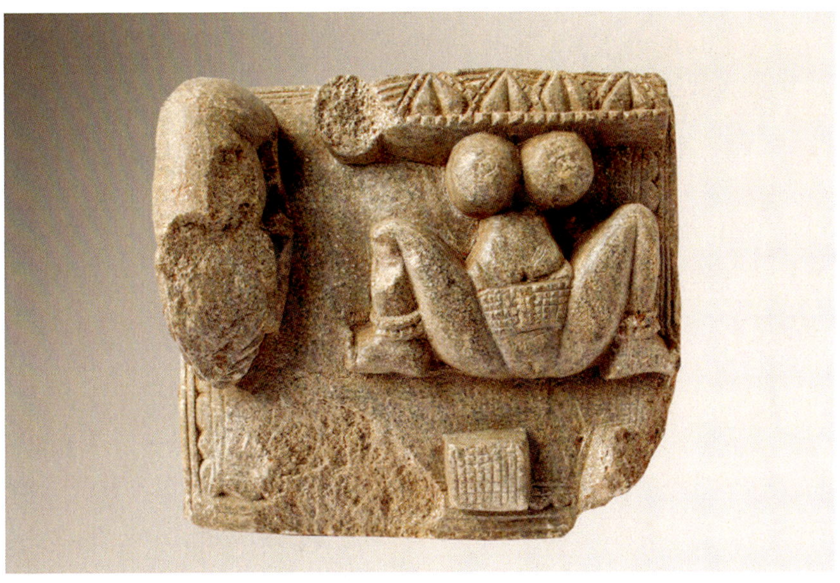

Plate 5: Lajjāgaurī image with a broken Nandī bull, Nagpur Museum, Mahārāṣṭra.
Courtesy Tejas Rege and Prasād Pawār

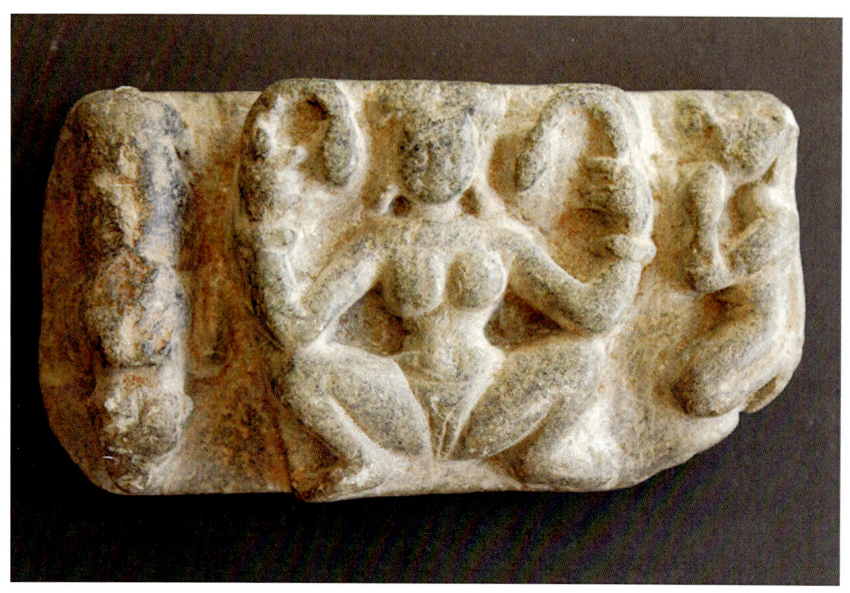

Plate 6: Small broken image, Department of Archaeology Collection.
M.S. University of Baroḍā.
Courtesy Professor V.H. Sonāvaṇe

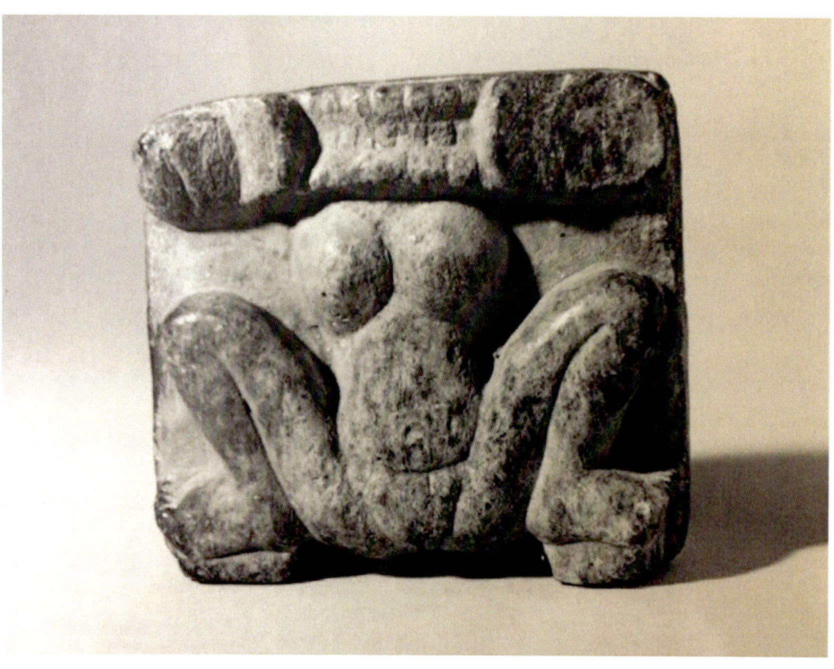

Plate 7: Lajjāgaurī image from Paunī, Nāgpūr District, Mahārāṣṭra, British Museum.
Courtesy Carol Bolon

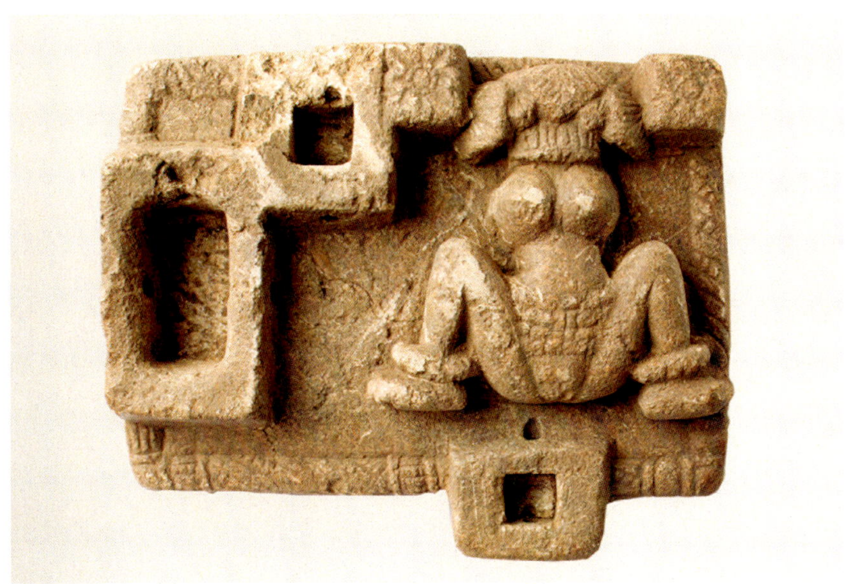

Plate 8: Lajjāgaurī image from Ramaṭolā, Bhaṇḍārā District, Mahārāṣṭra, Central Museum, Nāgpūr.
Courtesy Tejas Rege and Prasād Pawār

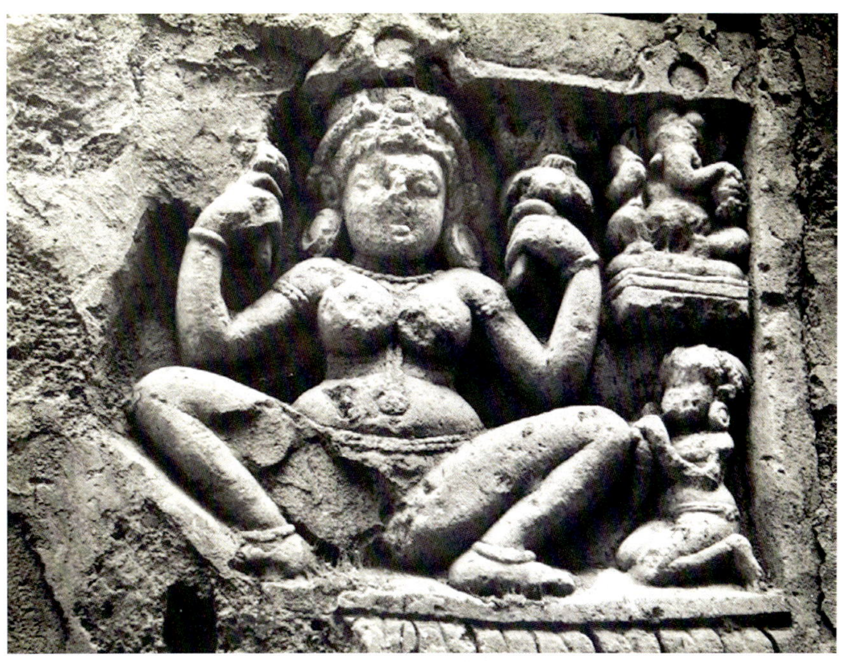

Plate 9: Lajjāgaurī image from Manjuśrī Vāpī, Dhānk, Gujarat.
Courtesy Professor V.H. Sonāvaṇe

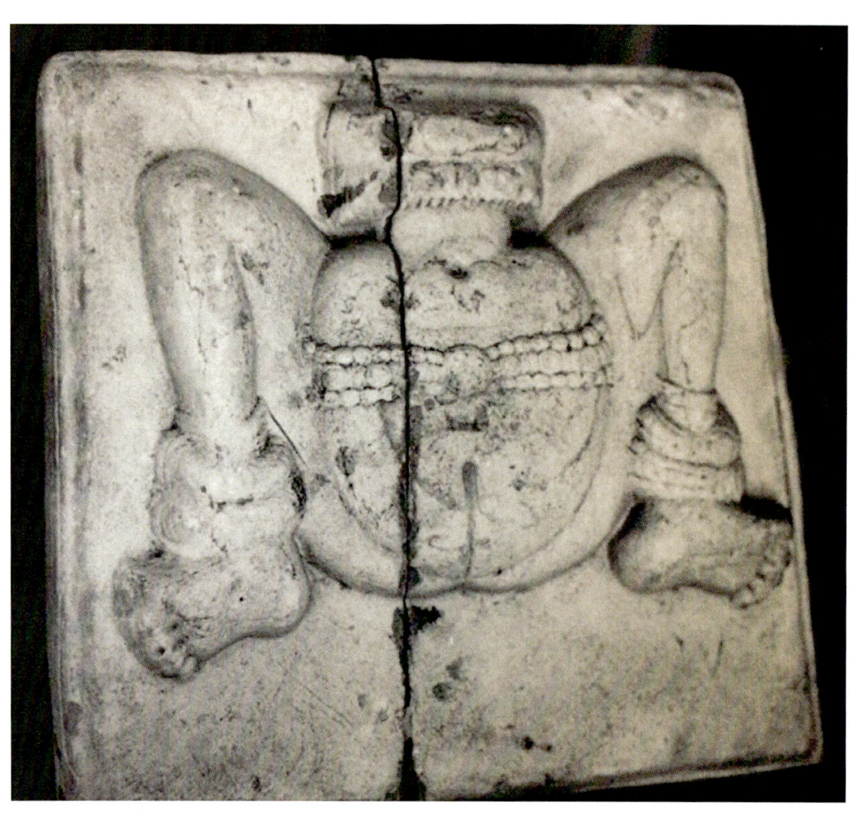

Plate 10: Lajjāgaurī image from Kārlāpelam, Guntur District, Āndhra Prades̀,
Victoria Jubilee Museum, Vijayawāḍā.
Courtesy Carol Bolon

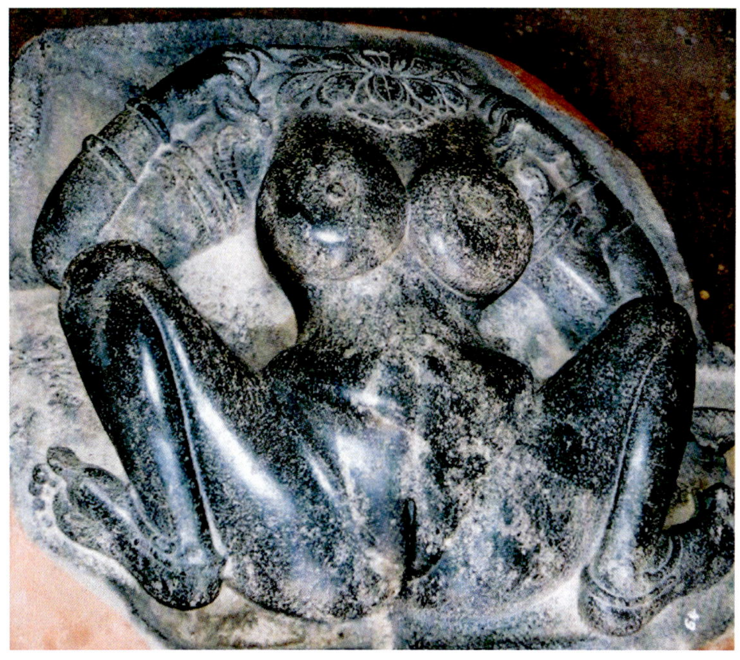

Plate 11: Image of life-size Lajjāgaurī sculpture at Ālampūr Museum, from Saṅgameśvara Temple, Kuḍuvelli, Āndhra Pradeś.
Courtesy Jayant Bhālcandra Bāpaṭ

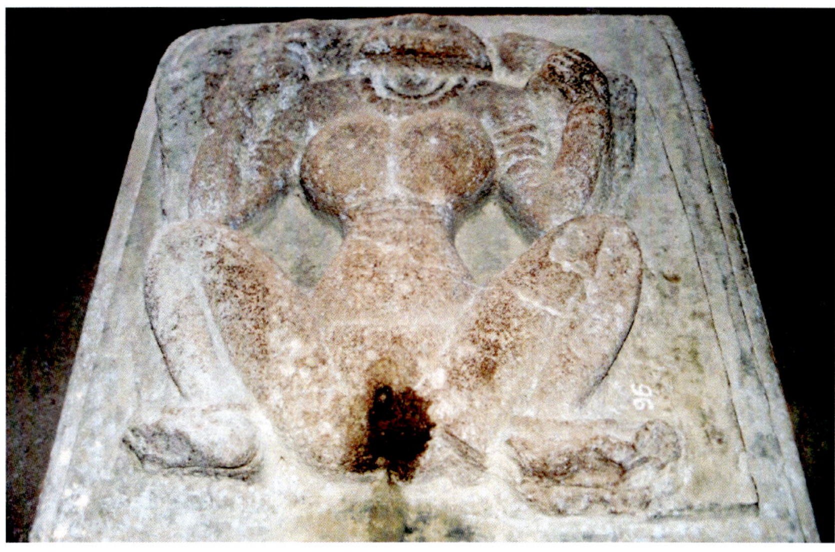

Plate 12: Image of life-size Lajjāgaurī sculpture at Ālampūr Museum, from Saṅgameśvara Temple, Kuḍuvelli, Āndhra Pradeś.
Courtesy Jayant Bhālcandra Bāpaṭ

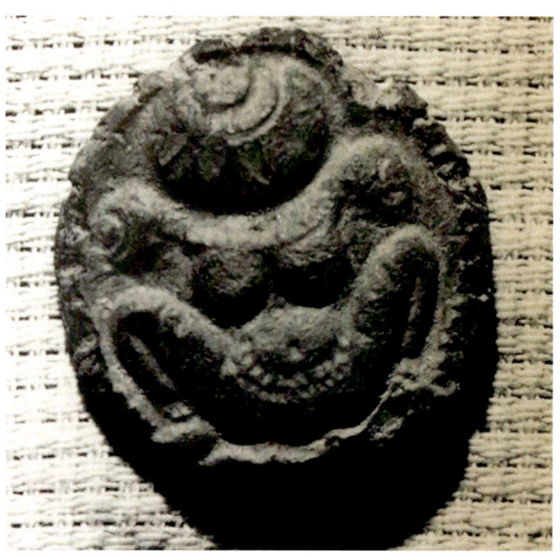

Plate 13: Lajjāgaurī image from Uttar Prades-Kanoria Collection, Pāṭnā, Bihār.
Courtesy Carol Bolon

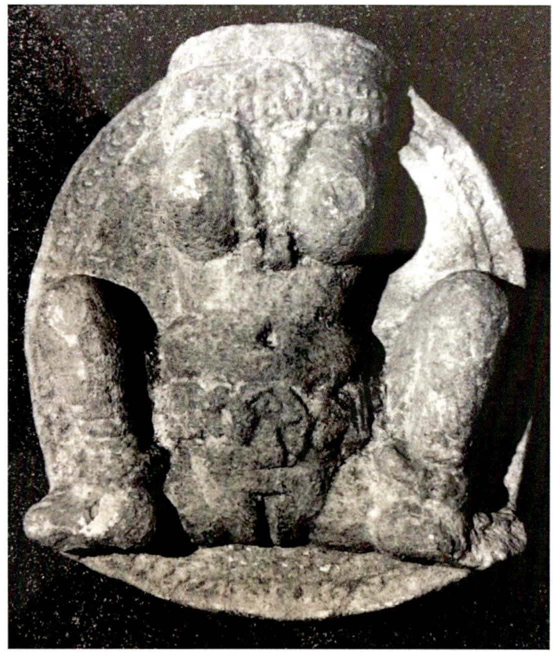

Plate 14: Lajjāgaurī image from Kausāmbī, Allāhābād District, Uttar Pradeś, Indian Museum Calcutta.
Courtesy Carol Bolon

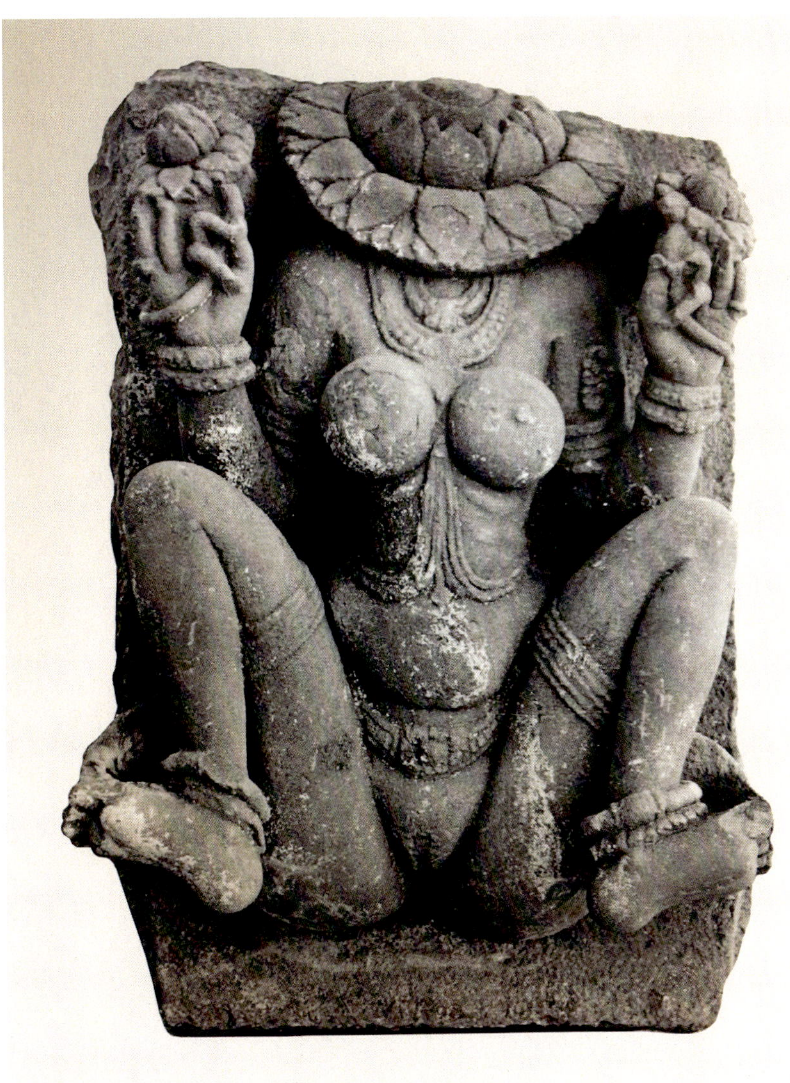

Plate 15: Image of life-size Lajjāgaurī sculpture from Nāganāth Temple, Nāgnāthkolla, Bijapur District, Badāmī Museum.
Courtesy Carol Bolon

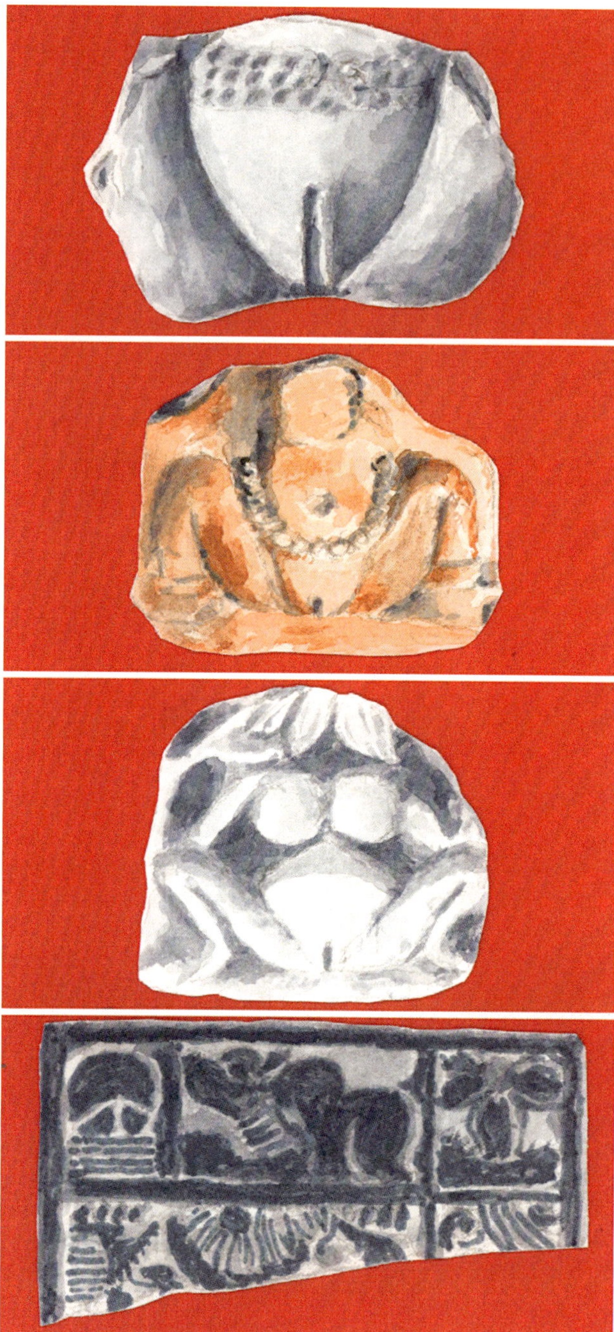

Plate 16: Paintings of broken image fragments from Ter Museum, Ter, Osmānābād District, Mahārāṣṭra.
Note the Nandī bull on the broken seal in the last image.
Paintings courtesy John Harris

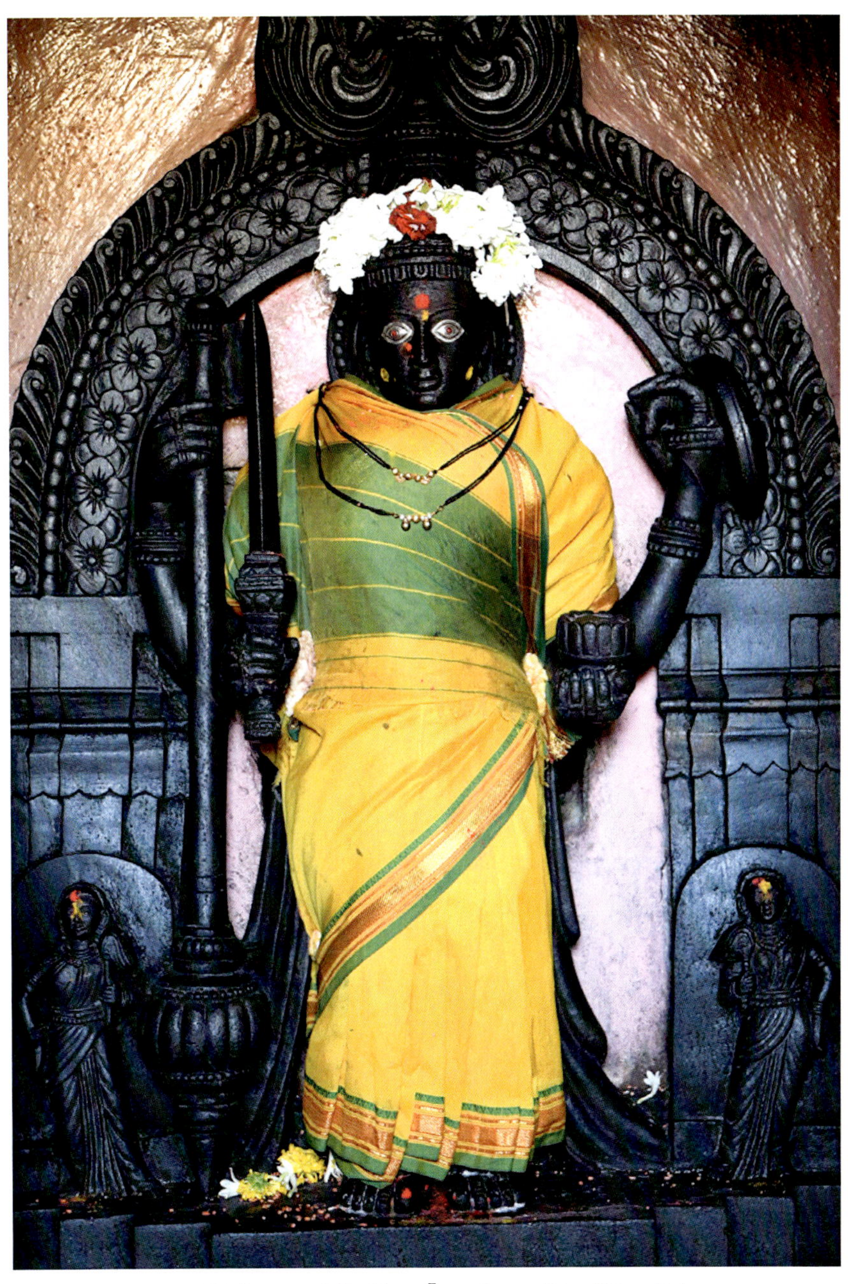

Plate 17: Image of Goddess Ānandanāyakī at Rāmatīrtha.
Courtesy Anuśā Gavāṇkar and Jayant Bhālcandra Bāpaṭ

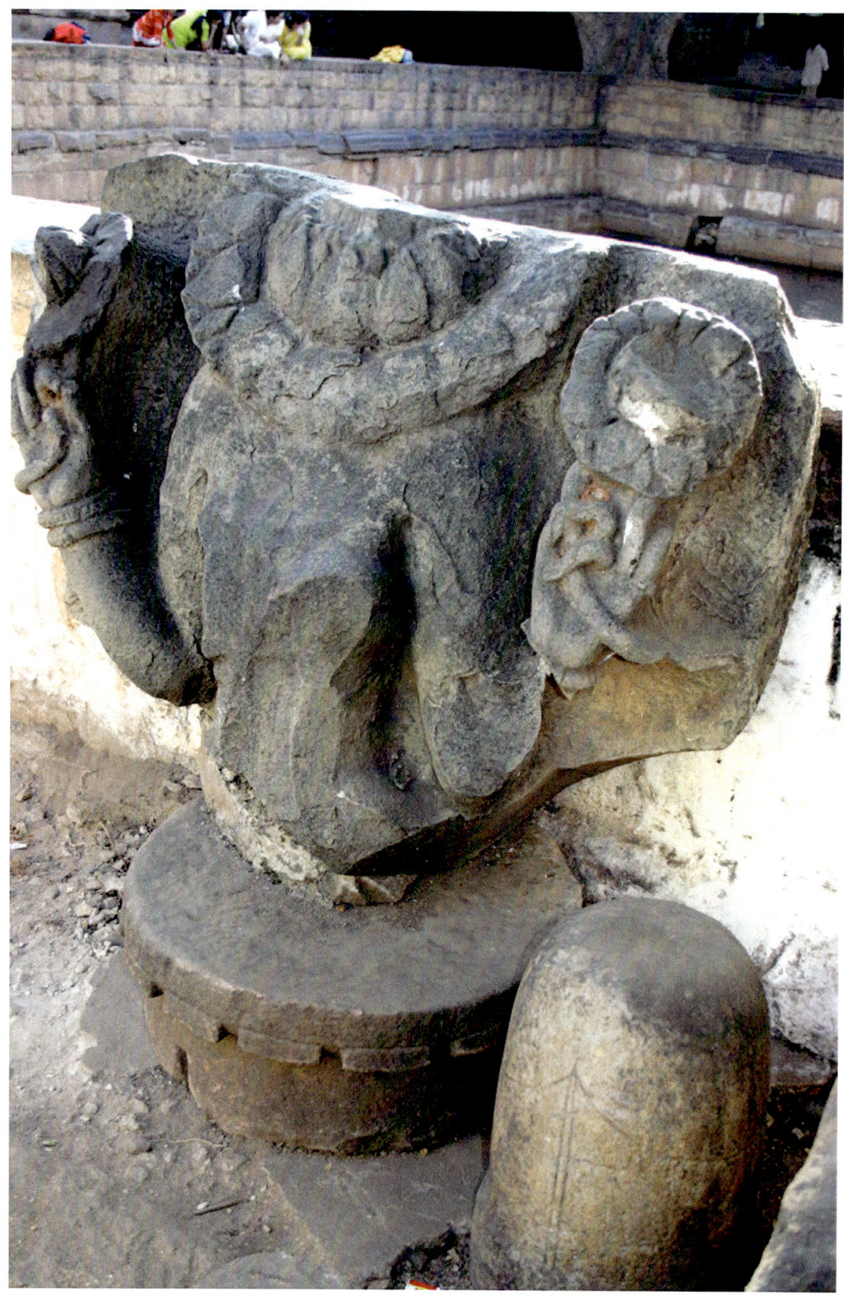

Plate 18: Broken image of Lajjāgaurī at Mahākūṭa.
Courtesy Jayant Bhālcandra Bāpaṭ

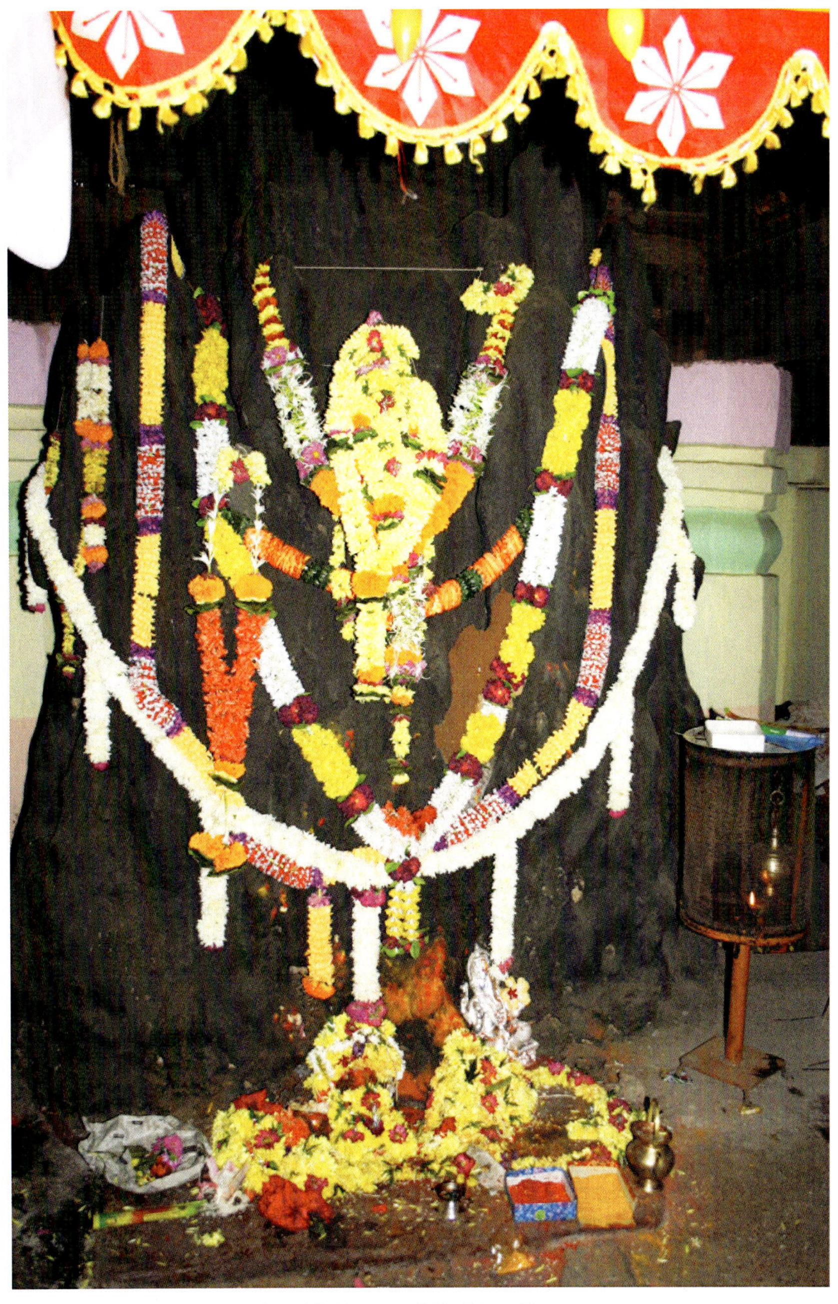

Plate 19: Image of Goddess Sānterī.
A giant anthill covered with black paint and decorated with flowers.
Courtesy Jayant Bhālcandra Bāpaṭ

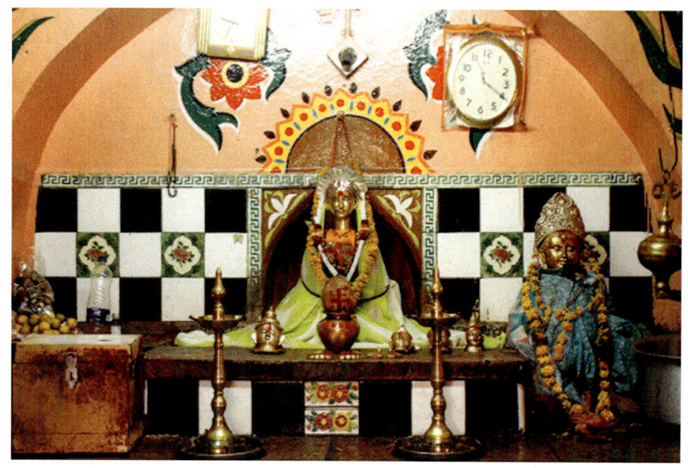

Plate 20: The present shrine of Goddess Āḷandī at Honhaḷḷī.
Courtesy Anuśā Gavāṇkar and Jayant Bhālcandra Bāpaṭ

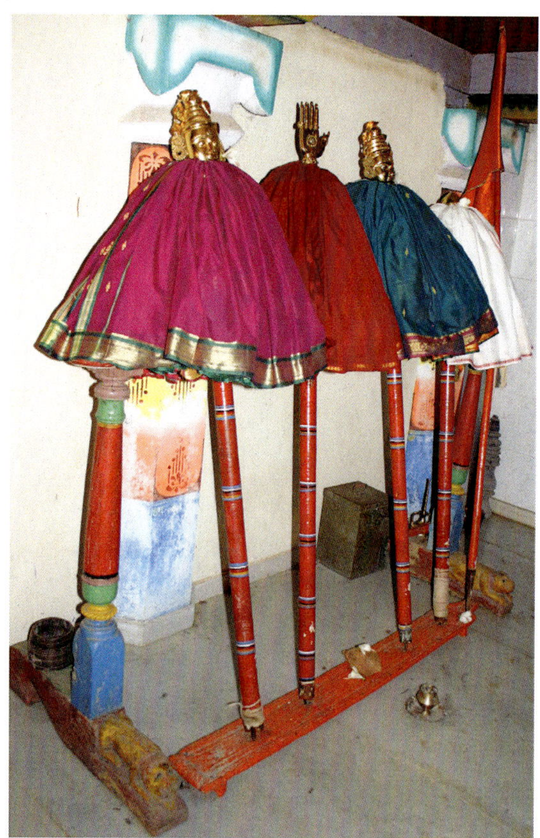

Plate 21: *Taraṅgas* in a goddess Temple.
Courtesy Jayant Bhālcandra Bāpaṭ

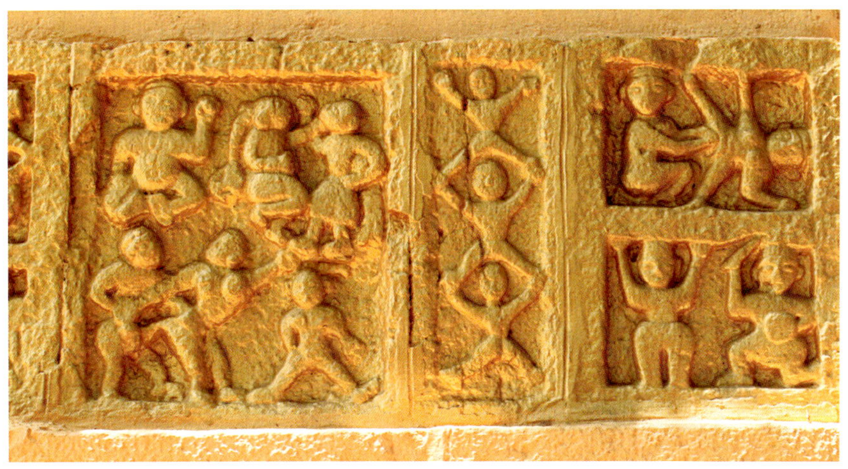

Plate 22: The parturition sculptures at Kurundwāḍ, Mahārāṣṭra.
Courtesy Anuśā Gavāṇkar and Jayant Bhālcandra Bāpaṭ

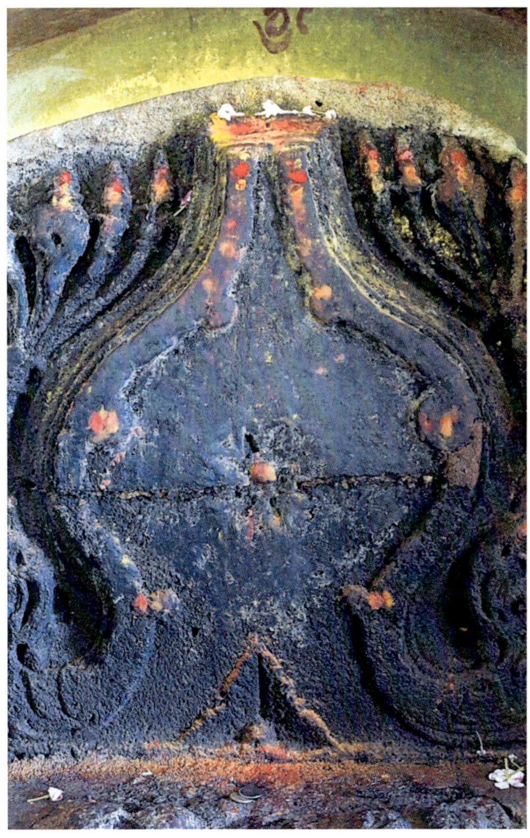

Plate 23: Image of Goddess Lakṣmī under the banyan tree.
Courtesy Anuśā Gavāṇkar and Jayant Bhālcandra Bāpaṭ

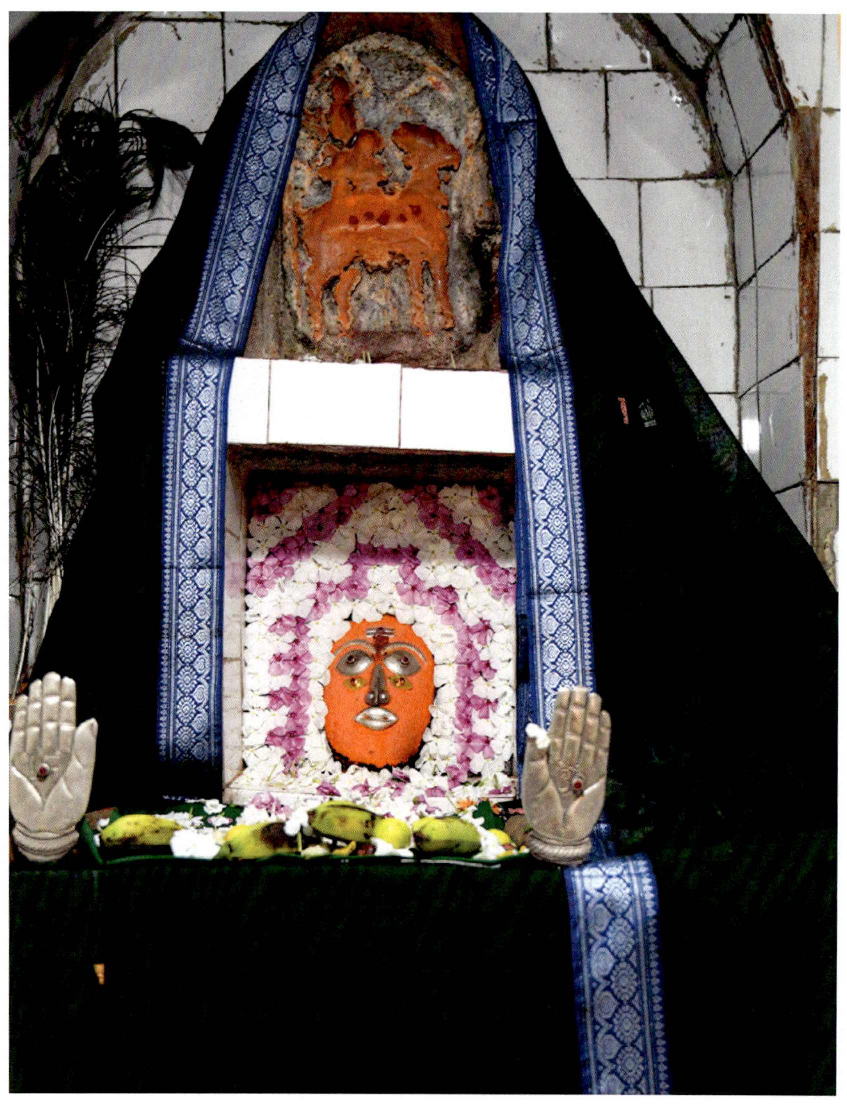

Plate 24: The Dhangar Goddess Kakmarī.
Courtesy Anuśā Gavāṇkar and Jayant Bhālcandra Bāpaṭ

on yourself. You are dressed in snow white and soft apparel and fragrant flower garlands. You are Bhagavatī, the favourite one of lord Viṣṇu. You are the one who grants wealth to the entire world. Please bless me.)

While it is true that, when the Purāṇas were written, Śrī-Devī in her original form of mother earth assumed two distinct forms as Lakṣmī and Bhūdevī and became part of the Viṣṇu pantheon, she is basically mother earth, and she also has a very special and firm relationship with the lotus. As a matter of fact, she is identical with the lotus and hence is known as Kamalā. Just as the lotus is a symbol of creation and plenitude, so is Lakṣmī.

Creation and Plenitude

In the majority of Indian cultural and religious traditions, Lakṣmī seated on a lotus and holding a lotus in her hand is a symbol of Plenitude. At the festival of Dīpāvalī (known commonly as Divālī), we worship her with Kubera, her partner and the master of the 'navanidhis'.[12] Kubera and Lakṣmī, the wealth- and plenitude-bestowing couple, have become the major objects of worship during the festival of Dīpāvalī. Formerly this festival was called 'yakṣarātrī'. The name itself illustrates the importance of Kubera during this festival. This is because Kubera is the leader of the Yakṣas and has often been called Yakṣarāj (*Lit*: the king of the Yakṣas). Kubera's prosperity-giving Śakti is Lakṣmī. The name of Kubera's chief general is Mahāpadma (*Lit*: the great lotus), once again showing the close relationship between Kubera and the lotus. The festival of Divālī thus preserves the tight-knit relationship between Lakṣmī, who is born from a lotus, and Kubera.

The close relationship between Kubera and Lakṣmī and their enormous capacity to grant plenitude to the world at large are naturally related to Lakṣmī's powers of regeneration. Plenitude is of course the end result of regeneration. For our ancestors, plenitude meant nothing more than the right amount of rain at the right time and the earth full of vegetation and a variety of grain. That is why they were full of admiration for household granaries that were full of grain and for cowpens full of cows and calves. They always yearned for fertile fields and cows and their calves. One can now see why the lotus that was closely associated with Lakṣmī became the symbol not only of regeneration but also of plenitude.

The Magnificent Earth-lotus

In the Vedic tradition, the earth is not merely a cog in the wheel of the universe but the mother of the entire universe. This is why she has been called *mahī* (*Lit*: the great one). We have seen how in the *Śrīsūkta*, this same primordial mother, *mahī,* appears as Padmā. The Purāṇas describe this lotus-like aspect of the earth in glowing terms. In the five essential topics covered in the Purāṇas (*pañcalakṣaṇāni*), description of the birth of the universe (*sṛṣṭyutpattī*) is prominent.[13] In this connection, the *Vāyupurāṇa* puts forward the following description of the birth of the mighty earth-lotus.

> *avyaktātpṛthivīpadmaṃ meruparvatakarṇikam* |
> *catuṣpathaṃ samutpannaṃ vyaktaṃ pañcaguṇaṃ mahat* ||
>
> *Vāyupurāṇa* (34.37)[14]

> (The earth in her lotus form was generated from the void. Mount Meru is the receptacle for the seed of this lotus. This lotus is endowed with five virtues and the four directions are its petals.)

In the process of this description, the *Vāyupurāṇa* also describes the earth as 'the one born with a lotus shape and containing dense forests.'[15] She has also been described as '*sanātana lokapadma*' (eternal lotus, 34.41, 45). The base and seed of this '*sanātana lokapadma*' is the eternal truth. All of the gods and goddesses were born out of this lotus; that is how magnificent it is.

The Milking of the Cow-Earth in the Lotus Pot

In the preceding paragraphs, we saw how some Purāṇas compare the earth to a magnificent lotus. However, they also compare her to a mighty cow. Furnishing considerable details, these Purāṇas explain that the Gods, Demons, Yakṣas, Gandharvas, Kinnaras and Nāgas milked the earth, the source of many gems, into many different receptacles and obtained the boons they sought. The *Matsyapurāṇa* (10.24) says that when the Gandharvas milked the earth-cow, the Gandharva named Vararucī, who was proficient in dramatics, became the milkman, the Gandharva Caitraratha became the calf and the receptacle used was made out of a lotus. With minor differences, the *Vāyupurāṇa* also puts forward a similar myth. It says:

padmapātre punardugdhā gandharvairapsaroganaiḥ |
vatsaṃ citrarathaṃ kṛtva śucīn gandhāstathaiva ca |
teṣāṃ viśvāvasustvāsīd dogdhā putro muneḥ śuciḥ |
gandharvarājo 'tibalo mahātmā sūryasannibhaḥ ||

Vāyupurāṇa (62. 191–192).[16]

(When the *Gandharvas* and *Apsaras* milked the earth-cow for her pure fragrant substances, the milkman was Viśvāvasū, the mighty *gandharva* king. He was as strong as the sun. The *Gandharva* Citraratha became the calf and the receptacle used was a lotus.)

In order to extract fragrant substances from the earth, the stories narrated by the composers of the Purāṇas employed the *Gandharvas*, known to have an intense liking for fragrant things. In employing the lotus as a receptacle for these fragrances, the Purāṇas have shown great imagination.

The Source of the Living and Non-Living

In concluding the section on the milking of the earth, the *Vāyupurāṇa* sings great praises of her. The idiom used is worth remembering:

saiṣā dhātrī vidhatrī ca dhāraṇī ca vasundharā |
dugdhā hitārthaṃ lokānāṃ pṛthunā iti naḥ śṛutam |
carācarasya lokasya pratiṣṭhā yonireva ca ||

Vāyupurāṇa (62.197)[17]

(We hear that the one who begets every living and non-living thing and sustains them, the one who is their constant support and the one who is the '*yoni*' that produces them all, is the one who has been milked by Pṛthu for the well-being of all.)

The composer of the Purāṇa calls this earth the honour of the living and non-living and the vagina that produces it all. This is entirely appropriate. The earth in this statement is not limited only to those who live on this planet. She is the mother of the entire universe. That is why she is called the vagina that produces the entire world.[18] Since the earth is equated with the lotus, the lotus is thus the creator of the universe. Indian religious literature frequently calls the vagina a *yonikamala* (*Lit*: vagina in the form of a lotus). One can now understand the symbolism behind this belief. It is the belief that the earth is a giant vagina in the shape of a lotus (*puṣkarākāra*).

Water and the Lotus

The lotus is a flower that is born out of water. That is why it is also known by other names related to water, such as *jalaja*, *vārija* and *abja*. As a matter of fact, Vedic symbolism equates water with the lotus. The Vedic seers and the composers of the Purāṇas repeatedly stress that water is the primordial element in nature. Because of the unity of water and the lotus, the latter becomes the root cause of creation. One of the Vedic seers declares that the lotus is the birthplace of Agni, the fire god as well:

> *tvāmagne puṣkarād adhyatharvā niramanthata* |
> *mūrdhno viśvasya vāghataḥ* ||
>
> *The Ṛgveda* (6.16.13)[19]

> (Oh Agni! The primordial waters in the form of the lotus are the cause of the universe. Prajāpati churned these and took you out from within.)

In explaining this *Ṛcā*,[20] the *Śathapatha Brāhmaṇa* [6, 4, 2, 2] equates water with the lotus by declaring that 'water is, in fact, the same as a lotus.'[21]

During Vedic times it was believed that Agni, the energy within the universe, was born out of the lotus or water. This belief strongly suggests the primordiality of water. The *Ṛgveda* declares that "All that is about is water only"[22] and "In the beginning, everything that existed was water."[23]

This kind of laudatory reference to the primordiality of water appears a number of times in Vedic literature. In the beginning, everything consisted of ever-changing, chaotic water. From this water – from the lotus that symbolised these waters, the energy of the universe was born. The *Taittirīya Saṃhitā* aptly describes this entire process as follows:

> *idamagre salilamāsīt* | *sa prajāpatiḥ puṣkaraparṇe vātobhūto 'lelāyat* |
> *sa pratiṣṭhāṃ nāvindata* | *sa etadapāṃ kulyāṃ apaśyat* |
> *tasminnagnimacinuta* | *tadiyamabhavat* | *tato vai sa pratyatiṣṭhat* ||
>
> *Taittirīya Saṃhitā* (5.6.4.2–3)[24]

> (In the beginning it was all waters. Prajāpati the creator was seated on and swinging on lotus petals. He was thus unable to achieve stability. He peeped into the depth of the waters and collected Agni, the fire, from there. After this, the earth itself

and the living and non-living things on the earth were born and Prajāpati came to eminence as a result.)

It can easily be seen that salila (water) here represents the constantly changing aspect of the primordial being, as against the lotus or lotus leaf, which stands for its stability in this ocean of change.

This myth about the birth of the universe in the *Taittirīya Saṃhitā* appears somewhat differently in the *Taittirīya Āraṇyaka,* which says:

āpo vā āsan salilameva | *sa prajāpatirekaḥ puṣkaraparṇe samabhavat* |
tasyāntaramanasi kāmaḥ samavartata | *'idam sṛjeyaṃ' iti* ||

Taittirīya Āraṇyaka (1.23.1)[25]

(In the beginning all was water. Prajāpati the creator then appeared on his own on the leaf of a lotus. In his mind, [sexual] desire appeared. He thought to himself that he would produce the universe.)

The primordiality and greatness of the waters and the lotus that are dealt with in great detail in the *Ṛgveda, Taittirīya Saṃhitā* and *Taittirīya Āraṇyaka* also appear in the *Śatapatha* and *Taittirīya Brāhmaṇas* with minor differences in explaining the myth of the Varāha (*Lit*: boar) Avatāra. Prajāpati assumed a boar incarnation and rescued the earth from the primordial waters. That is why he was called her 'master'. This myth about the birth of the earth and the nature within appears in the *Śatapatha Brāhmaṇa* (14.1.2.11).

The same myth appears in the *Taittirīya Brāhmaṇa*, which describes it in the following words:

apo vā idamagre salilamāsīt | *tena prajāpatiraśrāmyat* |
'kathamidam syād' iti |
so 'paśyat puṣkaraparṇam tiṣṭhat |
so 'manyat 'asti vai tadyasmin idamadhitiṣhatī 'ti |
sa varāho rūpaṃ kṛtvopanyamajjat |
sa pṛthivīm adha ārcchat |
tasya upahatyodamajjat |
tat puṣkaraparṇo 'prayatat |

Taittirīya Brāhmaṇa (1.1.3.5–6)[26]

> (In the beginning, all of the waters were in a state of flux. Prajāpati was unhappy because of this. He was worried as to how to deal with this constantly moving mass. Then he saw a lotus leaf floating on water. It appeared very stable. He assumed the form of a boar and dived into the deep waters near the lotus leaf. That is where he found the earth. He took away part of her and spread it on the lotus leaf.)

There is a well-known myth in the Purāṇas which says that Hiraṇyākṣa dumped the earth into the sea. To save her, Viṣṇu took the avatāra of a boar, killed Hiraṇyākṣa and brought the earth back on his tusk. It can be clearly seen from the discussion so far that this Purāṇic myth has its origins in the Vedic myths dealing with the birth of nature.

The idea that the lotus is a symbol of the procreative waters was already deeply entrenched in Vedic literature. As a matter of fact, the Vedic seers firmly believed that the lotus is the procreative symbol of water. To them, the lotus represented procreation.

Viṣṇu's Lotus Navel

The Vedic myth of the birth of the earth further matured and blossomed into poetry in the Purāṇas. According to them, Viṣṇu, the ultimate being, was contented, happily swimming in the enormous mass of the primordial waters. From his navel, he produced a golden lotus which had a thousand petals. That lotus had a lustre like the Sun. That beautiful lotus resembled the Sun in the autumn season, and shone as if it had petals of fire. From this enormous lotus, which spread over several *yojanas*,[27] the four-faced creator of the world, Brahmā, emerged. The wise have called this enormous lotus the perfect form of mother earth. That mother earth is Padmā (*Lit*: lotus like), also called Rasā, who produced the mighty mountains containing many precious things. Around this lotus-earth are the four seas. Thus, as a result of Nārāyaṇa's mere wish, this lotus-flower-like earth was born. It is because of this that myths about the earth's origin describe her as a flower. This lotus form of the earth and also her birth from the lotus are also described by the seers in discussing *yajña*, the fire sacrifice.[28]

The composers of the Purāṇas thus saw a relationship between the lotus that produced the earth and the navel of Viṣṇu lying in the ocean of milk. As a result of this, the relationship between the lotus, the earth, and Kamalā, the goddess Lakṣmī, became prominent in the worship regime of Viṣṇu.

The *Līlākamala*

The myth behind the *Līlākamala* also portrays the great symbolic quality of the lotus. In worshipping the devotees with the *Līlākamala* held in his own hand, Lord Kṛṣṇa indicates that the birth of the entire universe is the result of a mere powerplay (*līlā*) by him. A number of deities within Hindu iconography are shown holding a *Līlākamala* in their hands. Similarly, Saṃskṛt plays also contain examples of heroines holding the *Līlākamala* in their hands. In Saṃskṛt plays, just as we meet a Yakṣiṇī holding a lotus in her hand, we also meet a female lover who hits her lover gently with the *Līlākamala* and fills his eyes with lotus pollen. It is worth our while to note how the author of the *Yaśastilakacampū* describes the symbolic grandeur of the *Līlākamala* that the monarch held in his hand:

> *ṣrīlīlākamala tavāvanipate sāmrajyacihnaṃ mahat* |
> *kīrtyutpattiniketanaṃ kṣitivadhūviśrāmadhāmasvayam* |
> *lakṣmīvibhramadarpiṇaṃ kulagṛhaṃ rājyādhidevyāḥ punaḥ* |
> *krīḍāsthanamidaṃ vibhāti bhavanaṃ vāgdevatāyā iva* ||
>
> *Yaśastilakacampū*, Kāvyamālā edition (2.243–254)[29]

> (Oh Great Emperor! This *Līlākamala* in your hand is a lasting symbol of your empire. In it lies the origin of your fame. It is the resting place of the earth, who is in the form of your queen. It is the parental home of Lakṣmī, the goddess of wealth, who plays here. It is the playground of the presiding goddess of your empire. In fact, it is the home of the goddess of knowledge.)

Here one can once again see the symbolism of the thousand-petalled lotus.

Kamalaśīrṣā *Lajjāgaurī*[30]

The composers of the Purāṇas have often described mother earth, *bhūdevī*, as the *yoni* of the living and non-living things on this planet. It has already been mentioned in Chapter 1 that many of her images in the process of giving birth have been found at places such as Nevāse, Ter, Jayarāmasvāmice Vaḍgāv, Mahūrjharī, Mahākūṭa and others. Some of these images were discovered during excavations, while others are still being worshipped in temples around India. Ālampūr and Mahākūṭa were well-known places for the worship of this goddess. We know that even today, women pray to her in order to conceive.

This goddess has been called by various names such as Joguḷāmbā, Ellammā, Reṇukā and *Lajjāgaurī*. As I have shown in Chapter 1, the last of these names is a Saṃskṛtization of the words *Lañjā* or *Lañjikā* which are themselves derived from the Saṃskṛt word *nagnā* (naked). The whole reason for such a name, which hints at her peculiar form, is that all her images show her in the process of giving birth. Some of them show her up to her waist from below, while others include her shoulders as well. The latter display a lotus in place of her head. Both of her hands also hold lotuses. Some of the images that have been carved on rocks show four lotuses in the four corners of the rock. These images where the lotus replaces the head naturally hint at the identical procreative powers of the earth and the lotus.

The Mystery of the Name Vyāghreśvarī

One of the shrines for the goddess *Lajjāgaurī* is situated in South India and is known as Vyāghreśvarī. This place is situated on the banks of the Tuṅgabhadrā River about three miles from Hospeṭ station. Hospeṭ lies on the Macchalipaṭṭam-Bezwāḍā-Hubḷī line of the Southern Railway. The goddess's head is worshipped on one bank of the river, whereas her headless torso is worshipped on the other bank. The locals call this headless torso *Śrīrāmacaṇḍīśvarī* or the mother of Paraśurāma. The myth about the separate worship of the head and the torso of his mother Reṇukā after Paraśurāma beheaded her on the orders of his father is closely associated with this shrine.[31] This obviously means that the headless torso worshipped here as Reṇukā must be none other than the Uttānapāda[32] Aditi in her form showing her regenerative organs during the process of delivery. It is but natural for her to be called Reṇukā and for her headlessness to be explained in terms of the myth of Paraśurāma beheading his mother. Also, Reṇukā has also been considered an avatāra of *Aditi*.

Then why is it that this place was named Vyāghreśvarī? She is certainly not worshipped as Durgā with her traditional armour and traditional vehicle, the tiger. Why is it that an image showing only the generative organs is worshipped as Vyāghreśvarī? There is no doubt that there is no connection between the form of the goddess and the name given to her. However, it would be unwise to assume that the name Vyāghreśvarī has been given to this goddess by a mere mistake. It might be that, due to sheer ignorance on the part of the devotees, an image could be given the wrong name. However, even such an inadvertent mistake often has some logic behind it. To quote an example that comes to mind here, one of the well-known depictions of Viṣṇu shows him lying on the serpent Śeṣa while his consort goddess Lakṣmī massages his feet. During my research, I came across a strange myth prevalent among some folk in Mahārāṣṭra that suggests a totally different explanation for that type of sculpture.[33] The myth is as follows:

> Once a haughty brother kicked his loving sister. Because of this terrible sin, his foot became infested with worms. Because of her gentle nature, the sister forgot the insult perpetrated on her. She could not bear to see her brother's condition and resorted to physically removing the worms with her hands.

The village folk that I talked to told me that it is this story of the insolent brother and his sister that is depicted in the sculpture described above. It is easy to see how this myth would have come about. The sculpture does depict a man in the sleeping position and a woman holding one of his feet. That is adequate proof in the eyes of the village folk to invent this alternative myth.

However, the image of the goddess near Hospeṭ displays only the female generative organ. There is no hint of a tiger in any shape or form in this sculpture. The question therefore remains as to why she should be called Vyāghreśvarī.

This shrine of *Lajjāgaurī* happens to be in the state of Karnāṭaka, where the main language is Kannaḍa. Philologically, the Saṃskṛt word *vyāghra* becomes *bagga* in the Kannaḍa language. However, in folk Kannaḍa, *bagga* has another meaning as well, and that is 'lotus'. We already know that images of *Lajjāgaurī* very often have a lotus in place of her head and breasts. Lotuses are also carved around the image itself. With the prevalence of lotuses around her, one would be justified in calling her *Kamaleśvarī* (*Lit*: a goddess with lotuses) or *Baggeśvarī* in Kannaḍa. This latter word can be easily Saṃskṛtised to *Vyaghreśvarī*. Such Saṃskṛtization that changes the original meaning of the word is often seen in Indian literature.

A Symbol of Enchanting Beauty

In most Indian traditions, the lotus not only represents recreation and prosperity but softness, tenderness, delicacy, and bewitching beauty.[34] In describing female beauty, terms such as "lotus-faced" and "lotus-eyed" are often used. The lotus is used as the ultimate representation of female beauty.

In describing the beauty of many gods and goddesses too, the example of the lotus is often used. The ultimate respect one can show in the Bhakti tradition is to touch the feet of gods, godlike figures and elders. Their feet are venerated and are termed 'lotus-feet'. The devotee who touches such feet with his forehead is called 'a bee at the lotus feet'[35] and considers himself blessed. Many deities hold a lotus in their hands, and the seat of many deities is the lotus. The goddess Lakṣmī is always seated on a lotus. Similarly, in Buddhist iconography, the Buddha is also shown on a lotus seat. The well-known Bodhisattva Avalokiteśvara is known by the laudatory adjective *padmapāṇī* (one who holds a lotus in his hand). His famous representation at the Ajanṭā caves speaks for the enormous reputation of the lotus.

In this way, the lotus has become a symbolic embodiment of Indian tradition and is used in adjectives applied to the divinity. It would not at all be improper to describe it as the longest-lasting symbol of Indian culture and tradition.

Endnotes

1 The parental home (*Māher* in Marāṭhī) has had a very special place in Indian culture. Traditionally, marriages were arranged and the girls at the time of marriage very were young. As a result, they had a very special bond with their parents, especially the mother. Separation from the mother always produced a lot of sorrow and anxiety. Every so often, in the early days of marriage, newly married girls were sent to their parent's place on a kind of emotional holiday.

2 Translator's note: In Saṃskṛt, the words *kamala* and *kamalā* mean the lotus flower and the goddess Lakṣmī respectively.

3 Translator's note: The period between the months of September and November in India (the months of *Aświn* and *Kārtik* according to the Hindu calendar), when the monsoonal rains stop and the land is lush and green. The temperatures are mild and flowers bloom.

4 Translator's note: Ḍhere has given no details about the poet here.

5 Translator's note: Ḍhere has given no details about the poet here.

6 Saṃskṛt to Marāṭhī translation by Ḍhere. Marāṭhī to English translation by Jayant Bāpaṭ.

7 Zimmer, H. (1947). *Myth and Symbol in Indian Art and Civilization*, New York: 90–93.

8 Translator's note: In Hinduism, the word Śrī is used to describe goddess Lakṣmī, the consort of Viṣṇu. However, it appears that this was not the case in Vedic times. Thus, the *Ṛgveda* does not contain any reference to Śrī as a consort of Viṣṇu. According to a myth in the *Śatapatha Brāhmaṇa*, when Prajāpati was practising penance, Śrī came out from within his heart and appeared in front of him in the form of a beautiful, lustrous woman. This would mean that the goddess form of Śrī appeared after Vedic times. The

coalescence of Śrī with mother earth probably happened in post-Vedic times, after the Vedic and Indus-valley cultures mixed.

9 The word used here is *ciklīta*. It means moisture-bearing or slimy.

10 Alakṣmī is Lakṣmī's inauspicious sister. Many of the hymns pray for her destruction.

11 Saṃskṛt to Marāṭhī translation by Ḍhere. Marāṭhī to English translation by Jayant Bāpaṭ.

12 Translator's note: Kubera is said to be the master of nine generals who are known as *navanidhis*. Their names are: Mahāpadma, Padma, Śaṅkha, Makara, Kacchapa, Mukunda, Kunda, Nīla, and Kharva.

13 This criterion is described as a *sarga*.

14 Saṃskṛt to Marāṭhī translation by Ḍhere. Marāṭhī to English translation by Jayant Bāpaṭ.

15 *padmākārā samutpannā pṛthivī saghanadrumā* | (*vāyupurāṇa*, 34.44).

16 Saṃskṛt to Marāṭhī translation by Ḍhere. Marāṭhī to English translation by Jayant Bāpaṭ.

17 Saṃskṛt to Marāṭhī translation by Ḍhere. Marāṭhī to English translation by Jayant Bāpaṭ.

18 *carācarasya lokasya yoniḥ*.

19 Saṃskṛt to Marāṭhī translation by Ḍhere. Marāṭhī to English translation by Jayant Bāpaṭ.

20 Translator's note: a ṛc (Ṛcā in Marāṭhī) is a Vedic hymn.

21 *apo vai puṣkaram, Śatapatha Brāhmaṇa* | (6.4.2.2).

22 *salilaṃ sarvaṃ ā idam* | (*Ṛgveda*, 10.129.3).

23 *Idamagre salilamāsīt* | (*Taittirīya Samhitā*, 5.6.4.2–3).

24 Saṃskṛt to Marāṭhī translation by Ḍhere. Marāṭhī to English translation by Jayant Bāpaṭ.

25 Saṃskṛt to Marāṭhī translation by Ḍhere. Marāṭhī to English translation by Jayant Bāpaṭ.

26 Saṃskṛt to Marāṭhī translation by Ḍhere. Marāṭhī to English translation by Jayant Bāpaṭ.

27 Translator's note: a Yojana is a measure of distance. One Yojana is about 14 kilometres.

28 The *Matsyapurāṇa*, 168, 15–16 and 169, 1–18.

29 Saṃskṛt to Marāṭhī translation by Ḍhere. Marāṭhī to English translation by Jayant Bāpaṭ.

30 *Lit*: *Lajjāgaurī* with a lotus head.

31 *Kalyāṇ* magazine, Issue on *tīrthas*, January 1957, pp. 308–309.

32 Translator's note: *Uttānapāda* literally means one whose legs have been spread in order to extend the vagina. This is the typical position of a woman during the process of delivery.

33 At the Siddheśvara temple at Lātūr in Osmanābād district and at the Nageśvara temple at the village of Khireśwar situated at the base of Hariscandragaḍ, I was told this alternative myth about the sculpture of Lord Viṣṇu lying on the serpent Śeṣa.

34 *Artibus Asiae*, Vol. XIX, pp. 264–265.

35 *Caraṇakamalamilindāyamāna*.

Chapter 8

Jotibā

In developing the biography of Jogulāmbā in chapter 2, I made a definitive statement that following the methodology we adopted to study the *kṣetradevatās* (*Lit*: goddesses that are enshrined at a particular place), one should be able to study the *kṣetrapālas* (*Lit*: male deities that protect a holy place) in a similar fashion. With that in mind, in this chapter I study the popular deity Jotibā by examining the myths about him, the places of his worship, his iconography and the literature surrounding his worship. I am confident that the conclusions we derive from this study of Jotibā will be applicable to the study of the whole group of deities that are classed as *kṣetrapālas* in Mahārāṣṭra.

The main shrine of Jyotibā is at Wādī-Ratnāgirī near Kolhāpūr. Wādī-Ratnāgirī is also known as Jyotibācā Ḍoṅgar (*Lit*: Jotibā's hill). Jyotibā is the clan-deity of many castes and sub-castes within Mahārāṣṭra. Similar to Khaṇḍobā, Jotibā is a folk god, and hence he is popular all over Mahārāṣṭra among the rural folk. The popular *kṣetrapāla* deity Bhairava, who is to be found in villages all over Mahārāṣṭra, is closely associated with both Jotibā and Khaṇḍobā. Naturally, both of the latter belong to the genre of *kṣetrapālas.* Among the popular gods in Mahārāṣṭra, the male god Viṭhobā has coalesced with Viṣṇu. His status as Viṣṇu has now been accepted without question. Another god, one who originally belonged to Āndhra Pradeś, is Vyaṅkaṭeśa. He has become the clan-deity of many Mahārāṣṭrian families, most probably those Mahārāṣṭrians who came originally from Āndhra Pradeś and Karnāṭaka. Just like Viṭhobā, Vyaṅkaṭeśa, who goes by the folk name Vyaṅkobā, has also coalesced with Viṣṇu. Yet another name for Vyaṅkaṭeśa is Bālājī (*Lit*: the little child). Viṭhobā also lays claim to be the same as the child Kṛṣṇa, known for his childhood pranks. Vyaṅkaṭeśa's wife Padmāvatī is displeased with him. She has left him and has instead come to stay at the base of the hill. Viṭhobā's wife Rakhmāī is also unhappy with her husband and has chosen to live in another temple. According to a myth prevalent amongst the Dhangars, Viṭhobā's wife's name is Padubāī, a colloquial name for Padmāvatī. It is clear that these two gods who have so much in common have both coalesced with Viṣṇu. By contrast, Jotibā and Khaṇḍobā are two gods who, while attempting to coalesce with Śiva, have kept a great deal of their original character as well. The composers of *Māhātmyas* have tried their best to transform them into *avatāras* of Śiva, but these two have not given up their individualities, especially in the realms of their iconography and their worship and devotional regimen. If we closely examine these two gods who have maintained their singularities and attributes and hence opened their life history to us, it may well be possible to investigate Viṭhobā and Vyaṅkobā, the two gods who have more or less given up their original character.

Jotibā has given us one more clue. He tells us that his other name is Ravaḷanāth. The latter is one of the most favourite deities in Gomāntak (Goa) and South Konkaṇ. Just like our Bhairava, Ravaḷanāth's shrines are strewn all over the villages in these parts. He is worshipped there as a *kṣetrapāla*. Since it is firmly believed that Ravaḷanāth and Jotibā are one and the same, we should be able to find out more about Jotibā by studying Ravaḷanāth closely.

Khaṇḍobā, Jotibā and Ravaḷanāth are the three *kṣetrapāla* gods who appear similar. Of them, we are going to study Jotibā in detail. In association with this study, we will use iconographic attributes of Khaṇḍobā and Ravaḷanāth to help us on our way. In other words, we are going to examine the *kṣetrapāla* deities of Mahārāṣṭra by studying Jotibā in detail.

The Myth of Jotibā According to the Māhātmya

The *Māhātmya* of Jotibā has been composed in Saṃskṛt under the name of *Kedāramāhātmya*. Unfortunately, I have not been able to obtain a copy of it. Another work, *Kedāravijaya,*[1] was composed by a devotee of Jotibā named Harī Angāpūrkar in Śaka 1701 (1779 C.E.). This work consists of 36 chapters (*adhyāyas*) written in verse in *ovī* form.[2] It has been published three times. The author says that he has composed this work on the basis of the *Kedārakhaṇḍa* of the *Bhaviṣyottarapurāṇa*. This obviously means that the original *Kedāramāhātmya* in Saṃskṛt must have belonged to the *Kedārakhaṇḍa* of the *Bhaviṣyottarapurāṇa*. In rendering the original myth into Marāṭhī, Angāpūrkar may quite likely have resorted to adding a great deal of material of his own. In spite of that however, I think it is possible to distil the essence of *Kedāramāhātmya* from Angāpūrkar's Marāṭhī rendering.

Apart from the Māhātmya, a great number of devotional texts, such as a Kavaca,[3] a Sahasranāmastotra, some Aṣṭakas,[4] and other Stotras, have been composed in Saṃskṛt in praise of Kedāra (Jotibā). For instance, a Stotra composed in Saṃskṛt by Sakhārāmśāstrī Bāpuśāstrī Bhāgwat from Sātārā entitled *Śrikedāraliṅgamānasapūjāstotram* was published with a Marāṭhī translation in Śaka 1857 (C.E. 1935).[5] In addition, apart from the *Kedāravijaya* mentioned above, a great deal of other devotional literature, such as Stotras, Aṣṭakas, Abhaṅgas, songs and Āratis, has been published in Marāṭhī. A collection of thirty-two songs with the title *Śrīkeḍārapadaratnamālā* was published at Kolhāpūr in 1896 C.E.[6] Even in folk literature, *ovīs* in praise of Jotibā composed by women are also available. There used to be a keen devotee of Jotibā from the Bharāḍī tribe[7] called Bhujanganāth, who wrote under the pseudonym 'Nāth Bhujang'. He is known to have written beautiful songs such as *Jotibāce Kīrtanākhyāna*. However, I have been unable to get hold of his works.

The myth about Jotibā as it appears in the *Kedāravijaya* is as follows:

> In the holy place (*kṣetra*) of Badri-Kedāra, the couple Paugaṇḍa Ṛṣi and his wife Vimalāmbujā practiced penance in order to have a male child. Their penance paid off, and the son they got came to be known as Kedāra-Ravaḷeśvara. Since he was an *avatāra* of the Kedāranāth of the Himalayas, he was known as Kedāra, Kedāranāth, Kedāreśvara and Kedāraliṅga. Since the Kedāranāth of the Himalayas is a Jyotirliṅga, this child was often called Jyotirliṅga. In folk language, Jyotirliṅga became Jotibā, and that is the name by which he is known today.

Kedāra is also known as Ravaḷeśvara. The reason for his being given this name is the belief that he is the 'fire-like anger' (ravāgnī) *avatāra* of the Ṛṣi Jamadagni. The anger that Jamadagni had discarded after the killing of Reṇukā was taken up equally by Paraśurāma, the Navanāths, the sea, the forest, and the remaining world. Out of this the share that came to the Navanāths was taken up by Keḍāranāth, and hence he was named Ravaḷeśvara.[8]

> *nava ravāgnīcā avatāra | dharilā triguṇīṃ saguṇākāra |*
> *mhaṇūni nāma ravaḷeśvara | āgamottarīṃ ṭhevilem ||*

> (The anger distributed among the nine [Nāths] was taken up [by Keḍāra Nāth] and he held the three Guṇas in his Saguṇa form. That is why he was given the name Ravaḷeśvara by the Āgamas.)

Also known as *Himakedāra* (*Lit*: Kedāra from the Himalayas), Kedāra came to the south because of the insistence of goddess Mahālakṣmī. For this reason, he came to be known as *Dakṣiṇakedāra*. He took on the brief of reinstating Mahālakṣmī, who had been ejected from Karavīra by the calamities caused by the demon Kolhāsura. Many other demons, such as Ratnāsura, Raktabhoja and Mahiṣāsura, were in cahoots with Kolhāsura. On the side of Kedāranāth were many Siddhas, Bhairava and the Matṛkās. Also, on his side were the Śaktis Carpaṭāmbā alias Copaḍāī, Mahālakṣmī and Yamāī. Kedāranāth mounted his horse and cleaned up the army of the demons with the help of his own army. The mountain where Ratnāsura was killed came to be known as Ratnāgirī. The place where Kolhāsura died came to be known as Kolhāpūr. Goddess Mahālakṣmī was reinstated at Karavīra alias Kolhāpūr and because of her insistence, Kedāranāth stayed at Ratnāgirī for ever.

The original myth describes the battle in great detail. It also gives details of the origin of many other places apart from Kolhāpūr and Ratnāgirī. However, the only information from this myth that is worth our attention is as follows:

1) This god has two well-known names: Kedāranāth and Ravaḷeśvara.
2) The composers of the myth link Kedāranāth with the Jyotirliṅga Kedāranāth in the Himalayas.
3) In calling him Ravaḷeśvara, the composers attempt to connect Kedāranāth with the Ṛṣi Jamadagni.
4) The main shrine of this god is on a hill called Ratnāgirī near the town of Kolhāpūr.

Description of the Jotibā Kṣetra at Ratnāgirī

The main shrine of Jotibā, called 'Vāḍī Ratnāgirī' or 'Jotibācā Ḍoṅgar," lies 12 miles north-west of the town of Kolhāpūr and is surrounded by famous forts such as Panhāḷagaḍ and Pāvanagaḍ on the Sahyādri mountain range. Its height is 3,100 feet above sea level. There is a plateau with a circumference of two miles on top of the hill. Two miles to the east of the shrine are some Buddhist caves called 'Pohāḷyācī Leṇī' which date back to the 2nd century C.E.

There is a group of three main shrines on Ratnāgirī hill. These are Kedāraliṅga (Jotibā), Kedāreṣvara and Carpatāmbā (Copaḍāī Devī). Raṇojīrāv Śinde built the present Kedāraliṅga shrine in place of the old shrine in 1730 C.E. Daulatrāv Śinde built the shrine of Kedāreśvara in 1808 C.E. Prītirāv Cavhāṇ Himmatbahāddar built the Copaḍāī shrine in 1750 C.E. These three temples are enclosed by a wall whose dimensions are 234 feet from east to west and 270 feet from north to south. All of these enclosing walls have small enclosures (*ovarīs*) built within them. The complex is approached via three grand entrances. There is a stone inscription of 32 lines in Saṃskṛt on the wall to the north of the western entrance. Apart from these three shrines, another-well known shrine is that of Rāmeśvara, which was built by Māḷjī Nikam Panhāḷkar in 1780 C.E. Two furlongs[9] away to the north of the main Jotibā shrine is the temple of the goddess Yamāī, which was also built by the Śindes. Near the southern door of the Jotibā temple, there is a platform for a *bagāḍ*.[10] Situated on this platform about 30 feet away is a five feet high hexagonal post. It is engraved with the information that the Pāṭil from the village of Sātve received the honour of being the Bagāḍkarī (Lit: one who has successfully performed a Bagāḍ).

Apart from this, outside the enclosure for these main temples, there is the temple of the goddess Ṣaṣṭhī (Saṭvāī) on the east. On the western side are temples of Dattātreya and Rāmliṅga. On the hill there are many other temples, such as those of Tukāī, Maṅgḷāī, Mahiṣāsuramardinī, Bāḷabhairava, Kāḷabhairava and Toraṇabhairava. There are also many tīrthas (sacred water tanks), such as the Jāmadāgnyatīrtha.

The Significance of the Peripheral Deities

In order to investigate the function and nature of Jotibā, I feel it is necessary to look at the other deities that are his neighbours on the Ratnāgirī hill. We are certainly going to look at the goddess Yamāī, whom Jotibā visits every year on the full-moon day of the month of Caitra in the hope of marrying her. We need to know what place she has in his life-history. The goddess Ṣaṣṭhī (Saṭvāī) is the wife of Skanda, the chief of the *kṣetrapāla* gods in the south. She is also known as the goddess who rules over matters concerning the delivery of a child. The shrine of Rāmliṅga is also important. It has been observed that this shrine is always associated with the myth of Reṇukā, Paraśurāma and Dattātreya, which has its origin at the place Kṣetra Māhūr. It is generally believed that Rāmliṅga and Paraśurāma are one and the same. It is also worth pointing out that the word *liṅga* is common to both names Kedāraliṅga and Rāmliṅga.

Devotion and Devotees

The devotees of Jotibā comprise of people of almost every Hindu caste in Mahārāṣṭra. They also include Muslims and Jains. Jotibā is the clan-god (Kuladaivat) for many families. Two well-known clans of Mahārāṣṭra, the Śindes (Scindiās) of Gwalior and Himmat Bahāddūr Cavhān of Kolhāpūr, have a special affection for Jotibā. Both of these clans have supported the shrine in many ways. The Rājājñe clan of Kolhāpūr proudly exhibit Jotibā's name on their seal. The seal declares

> *śrījanoddhārāvatārasya ratnaśailanivāsane* |
> *rājā-ravalanāthasya bhadrā mudrā vijāyate* ||
>
> (This is the auspicious and precious seal of King Ravaḷanāth, who took an *avatāra* for the upliftment of the masses, and who resides on the peak of the mountain where precious stones abound.)

In order to make sure that the worship at the shrine continues without interruption, the Śindes and Cavhāṇs have donated the proceeds of hundreds of acres of land in nearby villages to the service of the shrine.

Jotibā's official priests are Guravs. There are also many other people in the service of the shrine. These include workmen, clerks, Nāiks, Sepoys, flower-men, Motaddārs (horsekeepers), Cymbal players, Bhoīs (palanquin careers), Ayanewālās (mirror holders), Pānkars, Divaṭyās (lamp holders), Washermen, Tailors, Jāmdars, Goldsmiths, Gardiwālā, Samaiwālā and so on, who are designated officers of the shrine.[11] On the occasion of a festival, Parāṇḍekarbuvā performs a *kīrtana*[12] for which he uses material composed for this purpose by Nāth Bhujaṅg and also other poetry in the Bhakti tradition. In the month of Caitra, the *kīrtana* goes on for fifteen days. The Parāṇḍekars have the traditional honour and right to conduct the *kīrtana* at this shrine.

Many devotees take a vow[13] to undertake repeated trips (*kheṭe*) to the shrine in order to obtain special favours from the god. Judging from the stone inscriptions and available literature about the custom of *bagāḍa*, it appears that, as at many shrines of Khaṇḍobā, this custom was followed at Jotibā's shrine as well. *Bhaṇḍāra* (turmeric powder) and dried coconut are very important in the worship of Khaṇḍobā. At the shrine of Jotibā, *gulāl*[14] and *khārik-khobre* (dried dates and coconut) are important. The fragrant plant *davaṇā* is thought to be very dear to Jotibā.

Apart from the daily worship, Sundays and full-moon days are very important at this shrine. Devotees flock to the shrine in large numbers on these days. The full moon day of the month of Caitra is the main pilgrimage day for Jotibā. As many as a hundred and fifty thousand people flock to the shrine and spend several hundred thousand rupees on this day. Over twenty thousand rupees are collected by the state in pilgrimage taxes alone. The echoes of the chant '*cāṅg bhalā*' can be heard across the entire hill. Plays, *tamāśās* and shops selling many items are to be seen all over the place.

The main event at the Caitra Paurṇimā celebration is Jotibā's visit to Yamāī with the intention of asking for her hand in marriage. At 12 noon, his processional image is placed in his highly decorated palanquin. Then, accompanied by the tumultuous sounds of various musical instruments, graced by poles carrying the flags of a number of *mānkarīs*,[15] this palanquin reaches the shrine of Yamāī around 3 pm. As it moves along, people sprinkle *gulāl* and pieces of dried coconut in large amounts on this procession, and chants of *cāng bhalā* can be heard across the entire hill. The palanquin is then placed on the platform in front of Yamāī's temple. Surprisingly though, as soon as Yamāī hears that Jotibā has come to ask her hand in marriage, she closes the door to her shrine. (Obviously, the pujāris close the door, as per the requirement of the myth about the failed proposal of marriage). A dagger is then placed in front of the goddess's image and she is married to the dagger.

Apart from this main celebration (*Utsava*), other, smaller celebrations take place on days such as Guḍhī-Pāḍwā (the first day of the year according to the Hindu calendar), Dasarā and the full-moon days (Paurṇimā) in the months of Kārtika, Pauṣa and Māgha (November, January and February). It is worth noting that Nāga Pancamī, the day of serpent worship, which comes in the month of Śrāvana (July-August), is celebrated here as well.

The religious geography (*kṣetra*) of Jotibā, the surrounding deities and the festivals and celebrations that happen at this place convincingly tell us that although the myths try to establish a direct relationship of Jotibā with the Keḍāranāth in the Himalayas, Jotibā has very much maintained his local nature and character. Just like Khaṇḍobā, he is a god in the class of deities that are localised and that protect the surrounding area (*kṣetrapālas*). A folk goddess such as Yamāī is his wife. Dreadful and formidable worship rituals such as the *bagāḍa* inform us that he is a folk deity.

Name and Iconography

We have now examined the mythology of Jotibā and studied the geography and significance of the holy place (*kṣetra*) where he resides. We have also looked at the daily worship procedure followed at his shrine. We are now going to examine how closely this information relates to his name and iconography. Let me first start with his form as suggested by his iconography. Three devotional hymns, 'Stavarāja', 'Kavaca' and 'Sahasranāmastotra,' describe Jotibā's countenance in detail. The *Ravaḷanāthastavarāja* describes Jotibā's appearance as follows:

> *khadgaśūlaḍamarupātradadhānam* |
> *ratnabhūdharamaṇiṃ raṇadīkṣitam* |
> *turagavāhanamayaṃ hatadaityam*
> *tam namāmi satataṃ kuladaivatam* ||[16]

> (Forever I bow to the clan-deity (Ravaḷanāth) who holds in his four hands a sword,[17] a trident, an hour-glass drum[18] and a pot containing betel leaves, who is an ornament to the Ratnāgirī hill, who has learned the art and science of war, who rides a horse and who has destroyed the demons.)

The weapons Jotibā holds in his hands and the horse that he uses as his vehicle are the same as those of Bhairava. It is worth noting that Jotibā is also called the clan-deity here.

The *Kedārakavaca* describes the appearance of Jotibā in corrupt[19] Saṃskṛt as follows:

> *keyūrādivibhūṣitaiḥ karatalaiḥ ratnāṅkitaiḥ sundaram* |
> *nānāhāravicitrapannagayutairhemāmbarairmaṇḍitam* |
> *hastābhyāṃ dhṛtakhadgapātraḍamarūśūlaṃ sadā bibhratam* |
> *vājīvāhan-daityadarpadalanaṃ kedāramīśaṃ bhaje* ||[20]

> (I bow to Kedāreśvara, our clan-deity, who wears ornaments such as the keyūra and gemstones, who wears garlands of snakes, whose attire is golden, who has a sword, ḍamarū, trident and betel-leaf holder in his four hands, who rides a horse, and who conquers arrogant and haughty demons.)

The description in the above hymn is very similar to that given in the *Ravaḷanāthastavarāja* in terms of the iconography. On the other hand, the description given in the *Sahasranāmastotra*, while in agreement with the above two in terms of the weapons that the image carries, is different in terms of the vehicle of the god. It says:

> *dhyāyed devaṃ pareśaṃ triguṇaguṇamayaṃjyotirūpaṃ svarūpam |*
> *vāme pātraṃ triśūlaṃ ḍamarukasahitaṃ khaḍga dakṣe virājam |*
> *śeṣārūḍhaṃ kṛpāluṃ kamalapadayugaṃ bhaktakāruṇyagamyam |*
> *sarvāṅge liṅgabhūṣaṃ upavitasahitaṃ nāthamārgādhipatyam* ||[21]
>
> (A devotee should meditate in front of the god who holds the trident and the betel leaf pot in his left two hands, the ḍamarū and the sword in his right two hands and who is reclining on his vehicle, the serpent Śeṣā. This compassionate god represents the *liṅga* in its flame form (Jyotirliṅga) and is the presiding deity of the Nāth sect.)

According to the *Sahasranāmastotra*, Jotibā's vehicle is the serpent Śeṣā. However, if we leave aside the differences in the carrier, all three of these devotional hymns portray Jotibā as being identical to Bhairava. It is obvious that the devotees consider Jotibā as one of *kṣetrapālas* and it must be because of this particular belief that they equate him with Bhairava.

The suffix '*liṅga*' in one of Jotibā's names, 'Kedāraliṅga,' is indicative of his *liṅga* form. Compared to his longer names, Kedāranāth and Kedāreśvara, the shortened version 'Kedāra' is used much more often. However, one must remember that in devotional literature, he is always referred to by his honorific name Kedāraliṅga. The other name very common in folk literature and folk worship is Ravaḷanāth or Ravaḷeśvara. Ravaḷanāth is a well-known deity established as a *kṣetrapāḷa* in southern Konkaṇ and Goa. P.R. Behre has described his appearance as follows:[22]

> Ravaḷanāth's image is always shown standing. His left foot is slightly bent and projects forward. He has four hands and holds a sword in his front right hand and a bowl containing ambrosia in his front left hand. In his back right hand, he holds a trident and he has a ḍamarū drum in his rear left hand. He has a crown on his head and his gaze is directly in front. He wears a dhoti and is adorned with many garlands, including a garland of human skulls. Ravaḷanāth has a large curved moustache. Just like the other deities in these parts, he has eyes made out of silver. On both sides of the image, there are either two or

> four female attendants holding Chowrīes.[23] At times, a horse is carved on the right of the image.

Behere also reports that the Ravaḷanāth shrine at Oṭavaṇe-Candagaḍa is famous for curing devotees who have ingested poison. He states further that, similar to Jotibā's going to visit Yamāī's shrine to ask for her hand, the same happens with the *taraṅgas*[24] of Ravaḷanāth and Pāvṇāī. These *taraṅgas* are married to each other and the ceremony is called' Śivalagna. I have also heard from locals at the Sānterī shrine at Vengurle that there is an annual celebration of the wedding of Ravaḷanāth and Sānterī there. Because the rituals of the weddings of Ravaḷanāth and Jotibā are similar, Behere thinks that Yamāī and Pāvṇāī are identical. He thinks, however, that Sānterī is somehow different. In actual fact, both Yamāī and Sānterī are the same as mother earth, and we are soon going to see their similarity by looking at their images.

Jotibā's current image is obviously an evolved form. His *kṣetrapāla* status has obviously been taken into consideration and an attempt has been made here to establish a relationship between him and another *kṣetrapāla*, Bhairava. This has resulted in his particular form and iconography as we see it today. Earlier he was known only in his *liṅga* form. In his early life, the *kṣetrapāla* god Khaṅḍobā was also worshipped in his *liṅga* form. It was much later that his current iconographic form came about. In spite of this, Khaṅḍobā's original *liṅga* form can still be seen in the place well-known for his shrine, Jejurī. Similarly, at his famous shrine on Ratnāgirī hill, Jotibā's original *liṅga* form can still be seen right next to his now-popular image.

In many villages in the Konkaṇ region, I have personally seen many small stones shaped in their *liṅga* form. They do not have any particular names. Also, these *liṅgas* do not have the *Śāḷuṅkā*[25] base holding them. They look like roughly made pestles and come in various sizes and shapes. They are known only as *liṅgas* and worshipped as such. I believe that the *liṅgācī deuḷī* (*Lit*: a diminutive shrine for the *liṅga*) that Cakradhara, the subject of the *Līḷācaritra*, described in his wanderings, were definitely not major Śiva shrines but diminutive enclosures for such *liṅgas*.

Jotibā and the Nāth Sect

In devotional literature, Jotibā is often described wearing the typical Nāthpanthī attire: *Sailī*-Śṛṅgī-Kanthā-Jhoḷī.[26] A record has recently been discovered which states that during the reign of Ādilśāh, the worship of

Jotibā was in the hands of Gosāvis belonging to the Nāth sect. It is also believed that the current image of Jotibā was sculpted by a sādhū belonging to that sect. The work *Kedāravijaya* by Harī Aṅgāpūrkar hints at these beliefs as well.

I believe this relationship of Jotibā to the Nāth cult is due to the *kṣetrapāla* characteristics of Jotibā. My belief is based on the fact that the most important *kṣetrapāla* in Mahārāṣṭra, Bhairava, is the centre of devotion for the Bharāḍīs, who are followers of the Nāth sect. The Bharāḍīs, also known as Bharaṭakas, were originally involved in the maintenance and worship at Śiva and Bhairava temples. When the Pāśupatas were absorbed into the Nāth sect, the Bharāḍīs also became followers of the Nāth sect, and their deities changed accordingly.[27] Bhairava, the favourite deity of the Bharāḍīs, has also been described as a god of the Nāth sect. The well-known devotee of Jotibā called Bhujaṅga Nāth was also a Bharāḍī. He occupied a very important place in the devotional regime of Jotibā. Thus, Parāṇḍekar buvā, who claims the lineage of Bhujaṅga Nāth, still uses his material during the Kīrtana performances for the fifteen days of the celebration in the month of Caitra. He holds the exclusive right to do so.

Having seen this close relationship between Bhairava, the Bharāḍīs, the Nāth sect and Jotibā, we are left in no doubt that Jotibā is a god belonging to the same class of deities as Bhairava. My analysis of his individual characteristics from now on is thus based on my firm belief in his *kṣetrapāla* background.

Jotibā and Jyotirliṅga

Jotibā is the most common and popular name for this god. The suffix 'bā' in this name is also applied to many other village gods, such as Viṭhobā, Khaṇḍobā, Birobā, Ceḍobā etc., and is used as an honorific. Therefore, when one removes this honorific from his name, the root that remains is 'joti'(Jyoti). It is however possible that the root could be 'jot'. This can be discerned from the fact that the name Birobā comes from the root 'bīr', Ceḍobā comes from 'ceḍā' and Koṇḍibā comes from 'koṇḍā'.

The *kṣetrapāla* function of Jotibā is so obvious that it would be wrong to derive his name from the word 'jyoti or joti, both meaning 'a flame.'[28] To me, it would be more appropriate to connect it with *jot*, which means a plough pulled by a pair of bullocks. The commonly used word *jyotyā* derives from *jot* and it means a man who ploughs a field using a plough, i.e., a farmer. Also, it is interesting to observe that devotees of Jotibā frequently name their offspring either Jotibā or Jyotyājī. This latter name clearly tells us that the root in the word Jotibā is not 'jyoti,' meaning a flame, but is obviously '*jot*,' meaning a plough.

Just like the word *jokhaḍa*, the word *jot,* meaning "plough" (*nāṅgara* in Marāṭhī), obviously derives from the Saṃskṛt word *yoktra*. I am not aware of any Indian language that has a word meaning "plough" derived from the Saṃskṛt word *yoktra*. The letter k in the compound letter *ktra* in the word *yoktra* has obviously got preference in the formation of the Marāṭhī word *jokhaḍ*. It is therefore possible that the letter *t* got preference in the formation of the word *jot*. This transformation can be summarised as follows:

Yoktram > jokkha > jokhaḍ
Yoktram > jotta > jot

In the Marāṭhī language that is in use today, we use the verb *joṭaṇe,* which derives from the word *jot*. This verb is used to describe the process of attaching a bullock to the plough. This supports the suggestion that the word *jot* derives from the Saṃskṛt word *yoktra*.

In the present context, it is more important to examine the meaning of the word *jot* than to look at its etymology. The meaning of the word is definitely "a plough." I do not have to repeat now that the word *jot* is thus concerned with Jotibā's *kṣetrapāla* status. One of the names of this god, 'jyotirliṅga' is obviously a deliberate Saṃskṛtization, because Jotibā is phonetically similar to the words *jot* or *jotaliṅga*. It must be remembered that the word Jotibā is not connected in any way with the word Jyotirliṅga in the cult of lord Śiva.

Lāṅgala, *Liṅga*, *Lāṅgūla*, and *Lagula*

Having established the connection between the plough and the name Jotibā, it is now easy to see why this god is looked upon as a *kṣetrapāla*. With substantial evidence, philologists have shown that the word *nāṅgara* originates from the word *lāṅgala*, the latter coming from Niṣāda tribes. In taking stock of the cultural contributions of people belonging to Austric tribes, Sunitīkumār Caṭṭopādhyāy says:

> It appears that the Austric tribes of India have come from some of the tribal groups of South Asia, namely, kol, khāsi and mon-khmer. These civilizations belonged to the later stone age. In all probability, they learned the use of copper and iron after they

> entered India. They developed an agricultural style in which the mountain soil was cultivated using a wooden implement (which was called *laga, laṅga* or *liṅga*, all of which seem to be derived from the ancient word *lak).* They also were the first ones to cultivate rice on the tableland on mountaintops.[29]

Here Caṭṭopādhyāy clearly state that the Austric tribes used a special kind of wooden stick to sow the seed in the soil. With reference to this stick, he has used the ancient Austric word *luk* and its derivatives such as *lag, laṅg* and *liṅg*. The Saṃskṛt words for a stick are *lakuṭa* and *laguḍa*. One can clearly see that these words are connected with the Austric word *lak*. The word *nāṅgara* (< *lāṅgala*) obviously comes from this digging stick used to sow seed. The words lagula (stick used to sow seed), lāṅgala (*nāṅgar*, a plough), *lāṅgūla* (the tail of an animal), and *liṅga* (male generative organ) are all closely associated, and each one of them is directly or indirectly connected with the act of sowing the seed in the appropriate receptacle.

In this regard, the well-known philologist Śivaśekhar Miśra has discussed the etymologies of the words *lāṅgala, lāṅgūla* and *liṅga*. He says:

> The word lāṅgalam has no philological connection with Āryan languages. One must therefore deduce that this word must have come from non-Āryan tribes who predate Vedic times... Apart from hal (plough), the word lāṅgalam in Saṃskṛt also stands for *liṅga*. As opposed to this, in some of the sūtras and also in the Mahābhārata, one sees the word lāṅgūla which stands both for the tail of an animal as well as the generative organ of an animal. If then lāṅgala and lāṅgūla carry the same meaning, then it is easy to see how the word *liṅga* can also mean the tail of an animal. The similarity between the act of intercourse and the way the plough is used to cultivate the land is obvious. The plough digs the earth in order to sow the seed.
>
> It may sound somewhat strange that the Āryans incorporated some words from south-eastern languages. This is due to some unusual circumstances. Even today, some of these south-eastern tribes do not employ a plough to sow seed. Instead, they employ a pointed stick which has small holes in it. The seed is kept in the cavities made by these holes. The relationship between the penis and the implements used to sow seeds is quite obvious here. Professors Hubert[30] and Mauss[31] have shown that in Papua and Sagar islands, the stick employed to sow the seed is in the

> shape of a penis. In the languages belonging to these islands, the words 'digging stick' and 'penis' are synonymous. It is likely that the ancient tribes of India knew about this stick very early and even after the invention of the plough, the same name was applied to it.
>
> On the other side of the equation, it must be remembered that phallic worship in India and China was connected closely with Śaivism. It is therefore possible that the Āryans took phallic and image worship from the original tribes in the region. These rituals were despised by the Brāhmins and were not very common. If one thinks logically, it is possible to see how the words pertaining to the phallus, the *liṅga*, would have come into the language of the conquerors.[32]

Readers will understand why it was necessary to use this lengthy quote and I do hope they will appreciate its importance in our discussion. It was necessary to show the oneness of the three words: *lāṅgala, lāṅgūla* and *liṅga*. They have the same origin and mean the same thing. This has been adequately shown by the philologists mentioned above. With this background, the extraordinary importance of the word *jot* in the name Jotibā can be easily seen. Jotibā's name proves his importance as a *kṣetrapāla*.

Kedār, Kedāranāth and Kedāraliṅga

Although devotees refer to Jotibā simply as Kedāra, what they mean by that shortened name is one of the three names: Kedāranāth, Kedāreśvara or Kedāraliṅga. In the South, he is often referred to as Dakṣinakedāra (*Lit*: Kedāra from the south) or Dakṣinapati (*Lit*: leader of the South) Kedāra. When a devotee is addressing him this way, he is obviously comparing him with the Kedāranāth of the North, who reigns in the Himālayas. We have already come across the myth that declares that it is this Kedāranāth from the North who appeared in the South in order to destroy demons and then stayed there afterwards in order to please his devotees. Since the Himalayan Kedāranāth is one of the twelve Jyotirliṅgas[33] (*liṅga* in the form of a flame), there has always been an attempt both by the devotees and by scholars to explain the name Jotibā as relating to the Himālayan Kedāranāth. I have, however, shown here that the name Jotibā has no connection with *Jyot* (Skt: flame). It is connected with the word *jot* meaning "plough." What this means is that the word Jotaliṅga has been Saṃskṛtized to Jyotirliṅga. The compound word *Jotaliṅga* is made of two words with the same meaning, *jot* and *liṅga* (*lāṅgal* + *liṅga*). This belief, that the two words are identical, is consistent with Jotibā's role as the master and protector of the *kṣetra*, meaning the earth.

This role of Jotibā must always be kept in mind in studying his iconography, the stories and myths associated with him and the way his worship is performed. Once this is done, the etymology of his other names, namely, Kedāranāth and Kedāraliṅga, automatically becomes clear.

Both of the suffixes, *-liṅga* and *-Nāth*, in these names denote his status as the male principle and the master. Obviously, he is in union with the *yonī* who is the genetrix of this world, and that *yonī* must therefore have been referred to as Kedāra in these names. One can also say that the *kṣetra* (the piece of land) where Jotibā is the master must be referred to as Kedāra. This logical conclusion is in fact the truth. Saṃskṛt dictionaries and literature declare unequivocally that the word Kedāra means a *kṣetra*, a piece of land. Ancient works on agriculture such as the *Kṛṣiparāśara* use the term Kedāra for land everywhere. It declares:

> *kṛṣāṇasāra-kedāra-vṛṣa-nīrada-sañcayāḥ* |
> *sarve te vandhyatāṃ yānti bīje vandhyatvamāgate* ||
> *na phalanti dṛḍhāḥ sarve bījāḥ kedārasaṃsthitāḥ* ||
> *tato mārge tu samprāpte kedāre śubhavāsare* |
> *dhānyasya lavanaṃ kuryāt sārddharmuṣṭidvayaṃ śuciḥ* ||
>
> (*Kṛṣiparāśaraḥ*, 166, 184, 206)

> (The ploughman, the soil (*kedāra*), the bull and the clouds; all of them are of no use if the seed itself is defective. Not every seed that is in the soil (*kedāra*) necessarily grows. Therefore, at the appropriate time and on an auspicious day, a fistful of seed should be sown in the field with both hands.)

As one can see, the word *kedāra* means the soil, the field or the land. Hence, all the three names of Jotibā, namely, Kedāraliṅga, Kedāranāth and Kedāreśvara, naturally speak of him as the master of the land. The name Jotibā is derived from a *jot* or *lāṅgala* (plough). It is therefore perfectly logical to call him the Nāth (master) of a Kedāra, i.e. Kedāranāth.

In the 5th Śloka of the *Kedārakavaca*, the adjective *medinīpati*[34] (*Lit*: master of the earth) is applied to Jotibā. The belief that Jotibā is the husband and master of the earth and that he is the one who impregnates her with his seed comes through again and again in many different forms in the devotional literature about Jotibā.

Jamadagni, the Lord of Reṇukā

The Stotras[35] *Kedārakavaca* and *Ravaḷanāthastavarāja* also address Jotibā as Jamadagni, Ekavīrāpatī and Reṇukānāth. Thus, the *Ravaḷanāthastavarāja* says:

> *devaṃ dakṣiṇakedāraṃ ratnācalanivāsinam |*
> *jamadagnimahaṃ vande ravaleśamabhīṣṭadam ||*
> *ekavīrāpatiṃ saumyaṃ jyotirliṅgaṃ parantapam |*
> *ravalākhyaṃ mahābhāgaṃ vande bhaktārtināśanam ||*
> *triśūlaṃ ḍamaruṃ khaḍgaṃ pātraṃ ca karapaṅkajaiḥ |*
> *bibhrāṇaṃ reṇukānāthṃ vande taṃ ravaleśvaram ||*

> (I bow to the god Jamadagni, who is the Kedāra of the South and who lives on the mountain adorned with precious stones. I bow to the Ravaleśa who grants the devotee's wishes. I bow to the husband of Ekavīra, who is mild by nature and whose name is Ravaḷa. He removes all the calamities that befall a devotee. He holds a trident, an hourglass drum known as Ḍamarū, a sword and a bowl in his lotus hands.)

The *Kedārakavaca* says:

> *śikhāyāṃ reṇukānātho mastake bhālalocanaḥ |*
> *bhālaṃ me rakṣa bhagavan bhrūmadhye medinīpatiḥ ||*

> (Reṇukā's husband is on the crest of hair, he who is the eye in the brow is on the head. That illustrious god should protect my brow. That illustrious God should protect my brow, the husband of Medinī, who is in the midst of the brow.)

The repeated mention in the devotional literature of Jotibā being the husband both of Ekavīrā and Reṇukā and thereby equating him with the seer Jamadagni is worth pondering upon. In reviewing the myths about Jotibā, we have already seen that each year there are elaborate preparations on Ratnāgirī hill for the wedding of Jotibā and Yamāī. Jotibā's palanquin goes to the temple of Yamāī amid the sounds of drums and cymbals, but Yamāī closes the door on him as soon as he arrives at her doorstep. Let us now put aside the aspect of Yamāī closing the door on Jotibā and think more about the myth. The idea that Yamāī is Jotibā's wife holds sway throughout the myth. The alternate names for Yamāī alias Yallamā are Reṇukā and Ekavīrā. Devotional literature, stories and myths contain many proofs of this. In Āndhra Pradeś, she is worshipped in the form of an anthill, which is always considered to be a symbol of the earth's vagina or uterus. In south Indian languages, the word *poṭṭu* has two meanings: the stomach or an anthill. Her name Reṇukā (*reṇu* + *kā*) means 'something made up of Reṇu or very fine sand'. Obviously, this hints at her form as an anthill made of very fine sand. Thus, the goddess worshipped all over south India as Yamāī, Yallamā, Reṇukā and Ekavīrā is nothing but Bhūdevī, mother earth. Naturally, Jotibā's other names, such as Jamadagni, Ekavīrāpatī, and Reṇukānāth, resonate favourably with his name Medinīpatī (husband/master of the earth). They strengthen his role as a *kṣetrapāla,* the protector of the earth.[36] A Marāṭhī hymn called 'Jyotirliṅgāṣṭaka' composed by a Mahārāṣṭrian devotee called Mādhav, addresses Jotibā as an *avatāra* of Jamadagni as follows, in Marāṭhī:

jo jāmadagni-avatāra udāra krūrām |
jyāce bhaya tribhuvani bahudhā asūran ||
dasaṃsi rakṣuni sadā padiṃ mukti deśī |
śrijyotirliṅga smaratāṃ bhavaḥdukha nāśī ||

(The one who is an *avatāra* of Jamadagni, who is generous [to his devotees] but who is feared by the demons and the cruel, the one who protects the devotees and liberates them from the cycles of birth and death [is the Śrījyotirliṅga]. When one chants His name, all human miseries disappear.)

The Story of the Marriage of Jotibā and Yamāī

As we have already seen, the ritual of the unsuccessful wedding of Jotibā with Yamāī is enacted each year on the hill of Ratnāgirī on the full moon day of the month of Caitra. Many researchers, traditional and modern, have tried to deconstruct the myth in order to understand the reasons behind Yamāī's refusal to marry Jotibā. Some of them do not accept their proposed relationship at all. Others are uneasy with the traditional myth requiring Jotibā to go to Yamāī to seek her hand in marriage. Marāṭhī women, when attending to household chores, often sing *ovīs* composed either by saints or by women themselves. In one such *ovī*, there is a hint of a possible reason for this unease. The *ovī* says:

caitācyā mahinyāṃt |
deva jotibā ābāgalā[37]|

paṭhīcyā bhainīsaṅgam |
gelā lagīna lāvāyalā ||

(In the month of Caitra, god Jotibā acted strangely. He decided to propose marriage to his own younger sister.)

This *ovī* hints that Yamāī is Jotibā's younger sister and that without thinking about this prohibited relationship, Jotibā wanted to marry her.

Yamāī is Śakti in the form of a mother. According to the pattern of mother goddesses, she is considered to be a virgin. Although she has, on occasion, used the male principle in order to procreate, she is certainly not bound to him.[38] She is on her own, totally free. The male has come into her life as a father, a husband or a brother, but none of these relationships has ever curtailed her total freedom.

When this inordinate power of the female and goddesses became a challenge for males and male gods, there seems to have been an attempt to bring the powerful goddesses into the male fold as wives of the male gods, thereby reducing their importance and power. However, this attempt at a forced marriage has not at all been accepted by these virgin mother goddesses. Take for example the goddess Yogeśvarī, who was on the way to her marriage with Vaijanāth (Śiva) at Paraḷī. Before reaching Paraḷī, she deliberately stopped at Āmbe under the pretext of doing her hair and attending to her toilet. That way she avoided the auspicious time (*muhūrta*) for the wedding and stayed at Āmbe for good, creating her own shrine at that place. There are other examples where such goddesses have stayed separately on their own even after their wedding. Thus, Padmāvatī, the wife of god Vyaṅkaṭeśa of Giri hill at Tirupatī, became angry and left him, establishing her own shrine at the base of the hill. Similarly, the goddess Rukmiṇī is still angry with the god Viṭṭhala at Pandharpūr.

The stories of Yamāī and Yogeśvarī, who rebelled before their weddings, and Padubāī (Padmāvatī) and Rakhmāī (Rukmiṇī), who left their husbands after their weddings, are examples of ancient mother goddesses who proclaimed their freedom, albeit somewhat feebly. This then is the true reason behind Yamāī's refusal to marry Jotibā.

Bhāskarrāv Jādhav's Discussion about Jotibā

Since Jotibā is a favourite god of the village population in Mahārāṣṭra, it was but natural that the god received attention from those who wanted to educate the masses. Such attention worked both ways: at times it was used to explain the myths associated with the deity; at other times it was also a vehicle for criticising some aspects associated with the deity. More often than not, during such times, the researcher's point of view does not necessarily coincide with the actual state of affairs.

Bhaskarrāv Jādhav from Kolhāpūr was one such researcher who consistently tried to educate the masses through his writing about traditions. In his booklet called '*Marāṭhe āṇi tyāncī bhāṣā*' (*Lit*: the Marāṭhī people and their language), he expresses certain views about the origin of Jotibā. He says:[39]

> In the word Jotibā, the main element is 'Jot'. Jot is the clan deity (*kuladaivat*) of many Marāṭhā families. Among them, the Śindes and Cavhāṇs are well-known ones. It is important to consider the surname Śinde, the clan deity Jot and the salt water plant, 'Samudravel' together. The name Śinde started appearing on stone inscriptions in the tenth century, and the bards of that time connected this name to the river Sindhu. They also said that, etymologically, the name Śinde came from the region of Sindh. This is mentioned in a stone inscription at Karād. The clan deity of the Śindes is Jot. Even today, there are many ancient Jot temples in Sindh. In the annual festival for Jotibā on Ratnagirī hill, the devotees constantly shout, '*cāṅga bhalā*'. It is interesting to note that in Sindh, the expression, '*caṅgā bhalā*[40] is used as a greeting when two people meet. When two Sindhis meet, no matter what their caste or religion is, they always greet each other with '*caṅgā bhalā*'. This observation strengthens the argument of the bards that the Śindes came originally from the region of Sindh. Their Devak[41] is a plant that thrives in the sea. This vine shows the extent of the full tide. When the Śindes came to Mahārāṣṭra and took a new totemic emblem, they chose the leaf of this plant as their Devak. It therefore appears that they came by sea, landing near the port of Ratnāgirī. The present hill of Jotibā is approximately 75 miles by road from the port of Ratnāgirī. The distance would be much less if one walked. It was the Śindes who named this hill Ratnāgirī. The Śindes ruled over the district of Karād, which is not far from here.

One can summarise Bhaskarrāv Jadhav's views as follows:

1) Jotibā is the clan deity of the Śinde family.
2) The Śindes came to the port of Ratnāgirī by sea and then travelled to Jotibā by road. They named the hill that holds Jotibā's shrine, 'Ratnāgirī hill'.
3) In the name Jotibā, the main word is Jot. In the original land the Śindes came from (Sindh), Jot (*jyoti* = flame) is an ancient deity.
4) The phrase 'cāṅga bhalā' has its origin in the language of Sindh.
5) With the passage of time, the flame (Jot, Jyoti) was replaced by an image.

Jādhav also states:

> There are ancient shrines of 'Jot' in Sindh. There is no image there. Instead, a lamp burns there twenty-four hours a day. That lamp is considered to be the god. There were similar shrines in Kolhāpūr district. We have ourselves seen one such shrine on the Rāmliṅga hill. There used to be just a lamp there and it was protected from all sides against wind. I hear that it has not been there any more for the past ten or fifteen years. In Sindh, there is such a lamp shrine at each of the Hindu settlements. A lamp burns there constantly. The *pañcāyat* (local government) of the village provides for the oil for the lamp and also organizes someone to look after it.[42]

Bhāskarrāv Jādhav thus suggests that the worship of the flame originated in the Sindh area of India and was brought to Mahārāṣṭra by the Śinde family. He also says that the clan deity of the Śindes to this day is Jotibā. He reports that the Śinde family from Gwālior spends a large amount of money at Wādī-Ratnāgirī during the Jotibā annual festival and that they have built a large temple of Jotibā at Gwalior. Jādhav believes that the word *jyotirliṅga* denotes a deity (*liṅga*) who is in the form of a flame (*jyoti*).

Jādhav then discusses the Cavāṇ family, whose clan deity is *jvālāmukhī*.[43] The word *jvālā* means a flame. Jādhav describes this as the evidence that shows that Jvālāmukhī and Jotibā are identical. He believes the Cavāṇs were worshippers of the flame and when they came to Mahārāṣṭra from their erstwhile abode in the Kāṅgḍā valley of the Himalayas, they brought the representative of Jvālāmukhī, the Jot, in the form of a lamp with them.

Jadhav's argument can now be summarized as follows: 'Jyot' is the male deity of the Āryans. His original place was at Jvālāmukhī in the

Himalayas. As a representative of this deity, the flame came initially into Sindh. From there, it went to Mahārāṣṭra with migrants. The deity was originally worshipped solely in the form of a flame. Later, when image worship became popular, a distinctive image was created. This is the form we see today. The original deity in the form of a flame was then reduced to the position of the oil lamp that constantly burns by the side of the image.

I have quoted Jādhav's discussion in some detail because I feel that it is very important for unravelling Jotibā's origins. In the light of his arguments, a few other points also come to mind:

- The *nandādīpa* (*Lit*: the flame that imparts joy) which constantly burns in the sanctum sanctorum of any temple is not only confined to Jotibā shrines but found in all *grāmadevatā* and *kuladevatā* (village gods and clan gods) shrines throughout Mahārāṣṭra. During special festivals such as the *navarātrī* celebration, the *nandādīpa* is found in household shrines as well. Also, when lighting this lamp, no distinction is made between a male deity and a female deity. This obviously means that the *nandādīpa* is not a representation of Jotibā, nor is it a requirement for his worship alone. Therefore, it sheds no light on the iconography of Jotibā.
- Similarly, the traditional myths associated with Jotibā, the deities associated with him and the mode of his worship all point to his being a *kṣetrapāla*, the protector of a village or land. In this way, he is similar to other gods who act as *kṣetrapālas* in Mahārāṣṭra and south India, such as Bhairava, Khaṇḍobā, Ravalanāth, Ayyappam and Murugan.

The Śinde Clan and Jotibā

We have seen that Bhāskar Jādhav attempted to discover the origins of Jotibā by looking at the involvement of the Śinde clan in his worship. The Śindes of Gwālior are very devoted to this deity and have made a major contribution to the erection and maintenance of the shrine for Jotibā at Vāḍī-Ratnāgirī. It was Raṇojī Śinde who erected the present temple of Jotibā and also the Jāmadagnya Tīrtha next door. The Kedāreśvara temple, however, was built by Daulatrāv Śinde, and the Śindes contribute a substantial amount of money to the daily maintenance and worship of Jotibā. We naturally wonder about the reasons behind this fervent devotion on the part of the Śinde clan. Does it have any connection with the name Śinde, the district of Sindh and the deity Jot in that area? Before we answer this question, it is worth looking at the early history of the Śindes.

Inscriptions have been found stating that a clan by the name of *Sinda* used to rule as ministers in an area called *Kuntal* near Vāḍī-Ratnāgirī in the 8th and 9th centuries. For instance, a minister calleed Īśvara who belonged to the Sinda clan ruled the region of Vanavāsī-Santaliṅge in the present-day Karnāṭaka state between 1165 and 1172 C.E. He called himself '*karahāṭapuravarādhīśvara*'.[44] This obviously does not mean that he himself ruled over Karhād. It can however mean that his ancestors at one stage ruled over the Karhād region.[45]

An incomplete copper plate inscription refers to (the minister) Ādityavarman, the grandson of Bhīma and the son of Muñj. While he was at Junninagara (the present day Junnar), he gave a grant of the village of Kinhaī on the banks of the Indrāyaṇī river to a Brāhmin by the name of Navaśiva. This Ādityavarman called himself a *mahāsāmant* (supreme minister). V.V. Mirāśī thinks that in view of the fact that Ādityavarman mentions some of his ancestors in this inscription, this family probably lived in the Karhād-Kolhāpūr area from the 8th and 9th centuries onwards. Also, since the famous Mahālakṣmī temple at Kolhāpūr is thought to date back to the time before the Śilāhār dynasty, Mirāśī feels that it was probably built by kings of the Sind family.

It would therefore be reasonable to say that the close connection between the Śindes and the shrine of Jotibā at Wāḍī-Ratnāgirī must go back historically to the time of the Sāmants of the Sind clan who ruled the area of Kuntal. The kings of the Sind dynasty claim that they come from the Cobra clan (*phaṇīndravaṃśīya*). The present Śinde family also calls the *nāga* or cobra–the king of serpents–their original ancestor (*mūḷapuruṣa*). The royal emblem of the Śindes is also the *nāga*. I have always felt that this devotion to the cobra (the *nāga*) that runs in the Śinde family may well be connected to their devotion to Jotibā. I must therefore investigate to see if there is any connection between Jotibā and cobras.

Jotibā's Form as a Cobra

Although Jotibā's present vehicle is a horse, his secondary vehicle is the cobra. The two vehicles are found in the devotional literature about Jotibā as well. Thus, in his *Jyotirliṅgastotra* (*Lit*: the hymn of the *liṅga* in the form of fire), the devotional poet Bāḷakriṣṇa, in describing Jotibā, admiringly exclaims, 'Who is the god on the horse?' However, in the very next line he describes Jotibā as seated on a cobra.[46] In Saṃskṛt devotional literature also, both of these vehicles are mentioned. There, however, the cobra gets a prestigious mention. The *Ravalanāthastavarājaḥ* describes Jotibā as follows

> *śeṣasthaṃ karuṇāsindhuṃ kāruṇyaṃ kavitāpradam |*
> *daityaghnaṃ vasudaṃ vipraṃ vande vairivimardanam |*
> *kuṅḍalīnaṃ virūpinaṃ śubhaṃ yajnopavītinam |*
> *nūpūrārāvasaṃyuktaṃ vande pannagavāhanam ||*

> I bow to the one who is seated on the serpent Śeṣa, who is an ocean of compassion (for his devotees), who bestows knowledge, who destroys demons, who grants wealth, whose carrier is a serpent, and who is a Brāhmin who destroys enemies. I bow to the one whose name is Kuṇḍalin (or who wears earrings), who changes his colours, who wears a white and auspicious sacred thread, who wears anklets, and whose vehicle is a snake.

In this Śloka, two names of Jotibā, Śeṣastha and Pannagavāhana, both point to the serpent as his vehicle. However, his name Kuṇḍalin hints, further, at his being a serpent himself.

In describing Jotibā's form as a serpent, the *Kedārakavaca* goes even further. In describing his form for the devotee to meditate upon, it says:

> *paścime pannageśca vāyavyāṃ daityanāśakaḥ |*
> *uttare uttareśaśca īśānyaṃ īśa evaca |*
> *kuṇḍalīnaḥ kapolau ca nāsikāṃ vighnanāśanaḥ |*
> *oṣṭhadvayaṃ umānātho dantayordharaṇīdharaḥ ||*

> (His west side represents the king of snakes (*pannageśa*), his north-west represents his aspect as the destroyer of demons. His northern aspect is that of the master of that direction, his southwest aspect is that of god *Īśvara*. His cheeks represent his form as a coiled serpent (*kuṇḍalin*), while his nose stands for him as the destroyer of calamities. His two lips reveal him as the husband of Umā (Pārvatī), whereas his teeth reveal him as the one who holds the earth on his head.)[47]

In this śloka, *pannageśa* (king of serpents), *kuṇḍalin* (a coiled serpent) and *dharaṇīdhara* (the snake Śeṣa who holds the earth on his head) are three names used for Jotibā. All of these denote his form as a serpent. We may note here that the celebration of Nāgapañcamī[48] is a part of Jotibā's annual festival. We may also note now, an important observation well-known among scholars of Indian deities, that many gods were worshipped earlier in non-human form. When they acquired human form later, their original non-human form became their vehicle. Thus Śiva, who was originally worshipped as a bull, later came to have the bull as his vehicle. Similarly, Viṣṇu, who was worshipped as an eagle, later came to have the eagle as his vehicle.

The Cobra: Jotibā and Other *Kṣetrapāla* Gods

The existence of Jotibā in an alternative, serpent form is an extraordinary characteristic of *kṣetrapāla* gods. In the Indian tradition, a serpent is a *kṣetrapāla*. The anthill is thought to be a representation of the female sex organ and the serpent is the symbol of the male sex organ, the phallus. The snake has always been worshipped primarily as a child-giving deity. In south India, in many castes and tribes, a bride worships a snake at the time of her marriage. In some places, married women worship an anthill at the time of a wedding and bring a sample of the soil home as *prasāda*. Women desirous of bearing children often worship a snake or an image of a male snake and his female counterpart. Many such women take a vow and, to fulfil it when a child is born, they bury an image of a snake (*nāgakaḷa* = *nāgaśiḷā*) in the precincts of a temple or under a tree.

The perceived ability of snakes to give progeny to a childless woman has long been evident in Indian folklore and has been expressed in many ways. Almost all of the south Indian *kṣetrapāla* gods have retained their serpent character. For instance, the well-known *kṣetrapāla* god of the south, Murugan, is believed to visit his devotees in the guise of a snake. If they see a snake, even today people rejoice in the belief that their god Murugan has given them *darśana*. Similar to Murugan, the god Subrahmaṇya, who has coalesced with Kārtikeya, is worshipped in the form of a snake inside an anthill. In many of the well-known temples of Subrahmaṇya, in place of his image as Kārtikeya, he is worshipped in the form of a huge anthill and an image of a snake. The popular alternative name for Subrahmaṇya is Subbarāya, which means Nāgarāja, the king of serpents.[49]

In Mahārāṣṭra, the close relationship of the god Bhairava with snakes is well known. It is a common belief in village Mahārāṣṭra even today that, because Bhairava is adorned with snakes and one of his forms is a snake, he can remove the poison of a snake. The same applies to the god Ravaḷanāth. One of his vehicles is said to be a snake, and in view of his power to remove snake poison, one is left in no doubt of his close relationship with snakes. The Marāṭhī god Khaṇḍobā is closely aligned to Kārtikeya, like the south Indian Subrahmaṇya. At Khaṇḍobā's shrine in Jejuri on the bank of the river Karhā, Khaṇḍobā is worshipped as a symbolic anthill with *bel-bhaṇḍāra*.[50] Here he is called *Ādimailāra*, the orginal Mailāra, probably due to his anthill form. I believe that the *Maṇmailāra* (*maṇṇu mailāra* = māticā *mailāra, Lit.*: made out of earth) at Bellārī in Karnāṭaka must have originally been an anthill. In our folk religious tradition, there is ample evidence to show that a serpent and a plough are thought to be identical with each other. Balarāma, who is considered to be an *avatāra* of the mythical snake Śeṣa, is also known as *hala-dhara* (*Lit*: one who holds a plough). Finally, in Kāśmīr, the symbol for Śeṣa is the plough.[51]

To summarise then, the symbols used in the worship of the *kṣetra* (the earth) and the *kṣetrapāla* (the master and protector of the earth) are the anthill and snake respectively. It is obvious that they are symbols of the female and male principles. These symbolic 'genetrix and genitor' of the world are without doubt indispensable for unravelling the mysteries of folk deities.

Ravaḷanāth and Sānterī

In the context of the symbolism of the anthill and the serpent, we need to consider Jotibā's other name, Ravaḷanāth. This is because, just as Jotibā's consort Yamāī is the same as Reṇukā (composed of *reṇu*, small particles of soil – in other words, the earth), in the same way, Ravaḷanāth's consort, Sānterī, is well known in Goa and South Konkaṇ by her other name, Bhūmikā (the earth). In the state of Āndhra Pradeś, Reṇukā is worshipped in the form of an anthill. In the same way, in Goa and south Konkaṇ, Sānterī is worshipped in her Royaṇa-Ravaṇa form, i.e. in the form of an anthill (see Plate 19).

Although in some places Ravaḷanāth's vehicle is said to be the tortoise, in many other places, just like Jotibā, his vehicles are the horse and the serpent. The first element, *Kedāra*, in the names Kedāranāth and Kedāreśvara denotes a *kṣetra* (land or soil or the earth). Similarly, the first element, Ravaḷa, in the names Ravaḷanāth and Ravaḷeśvara also denotes a *kṣetra*. The word *ravaḷa* comes from the word *royaṇa*. In the colloquial Marāṭhī used in Goa, Ravaḷa means an anthill. Naturally, Ravaḷa

(Ravaṇa < Royaṇa) stands for Sānterī, and Ravaḷanāth is her husband or master. Just like the names Keḍāranāth and Keḍāreśvara, Ravaḷanāth and Ravaḷeśvara also show this god's role as a *kṣetrapāla*. Since the anthill is taken as a symbol for the earth, the *kṣetrapāla* takes the form of a serpent here.

At this point, we must think about Jogeśvarī, the consort of the main *kṣetrapāla* in Mahārāṣṭra, Bhairava. In Marāṭhī devotional literature composed in praise of him, Bhairava is termed *Skandabāndhava* (*Lit*: brother of Skanda) as well as *Śeṣajādhava* (*Lit*: husband of Śeṣa's daughter). In singing the *āratī*[52] of Jogeśvarī, devotees say, 'You call yourself the daughter of Śeṣa. Your play is beyond description'[53]. This means that in the minds of the Marāṭhī devotees, Jogeśvarī is without a doubt the daughter of the great mythical snake, Śeṣa. We have already seen that in the biography of Śakti, the mother, the male principle appears as her father, brother, husband or son. Jogeśvarī is thus the daughter of Śeṣa and also the consort of Śeṣa.

Because Bhairava is a *kṣetrapāla*, Jogeśvarī automatically becomes the *kṣetra*, the earth that he is the master of. It would be natural to think that her name came from the Saṃskṛt *Yogeśvarī*. One must however remember that the name Yogeśvarī is not at all consistent with her form as earth. The name Yogeśvarī-Jogeśvarī is a Saṃskṛtization of the south Indian name Joguḷāmbā. As we have seen in Chapter 2, Joguḷāmbā is the mother goddess who grants children. Since this name is indicative of her child-giving powers, it is the appropriate name to connect her to and consider her as the *kṣetra*, the earth. Bhairava's role as the *kṣetrapāla* would then be consistent with her being the *kṣetra*. Although the Yoginī-Yogeśvarī at Ālampūr in Āndhra Pradeś has coalesced with the eighteen Śaktis, local devotees know her only as Joguḷāmbā.[54]

Kṣetra and *Kṣetrapāla*

The story of Jotibā that we have examined through the myths about his name, through his iconography, through the rituals used in his worship and through the devotional literature about him is very telling in a number of ways. During our search for Jotibā, we have discovered that he is very similar to the well-known south Indian *kṣetrapālas* such as Murugan, Ayyapan and Śāstā; and Khaṇḍobā and Ravaḷanāth in Mahārāṣṭra. Although these gods have attempted to coalesce with Skanda and Bhairava in Śiva's pantheon, their role as *kṣetrapālas* and *kṣetrapatīs* has not at all changed. We have also discovered that, due to these gods, the goddesses that they are connected to have automatically been revealed as representatives of the land and the earth. Naturally, these deities who are worshipped as the 'parents of the world' are forever celebrating the festivities associated with the creation of the world. That may be why humans have consistently worshipped their procreative powers since the beginning of civilization.

Endnotes

1 Sāvant, Śivājīrāv Ābājīrāv. Śaka1893, 1971 C.E. *Śrīkedāravijaya*. 3rd Edition. Beḷgāv: Śrirāmatatva Prakāśan.

2 Translator's note: An *Ovī* is a form of Marāṭhī poetic metre generally made of four lines. Most of the Marāṭhī Saints wrote their works in the *Ovī* form.

3 Translator's note: A *Kavaca* is the very first part of a hymn which is composed in praise of a god. The word literally means a 'protective shield'. The hymn usually starts with the *Kavaca* part which seeks a shield of protection from the deity for various limbs of the devotee. At the end of the *Kavaca* part, the hymn describes the greatness of the deity etc.

4 Translator's note: An *Aṣṭaka* is a hymn containing eight couplets.

5 Bhāgwat, Sakhārāmśāstrī Bāpūśāstrī. Śaka 1857, 1935 C.E. *Śrikedāraliṅgamānasapūjāstotram* (with Marāṭhī translation), Sātārā.

6 Sāgāvakar, Ganeśaśāstrī Tāyātaśāstrī. 1896. *Ṣrīkeḍārapadaratnamālā,* Kolhāpūr.

7 Translator's note: Bharādi is a nomadic tribe in Mahārāṣṭra. Bharādis roam around the countryside, play their traditional drums and sing songs in praise of deities while asking for alms.

8 Translator's note: Ḍhere has not given the source of this verse in here.

9 Translator's note: A furlong is a measure of distance in imperial units. It is an eighth of a mile.

10 Translator's note: The word *bagāḍ* refers to piercing the back of a man with iron hooks and suspending him from a wooden post at a great height. It is performed by a devotee to thank the deity for fulfilling his wishes. The person who swings from the metal hook is called a 'gaḷkari'. Each year, one person is chosen by the village to be the Bagāḍ *gaḷkari* during the procession for the village deity. The *bagāḍ* is assembled before the procession. In Mahārāṣṭra, it is made of five metals with a golden hook. The head of the village inserts the hook in the *gaḷkari*'s back. At the end of the procession, the person's family hosts a feast for the entire village.

11 Translator's note: Large temples have several designated servants who are in the permanent employment of the shrine trust. For example, a *Motaddār* is a horse's attendant, a *Nāik* is a chief of the guards, a *Bhoī* is a palanquin carrier, an *Ayanewālā* is a mirror supplier, a *Divṭyā* is a lamp holder, a *Samaiwālā* is a person who looks after the large lamps by the side of the god, a *Jāmdār* is the keeper of the wardrobe and so on.

12 Translator's note: *Kīrtana* is a performance, usually in temples, which includes the narration of a religious topic by singing, telling popular purāṇic stories about the deeds of gods, and at the same time, instructing people about moral and spiritual conduct and observing of social norms. It is part of the Bhakti tradition. The performer is known variously as *Haridāsa, Kīrtanakāra* or *Kathekarī*.

13 Translator's note: Called *navas karaṇe*, devotees promise to do special and often arduous tasks in order to please the god so that he/she will give them the boons they seek. Once their wishes are fulfilled, they make sure that they perform those tasks as promised.

14 An orange-red powder offered to deities as a beautifying symbol.

15 Translator's note: *Mānkarī* (lit: one who has the privilege/honour) is a term that was used for people who had traditional privileges in the king's court or in a shrine. In the king's court this could take the form of sitting in the front row in front of the royalty. In a temple, this could involve making offerings to the god ahead of everyone else.

16 Saṃskṛt to Marāṭhī translation by Ḍhere. Marāṭhī to English translation by Jayant Bāpaṭ.

17 Translator's note: A sword.

18 Translator's note: A musical drum which is a part of the iconography of Śiva.

19 Translator's note: Grammatically and composition-wise, this is incorrect Saṃskṛt. It goes to show that the person who composed the Kavaca was not well versed in Saṃskṛt language.

20 Saṃskṛt to Marāṭhī translation by Ḍhere. Marāṭhī to English translation by Jayant Bāpaṭ.

21 Saṃskṛt to Marāṭhī translation by Ḍhere. Marāṭhī to English translation by Jayant Bāpaṭ.

22 Behre, P.R. 1955. *Śrī ravaḷnāth aṇi konkaṇātīl devaskī*, Borivlī: 17–20. (In Marāṭhī; translated by Jayant Bāpaṭ).

23 Translator's note: A *Caurī* is a fly whisk held by attendants of gods or royalty.

24 Translator's note: A *Taraṅga* is a decorated post that represents a god or a goddess. These are important representations of the deities at the time of processions. *Taraṅgas* take the first place in the procession. This is followed by the palanquin of the god and then the devotees who dance and chant the god's name.

25 Translator's note: The *Śāḷuṅkā* represents the *yoni* which holds the *liṅga*.

26 A Nāth ascetic traditionally wears a *kaṇṭha*, a saffron coloured cloth. It is also known as *godhaḍī* or *guḍarī*. It is made up of rags. According to legend, goddess Pārvatī painted this cloth with her own blood and gave it to Gorakṣanāth. *Śailī* is a sacred thread made out of wool. One end of this has a ball made out of woollen thread. It is called a Goṇḍā in Marāṭhī. A Nāth ascetic carries a small horn (śṛṅga) around his neck, which is blown during worship rituals. He also carries a loose cotton bag (Jhoḷī) tied around his neck in which he carries food and other items.

27 Translator's note: Ḍhere, R.C. and Kāmat A.P., *Śrī Nāmadev - Eka Vijayayātrā*. 1970. Pune: 58–59. (In Marāṭhī)

28 Translator's note: The word *jyoti* (also known with the alternative pronunciaton Jotī) means a flame.
29 Translator's note: See chapter 2, Joguḷāmbā.
30 Translator's note: Although Ḍhere does not quote a reference here, this could be Professor René Hubert, the French philosopher and sociologist.
31 Translator's note: Ḍhere does not quote a reference here either. This may be the well-known French sociologist, Marcel Mauss.
32 Miśrā, Śivaśekhar. 1952. *Bhāratīya Saṃskṛtime Aryetarāṅśa*, Lakhnau: 49–53 (in Hindi).
33 Translator's note: While every shrine of Śiva is sacred, of special importance are the most revered twelve *Jyotirliṅgas*, the liṅgas of Śiva in the form of a flame.
34 *Bhālaṃ me rakṣa bhagavan bhrūmadhye medinīpatiḥ* | (*Lit*: Oh Bhagavān, protect my forehead. Oh, Master of the Earth, protect my eyebrows).
35 Translator's note: Short devotional hymns.
36 Ḍhere, R.C. *Śaktipīṭhāncā Śodha*. 1973. Puṇe and Kolhāpūr: 30–36, 42–46. (In Marāṭhī)
37 Translator's note: The verb form *ābāgalā* needs to be taken as meaning 'became strange, ridiculous'. It probably comes from the Kannada word ābā meaning 'ridicule'. The verb root ābāgaṇe must then mean 'to be ridiculous'.
38 When she did require a male counterpart, the latter was secularised and subsumed to her. See Coburn, T. Devi, the great Goddess, in Hawley and Wulff. 1996. *Devī, Goddesses of India*. University of California Press: pp. 31–48.
39 Jādhav, Bhaskarrāv (1932). *Marāṭhe āṇi tyāncī bhāṣā*, Kolhāpūr: 43–45 (In Marāṭhī)
40 Translator's note: The literal meaning of the phrases 'cāṅga bhalā' or 'cangā bhalā' is, 'Are you okay?'
41 Translator's note: Devak is a clan emblem. This can be a tree, an animal or a god.
42 Jādhav, Bhāskarrāv. *op.cit.* 45.
43 Translator's note: The literal meaning of *jwālāmukhī* is one who has flames emanating from his/her mouth.
44 The compound word karahāṭapurawarādhīśvara can be interpreted in two ways: Firstly, it can mean the (king) one who used to rule over Karahāṭapura (present day Karhāḍ in Mahārāṣṭra), or one whose ancestors ruled over Karhāḍ in the past.
45 Mirāśī, V.V. 1974. Kolhāpūracyā Mahālakṣmīce Devālaya. *Navabharat*, Year 27 (Issue No. 5, February), 65–71 (In Marāṭhī)
46 *bhujaṅgāvarī āsana nāthjīce* (In Marāṭhī)
47 Translator's note: The use of the word *dharaṇīdhara* and the reference to his teeth, hint at his character as Viṣṇu in his boar incarnation who held the earth with his tusks.
48 Translator's note: *Nāgpañcamī* is a traditional festival in honour of serpents observed by Hindus throughout India. The festival is observed on the fifth day of bright half of Lunar month of Śrāvaṇa (July/August), according to the Hindu calendar. Women, especially married ones, flock to known anthills and worship the snake who occupies the anthill. Snake-charmers also visit households holding cobras in their cane-basket and asking for alms.

49 Translator's note: See chapter 9, 'Subrahmaṇya'.

50 Translator's note: *Bel* (leaves of the tree *Aegle marmelos*) and *bhaṇḍāra* (tumeric powder) are used exclusively for the worship of Khaṇḍobā, the fierce deity, mainly by the peasants in Mahārāṣṭra and Karnāṭaka. It is Śiva who is supposed to be fond of *Bel,* and since Khaṇḍobā has coalesced with Śiva, *Bel* leaves were probably adopted later in the worship of Khaṇḍobā.

51 Tavkar, N.G. *Nāgabhūmī Kāśmīr.* 1974. Mumbai: 19 (In Marāṭhī)

52 Devotional group songs sung at the end of a pūjā.

53 *śeṣakanyā mhaṇavisī, tujhī agādha līḷā.* (In Marāṭhī)

54 See Chapter 2, *Joguḷāmbā.*

Chapter 9

Subrahmaṇya

During my investigations on Jotibā in the previous chapter, I have referred to Subrahmaṇya, a god similar in many respects to Jotibā. It is well known that in Southern India, Subrahmaṇya is a popular name for the god Skanda. Skanda holds a unique position in the galaxy of Hindu gods. The myth about his birth is mysterious and strange. He is also known for his valour. The devotional regime surrounding Skanda involves several perplexing mysteries. The adjectives 'cunning and crafty' have been applied to him by some devotees. Thieves call him their favourite deity. He is considered to be the leader of the *bālagrahas*,[1] who are troublemakers that produce ailments in newborn babies. The purāṇic myth about Agni, the god of fire, holding Skanda's foetus in his stomach, is well known. His name Kumāra is in fact synonymous with Agni. Although Skanda is the elder son of Śiva and Śakti, his relationship with Śakti is much stronger than that with his father. He is regularly found with the Mātṛkās. Goddess Ṣaṣṭhī, who rules over the moment of the birth of a child, is Skanda's wife. The peacock or the rooster are his vehicles. Śakti is his main weapon. Six Kṛttikās are associated with Skanda's birth, and this is the reason his other names are Kārtikeya and Ṣaṇmukha. In the realm of world mythology, Skanda-Kārtikeya occupies a special position, especially when one examines myths associated with child gods (bālagrahas).

Skanda and the *Kṣetrapāla* Gods

It is my belief that unravelling the mythology of Skanda-Kārtikeya may lead us automatically to the resolution of many other mysteries in the realm of pan-Indian deities. However, here we will consider only a very small part of that great mystery, and that too in an indirect way.

Even to this date, Skanda worship is widely prevalent in South India. There are several *kṣetra* places that are of particular importance for his worship, and there are many temples devoted only to Skanda. He also has an important place within the pantheon associated with Śiva. Images of his two wives, Devasenā and Vallī, are always shown with him in South Indian temples.

Even a superficial look at the South Indian worship of Skanda informs us of an important detail about him. It tells us that the earlier worship of the very popular *kṣetrapāla* gods, such as Ayyappan, Śāstā and Murugan, was a precursor to the present worship of Skanda. Although these gods have acquired the characteristics of Skanda, have copied many biographical details of Skanda, and are now being worshipped as Skanda, they still hold onto their own forms, their original myths and their original names in the minds of the people who worship them. On the other hand, one cannot but notice that the mythology and religious literature that have been developed for the worship of these *kṣetrapāla* gods have coalesced appositely with those of Skanda-Kārtikeya. Similarly, the well-known Marāṭhī folk deity Khaṇḍobā appears to be identified with Skanda on the one hand and with Bhairava on the other. Thus, the festival of Skandaṣaṣṭhī[2] is observed all over Mahārāṣṭra as a special day for Khaṇḍobā. The fact that the *kṣetrapāla* gods have eventually coalesced with Skanda says a great deal about his original character.

Subrahmaṇya: A Very Popular Name in South India

Subrahmaṇya, Skanda's other name, is very popular all over South India in literature and in the naming of newborn male children. The custom of using a deity's name for the newly born is very prevalent in India. Subrahmaṇya, Bāla-Subrahmaṇya, Subbārāv, Subbarāy, Subbalakṣmī are some of the names used very frequently in South India. It is of course quite natural for this to happen. A parallel in Mahārāṣṭra is the naming of children after Khaṇḍobā, whose worship is highly prevalent in folk culture. Common village personal names such as Khaṇḍerāy, Mhāḷsākānt, Haibatī (Hayapatī), Mahipatī, Mailāra, and Mālojī; all refer to Khaṇḍobā.

Although the name Subrahmaṇya seems respectful on the surface, to me it is not as straightforward as it looks. The word *brāhmaṇya*[3] means sacred. Subrahmaṇya would therefore mean highly sacred. What is not clear is why is this name used for Skanda alone? In principle it should be applicable to any god. What then is the mystery behind this name?

Subrahmaṇya's Icon

The mystery about Subrahmaṇya deepened further for me when I browsed through an old travelogue in Marāṭhī with the title *Yātrākalpalatā*. This book describes the travels of one Sardār Raghunāthrāv Vincūrkar in northern and southern Karnāṭaka between 1881 and 1883. The pilgrimages he undertook during this period were recorded by Gauriśāstrī Anantaśāstrī. During this period, Raghunāthrāv visited a *kṣetra* of Subrahmaṇya. In this connection, I found the following passage by Gauriśāstrī most interesting:

> When we left the main road to go to the Subrahmaṇya *kṣetra*, we encountered such dense jungle that at times it was difficult to see the sun in the sky. In this dense forest, there is a place close to the temple of Subrahmaṇya that houses another ancient temple. This temple has no image as such, but houses a very tall anthill instead, in the sanctum. A Brāhmin from a village about a mile away comes and performs the pūjā of this anthill. A small river runs past this temple. Locals told us that a very large number of snakes are found in the temple area and near the river. Raghunāthrāv stayed here overnight. The people in his entourage did see a number of snakes, but no one suffered from snake bite.
>
> The place called Subrahmaṇya is a very small village. It houses the Subrahmaṇya shrine. It is also known by the name of Kumārādrī. The river Kumāradhārā runs past this shrine. In addition to the main shrine, there is another shrine called Ādi-Subrahmaṇya. This shrine houses a termite nest, and it is this nest that people worship here.[4]
>
> The main Subrahmaṇya shrine is very large. However, devotees are able to view the image only from a certain distance; they are prevented from going any closer. When one takes *darśan* of the deity in the sanctum from such a distance, one sees a gold-plated shrine that contains an image of a golden cobra and an image of Subrahmaṇya with six heads seated on a peacock. The priests in the temple do not divulge any information as to what else the sanctum contains. The reason for this reticence on the part of the priests is not known.
>
> It has, however been said that in earlier times, the main icon in the sanctum was the anthill. In front of this was an autochthonous image of Subrahmaṇya. Later, when Ṭipu Sultān's rule was established in this region, Muslims destroyed the Subrahmaṇya image and dug out the termite nest. After that, devotees installed the present images and started worshipping

> them. The pujārīs may have thought that if people came to know about this history, it could reduce their belief in the power of the shrine, and as a result, they do not divulge the description of the sanctum or the history of this shrine.

It is clear from the description given by Gauriśāstrī that it was the termite nest that was worshipped as the main deity in the Subrahmaṇya shrine, the Ādi-Subrahmaṇya shrine next door and the old temple in the forest. This is still the case. Also, along with the termite nest, an image of a cobra is also worshipped. According to the description in the '*Tīrthāṅka*' issue of *Kalyāṇa* magazine, Ṣaḍānana's (Kārtikeya's/Subrahmaṇya's) image, seated on the peacock occupies the upper half of the centre of the sanctum. The middle is occupied by the mighty snake Vāsuki and the lower half is occupied by Śeṣa, the seat of Viṣṇu. This means that the termite nest and serpents are the subjects of devotion at this temple. These icons are worshipped as Subrahmaṇya at this shrine. The devotees believe that Subrahmaṇya is another name for Kārtikeya.

The question that arises now is that, if Subrahmaṇya is another name for Kārtikeya, why is he worshipped in the form of a termite nest, and also as a serpent? What is the relationship between Subrahmaṇya, the anthill and the serpent? The answer to this question can be easily found in the realm of devotion. One can say that, whenever such questions arise, their answers are provided by the explanatory tales about the god in question, traditionally constructed by the devotees associated with the cult.

The Traditional Etymology of the Word Subrahmaṇya

The name Subrahmaṇya is thought to have been derived from the prefix *su* and the noun *brahmaṇya*. That is, the pure lustrous *brahman* which is beyond *māyā* and which removes the shackles of *māyā*, is, according to his devotees, Subrahmaṇya. It is essential that on this higher plane of devotion, construction of such a belief is an important step. In order to establish these new constructs, it often becomes necessary to either forget or overlook the early stages of the development of the mythology of the deity in question.

There is a myth[5] which tries to explain the importance given to serpents and the occurrence of a large number of them in and around the temple of Subrahmaṇya. It says that in ancient times, there was a fierce battle between the snake Vāsuki and Garuḍa, the eagle. Vāsuki was severely injured during this battle and was wailing loudly, begging for someone to save him. Hearing his cry for help, the sage Nārada came there and tried to make peace between Garuḍa and Vāsuki. He told them that such a conflict between brothers was not in their best interest. Although Garuḍa listened to Nārada's advice at the time, he made a threat to Vāsuki. He said that, although he had let Vāsuki go that time, he would surely kill him at a later stage. Frightened Vāsuki asked for Nārada's help in finding a safe place. The sage advised him to go to a cave near the mountain Kumārādrī and practise penance in order to propitiate Śiva. Vāsuki did so and pleased Śiva. When Śiva appeared before him, Vāsuki sought, as a boon, protection from Garuḍa. Śiva told Vāsuki that, after the destruction of Tārakāsura, Kārtikeya would come to Kumārādrī mountain to rest. At that time, Vāsuki should submit to him and seek his protection. After doing penance and killing the demon Tārakāsura, Kārtikeya arrived at Kumārādrī. Vāsuki submitted to him, told him what had happened and sought his protection from Garuḍa. Kārtikeya granted his wish. From then on, serpents have been able to live in the Subrahmaṇya *kṣetra* without the fear of eagles.

Subrahmaṇya: The King of Serpents

While the above myth explains, on the devotional level, the presence of serpents and serpent images around the temple of Subrahmaṇya, it sounds somewhat illogical and stretched when one ponders upon it. This is because, in the Subrahmaṇya temple, a serpent is not worshipped as a subordinate godling who has come for shelter to Lord Subrahmaṇya. Instead, at this temple, Subrahmaṇya is actually worshipped as a serpent.

I have a feeling that the fact that Subrahmaṇya is worshipped in the form of a snake should enable me to solve the mystery behind his name. The name Subrahmaṇya, used as an alternative name for Skanda, seems to be of Saṃskṛt origin but appears to me to be somewhat artificial. Rāvbahādūr Viśvanāth Nārāyaṇ Maṇḍalīk, in one of his beautiful essays read at the Bombay Branch of the Royal Asiatic Society on 13th May 1869, explored the mystery of the name Subrahmaṇya.[6] In his thought-provoking essay, 'Serpent Worship in Western India,' Maṇḍalīk has discussed in great detail the tradition of serpent worship and many of the peculiarities associated with this tradition. In this essay, Maṇḍalīk suggests an etymology of the name Subrahmaṇya. He opines that *Subbar* and *Maṇi* are the two words that make up this name, and that it signifies the chief or jewel of serpents. The words Subbarāya or Subbarāja mean the sovereign serpent. Thus, in Maṇḍalīk's opinion, Subrahmaṇya, which is an alternative name for Skanda, is an artificially Saṃskṛtized form of the Tamil word *subbaramaṇi* with which it rhymes. The original meaning of the word is *nāgarāja* (king of serpents) or *nāgaśreṣṭha* (the excellent serpent). I have no doubt that the prefix '*subba*' in the South Indian names Subbarāja, Subbārāv and Subbalakṣmī refers to a serpent. It is worth noting that another name, Nāgarājan,[7] is also very popular in South India.

Undoubtedly, Maṇḍalīk must have arrived at the etymology of Subrahmaṇya after exhaustive research. Many South Indian scholars have also come to the same conclusion. For example, in his book *Dravidian India*, T.R. Śeṣa Iyengār states:[8]

> There exists a close connection between the worship of Subrahmanya and that of the serpent. The common name Subba or Subbaraya found among the Telugu, Canarese and Tamil people is explained to be both a contraction of Subramanya and a synonym for a serpent. The sixth day of the lunar month (Śaṣṭhī) is held as peculiarly sacred to Subrahmanya as to the Serpent God. His riding on a peacock, his marriage with the forest maid Valliyāmman, and the fact that his most famous temples are on the hill tops show that he is connected with the ancient tree-and-serpent worship.

In this quote, Iyengār shows that the prefix *subba* in the Telugu, Tamil and Kannada languages is indicative of a snake, and also that Skandaśaṣṭhī is the same as Nāgaśaṣṭhī. Although Iyengār did not have the courage to point out that Skanda and *nāga* (serpent) are the same, he did point out many close similarities between them.

The facts that Subrahmaṇya is worshipped in the form of a snake, that his name means "snake," and that the sixth day of the lunar month is taken as a special day for the worship of both the snake and Subrahmaṇya, suggest to me that those *kṣetrapāla* gods who have coalesced with Skanda in the South must themselves possess the characteristics of a serpent. The proof for my deduction can be found in a recent book in English called '*Karttikeya*' written by Ratnā Navaratnam and published by Bhāratīya Vidyā Bhavan. In this book, Navaratnam writes:[9]

> There is a popular belief that Muruga manifests himself in the form of serpents to exhibit his grace to his devotees. Paripadal refers to a fearful sight of a five-headed serpent and its tender young one which frightened the young devotees at the temple

> of Tirupparankundram. It is interesting to note that this fearful sight was later discovered to be a water-flower nestling of the hill pool.[10] Anyhow, the imaginary fear suggests the existence of belief in the five headed serpents in the abode of Muruga.

Navaratnam thus records that the devotees of the highly popular South Indian *kṣetrapāla* god Muruga firmly believe that he blesses them by appearing before them in the form of a cobra. She also notes an ancient record mentioning the appearance of Muruga in the form of a cobra with five heads in the temple of Tirupparankundram.

K.R. Venkaṭaramaṇ noted that, even today, 'the appearance of a serpent is considered by common folk as betokening the presence of Murugan'.[11]

People belonging to the 'Vaidya' caste in Bengal perform the *nāga-maṇḍala* dance in order to propitiate the cobra. At that time, a great snake is drawn with coloured powder[12] on the floor in the pūjā marquee. The devotees call this snake 'Śubharāy'.[13]

All of the above evidence clearly shows that, although Subrahmaṇya, who is worshipped in South India in the form of a snake around termite nests is presently considered to be Skanda-Kārtikeya, he is originally a serpent-god. His name Subrahmaṇya signifies a snake. The well-known South Indian *kṣetrapāla* god Murugan, who has coalesced with Skanda, is also seen by devotees as a serpent. This relationship among Muruga, Subrahmaṇya and the *nāga* is crucial for understanding the *kṣetrapāla* deities.

Kṣetrapālas Gods and Serpents

The relationship between Murugā, who has coalesced with Subrahmaṇya, and serpents is not confined only to South India. It can be clearly seen all over India when one looks at the nature of *kṣetrapāla* deities and their cults. Thus, the well-known *kṣetrapāla* god Bhairava is known for his special relationship with serpents. Serpents are always found in the sanctum sanctorum of a Bhairava temple. Bhairava appears before his devotees in the form of a serpent. There is a firm belief among his devotees that this Bhairava in snake form protects them and cures them of snake bite. One hears this same myth about Jotibā in Mahārāṣṭra and Ravaḷanātha in the Konkaṇ-Goa region. These latter gods are thought to be incarnations of snakes, they have snakes on their body and they cure people of snake bites. We have already seen in the previous chapter that, in the hymns composed in his praise, Jotibā is also addressed by other names, such as Pannageśa (*Lit*: king of serpents), Dharaṇīdhara (*Lit*: one who holds the earth) and Kuṇḍalin, all of which signify his serpent character. The fact that *kṣetrapāla* gods such as Bhairava, Jotibā, Ravaḷanātha and Muruga have characteristics of serpents will be highly useful in exploring the mysteries of many of the deities of India.

Nāga: *Kṣetrapāla* and *Kṣetrapatī*

The reason why *kṣetrapālas* have a close association with Nāgas is that Nāgas are themselves *kṣetrapatīs*. The termite nest is the symbol of the generative organ of the earth, whereas *nāga*, the serpent, symbolizes the male generative organ. The *nāga* is worshipped primarily as the giver of progeny. In the village of Subrahmaṇya, where god Subrahmaṇya is worshipped in his snake-form near the termite nest, devotees worship him and make vows in order to get children. On the day of Skanda-Ṣaṣṭhī (also known as Nāgaṣaṣṭhī and Campāṣaṣṭhī), there is a major religious festival at this place. The main priest covers his hand with a leather glove, puts his hand inside the termite nest and takes out three handfuls of earth. The earth is called *mūlamṛttikā* and is distributed among the devotees as *prasāda*. It is thought to have the power to give children to the devotees. It should by now be clear that the earth, which is impregnated with the potent seed of the great male, is also considered capable of giving children to devotees.

The belief in the progeny-giving powers of the serpent is deeply rooted in Indian religious tradition. All over India, there are many myths and stories that elaborate this belief again and again. Among many castes in South India, brides and married women worship a snake at the time of a wedding. In some places, at the time of a wedding, married women worship an anthill and bring the soil from it to be distributed as *prasāda*. Women desirous of conceiving a child worship a snake or a snake-couple. They make a vow (*navas*) to get an image of a snake sculpted. This image is then ceremoniously established under a tree or in the precincts of a temple. This discussion reminds me of a tale that a close friend of mine, Moreśvar Wāḷimbe, heard from his mother. His mother told him that it was a firm belief that if a snake looks at a pregnant woman, he loses his eyesight. It is only after she delivers the baby and takes her post-parturition bath that the snake gets his eyesight back, when he smells the typical fragrance in the bathroom.[14] It is obvious that this belief is intended to ensure that a pregnant woman does not have a sexual relationship with a male. The belief obviously hints that all males correspond to the snake, who himself is the representative of the male principle.

It seems that this belief in the amazing potency of the serpent has been prevalent since ancient times, not only in India but also in other countries. In showing that the serpent is held to be responsible for menstruation in human females, Briffault states:[15]

> This notion has been thought to derive from the phallic shape of the animal, and that idea is undoubtedly present in those worldwide beliefs. It was thought by the ancients, and is still believed by the European peasantry, that during sexual conjunction the male serpent introduces its head in the mouth of the female, and that the latter gnaws and bites it off, thus becoming fecundated.

In view of the fact that a serpent is shaped like a phallus, the statement by Briffault that people other than Indians also think of the snake as a symbol of the human male sex organ makes perfect sense.

It is not necessary for us to examine here every aspect of the mythology associated with serpents. All that we are concerned with is to demonstrate the serpent's position as a *kṣetrapāla* and a *kṣetrapatī*. Even if we limit ourselves only to South India, we know for certain that the *kṣetrapālas* take the form of Nāgas. We have also observed that Bhūdevī–mother earth is closely linked with them at these places. In the cults of such well-known South Indian goddesses as Ellammā, Mātaṅgī, Reṇukā, Sānterī, and Bhūmikā, the *nāga* or his symbol holds an important position. Female devotees of Ellammā and Reṇukā hold a staff called *nāgaphaṇī*.[16] The importance of the *nāga* in the worship of the goddess Sānterī in South Konkaṇ and Goa is well known. The sculpted image of Bhūmikā shows her holding a *nāga* in her hand.[17] In one of her thousand auspicious names, goddess Banaśaṅkarī (known also as Śākambharī) has been called *nāgaliṅgabhagāṅkāḍhyamauliḥ* (*Lit*: a goddess whose head has been adorned with a phallus in the form of a *nāga*, and a vagina).[18]

Thus, in researching the mystery of the god Subrahmaṇya in the village with the same name, we have unravelled the great mystery of the father and mother of the world.

Endnotes

1 Ḍhere, R.C. 1996. *Lokadaivatānce Viśva*. Pune: Padmagandhā Prakashan. Chapter 6 with the title, 'Bālagrahāncī Upāsanā' (Lit: The worship of *Bālagrahas*): 95–111 (In Marāṭhī).
2 Translator's note: Skandaṣaṣṭhī is a *vrata* (religious observance) observed on the sixth day of the *Śuklapakṣa* (first half of the month) of Kārtika. Offerings are made to Skanda on this day.
3 Translator's note: The three other meanings of this Saṃskṛt word are: *vaḍa*, the ficus religiosa tree; Saturn; and Viṣṇu.
4 Translator's note: From the description here, it is certain that the place Raghunāthrāv visited was the village of Subrahmaṇya situated in the western ghats of Karnāṭaka. This place has two ancient temples. The first one is called Kukke Subrahmaṇya temple at present and the second one is the Ādi-Subrahmaṇya temple. The latter houses a termite nest. I have been unable to get hold of a copy of *Yātrākalpalatā*.
5 *Yātrākalpalatā*, *Ibid*., pp. 41–42.
6 Maṇḍlīk, N.V., ed. 1896. *Writings and Speeches of the late Hon. R.B. Viśwanāth Nārāyaṇ Maṇḍalīk*, Bombay: 245.
7 The name Nāgārjuna consists of two parts, *nāga*, meaning serpent and Arjuna, the great warrior of the Mahābharāta.
8 Śeśa Iyengār, T.R. 1925. *Dravidian India*, Vol. 1, Madras: 110.
9 Navaratnam, Ratnā. 1973. *Kartikeya – The Divine Child*, Bombay: 143.
10 Translator's note: The water-flower that Navaratnam mentions must be a lotus. As to how a lotus could be mistaken for a five-headed serpent with its offspring is hard to understand. The translator has been unable to locate the book by Navaratnam.
11 Venkaṭaraman, K.R. 1956. Skanda Cult in South India. In: Haridās Bhaṭṭācārya, ed., *The Cultural Heritage of India,* Calcutta, Vol. 4: 309.
12 Translator's note: Such a diagram is called *rāṅgoḷī* in Marāṭhī (*Skt*: *raṅgāvalī*). It is customary to draw such diagrams in front of the house or around the worship area during religious festivals and on auspicious occasions.
13 Jośī, Paṇḍit Mahādevaśāstrī. 1967. ed., *Bhāratīya Saṃskṛti Kośa,* Pune: Vol. 4: 745–746.
14 Translator's note: Ḍhere uses the Marāṭhī word *gandha* for the smell emanating from a woman's delivery area and bathroom immediately after she delivers a child. In the olden days in Mahārāṣṭra, a pregnant woman was isolated in a small corner of the house that was traditionally dark. For a few weeks before the delivery, she was massaged every day with medicinal oils. For many hours during the day, she was asked to rest on her coir bed. Embers were placed beneath the bed to ensure that she was warm. Incense (*dhūpa*) was burned on these embers, which produced a hot, smoky smell in the area. The combined smell of embers, incense and massage oils is what Ḍhere is referring to as *gandha*. Upon delivery, the woman and the baby were massaged and bathed in the same area.
15 Briffault, Robert. 1959. *The Mothers*, London: 315.
16 *Lit*. a cobra-hood.

17 Translator's note: I have been unable to confirm details of the iconography of goddess Bhūmikā as described by Ḍhere. Bhūmikā (Bhūmī), is goddess earth, who is considered to be the second wife of Viṣṇu. Textbooks of Hindu iconography show her with two hands, one holding a lotus and the other being free. None of the references I checked show her holding a serpent in one of her hands.

18 Translator's note: *nāgaliñgabhagāñkādhyamaulī* in Saṃskṛt.

Chapter 10

Forms of the Vedic Goddess Aditi in Nature

When the great mother earth rests contentedly in union with the primordial father who embraces her with his thousand rays,[1] she is satiated in the extreme, and, as a result, she holds in her womb a foetus made up of highly nutritious grains and juicy fruit. Every part of her body is beautified by green ornaments. The human female, who is a miniature form of the mother earth, appears identical when she is pregnant. This mother of tomorrow wears a silken green Saree (*Śālū*[2]) and green bangles stretching up to her elbows. When she starts her walk in slow majestic steps because of the extra weight she carries, she appears as if the earth is moving in a miniature form for the appreciation of the onlookers. Whether it is mother earth or the human mother, both can be thought of as giving birth to that which is divine in nature. This divinity in nature is expressed in an array of colours, smells, sounds, spirits and movements. Just like the external nature around us, which is a part of the divine, so is the inner human world of many beliefs and feelings, resolves and options, love and hate and creative intellect and imaginative power. That is why the Vedas have aptly called this divine quality in nature, which gives rise to the inner world of us humans, *Aditi*, the imperishable. Seasons come and go; their cycles move continually. The natural landscape that is almost totally burnt in Summer (Grīṣma), gets drenched by the thousandfold currents of water in the season of monsoon (Varṣā)[3] and appears time and time again as a foetus in the womb of mother earth, only to be reborn and blossom in the form of millions of leaves and flowers by the time autumn (Śarada) arrives. Once again, when winter (Śiśira)[4] comes, leaves start falling off the plants and a lot of plant life dies. The fierce Summer then roasts everything in sight, only to be replaced by the rainy season, which brings in rebirth. The wheel of birth, death and re-birth, similar to the wheel of the seasons, rotates endlessly. In spite of this, mother earth is ever ready to carry the new foetus with fresh enthusiasm. Her magnificent motherhood is eternal and endless. She is *Aditi* the imperishable, and the mother of gods. Manu describes aptly the amazing similarity between the great mother earth and the human mother:

> *kṣetrabhūtā smṛtā nārī, bījabhūtāḥ smṛtaḥ pumān* |
> *kṣetrabījasamāyogāt saṃbhavaḥ sarvadehinām* ||
>
> *Manusmṛti* (9.33)[5]

> (The female is thought to be the field and the male is the seed. It is the union of the field and the seed that produces all living beings.)

Aditi: The Earth

Vedic seers considered the earth and Aditi – the mother of gods – as the same at some times, but totally different on other occasions, and having coalesced together into one on yet other occasions. The earth is *janayitrī* (the producer) and *dhātrī* (the sustainer). She is also *Pṛthivī* (ample, broad) and *mahī* (great). Similar to the earth, Aditi is also *mahī mātā* (the great mother).[6] Aditi is *aṣṭayonī* (one with eight vaginas) and *aṣṭaputrā* (one who has given birth to eight sons). She gave birth to seven divine sons, the *Ādityas*, and broke the eighth egg. The *Ādityas*, however, refused to take part in natural procreation, and Aditi was therefore forced to bring life into this eighth egg, '*mṛta garbhāṇḍa*'[7](mārtāṇḍa) and nourish it. However, in order to continue the cycle of birth and death, she had to make sure that this *mārtāṇḍa* died.

> *prajāyai mṛtyave tvat punarmārtāṇḍamabhibharat* ||[8]
>
> *Ṛgveda* (10,72, 9)[9]

> (Oh Mārtāṇḍa! in order to maintain the cycle of birth and death, I made sure that you died.)

There is no doubt that this episode in the biography of Aditi as described by the Vedic seers proves that the earth and Aditi are identical to each other. For nature to take its course, it is important that the cycle of birth, death and re-birth must continue. That is why Aditi, who brought the dead '*garbhāṇḍa*' to life in order to continue the cycles of life and death, is the same as the earth, who continues to do this through the cycles of nature.

Pṛthivī, Yajñavedī and Sṛṣṭī

In the opinion of the Vedic seers, the whole universe was formed as the result of a sacrifice, and it was in itself an ingredient of that sacrifice. For them, the 'sacrificial altar' for this sacrifice was the earth.[10] In their eyes, for a new life to be born, offerings of the old one on this altar was necessary. The only way this could be achieved was through death. This lofty thought of the Vedic seers in imagining the earth as the sacrificial altar where death and motherhood are put on an equal footing must be considered as an expression of a great universal truth. It is the unfolding of a divine mystery. Not only in India, but all over the world, there is a common belief among human groups that creation takes place either through the intercourse of a divine couple or through sacrifice – death, voluntarily entered into.[11] In explaining this two-fold act of creation, Dr Eliade has said:[12]

> Let us especially note that the creation is completed and perfected either by a hierogamy or else by a violent death; which means that the creation depends both upon sexuality and upon sacrifice, voluntary sacrifice above all. The myth of the origin of edible plants – a myth very widely distributed – always has to do with the spontaneous sacrifice of a divine being.

I feel that it is essential at this juncture to quote Dr Eliade's comments in their entirety in order to show the relationship between voluntary martyrdom and creation:

> The myth of creation by a violent death transcends, therefore, the mythology of the Earth-mother. The fundamental idea is that life can only take birth from another life which is sacrificed. The violent death is creative – in this sense, that the life which is sacrificed manifests itself in a more brilliant form upon another plane of existence. The sacrifice brings about a tremendous transference: the life concentrated in one person overflows that person and manifests itself on the cosmic or collective scale. A single being transforms itself into a cosmos or takes multiple re-birth in a whole vegetable species or race of mankind. A living 'whole' bursts into fragments and disperses itself in a myriad of animated forms. In other terms, here again we find the well-known cosmogenic pattern of the primordial 'wholeness' broken into fragments by the act of creation.

Eliade's discussion of the relationship of sacrifice and creation is certainly thought-provoking and revealing. When one thinks about the relationship of the two aspects of creation, one naturally asks the question whether there is actually a relation between the intercourse of the primordial beings and the voluntary death or sacrifice of these divine beings. On the face of it, the two processes are very different. In this context, it is important to remember that the Vedic seers experienced and appreciated the primordial intercourse in the form of (fire) sacrifice. Thus, the *Bṛhadāraṇyaka Upaniṣad* (6.2.9–13) puts forward a wonderful idea that explains in detail the creation of the world through five consecutive sacrifices (yajñas):

1) The divine abode (Divya-loka) is the fire of sacrifice (*agni*). Āditya is its firewood (samidhā). The rays of the sun are the smoke that emanates from this fire. The day is the flame of this sacrifice. The four main directions are the burning coals and the other directions are the embers. Gods make offerings of their firm devotion into this fire. King Soma is born from these fire offerings.
2) The rains are the fire for the sacrifice. The year (Saṃvatsara) is the firewood and the clouds are the smoke of this fire. Lightning is the flame, thunderbolt is the burning coals and the thundering of the clouds is the embers. The gods make an offering of King Soma in this fire. Nature gets born from these offerings.
3) This world is the fire for the sacrifice. The earth is the firewood. Agni, the fire itself, is the smoke. The moon represents the burning coals for this fire and the constellations are the embers. The gods make offerings of rain into this fire. From it, food is born.
4) A human male is the fire for the sacrifice. His open mouth is the firewood. His life-force is the smoke. His eyes are the burning coals and his ears are the embers. The gods make offerings of food into this fire. From these offerings, the male seed is born.
5) A woman is the fire for this sacrifice. Her middle is the firewood. The hair on her body is the smoke. Her vagina is the flame. The process of intercourse in the vagina is the burning coal. The orgasm she achieves is the embers. Gods make offerings of semen into this fire. Out of this a male is born. He lives for a number of years. When he dies, the gods put him into the fire again.

There is no doubt that this cycle of generation described by the Ṛṣis, the composers of the Upaniṣads, brings together the two interrelated streams of death and regeneration. The Ṛsis believed that the process of intercourse was a sacrifice and hence had a sacred aura of divinity about it. This same idea of sexual intercourse as a sacrifice has been described by the same Upaniṣad in another place as well.[13] Prajāpati wanted some place for his seed. That is why he created woman. Her lower portion is the sacrificial altar. The hairs on her body are the flames of the fire.

Once one accepts this extraordinary idea of seeing sexual intercourse as a sacrifice, one can readily see why the word *yajamāna* is commonly used to describe a husband.[14] A *yajamāna* is the one who performs a *yajna*, a sacrifice. A husband makes an offering of his semen in the fire that is his wife. Progeny is born out of this offering. That is why a husband (*pati*) is called a *yajamāna*. Also, one who wishes to be a *yajamāna* has to undergo an initiation to perform such a sacrifice and has to be born again on a divine level. It is only then that he attains the right to perform sacrifices and to obtain worldly pleasures. It therefore follows that a *yajamāna* is a person who marries in the traditional way by following the required rituals and deposits his seed into his wife. This resonates well with the fundamental idea behind sacrifice. This vision of our ancestors that looks at regeneration in this light is amazing indeed!

Go-Vṛaṣabha

We have now seen the relationship between the earth (Pṛthivī) and Aditi. We have also noticed how they often coalesce. In the same vein, we also saw how the Vedic Ṛṣis thought about the procreational aspect of both women and the earth in the form of a sacrifice. These Vedic seers used the term *mahānagna* (*Lit*: the great male nude) for the male principle used by both the earth and a human female for procreation. The female principle that unites with him is called *mahānagnī* (Lit. the great female nude). In his masterpiece, *Śiva Mahādeva* published in 1966,[15] the great scholar Dr Vāsudevśaraṇ Agrawāl comments very effectively on these two adjectives. He says:

> One of the original, fundamental and mysterious forms of Siva is *mahānagna* or *digambar* (*Lit*: one whose clothes are the sky). The origin of this iconic adjective is to be found in the Vedic interpretation of the word, *mahānagna* (*Atharvaveda*,

> 20.136.11). This adjective describes the great procreative male. His consort has been called *mahānagnī*. ... This *mahānagnī* runs after the *mahānagna* and says to him, 'eat this rice and then have sexual intercourse with me'. All of this imagery has naturally been created in the sexual mould. In order to procreate the world, the creator first developed sexual desire. The language of that ancient time has been aptly described by this explicit imagery.

Agrawāl hints that Śiva's vehicle Nandī – the bull, or Śiva himself in the form of a bull – was termed *mahānagna.* The word Nandī literally means one who is satiated or one who is the source of joy. In the process of procreation, during sexual intercourse with the female principle, this satiated aspect of Nandī is expressed. Dr Agrawāl has called this aspect of Nandī, 'a joy-giving procreative seed'.

As a logical corollary, one would be tempted to conclude that if the male principle is to be visualised in the form of a bull, the earth or the human female would naturally be in the form of a cow. This expectation is totally consonant with the imagery created by the Vedas. Thus, the Vedas named both Aditi and Pṛthivī, as earth-cows.[16] According to *Nirukta*, "cow" is an alternative name for Pṛthivī.

> *gauriti pṛthivyā nāmadheyam* ।
> *yadasyām bhūtāni gacchanti*॥
>
> *Nirukta* (2.1.1)[17]
>
> (Gau is another name for Pṛthivī, the earth, because all living beings coalesce with her.)

In explaining the interpretation of the word *gau* as the earth, the composers of *Nirukta* suggested that etymologically the word *gau* comes from the verb *gam,* to go. The composers of *Nighaṇṭu* give the etymology of this word in the same way:

> *gauriti pṛthivyā nāmadheyam* ।
> *yaddūram gatā bhavati yaccāsyāṃ bhūtani gacchanti* ॥
>
> *Nighaṇṭu* (2.5)[18]
>
> (*gau* is the name of 'the earth'. This is because she keeps going away and because of that, all the living dissolve into her.)

The Purāṇas further extended this imagery of Pṛthivī – the earth as a cow. They give detailed descriptions of how various material gains were obtained by milking this cow at various times. They also describe who enacted the parts of the calf, the milkman and the container used to collect the milk each time. In examining the imagery of the lotus, we have already seen how the Gandharvas, who very much liked fragrances, made Citraratha the calf and milked the earth-cow in a lotus pot to obtain them. We are well aware that the Purāṇas contain many myths describing how the earth-mother, overburdened by the sins of the demons or by other violence and atrocities, assumes the form of a cow and goes to Paramātmā, the ultimate being. She persuades him to take an *avatāra* to destroy both the evil and the demons.

At a place called 'Jayarāmaswamīnce Vaḍagāv' in the Sātārā district of Mahārāṣṭra, a most interesting image of *Lajjāgaurī* has been found. On the right-hand side of this image is Nandī the bull.[19] *Lajjāgaurī* is of course '*mahāmātā*', the great earth mother. She is often imagined in the form of a cow. That is why Nandī is shown next to her in this image.

In Marāṭhi weddings, the groom often wears a *bāśiṅga* on his head. This custom has its origin in the belief that bulls represent the male principle in nature. These days, the *bāśiṅga* is nothing more than a fancy male and female ornament in wedding rituals. However, in the past, the *bāśiṅga* was a ritual necessity. A *bāśiṅga* is a crown with two horns. The word is made of two fragments: *bā* and *śiṅga*. *Bā* means two. For instance, in the Marāṭhi words bāvan (fifty-two), bāsaṣta (sixty-two) and bāhāttar (seventy-two), the prefix *bā* means two. It is obvious that the word *śiṅga* comes from the Saṃskṛt word *śṛṅga*. Therefore, the word *bāśiṅga*, which has the literal meaning 'two horns', denotes a headpiece with two horns. It is commonly known in English as a 'horn-dress'. Although a horn is a characteristic of an animal, why do we commonly use it as an ornament for the groom? We need to investigate why humans would want to assume the character of an animal at the time of their wedding.

Śṛṅga: The Mark of Manhood

The relationship between the *bāśiṅga* and the wedding ceremony is considered to be so close that when the time is ripe for a wedding to take place, Marāṭhī speakers use the idiom, '*bāśiṅgabaḷa ubhe rāhaṇe* (*Lit*: letting the strength of the *bāśiṅga* stand). When the wedding is over, they use the phrase, '*bāśiṅga suṭne*' (*Lit*: the *bāśiṅga* is now free to for use). If we think that a person is particularly suitable for a certain job, we say that the *bāśiṅga* for this job is written on his forehead. All of this means that, in a wedding ceremony, the *bāśiṅga* is a symbol of the groom's manhood. This obviously means that the animals whose characteristic mark is the *bāśiṅga* have traditionally been taken as symbols of manhood.

The bull, the he-buffalo and the stag are well-known as animals with horns. Among them, the bull occupies an extraordinarily important position in Indian culture. In our agrarian land, the bull has always been considered sacred. The Purāṇas consider him the vehicle of Śiva. With a great deal of respect, we refer to a valorous person as someone who is like a bull. In saying this, we most certainly do not wish to demean him by comparing him to an animal. Rather, we are proud of him this way. This inordinate importance given to the bull in Indian literature and in daily living has been so, since pre-Vedic times. This greatness of the bull in cultural traditions is certainly worthy of a major doctoral thesis. There is no need to provide superficial evidence to prove this point.

Etymologically the word *vṛṣabha* comes from the root *vṛṣa*, which means 'to sprinkle, to discharge, to shed'. Thus, the intended meaning is 'someone who discharges or sheds his seed'. Naturally, the *vṛṣabha*, because of his ability and innate tendency to shed his seed, has become the symbol of manhood. In relation to the earth and the sky, the *vṛṣabha* is a representative of the sky. By showering rain, he impregnates the earth. Thus, in an individual sense, he is the male who sheds his seed, while as a metaphor, he is the sky that showers the earth with rain. The notion that the waters from the sky are the seed that impregnates the earth and creates the vegetable kingdom has been expressed many times in various texts.[20] This close, loving and eternal relationship between the heavens and the earth is the subject of many hymns in the Vedas. Many a poet has sung a description of the everlasting relationship between mother earth and the heavens.

Power and Might for the Creation of the World

Although the *vṛṣabha* has been described by the Purāṇas as the vehicle of Śiva, it appears from Vedic references that, in earlier times, Rudra-Śiva was considered to be a *vṛṣabha*.[21] There are several instances in Indian mythology where a figure that was worshipped in a non-human form in the beginning was later worshipped in human form. In such cases, the image's earlier non-human form has been appropriated as the vehicle of the image in human form. This is what has happened in the case of Rudra-Śiva. In the beginning, he was in the form of a *vṛṣabha*. Later, the *vṛṣabha* became his vehicle. In the beginning, Viṣṇu himself was *suparṇa*, the eagle. Later, the eagle became his vehicle. Signs of Śiva being identified as *vṛṣabha,* the bull, can be seen in later Śaivite literature. Thus, the *Liṅgapurāṇa* gives Śiva various names that are connected with a horn, Śṛnga, viz. Dīptaśṛṅga, Ekaśṛṅga, and Śṛṅgin. The father of the world, according to Hindu mythology, is thus identified as one who possesses the *Śṛṅga*. This *Śṛṅga* is the symbol of his creative power and might.

The *liṅga* is the symbol of manhood and is capable of impregnating the earth and a woman. One sees a very direct manifestation of this belief in the *Bālakāṇḍa* of the *Rāmāyaṇa*, Sarga 9–10. According to this passage, a king named Romapāda ruled the kingdom of Aṅga. Because of a sin he had committed, there was a long drought in his kingdom. As a result, there was chaos everywhere. The king summoned his Brāhmins and asked them to perform a ritual to invoke rain. The Brāhmins advised him that Ṛṣyaśṛṅga, the son of the sage Vibhāṇḍaka, was a strict bachelor who had never yet seen a woman. They asked the king to send a prostitute to Ṛṣyaśraṅga in order to tempt him. That way, she could bring him to the king's kingdom. The king was further asked to give his daughter in marriage to Ṛṣyaśraṅga. The Brāhmins assured the king that, if he succeeded in doing so, the rains would come. The king did as they advised and gave his daughter Śāntā, in marriage to Ṛṣyaśraṅga. This resulted in breaking the drought in the country of Aṅga.

When king Daśaratha found out about this extraordinary regenerative potency of Ṛṣyaṣraṅga, he brought him to his capital, Ayodhyā, and performed the Putrakāmeṣṭī fire sacrifice with Ṛṣyaṣraṅga as the head priest.[22]

The inner meaning of these two tales from the *Rāmāyaṇa* is that the sage Ṛṣyaṣraṅga was able to produce rain and remove the barrenness of Daśaratha's queens. Ṛṣyaṣraṅga was a male with a Śṛṅga and his Śṛṅga came from a stag. This tale of Ṛṣyaṣraṅga sheds important light on the relationship of the horn (Śṛaṅga) and the ability of a potent male to produce children.

A Meaningful Term (*Arthavāhī Saṃjñā*)

One of the hymns of the *Ṛgveda* discusses the relationship of the gods Agnī, Soma and Indra and with the Śṛṅga.[23] The image of horn-wearing Paśupati found in the excavations at Mohenjo-daro is of course well-known. It is also well-known that other horned images have also been found at Mohenjo-Daro. There are many castes and sub-castes in India who make use of horns or a crown with horns for many of their celebrations, in particular weddings, even today. As a matter of fact, ancient civilizations in the world made the connection between a horn and the phallus. Marāṭhī proverbs such as '*śiṅga phuṭṇe*' (*Lit*: become extra smart), and '*śinge moḍūn vāsarāt śirṇe*' (*Lit*: break one's horn in order to be one with the young) also hint at a relationship between male potency and the horn. We have, however, lost the significance of the colourful *bāśiṅga* that adorns a groom at the time of the wedding. It spells out this ancient and all-pervading tradition. The *Viṣṇudharmottara Purāṇa* describes the horns of a bull with the beautiful and meaningful term, '*nidhiśṛṅga,*' the horn of plenty (cornucopia). If the bull represents virility, the power to impregnate and create and hence to generate plenty and prosperity, then his horn must be aptly recognised as the horn of plenty. Water sprinkled out of a horn is considered to be highly sacred and powerful.

When village women sing the exciting tale of Rukmiṇī's wedding (Svayaṃvar) to Kṛṣṇa while they grind grain under their grinding stone, we can see the importance of the *bāśiṅga* as they describe the defeat of the other suitor, Śiśupāla.

navarā śiśupāla |
yāca bāśiṅga moḍalam |
gelā rukmiṇa jitāyalā |
yālā apayaśa ghaḍalam ||
navarā śiśupāla |
bāśiṅga paḍala pāyānta |
rukmiṇī navarī |
nāhī tyācyā daivāta || [24]

(The groom Śiśupāla broke his *bāśiṅga*. He went to conquer Rukmiṇī but met with defeat. The groom Śiśupāla, his *bāśiṅga* fell on his feet. He was not destined to have Rukmiṇī as his bride.)

There is no need for me to explain further the relationship evident in these *ovīs* between the bāśiṅga and the manliness required to win a bride. It can be seen that this symbol of virility has achieved a deep-seated respect in folk culture and religion.

Aditi: Reṇukā

In order to make sure that the eternal wheel of life with its spokes of birth, death and re-birth keeps spinning, Aditi nourished the dead foetus in her womb once again. This phase of her life is indicative of her oneness with mother earth. Aditi is the same as mother earth, because she is the one responsible for the continuation of the wheel of life. By contrast, Reṇukā, worshipped only in the form of her generative organs, is mother earth in both her form and her name. It is therefore hardly surprising that the devotional literature about Reṇukā considers her identical with Aditi.

The Reṇukā-Māhātmya, which claims to be a part of the Sahyādrikhaṇḍa of the *Skandapurāṇa* claims that Reṇukā is an incarnation (*avatāra*) of Aditi. As the story goes, the gods were defeated in a battle with the demons. The worried gods surrendered to Viṣṇu and begged him to assume an *avatāra* in order to destroy the demons. Upon this, Viṣṇu promised the gods that:

aditeḥ sambhaviṣyāmi yadā garbhe surottamāḥ |
tadāhaṃ dvijarūpeṇa ghātayiṣyāmi dānavān ||
triḥsaptakṛtvaḥ pṛthivīṃ kṛtvā niḥkṣātriyāmaham |
brāhmaṇebhyaḥ pradāsyāmi dakṣiṇārthaṃ makhe śubhe ||
ekavīreti vikhyātā sarvakāmapradāyinī |
aditiryā madambā sā sambhaviṣyati bhūtale ||
tathāpi tāṃ prārthayadhvaṃ gacchadhvamadhunā surāḥ |
tatasyāṃ bhaviṣyāmi yadi sā dhārayiṣyati ||

Sahyādrikhaṇḍa, Renukāmāhātmya (1.14–17)[25]

(Oh great gods! When I take birth in Aditi's womb, I will be born as a Brāhmin who will destroy the demons. I shall annihilate all the Kṣatriyas from this earth twenty-one times. And I shall perform a fire sacrifice at which I shall donate that earth, devoid of the Kṣatriyas, to the Brāhmins. My mother Aditi, who is known to be the bestower of every wish (of the devotee), will be born as Ekvīrā and will be famous on this earth. I ask you to go to her right now and worship her. If she is prepared to carry my foetus in her womb, then I will be born as her son.)

Paraśurāma, one of the *avatāras* of Viṣṇu, is well-known to be the son of Reṇukā. Reṇukā is also Bhūdevī, mother earth. Her representation either in the form of her vagina or as an image displaying her vagina and her breasts, is highly significant. We have already discussed the myth that tries to explain her headlessness as being due to Paraśurāma, her son, cutting off her head.

As a matter of fact, all three 'Rāmas' are associated with Bhūdevī, mother earth. Bhārgava Rāma, alias Paraśurāma, is the son of the Bhūdevī named Reṇukā. Rāghava Rāma of the Rāmāyaṇa is the husband of the Bhūdevī named Sītā (Sītā literally means 'furrowed land'). Right from Vedic times, Sītā has been well known as 'fertile earth'. The author of the *Rāmāyaṇa*, Vālmīki, has described how both the birth and demise of Sītā, the heroine of the epic, is associated with mother earth. One also knows that the very name Vālmikī is derived from an anthill,[26] once again connecting it to the earth. The third Rāma is the Yādava Rāma, Balarāma. The name of his wife was Revatī, which is also the name of a mother goddess. Balarāma's weapon of choice is the *lāṅgala*, the plough. It is worth remembering that he himself is an *avatāra* of the mighty serpent Śeṣa. These three Rāmas, who are associated with Reṇukā, Sītā and Revatī, all have their names derived from the Saṃskṛt root, *ram*.[27] I have a strong feeling that the name Rāvaṇa is also derived from the same root. Rāvaṇa's wife is Maṇḍodarī (*Lit*: one who is sterile/infertile). If one ignores the details of the story of Rāma as described by Vālmikī and concentrates only on the meanings behind these names, one can say that Rāma is *ramaṇa*, the delightful one. His name signifies that his consort is appropriately pleased with him. On the other hand, the name Rāvaṇa is indicative of force. His beloved is Maṇḍodarī (*Lit*: infertile) and that is why he forcefully abducted Sītā (*Lit*: fertile).

I am well aware of my digression from the topic under discussion. It is just that after discussing Paraśurāma, the son of Reṇukā, I thought of the other three Rāmas, and my mind was filled with wave after wave of the myths about them. This discussion was therefore hard for me to contain. If these myths become historical truths tomorrow because of an appropriate piece of evidence, then I shall be more than happy. On the other hand, if they prove to be without substance, I am sure the intelligent readers will forgive me.

In the present context, the most important subject is of course Aditi, the mother earth. Having looked at her varied aspects and many splendoured forms, the possibility of finding even more of her forms cannot be discounted.

Rāṇḍāv Punav: Aheva Punav

In examining the history of *Mataṅgīpaṭṭa*, we had occasion to discuss Mātaṅgī, the one who has coalesced with Reṇukā, and Mātaṅgī's human representative, the Devadāsī. In addition, we have also seen how the three goddesses, Reṇukā, Yallammā and Mātaṅgī are identical with one another. Further, we have looked at the myths that give credence to the belief about the oneness of these deities. One gets a similar sense of *déjà vu* when one studies goddess Yallammā of Saundattī and her devadasī devotee called the Jogtīṇ (plural: Jogtīṇī). The latter tell us a lot about the cult of Yallammā.

The most famous shrine of Yallammā is at Saundattī, 110 miles from Kolhāpūr and 40 miles from the town of Hubḷī in Karnāṭaka. Thousands of devotees of Yallammā are spread throughout the districts of Beḷgāv, Vijāpūr and Hubḷī in Karnāṭaka, and at Kolhāpūr, Solāpūr, Sānglī and Miraj in the state of Mahārāṣṭra.

Just like the Mātaṅgīs, Jogtīṇi are also considered to be special devotees of Yallammā. As a matter of fact, they are looked upon as representatives of Yallammā in human form.[28] Everything to do with Jogtīṇi such as their initiation into Jogtīṇ-hood, the alms they ask for, the clothes they wear and their myths and songs is highly significant in the context of the worship of the mother-goddess. However, at this stage, rather than going into such matters in detail, we are going to look at an important ritual connected with the Jogtīṇi. This ritual involves breaking the bangles worn by a Jogtīṇ on a particular day and giving her fresh bangles on another day. Both of these days are chosen according to the Hindu calendar. The 'breaking of the bangles' ritual is called *raṇḍāv punav* and is performed on the full-moon day of the month of Māgha (February-March). The offering of new bangles is performed on the full-moon day of the month of Jyeṣṭha (June) and is called *aheva punav.* The four-month period from Māgha to Jyeṣṭha is considered to be the period of the goddess' widowhood. When one thinks about the timing of these rituals in relation to the earth mother, it becomes abundantly clear that the state of the earth after the crops have been harvested is very much suggestive of her 'widowhood'. On the other hand, when new crops are sown at the beginning of the agricultural year, her ability to bear their foetuses is indicative of her 'happily married (*saubhāgya*)' status. In the *Reṇukāmāhātmya*, which is composed in the *ovī* meter and which describes the importance of the holy place Saundattī, the idea of the four-month widowhood of Reṇukā has been discussed in relation to an episode in her biography. When king Kārtavīrya murdered Paraśurāma's father, Jamadagni, Paraśurāma took vengeance, came back to his mother after four months and brought his father back to life. The Ṛṣis then performed the marriage of Jamadagni and Reṇukā once again. However, by making slight changes to the tithī,[29] the custom of observing the widowhood of Reṇukā for four months during the period of Cāturmāsa remained with her devotees. That is the way myths work.

Potrāj and *Hijḍā*[30]

At this juncture, we must consider two classes of Goddess' devotees who are totally different from the Jogtīṇi. These are the *Potrāj* and the *Hijḍā*. It is important to know that both of these are males who move about in female form. The *Potrāj* becomes a female simply by changing his dress, but the *Hijḍā* becomes a woman by cutting off his male generative organ and thereby rejecting his maleness.

A *Potrāj* is a devotee of Marīāī or Māriammā, the mother goddess in South India. Only those belonging to the Mahār and Māṅga castes seek initiation as Potrājas. The *Potrāj* is also known as Kaḍakalakṣmī or Marīāī, the latter identifying him with the deity he worships. When a *Potrāj* comes to your doorstep, it is said that "the Marīāī's entourage has come".[31] While it is tempting, one must refrain at this stage from examining *baḍhaṇ*, the ritual used as an initiation ceremony for a *Potrāj*, the songs that he sings in praise of goddess Marīāī, the myths associated with those songs, his right to officiate at the worship of the goddess and the rituals he uses in doing so. It is, however, worth noting that the *vahyā*[32] that he knows by heart are very similar to folk songs sung by village women. In the words of Prabhākar Māṇḍe, the *Potrāj*'s songs are so similar to women's folk songs that they may actually be identified as such.[33]

Etymologically, the word *Potrāj* can be derived from two words, Poṭṭurāju and Poturāju, both having different meanings. Poṭṭu means either an anthill or the stomach. Potu means a male buffalo (*Skt.* Mahiṣa). A devotee of the goddess Mahiṣāsuramardinī would be tempted to derive the word *Potrāj* from Poturāju, the male buffalo, or the Mahiṣarāj, the king of the Mahiṣa. However, this etymology does not sit well with the female form that *Potrāj* normally assumes. If we start with the word Poṭṭu meaning stomach (*udara* in Saṃskṛt, also meaning the womb) then he becomes udararāj, the king of the stomach. The suffix rāj is commonly applied to feminine words in order to convert them to the masculine gender. Thus, Mohinī is the female *avatāra* of Viṣṇu and Mohinīrāj is another name for Viṣṇu. I therefore feel that in this instance, the word Poṭṭu, meaning the stomach (womb) is the origin. And since the *Potrāj* is the representative of the goddess in the form of an anthill or womb, he is called Poṭṭurāju, which later became *Potrāj*.

The other devotee of the goddess, *Hijḍā*, is originally a male. However, at the time of his initiation, he cuts off his sex-organ in order to become a female. Impotent men hide their impotence and often try to show their maleness in public. But these devotees of the goddess voluntarily cut off their male sex organ in order to assume the female form. Hijḍās are the devotee of a goddess by the name Becarā. It is thought that this name is derived from the word Bahucarā. However, with good reason, I feel that Becarā is derived from the word dvicarā. It is common knowledge that the Saṃskṛt word *dvi* becomes *be* in many languages. Dvicarā would therefore mean *ardhanārīsvarūpiṇī*, the goddess who moves about in both the male and female forms. As a name, Dvicarā resonates well the hermaphrodite form taken by the *Hijḍā*.

Another aspect of both the *Potrāj* and the *Hijḍā* is the fact that they have both chosen the female gender in spite of being males beforehand. Why did they choose to do so? Was there a time when the devotee of a goddess was forced to do so? Is this a relic of an ancient custom? To answer these questions, we will have to go far back in history, not a hundred, but thousands of years.

In ancient society in the distant past, mothers and mother goddesses reigned supreme. In the cults of these mother goddesses, only priestesses were allowed. Males were not only forbidden to enter the sacred area, but it was also decreed that if they did so by mistake, they would be converted to females. Tales of forests inhabited only by women, where men were not allowed, appear many times in the Purāṇas.[34] Later on, when men took hold of the priesthoods in such places, the idea of forbidding such encroachments still remained. It was for this reason that those men who undertook priestly duties at such places chose to transform themselves into females. The *Potrāj* and the *Hijḍā* are two living examples of such devotees who converted themselves into females in order to become the goddess' priests. One of them did so by simply changing his attire, the other by cutting his male organ. The dictum of the Tāntrics, 'one should worship *parā* (Śakti) by becoming a female,' is an example of this ancient tradition.

The belief and tradition of excluding men from the cults of goddesses is reflected indirectly in the myth associated with the birth of

Skanda in the *Bṛhaddharmottarapurāṇa*. In order to destroy the demon Tāraka, a general with the lustre and valour of Śiva needed to be born. For this reason, the gods plotted and organized the union of Śiva and Umā. However, even though a hundred god-years elapsed, their intercourse would not stop. The gods therefore got very worried and sent some Brāhmins to disturb their privacy.

The *Bṛhaddharmottara* Purāṇa says:

> *viprān dṛṣtvā tadā devī vrīḍitā pidadheṃ 'śukam* |
> *devīprītyai sthalaṃ tattu śivaśaptaṃ tato 'vadhi* ||
> *puṃsāmagamyaṃ samabhūt puṃsām strītvakaraṃ dvija* |
> *sthānabhraṣṭha śivastejastatyāja pṛthivītale* ||
>
> *Bṛhaddharmottarapurāṇa* (53.54–55)[35]
>
> (After seeing the Brāhmins in that private place, the goddess was highly abashed and immediately put her clothes on. Because of the fact that he was interrupted at the height of coition, Śiva spilled his seed on earth. In order to please the goddess, he uttered a curse that, from now on, no man would be able to enter this place. If a man does come here in spite of this injunction, he will be transformed into a female.)

There is no doubt that there lies behind this myth the thought that males ought to be forbidden from the place where the Devī reigns, and the subsequent transformation of the male into a female if a male transgresses this rule. It is but natural that the authority of priesthood for the worship of the mother goddess should rest with females alone. When males did encroach on this territory, they were unable to totally do away with this prohibition. In order to find a way out of this situation, they symbolically accepted their transformation into females. They did this symbolically either by wearing women's clothes or by destroying their male sexual organs.

The *Bṛhaddharmottarapurāṇa* thus describes two conditions necessary for obtaining the rights to the worship of mother earth and allied deities. The first is that the devotee must be a female and the second is for the male to symbolically turn himself into a female. The two adjectives used in this context, *puṃsāmagamyaṃ* (*Lit*: forbidden for males) and *puṃsām strītvakaraṃ* (*Lit*: by changing the male into a female) are used to describe the worship at goddess shrines, and they precisely describe the above.

Let us now look at two places of the worship of such a goddess, which are both more or less neglected. In that process, we will also look at two other goddesses in her class and also at the *kṣetrapatī*. It is only then that we will be able to satisfactorily conclude this discussion.

The Goddess Ānandī at Āḷand

There was an ancient place of worship for the goddess *Lajjāgaurī* at Āḷand (Āḷand-Gunjoṭī), 16 miles from Gulbargā in the state of Karnāṭaka. Mahārāṣṭrians however know this place for a different reason: it is the place which houses the memorial stone of saint Tukāram's parātpara-guru,[36] Rāghava-Caitanya.

From the 11th century C.E. onwards, Āḷand was known as a wealthy and cultured town.[37] A goddess with the name Alandī or Ānandī was the tutelary deity of this town, and the town's name was probably derived from her name. This goddess and Śiva with the name of Someśvara were housed in the same compound in two separate large temples. On one of the walls of the goddess temple, there is an inscription dated '*pauṣa śuddha pancamī*' in the Śaka 1005 (27th December 1082 C.E.), inscribed by the Cālukya king Tribhuvanamalla Vikramāditya. The inscription mentions Someśvara, goddess Ālandī and a highly regarded Vedic school run by one Sureśvarācārya. Another inscription, this one found at Ablūr and dated around the same time (1200 C.E.), describes in a flowery and poetic style, the beauty, exuberance and plenitude of this city. The inscription says that the city of Āḷand is an ornament to Kuntal Pradeś and is home to various arts and religious preceptors. We have seen that the place was known as Āḷand (because of the tutelary goddess Ālandī) or Ānandavana. Similarly, it was also known as Somanāthapurī because of the presence of Śiva, present there as Somanātha. The place was also known as 'Ālanda hajārī', perhaps because it was the place from where a thousand (hajār) smaller towns were governed.

The shrine of goddess Ālandī at this place must have been very well known. It also appears to have been under the influence of Śākta tāntrics for a long time. We have stated earlier that Saint Tukāram's parātpara-Guru, Rāghava-Caitanya, who was a tāntric, stayed here around 1500 C.E. In the early part of the 16th century, he took his Mahāsamādhi[38] in the same compound as the goddess' temple. Rāghav-Caitanya is known to have composed tāntric hymns for Gaṇeśa and the goddess Jvālāmukhī. The fact that he chose, not only to stay within the temple complex, but also to end his mortal life at the place, tells us a great deal about the importance of this shrine for the tāntrics of the time.

Not long after Rāghav-Caitanya's demise, in the latter part of the 16th century, Muslim invaders occupied this place and destroyed the temples. Rāghav-Caitanya's memorial was converted into the shrine of a fictitious Sufi saint (avaliyā). The biography of this imaginary Sufi saint was elaborately constructed, and he was given the name Lāḍale Maśāyakha. Both Someśwara and Ālandī were completely uprooted from this place. Today, this same Goddess Ālandī can be found in a small village called Honnahaḷī, about 3 kilometres from the town of Āḷand. Her little shrine is in a totally neglected state (see Plate 20).

The locals at this place call her Yallammā. They call Someśwara by the name Iraṇṇā. In the present context, it is most important to remember that the form of goddess Ālandī at Honnahaḷḷī is identical to that of *Lajjāgaurī*. In folk religion, she is called Yallamā. This strange image of the goddess is explained quite differently within the Hindu and Muslim traditions. The myth according to the Hindu tradition is given in a work by the name *Nāgeśalīlāmṛta*. It says:

> This savage and cruel goddess used to reside on the outskirts of the town. Every three years, she demanded the sacrifice of a Brāhmin and also some other food. When one of Rāghav-Caitanya's disciples went into the town to seek alms, he heard loud wailing from a Brāhmin family's home. When he went to investigate the cause of the wailing, he was told that the old woman in the family was crying because her son was going to be sacrificed to the goddess on that day. Upon hearing this, the disciple went back to Rāghav-Caitanya, sought his permission to intervene and came back to the village with a staff and some ashes collected from Rāghav-Caitanya's feet. With the Brāhmin boy, he went to see the goddess' shrine. When they were near the goddess, the disciple threw the ashes and the staff at her. The staff repeatedly hit the goddess on her back while the ashes hit her on her face. The goddess was so harassed by this that she started fleeing the scene. Finally, she fell flat on her face on the outskirts of Honnahaḷī and surrendered to Rāghav-Caitanya. Thereupon, he established her in a shrine in the same position that he had found her in (lying prostrate on her face). People started worshipping her again.

> After that, the goddess discontinued her custom of requiring human sacrifice.

The Muslim myth by contrast, says that when the Sufi Saint Lāḍle Maśāyakh came and stayed in the compound of the goddess temple, the goddess was scared of him and started running away. While running, she became unconscious and fell on her face. She is found in the same position today.

During his research on the guru-tradition of Sant Tukāram, B.C. Bendre collected a great deal of information about the biography of Rāghav-Caitanya. Based on that information, he comments that:

> In the precinct of the Someśvara temple at Āḷand, there used to be a shrine for goddess Āḷandī as well. After 1562, the Sultans in the Deccan probably got together and destroyed Hindu temples *en masse*. This was particularly true in the area of Āḷand-Gunjoṭī. During this time, the well-known temples at Āḷand were also destroyed. Either the Muslim soldiers removed and threw away the goddess image or the townsfolk may have deliberately spirited it away in order to protect it. In any case, the goddess image was taken to the village of Honnahaḷī, one and half miles from Āḷand. It was probably removed in a great hurry and the locals then must have tried to bury it face down so as to protect it. To this day, the Goddess image is still in the same position, and the image's posterior is what is worshipped at present. Annual celebrations are also held.

The facts that this goddess carries the popular name Yallammā and that it is her posterior that is worshipped tell us that her present physical state is not due to any calamities but, on the other hand, is quite natural. Attempts to explain away her strange, unconventional and almost obscene image have obviously resulted in the creation of these myths and other explanations. When Brāhmins took control of her shrine, she was denigrated and even cast aside. It is clear that the explanations for her lower status, her neglect and her being cast aside from Brāhminic Hindu practices would have been supported by convenient explanations and myths.

The name Āḷandī (Ānandī) for this goddess is obviously artificial. It is nothing but a transformation of the popular name Yallammā. Just as Ālampūr is a transformation of the word Ellammāpura, so is Āḷand (Āland), which is the name of the place, so named after its tutelary deity, the goddess Āḷandī. The name Āḷandī Devī is based on the transformation l -> ḷ-> n. Similarly, the *Nāgeśalīlāmṛta* has transformed Āḷand into Anand. This reminds me of the town of Āḷandī in Mahārāṣṭra, known solely because of saint Jñāneśvar. Just as the words Āḷand and Āḷandī are very similar, in the same way, the work *Āḷandīmāhātmya* discusses the words Anandavipin and Anandawana. The place Anandavipin is mentioned in the *Āḷandīmāhātmya*. I am therefore tempted to ask myself whether the tutelary deity of Jñāneśvara's Āḷandī was at some stage Yallammā in the form of *Lajjāgaurī*, similar to the Āḷandī Devī of Āḷand. Yallammā, in her form as *Lajjāgaurī*, assumed the respectable name Āḷandī Devī at Āḷand and stayed with her consort Someśvara. Is it then possible that Ellammā, in her form of *Lajjāgaurī*, stayed at Jñāneśvara's Āḷandī with her consort Siddheśvara? At this stage, we do not have enough evidence to express any opinion about this. If, however, we do obtain such evidence, we would be able to study her relationship to Jñāneśvara's writing and scholarship.

The *Lajjāgaurī* at Ālāpura[39]

In 1973, at a place called Bhokardan in the Aurangābād district of Marāṭhawāḍā, several images of goddess *Lajjāgaurī* were found. Although Bhokardan is a Talukā place, today it is only an ordinary small town with a population of about 10,000 which still holds the shattered remains of its glorious past. In the ancient past, even before the time of the Sātavāhanas, it was a great city that was a centre of culture and wealth lying on the main road from Ujjayinī to Pratiṣṭhān. The present name, Bhokardan, has come from its ancient name, Bhogavardhan (*Lit*: that which augments one's worldly pleasures) which aptly describes its prosperity and exuberance in the hoary past. The prevalent local myth considers the city to be the capital of king Bhaumāsura, who was an arch enemy of Lord Kṛṣṇa. Plenty of stone inscriptional evidence indicates that many of the rich and pious citizens of this city financially supported the construction of the famous Sāñci and Bhārhut *stūpas*.

A Śaivite cave temple constructed in the heydays of the Raṣṭrakūṭa kings, around the 8th century C.E., can be found on the left bank of the river Keḷṇā here. There is enough evidence to suggest that the beginnings of Śaivism in this area are a great deal older than this. A stone inscription that has been recently found records the donation of a piece of land in Bhokardan by the Mahiṣmatī Kalacūrī king Śaṅkaragaṇa, to a Brāhmin in 597 C.E.

All of this goes to show that, even before the reign of the Sātavāhanas, Bhokardan was a prosperous city. There were a large number of businessmen at Bhokardan, who were followers of Buddhism. After the reign of the Guptas, the influence of Buddhism waned and Śaivism rose in prominence.

With this background, we will now investigate the possibility of the worship of a folk goddess such as *Lajjāgaurī* in this area of prosperity and plenty. In the excavation around this area, two stone images have been discovered. Both are typical headless images displaying breasts and vagina. Experts are of the opinion that the reddish stone on which the first image is carved belongs to the period of around the 5th or 6th century C.E., i.e., it was carved after the rule of the Sātavāhanas. The other image is broken on its left-hand side. Lotuses are drawn on the right side of this image. Looking at the placement of these lotuses, one can reasonably conclude that they were carved on all three sides of this image. It has not been possible to date the image.

The information that is important for us is the fact that these two images were found not actually at Bhokardan, but at a place called Ālāpūr, a small village in the hills near Bhokardan. Present day Bhokardan is situated in the hills on the right bank of the river Keḷṇā, among several ancient ruins. Ālāpūr is situated on the left bank of the river and has not been encroached upon by the present-day population of the area.

As soon as I heard the name Ālāpūr, I was immediately reminded of the verse that lists the eighteen Śaktipīṭhas, namely, '*ālāpure yugulā devī*'. In chapter two of this volume, when we examined the mother goddess Joguḷāmbā at Ālampūr, we learned that, according to Paṇḍurangarāv Desāī, Joguḷāmbā was one of the eighteen Śakti goddesses and Ālampūr was the sacred seat (Śaktipīṭha) where her shrine was situated. However, now that we know that *Lajjāgaurī* images have been found at the place Ālāpūr near Bhokardan, there should be no doubt in our minds that goddess *Lajjāgaurī* was the presiding deity of this Ālāpūr near Bhokardan.[40] A Śaivite rock carved cave has been found at Ālāpūr, and there is an almost totally worn-out stone inscription on one of its walls. If only one could read this inscription, one may have been able to say what part the *Lajjāgaurī* image found at this place played in the development of the Śaiva and Śākta sects at this place.

I realise that it is futile talking about this now. The only thing one can say is that the name of the place Ālāpur, like the discovery of *Lajjāgaurī* images at this place near Bhokardan, resonates well with the verse, *'ālāpure yugulā devī'*. This description is equally valid for the place Ālampūr in Āndhra Pradeś as well.

Sānterī and Saptakoṭeśvara

In chapter 8, Jotibā, we saw that the relationship between Sānterī and Ravaḷanātha was that of a *Kṣetra* (*Lit*: field) and *Kṣetrapatī* (protector of the field). The name Sānterī for this goddess is thought to be derived from the word Sāntere, meaning an anthill. This view seems to have some substance. Thus, although goddess Sānterī is normally worshipped in the form of an image at many places, people in Goa and south Konkaṇ worship her in the form of an anthill. Since an anthill is formed from the soil of the earth (*bhūmī*), it is also called *bhom* (< *bhaum*) or *bhombāḍā*. And when this bhūmī is worshipped in the form of a goddess, the latter is often called 'bhūmikā devī'.

Sānterī is also worshipped as Śāntādurgā, a highly respected and popular goddess of Goa. In the state of Karnāṭaka, she is called Śāntalā Devī; a name commonly used to name newborn girls. On occasion, she has also been called Sateśvarī. The three names – Sānterī, Sateśvarī and Saptakoṭīśvara – sound phonetically similar to one another. When I looked at the phonetic similarity among these three names, I suddenly thought of a totally different possible etymology of the name Sānterī. The reader will remember that in the discussion about the maternal home of the earth in Chapter Seven, I looked at the significance of the lotus and its relationship with goddess Vyāghreśvarī and suddenly found a link there. In a similar manner, I thought that a similar logic may lead me to unravelling the mystery behind the similar-sounding names, Sānterī, Sateśvarī and Saptakoṭīśvara. The link here is the meaning of the word, *satta* in the Kannaḍā language. We have seen that the word *bagga* means either a tiger or a lotus in Kannaḍā. Similarly, *satta* is also a word with two meanings in the Kannaḍā language. It is possible to look at this word etymologically in two ways:

satta (< *sapta*: Saṃskṛt) = *sāt* (seven)
*satta (*originally a Kannaḍā word) = ashamed

The original Kannada word *satta* is closely related to the state of being ashamed due to nakedness. The transformation of the Saṃskṛt word *sapta* in Kannaḍā is *satta.* Conversely, the phonetic conversion of the Kannaḍā word *satta* (which means nakedness or being ashamed) would naturally be *sapta* in Saṃskṛt. We have seen previously that the lord and master (Nāth) of Mahākoṭeśvarī became Mahākoṭeśvara. It would therefore not be unreasonable to conclude that, by a similar process, the lord and master of Sattakoṭīśvarī became Saptakoṭīśvara.

It is often said that etymologically, the word *saptakoṭī* is derived from *yeḷkoṭī* (In Kannaḍā *yeḷ* = seven, *koṭī* = 100 lakhs). However, when we think of the way Sānterī is worshipped, we are left in no doubt that she is none other than the mother-goddess who is worshipped in her form as the genetrix, i.e., it is her vagina that is worshipped. With this background, one must then reason that the meaning of the word *yeḷkoṭī* would be 'the naked Yallammā (yeḷ = yallammā, koṭṭa = naked).

The *Taraṅgas* of Sānterī-Ravaḷanātha

In the worship regimen of Goan deities such as Sānterī, Pāvṇāī, Ravaḷanātha and Bhūtanātha (see Plate 21), the *taraṅg* plays an important part. The neuter word *taraṅg* is used to describe a one to two-metre decorated pole. The decorations involve bands painted in various colours. Other names for this pole are *khāmb* and *niśāṇa*. In Goa and the Southern Konkaṇ, most temples have deities called '*taraṅg*'. These *taraṅgs* have, attached to them, male or female brass or silver masks, the palm print of a hand, or a pot. According to information supplied by Mr. Bāmbarḍekar,[41] on special occasions, these *taraṅgs* are dressed in either a dhoti (for a male) or a saree (for a female) and worshipped as such. P.R. Behere[42] however says that the *taraṅgs* have either a cobra-hood, an impression of a hand or a female mask on them but there is never a male mask. In most places, these *taraṅgs* represent the three deities, Pāvṇāī, Ravaḷanātha and Bhūtanātha. The deities represented can vary according to the place of their worship and their number can be less than three as well. However, one can always be sure that a *taraṅg* for Ravaḷanātha will always be there. This obviously means that the main *taraṅg* is that of Ravaḷanātha. The pujārī who carries it during a procession is always the Gurav (the priest for the *kṣetrapālas* in charge of the field).

When I started analysing the information that the locals had about the *taraṅgas*, the thought came to my mind that a *taraṅg* is a piece of wood and it therefore bears a correlation with the hood of a cobra. We have already seen that the neuter word *taraṅg* is mainly associated with Ravaḷanātha, the god of the fields and the husband of the earth mother. When we looked at the devotees of Yallammā and Joguḷāmbā, we saw the great importance attached to the wooden post with a carved hood of the cobra on top. We also looked at the symbolism behind this. The Goan couple Sānterī and Ravaḷanātha are nothing but the *kṣetra* and *kṣetrapatī* (the field and her master). Also, Ravaḷanātha's consort Sānterī is worshipped as the 'Bhūmikā Devī' (mother earth) in her anthill form. It is well known that Yallammā and Mātaṅgī are also worshipped in their anthill forms. We can now understand why the *taraṅg* in the form of a wooden pole with a carved cobra hood on top holds such importance in the worship of Ravaḷanātha and the goddesses associated with him.

The only question that now remains is the etymology of the word *taraṅg*. We know that a *taraṅg* is in the shape of a wooden pole with a carved cobra hood on one end. We also know that a cobra-shaped pole is shaped like a phallus. It would not therefore be unreasonable to assume that symbolically, the *taraṅg* would be looked upon as a phallus. The words *liṅga*, *lāṅgal* and *lagula* have their origin in the Austric words *laga* and *laṅga*. One can think of a hypothetical alternative *tlaṅg* for these words as well. *tlaṅg* could become *talaṅga* by vowel transformation. The easy conversion between l and r could then produce the form *taraṅg* which would denote a phallus. One must remember that this etymology is based not only upon similar-sounding words but also upon the shape of the *taraṅg* itself.

Koṭṭavai: The Naked Mother Goddess

When we considered the etymology of the names Mahākoṭeśvarī, Mahākūṭa and Saptakoṭeśvarī, we directed our thoughts to the root *koṭṭa*, meaning naked, in all of these words. In old Tamil literature, there is a region of Tamilnadu called Pālai which had a goddess called Koṭṭavai, who belonged to the tribal people in the area. Koṭṭavai alias Korravai, was a goddess of the forest in the beginning. She used to ensure victory to her valorous devotees and was given human sacrifices in return. Although she had a ferocious character in the beginning, at a later stage she coalesced with Pārvatī. She became the consort of Śiva and became identical with Vindhyavāsinī and Mahiṣāsuramardinī. As a result, her only son, the well-known *kṣetrapāla* deity Muruga, coalesced with Skanda, the son of Śiva and Pārvatī.

Dr Vāsudevaśaraṇ Aggrawāl[43] describes Koṭṭavai succinctly. He writes:[44]

> Koṭṭavai was a mother goddess in South India and her worship was prevalent everywhere. Initially a demoness, she began to be worshipped either as Umā or Durgā at a later stage.

> Based on his study of Jain scriptures, Jagadīśacandra Jain has described the festival of goddess Koṭṭakiriyāmaha alias Koṭṭakriya. The *Nāyādhammaṭikā* mentions that when Durgā rides a mahiṣa,[45] she is called Koṭṭakriyā. This indicates that Mahiṣāsuramardinī and Koṭṭakriyā were goddesses belonging to either a similar or even the same retinue in the past. Their worship was prevalent amongst the tribes. The *Bhāgavata Purāṇa* has mentioned that the name of Bāṇāsura's mother was Koṭarā.[46] The naked goddess Koṭarā was one and the same as the South Indian Koṭṭavai. In his *Harṣacarita*, Bāṇabhaṭṭa has mentioned that the sight of Koṭavī was considered inauspicious. The commentator Śaṅkara says that the word Koṭavī means a 'naked woman'. The nakedness of Koṭavī in the commentary by the critic Śaṅkara resonates well with the description of Koṭarā given in the *Bhāgavata Purāṇa*. According to the composer Keśava of the Kalpadrukoṣa,[47] Koṭavī was one of the forms of goddess Ambikā. In his commentary on the Abhidhāna-Cintāmaṇī, Hemacandra (12th century C.E.), has described Koṭavī as a naked woman with loose hair.[48]

The worship of Koṭavī was prevalent among the ancient tribes. From there, she coalesced with many fierce and savage goddesses bearing various names and became popular from the south of India to the north. During my researches, when I was looking for evidence and artefacts about the worship of Yakṣas and goddesses in the ancient times, I was lucky enough to find a small shrine dedicated to Koṭmāī right on the grounds of the University of Benares. Koṭmāī is obviously none other than Koṭavī. Later on, I learned that in the district of Almorā there is a place called Koṭalgaḍh twelve miles from the place called Lohadhar. The local myth at this place says that this was the hillock which had the shrine of goddess Koṭṭavī. Koṭṭavī was the mother of the demon Bāṇāsura. The upper half of her body was clad with armour while the lower half was naked... This goes to show that the goddess variously called Koṭakriyā, Koṭarā, Koṭavī, Koṭmāī, Koṭṭavaī was worshipped from the south of India to the base of the Himālayas.

While he was surveying the archaeological finds in the state of Gujarat, Dr Sāṅkaliā mentioned a temple dedicated to the goddess Koṭṭamahikādevī.[49] An inscription mentions that Dhruvasena II renovated this temple in 639–640 CE. and re-instated the gift of a regular amount of money for the upkeep and worship at this temple, which had been discontinued by the State for some reason. Jackson, who first edited this inscription, mentions that this shrine was known as Koṭṭarādevi. The same inscription also states that the original temple was built by king Droṇasiṃha at a place called Trisaṅgamak, before it was renovated by Dhruvasena II. Trisaṅgamak is the present-day place called Tarasamiyā.[50]

When I was mulling over the name Koṭṭamahikādevī, it suddenly occurred to me that goddess Mahikāvatī, the presiding goddess of the town of Mahikāvatī (the present-day town of Keḷve-Māhīm near Mumbai) could possibly be goddess Koṭṭamahikādevī. This is because the large and imposing image of goddess Mahikāvatī, which lies horizontally, can still be seen in this shrine today.

Legend has it that Hanumān, the great devotee of Lord Rāma, kicked her, she fell flat on the ground and that is why she lies in this strange position.[51] It is also said that this goddess was worshipped regularly by Ahirāvaṇa and Mahirāvaṇa. The reasoning that has been offered to explain the strange position of the goddess at Āḷand is very similar to the explanation that is put forward here to comment on the unusual position of the goddess Mahikāvatī.

In 1973, I published a booklet called 'Śaktipīṭhāncā Śodha', that included the first two chapters of the present volume. I had sent this booklet to many scholars. In that context, it is worth noting what my researcher friend from Aurangābād, Brahmānanda Deśpāṇḍe, said in a letter to me dated 19th June 1975. Deśpāṇḍe says:

> Our family is originally from Karnāṭaka. My mother's grandmother was a Kannaḍā speaker. My mother's speech always contained a number of words from a village folk dialect from Kannaḍā language. When my little sister ran around without clothes on or laughed aloud shamelessly, my mother would always call her a '*Koṭakāi*'. While they were playing, her friends would make a big racket and my mother would address them as '*sāṭkāyā-koṭkāyā*'.[52]
>
> Therefore, it is possible that in our household, a shameless naked female was referred to as 'koṭkāī', without us being aware of the real meaning of the word.

The above information provided by Professor Brahmānanda Deśpāṇḍe is very definitely useful in throwing light on the original form of the goddess Koṭavī-Koṭṭakiriyā. In the same letter, Deśpāṇḍe also writes that he has in his possession an image of a naked female with raised legs from Māhurazarī. Finally, it is worth noting that Bahirā Jātaveda has, in his *Daśamaṭīkā* (6.156), mentioned Koṭarā as a 'Vighnadevatā' (calamity-causing goddess).

Mhaskobā: A Lord of the Field (*Kṣetrapatī*)

Similarly to Jotibā, who is the Lord of goddess Yamāī, to Ravaḷanāth, the Lord of Sānterī, and to Khaṇḍobā the Lord of goddess Mhāḷsā, Mhaskobā in his form as Bhairava is the Lord of goddess Jogeśvarī. He is very popular all over Mahārāṣtra with his main shrine being at Vīr in Purandar district. His main devotees are the Dhangars. Therefore, it is likely that he may be related to the god Birobā[53] of the Dhangars. Traditional information about Mhaskobā is contained in the Marāṭhī work, *Śrīnātha Mhaskobā devāce caritra* (*Lit*: The Biography of the god, Śrīnātha Mhaskobā), which has undergone several reprints.[54] On examining this work in detail, one is able to deduce the original form of this god.

According to the Dhangars, Mhaskobā of Vīr originated from the Bhairava of Sonārī. The myth that the Dhangars tell states that a Dhangar named Kamḷājī had his sheep and cattle[55] at Sonārī.[56] While at Sonārī, he visited the Bhairava shrine regularly and worshipped the god according to the Dhangar tradition. His sheep and cattle then moved away from Sonārī to a place called Borban on the banks of the Nīrā river. However, he was still very much devoted to the Bhairava at Sonārī. At the time of his regular daily worship, Kamḷājī used to meditate upon the Bhairava, and, in that state of trance, he would visit Sonārī and perform the pūjā there. The pujārīs at the temple could not make any sense of this mystery and decided to investigate this strange mode of worship. The god told Kamḷājī not to come all the way to see him at Sonārī. Instead, the god would come to Borban. When the dead Hivar tree next to Kamaḷājī's place would come alive and get fresh leaves, Kamaḷājī was to understand that the god had arrived at Borban. The god came in the form of a cobra with five heads. He would wrap himself around a virgin cow and drink milk from her four udders with four of his heads. Then he would assume a miniature form and happily settle himself on Kamaḷājī's woollen blanket. This kept happening for an entire year. When Kamaḷājī's father found out about this, he was petrified. Therefore, the god told Kamaḷājī that he should put him into a nearby anthill. Kamaḷājī did as he was told. The children of the farmer who owned the farm containing the anthill ploughed the farm and destroyed the anthill, in spite of Kamaḷājī's protestations. As a result of this, those children suddenly died. The farmer approached Kamaḷājī and sought his forgiveness for his children. Because of Kamaḷājī's devotion to the god, the children came alive again. When the plough near the anthill was removed, the god appeared there as an autochthonous stone. This stone is the present-day image of Mhaskobā.

This myth about the appearance of the God Mhaskobā at Vīr sheds important light on his original form. Originally, he is a *kṣetrapāla*, a Bhairava. He resides in an anthill and gives darśan to his devotees in the form of a cobra with five heads. The myth about his appearance in this form shows his similarity to the well-known *kṣetrapāla* gods Jotibā, Ravaḷanāth, Murugā and Subrahmaṇya. The distinguishing features that he has in common with these gods are certainly not limited to his often appearing as a cobra for his devotees. They also relate more to the special powers that he holds for them. Mhaskobā is considered by his devotees to be the remover of snake poison. However severe the snake bite is, if the affected person is taken to the temple of Śrināthа (Mhaskobā), given some lemon juice and made to circumambulate the sanctum, the person is most certainly cured. This is true not only for the place where his shrine is, but at other places as well. Thus, when a Dhangar goes to distant places such as Khāndeś and if he is affected there, he only has to look in the direction of the town of Vīr, utter the name of Śrinātha and pray, and he gets better. In addition to Mhaskobā's ability to remove snake poison, he is also known to have the munificence to grant children to those of his devotees who do not have them. With deep devotion, his biographer has noted that those women who had no children did conceive after they started worshipping God Śrināth.

Mhaskobā's annual fair starts on the full-moon day of the light half of the lunar month of Māgha[57] (Māgha Śukla Paurṇimā: *Lit:* full moon day in the month of Māgha) and lasts until the tenth day of the dark half of the same month. During this festival, Mhaskobā marries goddess Jogeśvarī. Thousands of Dhangars and devotees of other castes gather for this fair. The place resounds with the loud chanting of 'cāṅg bhale'. Grated coconut and gulāl[58] are sprinkled liberally. Men engage in the sport of swinging wooden poles. Devotees sing the *pavāḍs*[59] of the god. All of these characteristics of the annual fair of Mhaskobā are almost identical to those practised at the fair for Jotibā. As a matter of fact, the fairs are so similar that a devotee attending Mhaskobā's fair would feel that he is attending Jotibā's fair instead.

One more speciality of this fair that is worth noting is that a Kolhāṭīṇ[60] has the right of dancing in front of the god for nine days at the temple during this festival. This dancer firmly believes that the goddess will curse her if she does not perform during this festival.

The *Gaṅgotrī* of Yoginī Kaul Sect

The couple, *Kṣetra* and *Kṣetrapatī* in folk religion, was transformed into Śakti and her Bhairava by Śākta Tāntrikas. The story of how the devotional sect of a folk goddess at the Tryambakakṣetra in Mahārāṣtra was transformed into a Śākta tantric sect is both fascinating and revealing. Although the greatness of *Tryambakakṣetra* has often been expressed in our devotional literature, the collection of the stories, myths and Vedic background of this sacred place is to be found in the *Tryambakakṣetramāhātmya*.[61] This work claims to be a part of the *Padmapurāṇa* and consists of thirty-four chapters (*adhyāyas*) which contain a total of 1718 verses. This *Sthalamāhātmya* describes the religious significance and greatness of mountains such as Brahmagirī, sacred and meritorious waters such as the Godāvarī and deities such as Tryambakeśvara. Also incorporated into it are myths and stories about the cultural happenings and changes that took place here. While it is difficult to say with any certainty when this Māhātmya was composed, the cultural history of Tryambakeśvara Kṣetra that is described here definitely belongs to a period before the 12th or 13th century C.E.

The mountain Brahmagirī is thought to be Śiva himself. The left fork of this mountain is called Nīlagirī and is considered to be the left hand of Śiva.[62] It is said that Śiva held Pārvatī's hand with tender loving care and made her sit on the left side of his lap on the Nīlagirī mountain.[63] Pārvatī, known also as Bhavanī, is thus *nīlaparvatavāsinī* (one who lives on the Nīlagirī) here and is called Nīlāmbā. However, although the composer of this Māhātmya calls the mother of the world Nīlāmbā, he also says that she is none other than Reṇukā and describes the intense pleasure one obtains when one gets her darśan. He says:

> *nīlaparvatavāsinyā reṇukāyāḥ padāmbujam* |
> *ye paśyanti narā rājan na te yānti punarbhavam* ||
>
> *Śritryambakakṣetramāhātmyaṃ* (7.32)[64]

(Oh King! Those mortals who are fortunate enough to see the lotus-feet of goddess Reṇukā who resides on the Nīlaparvata, are

> without doubt rendered free from the repetitive cycles of birth and reach *mokṣa*.

The Nīlagirī mountain is not only the abode of Reṇukā, but it is also well-known as the *siddhikṣetra*[65] for the god Dattātreya. By reiterating its importance as a *siddhikṣetra* and an abode of God Dattātreya,[66] the composer of the māhātmya informs us that the great Paraśurāma obtained a *siddhi* here.[67]

After examining these details about the Nīlagirī mountain in the *Tryambakakśetramāhātmya*, one can see that on the left fork of Brahmagirī, there is an ancient and well-known shrine of the goddess Reṇukā. Also, similar to Māhūr, which is the most famous *kṣetra* for goddess Reṇukā, this shrine also shows the same mythological connections between Reṇukā, Dattātreya, and Paraśurāma.

On the southern side of Brahmagirī, there is a shrine for the goddess Kolāmbā. The author of the Māhātmya firmly believes that the goddess Kolāmbā is the same as the goddess Nīlāmbā on the Nīlaparvata. He narrates the following story. Long ago, a demon called Kolāsura, who was the brother-in-law of Hiraṇyākṣa, used to live in a cave at this place. On being entreated by the sage Gautama, Nīlāmbā-Reṇukā went to Gaṅgādvāra and killed the demon. On his death bed, the demon made a wish that he should be remembered in her name. Therefore, she took on the name Kolāmbā.[68] This story is of course a tale designed to explain the name Kolāmbā. To this date, the area of Brahmagirī around the shrine of Kolāmbā is known variously as Kolagirī, Kolācala or Kolāgaḍha.

The Mahānubhāva sect was well known at the time of Sant Jñāneśvara. It appears that its founder Cakradharasvāmī was also associated with Tryambakakṣetra. In the month of Āśvina in the Śaka 1189 (1257 C.E.), Cakradharasvamī went from Mehakar to Paiṭhaṇ. He did so only to visit Tryambakeśvara during the time of Siṃhastha.[69] After offering a *Viḍā*[70] to Lord Tryambakeśvara, the Svāmi went to Gaṅgādvāra and rested there for a while. At that time, Gaṅgādvāra had a shrine for the goddess Koḷāī. Water was oozing out of her navel. When one of Cakradharasvāmī's disciples called Ḍākhale saw this, he inserted his finger in the Goddess' navel and addressed the Goddess:

> You seem to appropriate the entire town to the banks of the Gaṅgā. Why don't you take my finger as well?

Cakradharasvāmī did not appreciate this insult of the goddess by one of his disciples. He told the disciple:

> Ḍākhalia! You should not speak to a deity that way.

This tale of Ḍakhale insulting goddess Koḷāī and the Svāmī telling him off for this mischief can be found in the *Līḷācaritra*. In the *Sthānapothī* of the *Līḷācaritra*, this goddess is also referred to as 'brahmagirīncā adhoparī koḷāī' (*Lit*: Goddess Koḷāī resides on the lower side of the mountain Brahmagirī). Needless to say, this Koḷāī is none other than the goddess Koḷāmbā, described in detail in the *Tryambakakṣetramāhātmya.*

The founder of the Śaiva Trika-Advaita sect was Tryambaka. One of the branches of his sect was located at Kāmarūpa.[71] This branch was called '*ardhatryambakamaṭhikā*' or '*uttaratryambakamaṭhikā*' and it was founded by a Siddha called Macchhanda or Mīna in the 5th century. Macchanda belonged to a Trika tradition which was a sister tradition to that established by Tryambaka. The tāntric sect connected with the '*ardhatryambakamaṭhikā*' tradition is known as '*yoginīkaulamata*'. This sect informs us that their original seat (*ādipīṭha*) was '*tryambakamaṭhikā*' as well. The name of the wife of the founder of this sect, Macchanda, has been recorded as Kukaṇāmbā. This name reminds us very much of Reṇukā. This is because Kuṅkaṇāmbā (Kukaṇā + ambā) is also one of the names of Reṇukā. The meaning of both of these names is the same. Kuṅkaṇā means someone made out of the particles of earth (Kuṅ = Prithivī, the earth, and Kaṇa = very small particles). Similarly, Reṇukā means made out of reṇus-specks. Obviously, both of these are the names of Bhūdevī, the mother earth. Reṇukā alias Kuṅkaṇā is worshipped in the form of an anthill in Southern India, especially in the states of Āndhra, Karnāṭaka, Konkaṇ and Gomantaka (Goa). As we have seen in previous chapters, an anthill symbolically represents the vagina of the earth. Therefore, a cobra, who often stays inside an anthill, is a representation of the male, the phallus, i.e. the *kṣetrapāla*. Kuṅkaṇā is the presiding deity of Konkaṇ. Within the borders of Tryambakeśvara, there is a tribal community called Konkaṇā. There is evidence to suggest that the worship of Kuṅkaṇā is prevalent in this tribal community even to this date.

Kaulamata has evolved out of the folk-religious worship of Kuṅkaṇā alias Reṇukā. 'Ku' means earth. The term *kula* has been formed by attaching the suffix *la* to this monosyllabic word. We know that in the language of the tāntrics, *kula* means Śakti. The word *Kula* is also related to the earth. It is from this word *kula* that the word *kaulamata* has been coined to denote the Kaula sect. The worship of the primordial mother in the form of her vagina has been in vogue in folk religion from ancient times. One can see the evidence of this even to this day. Tāntrics such as Macchanda transformed this folk worship into a tāntric ritual and coined the name Kaulamata to describe such worship. In this regard, it is important to know that the name of Macchanda's consort, Śakti and wife, was Kuṅkaṇāmbā.

We have already seen that the name of Macchhanda's *kaul* sect was '*Yoginīkaulamata*'. The Bhūdevī Reṇukā worshipped in the form of her vagina is commonly known as Joguḷāmbā in her seats such as Ālampūr. "Joguḷāmbā" literally means a mother (goddess) who gives children. The Saṃskṛtization of this southern term has resulted in names such as Yugulā, Yoginī and Yogeśvarī. Yogeśvarī of course is the consort of the *kṣetrapāla* god Bhairava. This background automatically suggests an explanation of the term *Yoginīkaulamata*. One would thus interpret the term *Yoginīkaulamata* as 'the sect of the worshippers of mother earth-Bhūdevī, in the form of a vagina. Such a conversion of folk religion into tāntric religion is worthy of much research.

I do not want to discuss either the history or the nature and character of *Kaulamata* at this juncture. All that I want to stress in this regard is the fact that *Tryambakamaṭhikā* is the source of *Yoginīkaulamata* and that this tāntric sect has evolved out of the folk tradition of the worship of mother earth in the form of a vagina. From the unsculpted stones of folk tradition have arisen the iconographic images of tāntric religion. As strong evidence of this truth, one needs to study the mystery of the creation of the Yoginīkaulamata.

With this background, it is no longer necessary to explain why Brahmagirī has been given the alternative names Kaulagirī and Kaulagaḍh. It is also unnecessary to explain further the particular importance of Reṇukā-Kolāmbikā, who resides on one of the branches of this mountain.

Uttānā Mahī[72]

Stella Kramrisch called *Lajjāgaurī* the spreadeagled Aditi. In her beautiful style, Kramarisch further commented that, because the lotus is considered to be the symbol of creation in the Indian tradition, it was most appropriate for it be located in place of the head in the iconographic representation of the goddess.[73] It was the perfect symbol that defined her personality. Earlier in this volume, in connection with the *Lajjāgaurī* image at Ālampūr, we have already discussed the contributions made by Stella Kramrisch. Although she was well aware of the Egyptian mother goddesses exemplified by Baubo, Kramrisch chose to connect *Lajjāgaurī* with Aditi. By doing so, she avoided the obvious temptation of saying that images such as *Lajjāgaurī* were copied from Baubo-type images during Roman times. There is no doubt that Kramrisch's correct identification is a tribute to her sound reasoning.

The only proofs before Ms. Kramrisch were the images of *Lajjāgaurī* at Ālampūr and at Mahākūṭa: nothing but the images. She was, however, well aware of the incredible and awe-inspiring form of Aditi in the Vedas. She was also well aware of Aditi's form as 'mother earth'. That is precisely why she strongly reasoned that these unusual images were those of the Vedic goddess Aditi. Due to the lack of evidence, Kramarisch was however unable to unequivocally demonstrate the process whereby the Vedic Aditi was transformed into *Lajjāgaurī*. That is perhaps why an important historical truth remained neglected in spite of the fact that it would have been possible to prove that truth by resorting to traditional methods. However, people such as Dr Sāṅkaliā believed only in ancient archaeology and totally neglected other available evidence. He opposed Kramrisch's interpretation and strongly put forward the view that the origin of the *Lajjāgaurī* lies in foreign goddesses such as Baubo.[74]

In our discussion so far, we have investigated the centres of worship of *Lajjāgaurī*, the traditions and modes of her worship and the thinking behind her worship by her devotees. We have examined the myths and stories that surround her and the symbolism that emanates from these myths. We have seen how the presence of this goddess and her various forms have pervaded our traditions right from Vedic times to this day. One would be justified in saying that Joguḷāmbā, Mātaṅgī, Yallammā, Reṇukā, Kuṅkaṇā, Kolāmbikā and Koṭavī are all forms of Aditi, the earth mother. Alternatively, one could say that these goddesses are forms of the same mother goddess who has tried to coalesce with Aditi.

Iconographically, the best image of goddess *Lajjāgaurī* that has been seen so far is at Ālampūr. In her exquisite style, Stella Kramrisch describes details of this very beautiful sculpture. One can easily see that, in the way it has been sculpted, this image has to be worshipped lying on her back. In this respect, she is similar to the *yoni* on which a *śivaliṅga* is placed. It is in this position that she has to be worshipped. After she is bathed with water, there is a spout on one side of her to take the water away. When one sees the spreadeagled position of this image, one is left in no doubt that she is worshipped in this position.

When one examines this peculiar posture of *Lajjāgaurī*, one is left in no doubt that this posture is the posture assumed either at the time of accepting the male seed or at the moment of giving birth to a child. Either of these postures is connected with motherhood, the process of recreation or on a larger scale, the regeneration of the universe. This is an everlasting and eternal truth. As the *Śatapatha Brāhmaṇa* says:

> *uttāneva vai yonirgarbhaṃ bibharti*
>
> *Śatapatha Brāhmaṇa* (3.2.1.29)[75]
>
> (Only a woman who is lying on her back [in a spread-eagled position] with her vagina extended [during intercourse] can bear a child.)

This statement in the *Śatapatha Brāhmaṇa* uses the words '*uttānā yonī*' (*Lit*: one with spread-out vagina). I feel that *Lajjāgaurī* cannot be described in any other way. This is especially true for the earlier images of *Lajjāgaurī*, which show only the part of the body up to the navel. They must be described only as '*uttānā yoni*' images. While they are images with a prominent vagina, one must remember that if the vagina is shown spread out and extended, the feet must be bent and turned sideways. In sculpting the images in this manner, I feel that the sculptor has shown appropriate decorum and propriety.

The term '*uttānā yonī*' (one with a spreadeagled vagina) in the *Śatapatha Brāhmaṇa* can mean both either the woman or the earth. However, I feel that it is the woman that is implied here. The Vedic Ṛṣis have said time and time again that just as a woman does, the earth also spreads herself in order to be able to receive seed.[76]

The identity between the spread-out earth and a spreadeagled woman is spelled out very clearly here. The only difference is their size. However, this difference between their sizes does not at all affect their similarity in terms of their motherly nature or their capacity to re-generate.

The Womb of Nature

The pure and primordial *yonī* form of Aditi, Pṛthivī or *Lajjāgaurī* is the womb of the entire universe. One may think that such a flowery description is a figment of my imagination. However, let me assure the reader that this is not my invention. It is a truth that has emanated from the imagination of the devotees. When one sees the transformation of *Lajjāgaurī* from a symbolic image of an anthill to a beautifully sculpted stone image bedecked with appropriate ornaments, one can clearly see the truth that has emerged from the devotees' ardent devotion. The belief that an anthill is the vagina of the earth, and hence it is the goddess earth in a *yoni* form, occurs not only in southern Indian folk religion and in the devotional regime of Yallammā-Santerī, but in Vedic literature as well. Durgā Bhāgwat recorded an incredible convention of togetherness between earth and the heavens as suggested in the *Śatapatha Brāhmaṇa* (1.1.1.17). A tale found in this Brāhmaṇa relates that, for some reason, the gods separated the earth and the heavens by forcing a wedge between them. When they were departing from each other, they gave each other some gifts. The heavens gave the earth salt (the semen of the skies). The earth on its part, gave the heavens fine sand from an anthill. Bhāgvat also found that in the *Aitareya Brāhmaṇa* (2.4.27) salt has been thought of as the semen of the heavens that fell on the earth. If salt is the semen of the heavens, then the fine fertile sand of an anthill can obviously be considered as the female *wetness* (*Śukra*) during intercourse. The anthill then becomes the vagina of the earth.

Thus far we have seen how the worship of the field deities (*kṣetrapālas*) has been consistently performed to this day in their forms such as the anthill and the cobra who resides within the anthill. Symbolically, we have experienced this in the worship of the field-goddesses Yallammā, Mātaṅgī, Reṇukā and Sānterī and the field-gods such as Muruga, Subrahmaṇya, Jotibā, Khaṇḍobā, Ravaḷanātha and Mhaskobā. The soil within an anthill has been considered particularly sacred not only in folk-religion but in the Vedic tradition as well. It has been considered an essential ingredient in many rituals.

The soil in an anthill is very fine and granular and hence very delicate. It is not stable enough to become an object of worship. It is impossible to construct a temple housing an anthill in its natural form. Every now and then, the anthill needs to be coated with a layer of clay. (I have myself seen such a clay layer put on the goddess Santerī in her anthill form at the town of Veṅgurlā). Because of this major limitation, when images of mother earth began to be constructed out of clay or stone, it is possible that, at one stage during this process, before they were made to resemble a vagina, they were made to resemble the conical shape of an anthill (see Plate 19). The image looks very much like an anthill, but the front of it looks more like a conch shell with an opening like a vagina. This conch shell like image is a womb. Its vagina-like opening is the entrance to the womb. It should now be clear why I called the pure vagina-like form of *Lajjāgaurī* as the 'womb of the universe'. It leads me to wonder if the origin of the sanctum sanctorum of a temple has evolved out of this idea.[77]

It is now necessary to establish a chronology of the development of *Lajjāgaurī* images starting from the conch-shell shaped, anthill-type images to those that are simply of the vagina-shaped and finally to the spreadeagled female torso showing the breasts and vagina. The images that show only the parts up to the navel from below are naturally those which represent only the regenerative aspect of the goddess. Although sustenance was implicit in these images, due to the fact that it was motherhood that was essentially being expressed, the organs of providing sustenance, i.e. the breasts, were not shown. Therefore, the next development was the creation of the images that prominently displayed both organs of creation and those of sustenance, i. e. the breasts and the vagina. These images were headless and had a lotus in place of the head. Some of them had lotuses surrounding the image. Others had lotuses in place of the breasts. As we have seen, in Indian religious thought, the lotus is seen as the very centre of the creation of nature; it is the home of generation. That is why the sculptors have shown a sense of artistic decorum in expressing the whole personality of *Lajjāgaurī* by replacing her head with a lotus. As we know, it is the head and the face that identify a person completely. The final stage of the development of *Lajjāgaurī*'s iconography was the creation of an image showing the whole torso, including the head.[78] It is true, that in the opinion of scholars, the available images of the *Lajjāgaurī* must be dated after the Sātavāhana period. However, if one takes into account the chronological development of the images, right from an anthill to the image of *yoni*, one must say that the worship of the *uttānā mahī* (spreadeagled mother earth) has been prevalent from Vedic times.

The Mother of the Family and the Populace

In the ways shown above, she is the mother of humans, birds and animals, insects and all vegetation. We have developed procedures for her worship according to our traditions and our beliefs. We have developed her images, her iconography and her symbols to suit our thinking and beliefs. One must however remember that it is not only us, but humans all over the world and in every period of history who have sung songs about the might of the 'Great Mother'.

The belief that humans have emerged from the earth is found all over the world. There are many languages that call human beings 'bhumi-ja.[79]' Mircea Eliade echoes this when he says:[80]

> That human beings were born from the Earth is a belief of universal distribution. In many languages, man is named 'the Earth Born'.

While I am fully aware of the universality of this truth, I have drawn a boundary for myself. I wanted to concentrate only upon the Indian tradition. Hence, I decided that I should study it first for myself and, having done so, give my readers a *darśan* of the goddess responsible for regeneration. This I have done by investigating a particular type of image. It is the manner in which I have completed this pilgrimage for the *darśan* of goddess *Lajjāgaurī*. I hope that the reader has stayed with me during this *yātrā*. If in this process I am fortunate enough to acquire the reader's love and affection as well, then this procession could be turned into something even bigger, a great pilgrimage (*mahā-yātrā*).

While I was engrossed in taking the *darśan* of this goddess, I came across two types of devotees. The first were the common folk who worshipped her in her original form as an autochthonous stone or a roughly sculpted image. The second were the elites in the society who sculpted elaborate images with a specific purpose in mind. I have however avoided to ask and seek answers to many a question that naturally comes to mind because of this division amongst the devotees. Some of these unanswered questions are:

- What, if any, was, or was there any, relationship between the folk worshippers and the elite ones?
- In converting her original form to an elaborately sculpted one, did members of the higher elite religion totally ignore the folk devotees, or did they share their cult with folk devotees?
- In worshipping the elaborately sculpted form, did the elite consider the purpose for which the original folk form was created? Was the original form incorporated into the new worship, or was the new form generated in order to totally ignore the old one? In other words, was the new form a clever and deliberate device to supersede the old one?

When a higher tradition incorporates folk worship or ritual, the manner in which it does this can either uplift the folk tradition or it can take unfair advantage of the lower tradition. We will have to find another occasion on which to discuss such matters. Until then, let us pray to the Great Mother in the very language of the Vedas. Hopefully, this will give us the strength and understanding to appreciate the anguish of the common man and the lower tradition.

> *matā būmiḥ putro ahaṃ pṛthivyāḥ* |
> *namo mātre pṛthivyai namo mātre pṛthivyai* ||
>
> *Atharvaveda* (12.1.12)[81]
>
> (Pṛthivī is the mother; I am her son. I bow to that Pṛthivīmātā, I bow to that Pṛthivīmātā.)

Endnotes

1 Translator's note: Sūrya, the Sun-god, is thought to produce a thousand rays. He is naturally the husband of earth. With his rays, he brings all the plant kingdom to life.
2 Translator's note: Śālū is a name of a traditional silk saree worn by women in the state of Mahārāṣtra. A bride traditionally wears a green Śālū which she receives from the groom's side.
3 Translator's note: Unlike the West which divides the year into four seasons, Hindus divide the year into six seasons, each one of two month's duration. These are: Vasant, Grīṣma, Varṣā, Śarad, Hemant and Śiśir. Grīṣma corresponds roughly to summer whereas Varṣā corresponds to the monsoon.
4 Translator's note: The season *Śiśira* corresponds roughly to winter.
5 Saṃskṛt to Marāṭhī translation by Ḍhere. Marāṭhī to English translation by Jayant Bāpaṭ.
6 *The Ṛgveda*, 1.72.9 and 9.74.5.
7 *Lit*: dead foetus in the form of an egg.
8 *The Ṛgveda*, 10.72.9.
9 Saṃskṛt to Marāṭhī translation by Ḍhere. Marāṭhī to English translation by Jayant Bāpaṭ.
10 Translator's note: *iyam vai vedī* (*Lit*: This earth is the sacrificial altar).
11 Translator's note: The imagery of the Goddess's twilight nature as both enlivening and mortifying seems to have its roots in ancient history, as seen from Celtic and Hindu sources. See Thomas Cleary and Sarta Aziz. 2000. *Twilight Goddess*, Shambhala: 12.
12 Eliade, Mircea. 1957. *Myths, Dreams and Mysteries*: 183.
13 *Bṛhadāraṇyaka Upaniṣad* (6.4.2–3); See also *Śatapatha Brāhmaṇa* (14.9.4.1–2).

14 *Śatapatha Brāhmaṇa* (11.3.2.1).
15 Agrawāl, V.S. 1966. *Śiva Mahādeva*, Vārāṇasī: 40–41.
16 *The Ṛgveda* 8.100.15; 1.164.8; 8.94.1.
17 Saṃskṛt to Marāṭhī translation by Ḍhere. Marāṭhī to English translation by Jayant Bāpaṭ.
18 Saṃskṛt to Marāṭhī translation by Ḍhere. Marāṭhī to English translation by Jayant Bāpaṭ.
19 Ḍhere published the first edition of his book *Lajjāgaurī* in June 1978. In that, he reproduced the image from Jayarāmasvamice Vaḍagāv discussed here. Although the image was of poor quality, the Nandī bull was still intact. The image now rests in the State Museum at Nāgpur and unfortunately, part of the mouth of the Nandī bull is now missing.
20 Translator's note: The elephant has often been equated with clouds and sculptures of an elephant having intercourse with a woman (symbol for earth) are common in Indian iconography. For example, see, Philip Rawson, *Oriental Erotic Art*, Gallery Books, 1981: 20.
21 *The Ṛgveda* 1.143.6, 2.33.7.
22 *The Rāmāyaṇa* (Sargas 11–18).
23 *The Ṛgveda* (1.163.9).
24 In Marāṭhī.
25 Saṃskṛt to Marāṭhī translation by Ḍhere. Marāṭhī to English translation by Jayant Bāpaṭ.
26 Translator's note: The Saṃskṛt word *Valmīka* means an anthill.
27 Translator's note: The verb root *ram* means to delight, to rejoice, to please.
28 Translator's note: For an excellent treatment of the devadāsis and their place and importance in the worship of Yallammā, refer to Lucinda Ramberg, *Given to the Goddess*, 2014. Duke University Press.
29 A *Tithī* is the date according to the Hindu lunar calendar.
30 Translator's note: In the Marāṭhī language, a *Hijḍā* is a hermaphrodite person.
31 Translator's note: '*marīāī cā ferā ālā*' in Marāṭhī.
32 *Vahyā* is the slang word for *ovyā* (plural of ovī), the couplets of folk songs.
33 Maṇḍe, Prabhākar. *Lokaprabhā weekly*. Mumbai: 6th of March 1977. p. 32. (In Marāṭhī).
34 Kosāmbi, D.D. *Myth and Reality* 1962. Bombay: 42, 46, 76–77, 80, 81, 99, 92, 115.
35 Saṃskṛt to Marāṭhī translation by Ḍhere. Marāṭhī to English translation by Jayant Bāpaṭ.
36 Translator's note: Parātpara Guru can mean two things: 1) the greatest of the greatest of Gurus, or 2) Guru's Guru's Guru.
37 Bendre, B. S. 1960. *tukārām mahāraj yāncī guruparamparā* (lit: The Guru lineage of Saint Tukāram), Mumbai: pp. 80, 81, 85, 86, 87, 92, 93, 97, 100, 103, 109, 120 (in Marāṭhī).
38 Translator's note: Although as a rule, Hindus cremate their dead, Saṃnyāsins and Saints are not normally cremated. Instead, they are known to choose a time and place of their demise and leave the body at a destined time. They may then be buried at that place or cremated and their

ashes buried under a memorial stone. Such a place is called Samādhī or Mahāsamādhī.

39 Translator's note: This section repeats some of the information from earlier chapters. However, for the sake of the flow of Ḍhere's argument, I have chosen not to omit anything.

40 Translator's note: This information clarifies a major question I have faced for quite a while. I visited Ālampūr in Āndhra Pradeś some years ago and went to the Darśan of goddess Joguḷāmbā. She was so far removed from the images of goddess *Lajjāgaurī* that I have come across that I felt somewhat shaken. Goddess Joguḷābā at Ālampūr has no resemblance whatsoever to the dozens of *Lajjāgaurī* images that I have come across during my field work. Joguḷāmbā at Alampur is a fierce deity. She has a lizard crawling on her forehead and has a fierce expression on her face. Obviously, she has no connection with *Lajjāgaurī*. Because of this, I find it difficult to accept her as a kind mother that Ḍhere portrays her to be.

41 Bāmbarḍekar, V. A. 1925. *Maṭhagāvacā Śilālekh* (Lit. The stone inscription at Maṭhgav). Mumbai: 158. (In Marāṭhī).

42 Behre, P.R. 1955. *Śrī Ravaḷnāth āṇi Konkaṇātīl Devaskī*. (Lit. God Ravaḷnāth and exorcism and black magic in Konkaṇ), Borivli, p. 13. (In Marāṭhī).

43 Translator's note: Aggrawāl wrote in Hindi. This is Ḍhere's translation of the original Hindi text.

44 Aggrawāl, Vāsudevaśaraṇ. 1964. *Pracīna Bhāratīya Lokadharma*, Ahmedabad: 113–114. See also, Ancient India, Vol. 4, p. 142, plates 202–203. Jagadīśacandra Jain, *Jain Āgama Sāhityame Bhāratīya Samāj*, 1965, Vārāṇasī, pp. 449–450 (in Hindi). Vasudevaśaraṇ Aggrawāl, *harṣacarit: eka sāunskṛtic adhayana*, Paṭṇā, 1953: 134–135. T.R. Śeśa Iyengar, *Dravidian India*, 1925, Madras: 97. K.A. Nilakaṇṭha Śāstrī, *The Sangam Age*, 1972, Maḍrās: 97. K.K. Pillāi, *A Social History of the Tamils*, Vol. 1: 497–498. J.N. Tiwārī, *Studies in Goddess Cults*, pp. 315–337. Translator's note: Tiwārī's thesis was published in book form with the same title in 1985, by Sandīp Prakāśan, Delhi.

45 Translator's note: A buffalo. Buffalo demon in this case.

46 *Tanmātā koṭarā nāma nagnā muktaśiroruhā* (Bhagavatam, 10.62.20).

47 Kalpadrumakośa, Śloka 127.

48 *nagnā tu koṭavī* | Abhidhāna Cintāmaṇī, 3.98; commentary: *nagnā vivsastrā yoṣit muktakeśītyāgamah, koṭane lajjāvaśāt yāti koṭavī*.

49 Sāṅkaliā, H.D. 1941. *Archaeology of Gujarat including Kathiawar,* Bombay: 218.

50 Tarasmiya is at present a locality within the city of Bhāvnagar in Gujarat State, India.

51 *Lokaprabhā* weekly magazine, Mumbai: 6th March 1977: 32. (In Marāṭhī).

52 Translator's note: This is similar to the Marāṭhī expression, '*sāḷkāyā-mhāḷkāyā*' with the same meaning.

53 The word Birobā is probably linked etymologically to the word Vīr (vīr-bā = Viroba -> Biroba).

54 Viz. Śrīmhaskobāce Caritra, 1889, See also Śrīnātha Mhaskobā devāce caritra, 1936 (in Marāṭhī).

55 The word *wāḍā* is used by the Dhangars to collectively refer to the sheep and cattle they possess.
56 Translator's note: *Sonārī* is a Village in Parāṇḍa Talukā in Osmanābād District of *Mahārāṣṭra* State.
57 Translator's note: The lunar month of Māgha occurs between February and March in the Gregorian calendar.
58 Translator's note: Gulāl is an orange-red dye sprinkled on god's images at the time of a pūjā.
59 Translator's note: A *Pavāḍ* or *Pavāḍa* is a type of alliterative poetry recounting the greatness or achievements of a warrior or a famous person.
60 Translator's note: The Kolhāṭī is an Indian nomadic tribal community. They belong to central India and Mahārāṣṭra. Traditionally, they are professional entertainers and acrobats and are classified as a 'nomadic tribe' by the government of Mahārāṣṭra. They have also been employed with tamāśā troupes. The Kolhāṭī lāvaṇī-tamāśā performers have got social prestige from the patronage of the art form by the Mahārāṣtra State government and this is vital to their identity as performing artists.
61 *Śritryambakakśetramāhātmyam,* Mumbai, Jagadīśwara Śilāpress, Śaka 1794 (1872 C.E.).
62 *ayaṃ nīlagiristasya śritryambakakśetramāhātmyam,* Mumbai, Jagadīśwara Śilāpress, Śaka 1794.
63 *Śritryambakakśetramāhātmyam*, 7.16.
64 Saṃskṛt to Marāṭhī translation by Ḍhere. Marāṭhī to English translation by Jayant Bāpaṭ.
65 Translator's note: A sacred place where one is able to obtain occult powers (*Siddhis*).
66 *siddhikṣetramidaṃ puṇyaṃ dattākṣayakārakam* |
dattātreyaṃ hariṃ sakṣāt vasantaṃ nīlaparvate || 7.20.
67 *jamadagñena rāmeṇa siddhiḥ prāptātra bhūmipa* | 7.32.
68 *Śritryambakakṣetramāhātmyam*, 14.41–65.
69 Translator's note: *Siṃhastha* is a very auspicious time according to the Hindu religious calendar. It occurs when the planet Jupiter enters the constellation of Leo once every 12 years.
70 Translator's note: The Indian practice of eating betel leaf with edible spices, prevalent all over India, has been very popular in Mahārāṣṭra as well, for a long time. Two betel leaves together, coated with Cunā (Calcium hydroxide), a vegetable gum called Kāt and then mixed with rose petal jam, saffron, grated coconut and other ingredients before folding them into a triangle, is traditionally called a *Viḍā* or *Pān* in Mahārāṣtra.
71 Translator's note: *Kāmarūpa* is the present area of western Āssām in India.
72 Translator's note: *Lit*: Spreadeagled Earth Mother.
73 Translator's note: By comparing the descriptions of goddess Aditi in the *Ṛgveda*, the Vājasaneyī Saṃhitā of the Śukla Yajurveda and the *Atharvaveda*, Kramrisch hypothesised that *Lajjāgaurī* is the mother earth Pṛthivī, who is the same as Aditi.
In her own words, 'As Aditi, she is the all-sustaining mother from whom the universe is born. The Vedas describe her as the wide one, the widely

spread bounteous earth who, with her legs spread open (uttānapāda), gives birth to all that is…

'She is "our Lady of Abundance." And she is earth, Pṛthivī, the broad one, spread on the water, the support of all living beings… As Earth, Womb and Altar, the image of Aditi is surrounded by the waters. The lotus flowers on them. Aditi is the Air, Aditi the mother, the same also Father and son'.

In describing the life-size image at Ālampūr, Kramrisch says:

'It lies facing upward on a nearly square plane. The rim frames the figure and allows water poured on it during worship to flow off through the spout to the left of the figure. Legs are drawn up laterally and bent at the knees. The soles of the feet are turned upward. Their modelling and contraction of the toes show the tension and struggle which attend the process of giving birth. The arms are bent upwards and the hands, each holding a lotus bud, are laid on the shoulders while the forefingers, in a sensitive and relaxed movement, touch upon the petal of the large and open lotus blossom that crowns the image, as its neck and head. A small and delicate bead necklace links chest and flower by the curve of its outline. It reposes on the surging modelling of the body, which gains powerful volume in the large, flattened globes of the breasts with their lotus nipples. – Thin anklets, quickened with serpentine energy, cling to the feet. But for these serpent ornaments, the figure is naked. The lower half of the body is modelled in the throes of muscular convulsion, from the palpitating flesh of hips and abdomen to their bud-like opening in the middle…

'Embedded and floating on the surging model mass, the lotus crowns the woman who is all body, gravid mass akin to that of the paleolithic Venus from Willendorf, who, though she has a head of hair, is without face…For the mother goddess is altogether body, incarnate purposive potentiality whose fulfilment, the womb, is between the symmetry, right and left, of the two breasts, hands and legs.

'Spread within, and coerced by the square limit of the base, the mass rises with curves, which are as tense as they are elastic. Their arcs hold the tidal waves of the life-giving body. Its boundless abundance is stemmed by the square field of relief. The overall conception of altar and life-giving body imparts monumental calm to the modelling. It is accentuated by a greater frequency of vibration in the modelling of the upturned soles, suggestive of muscular contractions in the agony of giving birth'.

74 Sāṅkaliā, H.D. *Artibus Asiae*, Vol. XXIII, p. 121. In here Sāṅkaliā states that 'In India, the inspiration was most probably received from Egypt through the Romans in about the first-second century A.Ḍ'.

75 Saṃskṛt to Marāṭhī translation by Ḍhere. Marāṭhī to English translation by Jayant Bāpaṭ.

76 *yatheyaṃ pṛthivī mahyuttānā garbhaṃ ā dadhe* |
eva tvaṃ garbhaṃ ā dadhe daśame māsi sūtave || (*Ṛ. Khil.* 4.132.3).
Lit: Just as the spread-out earth holds a foetus in her womb, you also should conceive in order to deliver in the 10th month.

77 Mookerji, Ajit. *Tantra Āsana*. p. 28. Translator's note: Ḍhere gives no further details of the particular edition of this popular book that he used. It is available in several editions.

78 Translator's note: The translator has a fundamental issue with the evolution of the image suggested by Ḍhere. In my opinion, it is reasonable to believe that any conjecture develops only after a certain amount of verbal corpus is generated; it is difficult to imagine it the other way around. It is true that verbal myths may be added or subtracted during the process of iconization. None the less, the priority must be given to the verbal myth. Given this, the fact that none of the myths quoted above mention or emphasize the Kalaśa suggests that the Kalaśa form cannot reasonably be assumed to be the progenitor of other forms. Further, all the *Lajjāgaurī* myths are about the loss of the head and its replacement with the lotus. The anonymity provided by the headlessness is the most important characteristic of this image. Therefore, to me, the fully anthropomorphic images do not fall within the scope of the myths and hence cannot be included in discussing the *Lajjāgaurī* either.

79 Translator's note: *Lit*: born out of the earth.

80 Eliade, Mircea. 1950. *Myths, Dreams and Mysteries*: 163.

81 Saṃskṛt to Marāṭhī translation by Ḍhere. Marāṭhī to English translation by Jayant Bāpaṭ.

Chapter 11

Śrī Ānandanāyakī

(Translation of Chapter 4 of Ḍhere's booklet *Śrī Ānandanāyakī*)

Translator's Introduction

The book *Lajjāgaurī* represented Aṇṇā Ḍhere's journey in trying to unravel the unusual iconography of the naked goddess named *Lajjāgaurī*, found in the Indian subcontinent. He convincingly interpreted the image as that of the divine mother, the genetrix of all beings, and hence her representation only in the form of a torso with breasts and vagina. Because of her nakedness, he felt awkward in approaching her and begged her forgiveness.

Ḍhere was well aware that early humans looked at natural caves as representations of the human vagina and that they worshipped them as such.[1] His researches now centred specifically on such worship in India. He was looking at the womb of the universal mother, namely, her organ of generation in the form of a cave. Ḍhere found one such cave at a place called Rāmatīrtha in Karnāṭaka. There is a small temple of goddess *Ānandanāyakī* here, at which she is situated in a small cave adjoining the main Śiva shrine. He was overwhelmed by this discovery and the visit led him to write the booklet, *Ānandanāyakī*.[2] He noted that in doing this research, he felt even more embarrassed, because he was now examining the Goddess's *yoni*. He therefore took the attitude of a foetus within that primordial womb. Because of this, the work is highly emotional and has strong poetic overtones. Many personal reactions of Ḍhere's intrude into this chapter. It is almost a form of participatory ethnography.

However, none of this detracts from the importance of this piece of research, and I have therefore included the most important chapter, chapter 4, from *Ānandanāyakī*, in this volume. To me, this chapter of Ḍhere's is an excellent example of how a highly evocative and emotional piece of writing can still be very analytical and searching.

Chapter Four of Ḍhere's *Śrī Ānandanāyakī*

I have always had an inner craving to visit the two goddess shrines associated with Jñānadeva's[3] world of experience: the sculptures of a female delivering a child in the temple complex at Kurundavāḍ and the *Lajjāgaurī* sculpture at a place called Rāmatīrtha. In the latter part of July 1988, I received a message from Dr Kusumtāī Koṭṇis from the town of Sānglī that there were sculptures of a female delivering a child on one of the walls of a temple at the town of Kurundavāḍ. She thought that they would be important for my research. She therefore advised me that I should go and visit the place. This made me resolve that I should go and see the one *Lajjāgaurī* shrine I had not yet visited. It also reminded me of A.R. Kulkarṇī, who worked at the Gokhale Institute in Puṇe. Kulkarṇī had informed me that at a place called Rāmatīrtha near the town of Athṇī, there is a totally different kind of sculpture of *Lajjāgaurī*. Kulkarṇī was attempting to decipher the unpublished stone inscriptions in the area. He was also planning to study the *Māhātmya* of this place. His idea was to collect all the documents associated with the cult at this place, so that he could record the historical importance of this Rāmatīrtha *kṣetra*. I hope that when he completes his study, researchers will have an important means to investigate the religious world of this important *kṣetra*, something that has not yet been done. My own interest in this place was limited only to inspecting the *Lajjāgaurī* sculpture and finding out more about her place in the overall scheme of things at Rāmatīrtha *kṣetra*.

In order to inspect the sculpture depicting parturition at the Śiva temple at Kurundavāḍ and also visit Rāmatīrtha *kṣetra*, I embarked on a tour of these places in the month of August 1988 with financial help from the 'Kesarī' organization. What I saw was beyond imagination and I was beside myself. In front of me stood the magical world which confirmed what I had been postulating all along in my book *Lajjāgaurī*.

The Mother-Goddess at Kurḍī

Before I saw the parturition sculpture at Kurundavāḍ, I suddenly remembered the recently discovered mother-goddess sculpture at Kurḍī in the state of Goa. Dr Śirodkar, who is in-charge of the Archaeology and Scriptology Department at Goa, publicised the find in newspapers and also wrote a research paper on the sculpture. From his paper, it is quite clear that this sculpture, in the form of a naked female, depicts the mother-goddess in the process of giving birth. Even though Śirodkar calls her *Lajjāgaurī*, strictly speaking she clearly does not fit the definition of those images that can be called *Lajjāgaurī*. As a matter of fact, there is no doubt whatsoever in the minds of researchers about the antiquity, the spread, the continuity to this date and the symbolism associated with the worship of *Lajjāgaurī*. Because of this, if there is a report of a new find of an image of *Lajjāgaurī* or an image of a mother goddess associated with fertility, not a great deal is going to be added to our knowledge about this topic. On the other hand, if we are able to discover the relationship of such an image with the religious history of the place where it was found, we may then be able to unravel some historical puzzles. Before visiting Kurundavāḍ and Rāmatīrtha, this was a challenge I faced.

The Parturition Sculpture at Kurundavāḍ

The series of sculptures depicting childbirth are to be found on one of the walls of the Śiva temple situated at the confluence of the Kṛṣṇā and Pañcagaṅga rivers. As soon as one climbs the steps of the famous Ghāṭ at Kurundavāḍ, one enters this temple. Although the renovation of this stone temple is comparatively recent, the renovators have managed to situate some of the old sculptures in such a way as to maintain the style of the old construction. The temple as it stands today has strong associations with the Ghorpaḍe family. It is most likely that this Ghorpaḍe family hails from the town of Soṇḍūra. This is because, although this is a Śiva temple, it goes by the name of Subrahmaṇyeśvara, and the Ghorpaḍes of Soṇḍūra are known to be great worshippers of Śiva's son Subrahmaṇya.

In the front portion of the temple, there are a series of sculptures on the walls on both sides. These have been fitted into the middle of the walls from the outside. They show a warrior on a battlefield, a horse-faced male who is riding a horse, a standing woman churning buttermilk and a couple engrossed in sexual intercourse. On the wall on the front right-hand side of the temple, there are a series of sculptures which depict the stages that a woman goes through when she is about to deliver a child. I knew of the existence of a wooden sculpture from South India that shows a woman in the process of delivery. Similarly, there is also a stone sculpture on the same theme on one of the walls of a temple at Chaprī in Madhya Pradesh. However, this was the first time I had seen a series of sculptures depicting various stages of parturition (see Plate 22).

I had not been aware of it before. On one of the pillars and also on the right-hand corner the entrance hall (*sabhāmaṇḍapa*) of this Subrahmaṇyeśvara temple, there are sculptures of cobras that are covered with red-lead. We know, of course, that the cobra is thought to be the most prominent and powerful representation of Subrahmaṇya. He is the arch-bestower of children. It is therefore but natural that sculptures of a woman in the process of delivery are found in a temple of Subrahmaṇya. It is in line with our ritual conventions.

Rāmatīrtha: A Śaivite *Kṣetra*

As I was mulling over the thought that this series of sculptures depicting parturition must have been important for devotees concerned with fertility, I was on my way to visit the *Lajjāgaurī* shrine at Rāmatīrtha. This Śaivite *kṣetra* is 35 kilometres[4] from the town of Athṇī on the Miraj-Bijāpūr Road in the district of Beḷgāv. As one starts toward the village of Kakmarī from Athṇī, one veers left towards the north about three kilometres before Kakmarī in order to reach Rāmatīrtha. The temple complex here is protected by walls on the east, west and south sides. On the north side, the existing stone hillock has been carved to accommodate the northern side of the temple construction. When one enters the temple complex from the eastern gate, one faces the temple of Rāmeśvara. He is the presiding deity here. Built probably eight or nine hundred years ago, this beautiful temple is known for its architecture and sculpture. The temple prospered during the time of the Cālukyas of Kalyāṇī and the Kalacurīs. Ācāryas belonging to the Pāśupata Śaivite sect were the preceptors here, and, under their leadership, the place developed as a great devotional centre as well as a teaching institution. Of the eight or ten inscriptions here, some are totally worn and a few have not yet been read. Two of the inscriptions are in Kannaḍā and have been deciphered and published by scholars. From these, we can glean a great deal of information about the kings and the religious preceptors who made this place famous.

As soon as one enters the temple complex, one sees a very beautiful and tall lamp pillar (*dīpamāḷa*)[5] in the right-hand corner. Every one of the lamp housings on this *dīpamāḷa* has been decorated with a sculpture of a peacock. On the night of Tripurī Paurṇimā[6] or during the festival of Dīpāvalī, when these peacocks display the lamps on their backs, the entire surrounding must look spectacular. Near this *dīpamāḷa* is a niche in the wall that has a sculpture of the god Subrahmaṇya riding on his carrier, the peacock. The devotees however seem to identify him with Bhairava and thus call him Bhairavanātha. They have written his name as such at the bottom of the niche. There are many such niches on the north side as well. One of them contains a number of images of Nāgas (cobras). The temple of Rāmeśvara has been constructed by slicing the rock on the northern side from the top to the level of the soil. Because of this, although there are some niches on the north, immediately after them one encounters the rock monolith. The niches on the southern side contain images of many gods, including Nṛsiṃha. In the central hall (*maṇḍapa*) of the Rāmeśvara temple itself, there are Śivaliṅgas that remind us of the gods Brahmā and Viṣṇu.[7] As one goes past this *maṇḍapa*, one comes to the image of Śiva in his *liṅga* form. Here he is known as 'Svayambhū' (autochthonous) Rāmeśvara.

The *Sthalapurāṇas* in Marāṭhī and Saṃskṛt

A *Sthalapurāṇa* extolling the religious importance of this place was composed in the 11th or 12th century in Saṃskṛt. A part of the *Svayambhūrāmeśvaramāhātmya* of the *Trikoṭakarudrasaṃhitā* of the *Śivamahāpurāṇa*, it describes the conversation between Dāśarathī Rāma and Kahola Ṛṣi. The name Kahola seems to be closely connected with the town of Kohaḷḷī near Rāmatīrtha *kṣetra*. Based on this Saṃskṛt work, a Saṃskṛt teacher named Anantarāv Deśpāṇḍe composed a Marāṭhī version of the Māhātmya in 1940 C.E. He was helped in this task by a devotee of Rāmeśvara called Govindarāv Kulkarṇī. I am grateful to Kulkarṇī's son Rājārām, who made a copy of the Marāṭhī Purāṇa available to me. This Māhātmya puts together several myths that describe the importance of Śiva and other gods installed here and also the greatness of the various tīrthas in this temple complex. According to this Māhātmya, the original name of Rāmeśvara was Omkāreśa (Omkāreśvara). However, Śiva took the name Rāmeśvara because of the devotion shown by Rāma. After Sītā was kidnapped, Rāma was wandering in a confused and unstable state. That is when Kahola Ṛṣi told him about the greatness of this place. According to the instructions of Kahola Ṛṣi, Rāma prayed to Śiva at this place, obtained his blessings, killed Rāvaṇa and went back to Ayodhyā with Sītā. This is the story the *Svayambhūrāmeśvaramāhātmya* tells about Rāmeśvara and Rāmatīrtha.

The Symbol of the Mother's Womb

When one starts going towards the west after taking *darśan* of god Svayambhūrāmeśvara, one sees another doorway. When I saw the writing, 'The temple of *Śrī Ānandanāyakī*' on its lintel, my wish to visit the goddess became intense. The name Ānandanāyakī as a name for Śiva's consort revived many old memories. I had a sense that I was about to unravel a great mystery. Where did the name Ānandanāyakī come from? Who was the unknown genius who thought of this name for Pārvatī? What were the cultural motifs that would have inspired him in coining this name? I entered the south-facing temple while I was thinking of these ambiguous questions and equally vague answers. Suddenly, all of the questions and answers dissolved into an amazing experience that transported me to another plane. This temple was not a temple in the traditional sense at all. It was a cave sculpted out of the tall rock called Ānandācala in the Sthalapurāṇa. Only the front of the cave had been built with a small door as the entrance. When I bent and entered through the small door, the image of Āndanāyakī with four arms stood in front of me. She had a sword in one hand, a mace in the second, a pot of water in the third and a shield in the fourth hand.

Śeṣappā Pujārī, who accompanied me, told me that the present image had been established in 1983–84 and the old broken one had been immersed in the waters of the Pāpanāśana Tīrtha. The Sthalapurāṇa of the place describes the image as follows:

> Her image looks as cool as a crore of moons. In her tender hands she holds the trident, a shield and a skull. She is wearing a silken garment.[8]

At that point, it occurred to me that neither the image that was directly in front of me at this temple, nor the image as described in the Sthalapurāṇa, resonated even remotely with the ever so beautiful and joyous name Ānandanāyakī. The moment I felt this, the image in front of me slowly became misty and went out of focus. A strange and intoxicating feeling filled my mind. As I stood there with some reserve and embarrassment,[9] I felt that the carved-out cave that housed the sanctum sanctorum for the image was in itself the image of the goddess. While the current image, with four arms, ornaments and weapons, serves the function of satisfying traditional devotees for their daily worship, I felt that the cave itself was the primordial form of goddess Ānandanāyakī. This feeling came from within the depths of my mind, and it consumed me. I felt my physical body disappearing and, in its place, a lustrous foetus, which had a memory of its own, occupied the womb of the great mother. This was an exquisite experience.

Behind this sanctum sanctorum, there is a narrow passage in the form of a cave that has been carved out of the rock. It is about two metres long. At the other end of this passage, there is yet another passage to the right, which hints at the space within. As we travelled from one passage to the other, the pujārī Śeṣappā said to me, 'it is through this inner passage that Śiva, in the form of an autochthonous *liṅga*, appeared here as Rameśvara'. When I heard this statement of his, I got goose-pimples all over my body. It is Śiva who dies again and again and assumes a corpse form. After his death, it is his partner, Ānandanāyakī, who holds his foetus again in her womb and bestows godliness on him. She is the source of his everlasting joy. I felt that, at that moment, the womb of the goddess was holding my foetus as well. The feeling made me dizzy with joy. For a short while, I thought that I too had been born from the 'golden foetus', the Hiraṇyagarbha. Śūdra kings, in order to rid themselves of their Śūdra status and achieve heavenly incarnation as members of the twice-born (*dvija*) castes, used to enclose themselves in a golden urn. They would then undergo a ritual symbolizing their re-birth as a foetus born out of the golden urn – the *Hiraṇyagarbha*. I felt that, like those kings, I too had come out of the golden womb. Unbeknownst to me, a feeling of being blessed swept over me. I said to myself:

> *mātrā 'haṃ janitaḥ pūrvaṃ martyadharmā surottama* |
> *tvadgarbhasaṃbhavād eṣa divyadeho bhavāmyaham* ||[10]
>
> (Oh Surottama! Previously I was born out of a mother's womb and hence I went through the cycles of life and death. Now that I have been born out of your womb, I have become a divine being.)

The Lover and the Mother

As we know, *Ānandanāyakī* is both the lover of Śiva and the genetrix of the entire world, which includes Śiva. The cave sculpture at Rāmatīrtha is a testimony to this divine and incredible truth. The devotee who experienced this divine truth and brought it to light through the agency of this cave sculpture must have been an amazing poet indeed! Because only a poet would be capable of imagining things at this subtle and elevated plane.

When I experienced this sensation through the cave-sculpture, I was reminded of the poet Kusumāgraj.[11] His imaginative power appreciated that at the dawn of creation, this mighty universe, resplendent with innumerable constellations, blooms like a mighty lotus with thousands of petals, looking for colours and forms. Similarly, through his plays and poems, he brought to light again and again the eternal truth that no matter what her relationship with the world around her is, a woman has motherhood ingrained in her; it is a part of her makeup. Through sexual love, she unveils the mystery of mother nature's primordial creation. However, through this very experience of sexual love, she invariably brings forth the intense experience of motherhood. Through his poetry and plays, Kusumāgraj has very powerfully portrayed this paradox of the intertwining of a woman's sexual and motherly love, which does not obey the rules of society. He has done so with such ease that one accepts it as a matter of course.

In Indian tradition, Rādhā, Kṛṣṇa's consort, has always been regarded as the ultimate ideal of a female lover. In one of his poems, Kusumāgraj calls her 'the eternal flame in the minds of males carried from the past to the present to the future'. Similarly, in imagining and describing the sexual experiences between Kṛṣṇa and her, he uses the words, 'the celebration of the touch of the female lips which express a mixture of the feelings of motherly love and sexual longing.' When he thinks of subjects dealing with sexual love, he says, 'one should love the tender and loving breasts of Rādhā'. Naturally, when he says this, he is merely wanting the reader to appreciate the eternal motherhood in the lover, a part and parcel of the female make-up. I am myself so happy to see that the inspired knowledge the Śaiva Ācāryas perceived over a thousand years ago is the same as the inspired thought that came to an accomplished Marāṭhī poet in our own day. Both of them share the same divine experience, although the medium through which they experience it is different. The

Śaivacāryas of their time experienced this divine celebration through grey granite stones, the great modern Marāṭhī poet experienced it through the medium of words.

When one walks out of *Ānandanāyakī's* sanctum sanctorum, and after experiencing her immanence, one's inner perceptions reach such divine planes that they are simply unable to be described by mere words. One has to experience that experience beyond words, through a wordless mind.

The Difference between the Name and the Form

After taking *darśan* of the goddess, I examined the surrounding area and the various buildings associated with the *kṣetra*. When I came out of the temple complex, one question still kept coming back to my mind again and again. Who named this lover of Śiva, Ānandanāyakī? I had already witnessed the sacred complex which was created by the leadership of the Śaiva Ācāryas. These Acāryas brought the wealth and blessings of the kings of the time for the benefit of the populace, who were devoted to this goddess. They broke through the hard rock and created a beautiful temple for Śiva with rich sculptural imagery. Why then did they not create a similar temple for Śiva's lover Ānandanāyakī? Instead, they sculpted a cave in her name. They did away with the norm where one erects a temple of one's favourite deity and installs an image that resonates with the mythology associated with it. Instead, they created this mysterious womb of the mother in the form of a deep cave. To me, this unusual form of Ānandanāyakī, while it gave me intense joy, demanded explanations.

The Lakṣmī under the Banyan Tree[12]

When I left Puṇe for Rāmatīrtha, I had no interest in experiencing the beauty and grace of the sculpture and images at this place. I was not at all interested in reading the stone inscriptions either. Nor was I interested in discovering the devotional make-up of the dynasties of kings who gave very large donations for the construction and maintenance of this amazing temple complex. Finally, I had no interest in discovering the history and traditions of the Śaiva Ācāryas who had given the temple complex great splendour and fame. This is not to say that if I found such information, I would have ignored it. I did want this information, but only if it was available in relation to my quest. I had been told that there was a *Lajjāgaurī* image at Rāmatīrtha, and that was the sole reason for my visiting this place.

That day, I took *darśan* of the presiding deity of Rāmatīrtha, the autochthonous Śiva known here as Rāmeśvara. I was also able to visit the shrines of other gods in his pantheon, such as Nṛsiṃha. I experienced the divine mystery within the *Ānandanāyakī* cave. In the mental process of trying to fathom the etymology of her unusual name, I kept thinking more and more about *Lajjāgaurī.* Sadly, however, I was unable to find anything about a *Lajjāgaurī* image within this temple complex. I asked the temple priest, Śeṣāppā Pujārī, many questions about *Lajjāgaurī.* I told him about the way this image is worshipped in the South. I told him the various names by which she was known. However, he was unable to give me any information about her. He simply did not know anything about a goddess who had no place in the temple complex as it exists today. Also, he did not appreciate the fact that I had come from far away in search of this image. I became thoroughly despondent with the thought that my trip was going to be in vain and that I would have to return home without seeing the *Lajjāgaurī* image here. Śeṣāppā suggested to me that Bāḷ Dixit, the elderly *purohit* in Rāmatīrtha, might have more information about this *kṣetra.* Unfortunately, he happened to be away that day. I was about to return home in my despondent state when I saw a young man carrying firewood on his head. Śeṣāppā informed me that the man was Śyām, the son of Bāḷ Dixit. I called him. He dropped the firewood on the platform built around the banyan tree and came over to me. He was eager to speak to me and was full of information. I showed him the photos of *Lajjāgaurī* in my book and asked him, 'I have heard that there is a shrine of *Lajjāgaurī* at Rāmatīrtha. Ever since I came here, I have been looking for it but no one seems to know anything about her.' In answer to my question, Śyām turned to Śeṣāppā and said, 'This man wants to see the Lakṣmī under the banyan tree. Let's go there'. All of us then hurried to the shrine under the banyan tree. On the same road that had brought us to Rāmatīrtha, there was a small shrine about a kilometre outside of town. Measuring only about eight feet by eight feet, it looked like a *grāmadevatā* shrine and was crudely built.

Nearby stood a large banyan tree and a neem tree. The shrine sits in the middle of an embankment about three feet in height. Near the steps going to the top of this embankment stands a small, rectangular sculpture of a cobra couple. As I bent down to enter the shrine, I noticed a carved sculpture near the back wall. Turmeric and vermillion had been smeared all over the sculpture. When I examined this sculpture in detail, I was overjoyed. There are many sculptures of *Lajjāgaurī* available today.

Among them, this one is undoubtedly very special. It has a unique theme. As a symbol, it is poetic (see Plate 23).

Although she is known here with the beautiful name Lakṣmī, the goddess of wealth, in view of this crude temple and the kind of devotees she attracts, she is far from wealthy at this shrine. I felt that it was very strange that in one of her forms with the beautiful name Ānandanāyakī, she sits next to the autochthonous Rāmeśvara and enjoys the luxury of daily worship. Why then does this Lakṣmī sit here in a totally ignored state? I kept thinking of the unknown and amazing sculptor who carved this symbolic image of *Lajjāgaurī* with poetic imagination. He may have done so out of his devotion or for some other reason. While I was impressed with his art, I could not understand why no one paid any attention to the goddess.

The Available Sculptures of *Lajjāgaurī*

All of the available sculptures of *Lajjāgaurī* portray her as a human female who is available and keen to have intercourse. At times, only the torso up to the navel is shown. At other times, her shoulders are also shown. In place of her head, there is often a lotus. Some images have lotuses in both of her hands, others have lotuses on all four corners of the sculpture. Some images portray a human female with a head as well. However, even these full images give prominence to the organ of creation, the vagina. Images that cover the shoulders as well prominently display both the vagina and the breasts. All of this goes to show that these sculptures portray the goddess responsible for creation and sustenance. She is the primordial mother of the world. Women believe that worshipping her will make them fertile. That is why they sincerely worship her sex-organ. They pray to her in order to protect their progeny.

The Symbolism of the Alternate Sculpture

To our analytical gaze, which is steeped in convention, tradition and perceived cultural norms, sculptures such as *Lajjāgaurī* appear obscene. We find worship of such images reprehensible. Although the thought behind the sculptures points to primordial motherhood, we cannot bring ourselves to think of them in such a light. In traditional society, the preceptors who dictate religious norms are not in favour of the worship of such images. By the same token, they are unable to deny the popularity of such worship. Under such circumstances, religious leaders belonging to the great tradition constantly and deliberately try to bring about changes in the practices of the little tradition. When they realized how enormously popular *Lajjāgaurī* worship was at Rāmatīrtha, they created a rich and lofty shrine of Ānandanāyakī along with her partner Rāmeśvara at this place. They also instituted a complex devotional cult here. Finally, they converted Ānandanāyakī's unconventional and "unacceptable" sculpture portraying a naked erotic female into a beautiful, symbolic and abstract image. Both images are intended to carry the same meaning; however, the latter is far more subtle and abstract.

The ancient sculptures found in the excavations at Ter, Nevāse and Bhokardan, as well as those that are worshipped even to this day at Jayarām Svāmice Vaḍgāv and Siddhankoṭṭe, prominently display the symbolism behind procreation. However, there is no finesse in these sculptures; they are rather crude. They cannot be proclaimed to be 'objets d'art.' In other places, though, where religious leaders elevated the devotional worship of the little tradition and brought it into the Brāhmaṇical tradition, a major change took place. In place of crude village images, they installed beautiful sculptures depicting the goddess. The images at Badāmī and Ālampūr are two such examples. The sculpture at Mahākūṭa must have been equally beautiful but now is seen only in the form of several broken pieces. At Rāmatīrtha, when they created the sacred complex, the Śaiva Ācāryas seem to have placed this new sculpture in place of the old one. Alternatively, they may have had the present one sculpted for some other purpose, but then it was installed here.

This sculpture is carved with finesse and is simply beautiful. But that is not its only distinguishing feature. The bland nakedness and the rather crude and prominent representation of the female sex organs that one observes in the well-known sculptures of *Lajjāgaurī* images has been purposefully avoided in this highly symbolic sculpture. Although nakedness of the image is no doubt hinted at, it has been achieved with a stylized poetic softness. Only those with an intimate knowledge of *Lajjāgaurī* images would be able to realise that this sculpture represents the headless *Lajjāgaurī* with vagina and breasts.

The sculpture is carved in the form of thick, raised lines on a flat rock measuring roughly two and half feet by two feet. The navel of the goddess is shown in the form of a lotus with eight stalks. At the base of this is a triangle with three petals suggestive of the generative organ. There is a horizontal and broken line at throat level suggestive of the absence of a head. From the two ends of this horizontal line, two thick lines, each with three strands, travel towards the two arched feet in the form of a little arched recess. The sculptor who thus showed the generative organ of this female in the form of a lotus surrounded by her body in the form of a circular arched recess, was no doubt her devotee. In sculpting her, he exhibited his highly evolved, cultured and rich upbringing and his inspired imagination.

The headless images of *Lajjāgaurī* often show either lotuses or lotus buds in her raised hands. Similarly, in this sculpture, there rest on her shoulders two sets of four lotus buds with long stems tied together. The stems then coalesce with the circular arches that represent the two sides of her torso. One of the four lotus buds on either side has the form of a conch shell. Unfortunately, part of the left-hand side of the sculpture has been badly worn, and some of it is also broken. There is also a large crack in the middle. The lotus-shaped navel, the half lotus below the navel representing the organ of generation and the lotus buds on her shoulders are obviously intended to show this goddess as Kamalā, Lakṣmī in the form of a lotus. The sculptor who produced this masterpiece no doubt considered her to be Kamalā, the consort of Viṣṇu. To complete her Vaiṣṇava character, he carved one of the lotus buds on her shoulders in the form of a conch shell.

The Myth of Lakṣmī in the Sthalapurāṇa

We have no means of finding out what the original devotees at this shrine called the *Lajjāgaurī* image at this place. Today, she is called the 'Lakṣmī under the banyan tree'. Although her image, albeit transformed, is highly suggestive of her original nature and purpose, the conch shell in her hand makes it obvious that an attempt has been made to give her a Vaiṣṇava character. We already know that the goddess Śrī, who assumed a lotus form and was therefore known as Kamalā, was not originally Viṣṇu's wife. When attempts were made to establish her relationship with male gods, she was at times connected with Kubera and at other times with Ganeśa, as can be seen from old sculptures that are available today. Eventually, she was given a permanent position as the wife of Viṣṇu. This can be seen from folk religion. When one thinks of the word Lakṣmī now, one does not think of an independent and free primordial mother. One only thinks of her as a consort of Viṣṇu. Through this new name Lakṣmī that shows its closeness to a lotus, and through the incorporation of a conch shell in her iconography, an attempt was made to successfully transform the name and form of *Lajjāgaurī* at this place. To seal this transformation forever, a myth was incorporated into the Sthalapurāṇa of Rāmatīrtha.

The composer of the myth wanted to ensure that the original name, form and purpose of the *Lajjāgaurī* image and the reasoning behind the erstwhile construction of the shrine would be lost forever. The myth in the Sthalapurāṇa is as follows:

Once upon a time, in Vaikuṇṭha, Viṣṇu's abode, there was a fierce argument between Lakṣmī and Bhūdevī, the two wives of Viṣṇu, over which of them was better. They created such a racket that Viṣṇu's yogic meditation was disturbed. He intervened and separated the two by holding Bhūdevī with his right hand and Lakṣmī with his left. Because she was held by his left (inferior) hand when he separated them, Lakṣmī became incensed with him. Saying that she did not want such a husband, she came to earth. She happened to come to Rāmeśvara Kṣetra, where she worshipped goddess Ānandanāyakī and practiced penance on the south bank of the Pāpanāśinī river at the place called Padmālaya. The purpose of her penance was to seek a boon from the goddess Ānandanāyakī in order to attract Viṣṇu to herself completely. The goddess was pleased with her penance and appeared before Lakṣmī, who sought the following boon:

> Oh Goddess Rāmaśaṅkarī! Just as a person seeking a favour from a *māntrik*[13] surrenders himself totally to him, similarly, let Viṣṇu surrender to me completely by the power of your boon (21.110.)

As soon as the goddess gave this boon to Lakṣmī, Viṣṇu became restless and pined for her. He left his abode at Vaikuṇṭha and, wandering in search of her, came to Rāmatīrtha Kṣetra. Lakṣmī regained her *saubhāgya*[14] in the form of Viṣṇu seeking her ardently. The Sthalapurāṇa says that (with the heat of her penance, she created a stream of sacred flowing water called Saubhāgyadāyinī (*Lit*: bestower of *saubhāgya*) at this place. Also, in one of the invocatory *āratis*[15] for him, Rāmeśvara, the autochthonus presiding deity of this place, is invoked with the adjective *lakṣmīsaubhāgya* (*Lit*: the good fortune of Lakṣmī).

The Distant Memories in Oral Tradition

We have seen that a deliberate effort has been made at this place to change the name, form and mythology of *Lajjāgaurī* and transform her into a Vaiṣṇava goddess. Also, she has been given a lower status; a minor goddess in the Śaivite pantheon. In spite of this, however, the oral tradition at this place still maintains memories of her erstwhile form and mythology. Śyāmrāv Ināmdār, the person who accompanied me to this shrine, said that 'the image here is the lower portion of the goddess. The head of the goddess is at a nearby village called Kakmarī'. As soon as I heard this statement of his, I was satisfied that I was once again hearing the myth of *Lajjāgaurī*. I remembered that *Lajjāgaurī* is Bhūdevī, that she is the great mother goddess in the form of a human mother and that she is worshipped as Reṇukā, Yallammā and Joguḷāmbā. I also remembered that the name Reṇukā denoted the earth and that the myth about Paraśurāma having killed his mother was connected with Bhūdevī. In this connection, I also remembered that in many shrines connected with *Lajjāgaurī*, an explanation of her headlessness is given as follows: After Paraśurāma killed his mother, Reṇukā, her headless torso was worshipped as Reṇukā, Yallammā, Joguḷāmbā and *Lajjāgaurī*, whereas her head was worshipped as Mātaṅgī. Therefore, Ināmdār's statement reminded me of *Lajjāgaurī* and the associated myths involving Paraśurāma.

Not the Dāśarathī Rāma but Bhārgavarāma[16]

From the discussion above, we know that a distant memory (of *Lajjāgaurī*) in the oral tradition is still very much alive in the family of the principal *purohits*[17] at Rāmakṣetra. On the other hand, in explaining the name of this *kṣetra*, the Sthalapurāṇa explicitly connects it to Rāma, the son of Daśaratha. It is obvious that if this place was supposed to be a holy place for the worship of Bhūdevī Reṇukā, who is the same as *Lajjāgaurī*, then it must be the Rāmatīrtha of Paraśurāma and not Dāśarathī Rāma. In this regard, one is always reminded of the fact that the coastal strip of the Konkaṇ and Gomantaka (Goa) is steeped in the worship of Bhūdevī. In many *Sthalapurāṇas* from this region, the place is regularly called 'Rāmakṣetra'. We need to remember that the name 'Rāma' stands not only for Rāma, the son of Daśaratha, but also for the Yādava 'Balarāma' (Kṛṣṇa's brother) and 'Bhārgavarāma' (Paraśurāma). In the Sthalapurāṇa of Rāmatīrtha, *Lajjāgaurī* is described as Lakṣmī, the wife of Viṣṇu. However, the adjective 'Bhārgavī' is often applied to her. Although Bhārgavī is one of the names of the goddess Lakṣmī, it is not a common name for her. We wonder, then, why the *Sthalapurāṇa* repeatedly calls her by this uncommon name. Is it possible that in attempting to deliberately refashion the age-old myth about *Lajjāgaurī*, the composer wanted to show her relationship with Bhārgava Rāma by calling her Bhārgavī?

The Goddess of the Dhangars at Kakmarī

The village of Kakmarī, where, according to the local oral myth, the head of the goddess is worshipped, is only four or five kilometres from the town of Rāmatīrtha. Shyāmrāv Ināmdār informed me that the goddess at Kakmarī is known as 'Amājava'. This was confirmed when I saw the name of the goddess on the lintel of the temple as 'Amājeśvarī'. The goddess, coated with red-lead, had eyes of silver buried deep in the red-lead. She was decorated with flowers and leaves that were artistically arranged. There was a brass image of a cobra in front of her image (see Plate 24).

Dhangars (Marāṭhī shepherds) have had the right to worship this image for many years. There is an important thirteenth-century stone inscription that mentions her name. The inscription is dated Śaka 1204 (1282 C.E.). It was found at the town of Maṅgalveḍhe. The inscription records the grant of this town along with six other towns, including Kavaṭhe, by one Siddhanāth, for the goddess Candikā. It also mentions that anyone who does not observe the terms of this grant (does not worship the goddess as per tradition), would need to explain his shortcoming personally to Goddess Kakmarī.

The inscription goes to show that an oath taken before the goddess Kakmarī carried a great deal of weight among the people of the time, to the extent that such an oath was thought inviolable.

The Mystery of Rāmeśvara

The goddess of Kakmarī is thought of as the head part of the entire goddess. At Rāmatīrtha she is known by the respectable name Lakṣmī. According to the myth in the Sthalapurāṇa, elite circles of devotees know her as the wife of Viṣṇu. In spite of all of this, her position within the Rāmeśvara-Ānandanāyakī pantheon is decidedly subordinate and neglected. Although her image in terms of her iconography is highly artistic, symbolic and representative of eternal motherhood, for all practical purposes, she is a minor local deity dependent on occasional worship by local women in their times of need. The artistically sculpted arches and lotuses on her image are now covered all over with turmeric and vermillion. They signify her roles as the one 'blessing married women in their role as eternally and happily married women' and as 'the bestower of children'.

Oral tradition still celebrates one particular instance where the worship of this *Lajjāgaurī* in the form of Lakṣmī enjoys a precious reminder of the past. That instance is the meeting of Rāmeśvara and Lakṣmī during the festival of Dīpāvalī. Once a year, at the time of Dīpāvalī, Rāmeśvara gets seated ceremoniously in a palanquin and taken to visit Lakṣmī. The occasion is celebrated by the lighting of several lamps. Locals describe this event as the meeting of a brother with his sister. How is this possible? The answer may lie in the fact that Ānandanāyakī developed into a goddess of the higher tradition from *Lajjāgaurī*. It is also true that, as the consort of Rāmeśvara, Ānandanāyakī occupies the cave temple on the west side of the Rāmeśvara shrine. However, in her new form under the banyan tree, she has become Lakṣmī, the consort of Viṣṇu. Because of this transformation, the only relationship she can now have with Rāmeśvara (Śiva) is as his sister.

One wonders if Rāmeśvara himself could be a local god. Thus, Mallaṇṇā, the son-in-law of the Cencu community in the Śrīśaila mountains, became the respectable Mallikārjuna Śiva, one of the twelve highly venerated Jyotirliṅgas. The godling Vīraṇṇā at Vijayanagara became the celebrated Virūpākṣa. Could it be that Rāmeśvara was a local godling who over time coalesced with Śiva? Goddess Kakmarī, who is thought to represent the head of *Lajjāgaurī* alias Lakṣmī under the banyan tree, is worshipped first and foremost by members of the Dhangar shepherd caste. However, to this date, she is still closely associated with the Lakṣmī at Rāmatīrtha. Could the present day Rāmeśvara be related to the Lakṣmī at Rāmatīrtha? A decisive answer to this question cannot be given at this point. However, it is worth our while to remember that one of the verses of the Sthalapurāṇa states:

> *saptakoṭī mahāmantra heci jayā mahāgātra* |
>
> (Verse 1270)
>
> (The great mantra of seven crores is the main limb of those…)

Although short and indirect, this is an important mention of Śiva. We already know that the '*saptakoṭī mahāmantra*' is the chant '*yeḷkoṭ yeḷkoṭ*'[18] Needless to say, Mailāra-Khaṇḍobā is considered an *avatāra* of Śiva in the *Sthalapurāṇas*.

Therefore, if we look through the small window of this mantra into the mysterious cavern of the unknown past, we may yet find the original form of the Rāmeśvara of today as one who was worshipped by the loud chants of *yeḷkoṭ yeḷkoṭ*, accompanied by Wāghyās covered in *bhaṇḍārā*.[19]

We do, however, need more evidence to fathom this and bring it to light. Until then, we must curtail our ardent desire for the truth.

The Śaiva Ācāryas who were responsible for transforming the folk worship of Rāmeśvara into traditional Śaiva worship are mentioned in the stone inscriptions that are found here, along with the kings who supported these Ācāryas.

The Śaiva Ācāryas of Rāmatīrtha

There are eight to ten extant stone inscriptions dealing with the autochthonous Rāmeśvara at this place. Two of these have been examined, read and edited by Vidyāratna R.S. Pancamukhī, in the second volume of the series 'Karnāṭaka Inscriptions'. Both of these inscriptions are located on the front wall of the Nṛsiṃha temple within the Rāmeśvara temple complex. The first of these inscriptions was carved during the reign of the well-known Cālukya king, Tribhuvanamalladeva (Vikramāditya VI). It deals with the worship of Rāmeśvara at Rāmatīrtha, the provision of food and lodging for holy men and the regular maintenance and repair of the shrine. It records the grant of the town of Nāgahaḷḷī for this purpose by the chief minister (Karaṇādhipa Mahāpradhāna) Cauvuṇayyā and Mahāmaṇḍaleśvara Permādiyaras. The gift was accepted by Ācārya Śivaśaktipaṇḍit, who belonged to the lineage of the Goṭakanūru Ācāryas and was a devotee of Nemeśvaradeva.[20] The gift was presented on February 10, 1115, which was a full-moon day, at the time of a lunar eclipse.[21] This Śivaśaktipaṇḍit was a Śaiva Ācārya belonging to the Kālāmukha branch of the Lākulīśa Pāśupata sect.

The second inscription records the donation of the town of Sindavur, situated in the area of Umbaravāṇī-Cḥattīs. The donation was made by the emperor (Bhujabalacakravartī) Bijjaladeva to the principal Ācārya at the Rāmeśvara temple, Ācārya Candrābharaṇapaṇḍita Deva. The inscription lauds Candrābharaṇapaṇḍita Deva as an Ācārya of universal fame and a leader of ascetics. The name of his Guru is given as Lokābharaṇapaṇḍita Deva. The date of this donation was Monday, May 2, 1166 (Vaiśākha Kṛṣṇa Amāvasya, Śaka 1089), which was a new-moon day, and the donation was made at the time of the solar eclipse on this day. The inscription also records some other donations for the offerings of sandalwood paste, incense sticks, lamps and food for the god Rāmeśvara.

The administrative centre Umbaravāṇī-Chattīs mentioned in the above inscription is the present town of Umrāṇī in the old State of Jat. This town has an ancient temple of Śiva called Hemaliṅga Mandir, which also has some inscriptions of the Cālukya-Kalacurī era. Pancamukhī has published two articles in the second volume of *Karnāṭaka Inscriptions*, cited above. In the first, the inscriptions are dated 1123 C.E. and 1142 C.E. respectively. The second article dates yet another inscription as having been recorded in 1174 C.E. In both of these articles, the Śiva shrine is called Hemmeśvara. It is also clear from the inscriptions that the name Hemmeśvara is closely connected with the name of one of the Mahāmaṇḍaleśvaras, Hemmāḍideva. It is worth noting that the first inscription in the shrine of Hemmeśvara was recorded during the reign of the Cālukya king Tribhuvanamalladeva. This inscription records the donation of all the property and wealth associated with the shrine of Hemmeśvara to the same Ācārya, Candrābharaṇapaṇḍita Deva, of the shrine of Rāmeśvara at Rāmatīrtha.

It should be amply clear from the above discussion that, during the reign of the Cālukyas of Kalyāṇī, the Śaiva Ācāryas of the Kālāmukha sect had attained great importance in Karnāṭaka and that their temples and Maṭhas were generously supported by ruling dynasties. These Śaiva Ācāryas erected several temples and Maṭhas in Karnāṭaka and the adjoining areas of Āndhra Pradesh and Mahārāṣtra during the 11th and 12th centuries, and even later during the Vijayanagara empire. The worship of Śiva attained great importance during this time. These temples and Maṭhas were also great centres of traditional learning. The majority of the stone inscriptions detailing the work of these Ācāryas are in Kannaḍā.

Although many of these inscriptions still remain unread, the ones that have been read inform us that the Kālāmukha Śaiva Ācāryas led an exemplary life as ascetics and had a profound knowledge of Śaivism. They excelled in imparting this traditional knowledge to their disciples. Along with the Kāpālikas, these Kālāmukha Ācāryas established the foundation of the Śiva-Dharma that resurfaced after Basaveśvara rejuvenated it in Karnāṭaka.

Many researchers have examined the inscriptions recorded in Kannaḍā in the 11th and 12th centuries C.E., and have noted the importance accorded in these to the Śaiva Ācāryas. Unfortunately, however, with the exception of David Lorenzen, an overseas scholar, no one within India has as yet attempted to put together an account of the work of these Śaiva Ācāryas. Furthermore, Lorenzen's work is based only on those inscriptions that had been read and edited by other scholars. It is, however, highly important to investigate the history and the circumstances that led to the construction of the Maṭhas and temples where these inscriptions were recorded, especially from the point of view of the then existing local traditions. This would shed light on the modus operandi of the Śaiva Ācāryas. Of course, such an investigation was not possible for Lorenzen. A task of such enormity is beyond the scope of one researcher working alone. What needs to happen is for a single expert researcher to concentrate on each temple or Maṭh in order to unravel the workings of the Śaiva Ācāryas at that place. Only when such combined and synergistic efforts have been undertaken, would we be able to throw light on how these Śaiva Ācāryas converted popular folk shrines into great centres of traditional Śaivism. Such research will unravel an exciting history that will bring to light the relationship of folk religion with the religion of the higher tradition. There are reasons to believe that, even at Rāmatīrtha *kṣetra*, a traditional centre for folk-religious worship of village deities has been transformed into a centre for higher Śaivism. In order to unravel the mystery behind such a transformation, one needs to examine the local traditions at Rāmatīrtha in fine detail. It is important to do so before the folk traditions vanish altogether. Even the minutest details of the folk tradition at the place need to be examined and recorded. That is the only way we can unravel the devotional character of the place before the Śaiva Ācāryas took over. It is important to do so for the sake of local cultural history as well.

Revelatory Signs of Folk Religion

Source materials that could be used to discover the details of how the Kālāmukha Śaiva Ācāryas transformed local village cults into the higher tradition of Śaivism are simply non-existent. However, some telling indications of how this may have happened are in existence to this day. Although I have mentioned them before, I take the liberty of re-listing them here for the benefit of the reader.

1) At this place, the Rāmatīrtha Kṣetra, *Lajjāgaurī*, the goddess of fertility, is still being worshipped in a small, insignificant and neglected shrine outside the town.
2) Her original form, showing her to be ever ready for accepting the male seed, has been converted here into a beautiful and highly symbolic image. However, because of the presence of the lotuses in the appropriate places (breasts and vagina), the main purpose of the image has been kept intact.

3) Her original form displaying her rather crude nudity must have been unacceptable to the devotees, and most certainly to the Śaiva Ācāryas. In order to address this, the beauty of the female form has been preserved and hinted at by sculpting it in the shape of vines forming semi-circular arches.
4) Her sculpture, adorned everywhere by vermillion and turmeric, is highly suggestive of the reasons for her worship. Similarly, the myth about her in the Sthalapurāṇa also suggests her close relationship with protecting a woman's status as someone blessed by having a husband. An ancient inscription about the *Lajjāgaurī* sculpture discovered at Nāgārjunakoṇḍā mentions a queen of the Ikṣvāku dynasty who worshipped the goddess. This queen has been called '*avidhavā* (*Lit*: not a widow) and '*jīvatputrā'* (*Lit*: one whose sons are alive). Even to this day, the *Lajjāgaurī* at Rāmatīrtha is considered to bestow *saubhāgya* and progeny.
5) The lower part of the goddess's body is thought to be at Rāmatīrtha, while the head is at the village of Kakmarī. The local myth explaining this is still very prevalent even among the higher castes at Rāmatīrtha. This oral tradition and belief suggest that, traditionally, the *Lajjāgaurī* here is also thought to be the same as Reṇukā.
6) The belief in the myth of the beheading of Reṇukā reminds us of the broader myth of Reṇukā and her son Paraśurāma. The latter is referred to here as Rāma, the short form of his full name.
7) Right from the beginning, this *kṣetra* has been known as Rāmatīrtha. The stone inscriptions call it simply *tīrtha.*
8) In the Sthalapurāṇa, although the name, form and biography of *Lajjāgaurī* have been completely transformed, she is called Bhārgavī again and again. Although her form as Lakṣmī is evident from this deliberately chosen name, the name alone hints at her true character as Reṇukā, the mother and wife of the Bhārgavas.
9) The Sthalapurāṇa mentions briefly that the god Rāmeśvara is very fond of the '*saptakoṭī mahāmantra*'. This mantra involves the constant chanting of '*yelkoṭ, yelkoṭ'*. We know very well that this chant is the favourite chant of Mailāra-Khaṇḍobā. We also know that Mailāra-Khaṇḍobā has been thought of as an *avatāra* of Śiva in all of his shrines.

10) *Lajjāgaurī*, known here as Lakṣmī, has been thought of as the sister of Rāmeśvara. Their annual visit to each other is celebrated each year during the festival of Dīpāvalī. The fact that Rāmeśvara, who is surrounded by riches, comes to visit this totally neglected goddess once a year throws light on their erstwhile close relationship.

It is important for researchers to keep in mind that Rāmatīrtha has been an important *kṣetra* for the worship of Rāmeśvara and his consort Ānandanāyakī for over a thousand years. In spite of this, there are vestiges in the folk-religious traditions here that hint at a relationship between Rāmeśvara and Lakṣmī. When we look at these signs seriously and ask ourselves why Rāmeśvara's consort has been given the significant and mysterious name Ānandanāyakī, one realises that unfolding the etymology of this name is itself the key to understanding the process of the elevation of the folk tradition to the higher, Brāhmanical tradition at this place.

Ānandīdevī and Ānandanāyakī

In my work *Lajjāgaurī*, I have explained that *Lajjāgaurī* was originally an independent goddess with her own mode of worship who granted progeny to her devotees. Even to this day, she is worshipped in her original form in places like Siddhanakoṭṭe. Depending on her whim, she chose whichever form of primordial male consort she fancied. However, with the passage of time, she has become the consort of Śiva. In her image at Jayarāmasvāmice Vaḍgāv, she is shown accompanied by the bull Nandi, the vehicle of Śiva. In an image currently kept at the museum at Nagpur, she is shown next to a *śivaliṅga*. This goes to show that, even in the worship directed solely to her, Śiva as the primordial male was seen as being connected to her. Scholars are now of the opinion that the Mahākūṭeśvara at Mahākūṭa and Navabrahmeśvara at Ālampūr, both very well known shrines of Śiva in the past and present, have become famous due to Śiva's supremacy and reign over the goddess *Lajjāgaurī*.

Historical Change in the Cult at Rāmatīrtha

In order to find out how the change in cult occurred at Rāmatīrtha, it is worth our while to look at another example of a place where a similar development seems to have occurred. This place is the village of Āḷand near the town of Gulbargā, in Karnāṭaka. Known today as the Dargā of Lāḍale Maśāyatkhā, this place, until the defeat of the Vijayanagara Kingdom, was a centre for the well-known God Someśvara and his consort Ānandīdevī. There were important and beautifully sculpted temples to both of these deities at this place. These temples were desecrated during the defeat of the Vijayanagara Kingdom. The images of the deities at these places were destroyed as well. However, until recently, many of the important remains of these temples were scattered around this place. During the reign of the Nizām and even after the liberation of Hyderabad, systematic attempts were made to destroy the ancient shrines and their remnants. Tukarām's Guru, Rāghava Caitanya, lived within the precinct of this ancient temple. His final resting place was also here. An inscription dated December 27, 1082 found at this temple tells us that it was the Cālukya King Tribhuvanamalla Vikramāditya of Kalyāṇī who brought prosperity to this temple. The name of the place, Āḷand, is also closely connected with the goddess Āḷandī. As a matter of fact, the name of this *kṣetra* explains the mystery behind the name of the goddess Āḷandī.

The Someśvara at Āḷand was known in the traditional folklore here as Iraṇṇā (Vīraṇṇā), and Goddess Āḷandī was known as Yallammā (Reṇukā). The image of goddess Āḷandī at this place was in the form of *Lajjāgaurī*. It was removed from here four centuries ago and is now worshipped as Yallammā at a place called Honhaḷḷī near Āḷand. At Honhaḷḷī, women desirous of having children worship Yallammā's generative organ.

Āḷandī (Ānandī) is an artificially constructed name. It is a transformation of her original popular name, Yallammā. Just as Āḷampūr is a conversion of the original name Yallammāpūr, Āḷand, the name of the town, has been adopted from the name of the presiding deity of the place, Yallammā. Similarly, the form Ānandī Devī has been derived from Āḷandī Devī because the letters l, ḷ and n are interchangeable. This would explain the transformation of the name Āḷand to Ānandavan in the work *Nāgeśa-Līlāmṛta*.

The transformation that was made at Rāmatīrtha was akin to the one that occurred at Āḷand. At Āḷand, the place associated with Yallammā, the name of the town was Saṃskṛtized to Ānandavan, albeit unsuccessfully. At Rāmatīrtha, a successful attempt has been made to associate the name that reminds one of Reṇukā, i.e. Rāmatīrtha, with Dāśarathi Rāma, instead of Paraśurāma. Similarly, the rock that holds the inside of the cave within which she stays in her form as a consort (of Śiva-Rāmeśvara) is called Ānandācala. At Āḷand, *Lajjāgaurī*, popularly known as Yallammā, has acquired the name Ānandī Devī. At Rāmatīrtha, she has acquired an equally beautiful name, Ānandanāyakī. The suffix '-nāyakī' in Ānandanāyakī serves to remind us vaguely of her original nudity. From the example of Ānandī Devī, one can easily conclude that the name Ānandanāyakī is a Saṃskṛtized version of Yallammā. It is therefore clear that the *Lajjāgaurī* at Rāmatīrtha was originally popularly known as Yallammā.

When Mailāra coalesced with Rāmeśvara, his temple obtained great riches but his cult became complex and highly Brāhminized. Because of this, he left his cowherd devotees behind. Ānandanāyakī, a Brāhminized version of *Lajjāgaurī*, acquired a cave temple of her own next to Rāmeśvara; the cave itself became the goddess. Her original image, by contrast, was given an insignificant shrine outside the town. She remains a minor goddess, recipient of simple worship by neglected, childless and hence unwanted women. Although she has coalesced with Śiva in her form as Ānandanāyakī, she has not been allowed to remain in her erstwhile original form in the new place given to her outside the town. Her form, unacceptable to some, has been transformed into a symbolic illustration. Her popular original name, Yallammā, has been changed to Lakṣmī due to the presence of lotuses in this stylized sculpture. In her new form adorned with lotuses, a conch shell has also been incorporated, thus converting her into a Vaiṣṇava goddess. A story has been incorporated in the Sthalapurāṇa about her obtaining a boon from her own consort form as Ānandanāyakī. This boon promises her the status of a woman whose husband is forever alive. This story has resulted in her incorporation into the Śaiva fold in a minor way. It is indeed fortunate for her that Mailāra in his form as Rāmeśvara visits her as her brother, albeit only once a year. At one time, she was the supreme goddess who offered shelter to her devotees. With the passage of time, it is she who has become a refugee. In terms of both history and sociology, this transformation is significant.

Although I am unhappy about this unfair sociological fact, I still have the same praise in my inner mind when I bow in front of the goddesses 'Vaḍākhālcī Lakṣmī'and the Ānandanāyakī in the cave. I say:

> *yā devī sarvabhūteṣu matṛrūpeṇa saṃsthitā* |
> *namas tasyai namas tasyai namas tasyai namo namaḥ* ||
>
> (I bow thrice to the goddess who resides in all living beings as the mother)

Tejogarbhā Guheśvarī[22]

Every time I witness the thousands of lamps lit at night during the festival of Dīpāvalī, I am reminded again and again of the Cave of Ānandanāyakī. This is mainly because, when I visited Rāmatīrtha, I understood the importance of the festival of Dīpāvalī and the lighting of the lamps during the annual celebration at the place. We have already seen how, more than eight or nine hundred years ago, the Śaiva Ācāryas constructed a grand, imposing temple of Rāmeśvara ornamented with beautiful sculptures at the *tīrtha* near the town of Athṇī. They did this by splitting vertically a huge boulder named Ānandācala and situating the temple next to it. Behind this temple, they sculpted the same boulder and, instead of a temple, created a cave for Śiva's consort. This dark, mysterious cave is inhabited by the primordial mother of the world, the Ādiśakti by the pleasing name of Ānandanāyakī. The sculptors who created this cave were fully aware of the darkness within. That is why they went to great lengths to stress the importance of lighting lamps during the worship of Ānandanāyakī. The poet who translated the Saṃskṛt Sthalapurāṇa into Marāṭhī states (in Marāṭhī):

> *dīpamāḷānī guhesī* |
> *alaṅkārije sāyāsī* ||
>
> (the cave should be adorned with lighted rows of lamps.)

Thus, the composer of the Sthalapurāṇa advises devotees who wish to obtain boons from Ānandanāyakī to make efforts to decorate the cave with lighted lamps. He also explains the importance of lighting lamps that use ghee made out of cow's milk or oil lamps using sesame oil at the entrance of the cave of Mahādevī, the great goddess.

> *bhṛguvāsarī to jana* | *akṣayyatīrthī yā snāna* |
> *karī dīpāvalī pradāna* | *ānandanāyakī pratī* ||[23]
>
> (That person bathes in the *Ākṣayatīrtha* every Friday and offers a row of lamps to Ānandanāyakī.)

This worship involving devotees offering lamps to Ānandanāyakī is especially noticeable at the time of Dīpāvalī. The sanctum sanctorum of the cave-goddess shines brilliantly with light and the moonless last night in the dark half of the month of Aśvina bears in its womb the beginning of the first day of Kārtika, the day of Balipratipadā.[24]

In imagining the seat of the mother goddess as a cave completely enveloped in mysterious darkness, there seems to be an attempt to direct our attention to the mystery of primordial creation. In the language of the Vedas, the place where the entire visible world lies dormant is called 'the cave'. The Vedas have thought of the cave as the earth's mysterious centre for the creation of the universe, which expresses itself with a myriad of names and forms.

The Womb of Mother Nature

The creative waters that were responsible for the birth of the universe were all enclosed in this cave. When they were freed from there, the birth of the universe started as an ongoing process. The very deep cave, the complete and total darkness within, and the creative waters that were engulfed inside are together considered to be the initial stage of the birth of the universe. This initial stage is responsible not only for the birth of the universe but also for everything that is born today. It is because of this that the dark cave that holds the foetus of creation and of the moonless night is especially important.

> *vidmā te nāma paramaṃ guhā yat* |[25]
>
> (O Agni, Lord of fire! We recognize your sacred presence in the cave.)

When the Vedic seers invoke Agni by addressing him this way, they are in fact describing the universal motherhood of the earth through the imagery of the cave and the foetus of the light enclosed within it.

The dark cave is the womb of mother nature, the womb of the great mother. The dark night is similarly an enormous and magnificent cave in the universe, a cave that is capable of enclosing the entire cosmos within itself. It is the lustrous cave that engulfs all the void. When one welcomes the lustrous foetus by lighting innumerable lamps, one is in dialogue with divine creation. Lamps in their thousands are lit within the self and surrounding the self. The experience is truly beyond description. In the course of this experience, the cave of Ānandanāyakī becomes an endless night. And, conversely, endless night becomes Ānandanāyakī.

Guheśvarī in Nepal

Strong evidence for the human perception of a cave as a goddess is seen in Nepal, where the goddess Guheśvarī (*Lit*: The Cave Goddess) has acquired great fame and reputation and is celebrated as a *kuladevatā* (clan goddess) even to this day. Insulted by her father Dakṣa at the time of the great sacrifice that he was performing, Satī threw herself into the sacrificial flames and died as a result. Maddened with grief and rage, Śiva took her lifeless body on his shoulder and roamed the earth. Parts of Satī's body fell in several places. All over India, there is a belief that the places where parts of her body fell became Śaktipīṭhas (*Lit*: seats of Śakti). There are, however, many versions as to where particular parts of Satī fell. The Nepalese firmly believe that the goddess' organ of generation fell at Guheśvarī and that is why the place became famous with that name. The very name Guheśvarī (*guhārūpā īśvarī*, the goddess in her form as a cave) is clearly the sign of her motherhood of the entire world. It symbolizes her being ever ready, in a state of primordial generation. It is because of this that the dark night lit by innumerable lamps in Dīpāvalī reminds me of the cave of goddess Ānandanāyakī.

The Cave: The Mother's Womb

This symbolism associated with a dark cave does not seem to be restricted to India alone. Many scholars of ancient history, anthropology and the history of religion all over the world have shown that for Stone-Age people who lived in caves, the caves were not only places for shelter; they were centres for meditation and reflection as well. These scholars have comprehensively examined the nature and geography of such caves and the beliefs about them among people of tribal heritage. Their researches show that tribals have looked at a cave as a maternal womb. It is the womb where one rests at the end of one's life in deep sleep and from where one enters this world again after re-birth.

Thinkers and philosophers all over the world have frequently expressed a poetic curiosity towards the darkness before light, the dark night before the sunrise and the mysterious gestatory state before creation. A scholar who comes to mind straightaway is the great psychologist, philosopher and critic, Eric Neumannn. Not only did he delve into the mysteries of the human mind, but he also had a lifelong interest in the workings of the human endeavour that have led to the enrichment of culture. He resorted to psychology in order to seek answers to many a problem in this area. In doing so, he examined the outlines and revealed emotions of the inner depths of the human mind. With his sharp intellect and wisdom, he travelled with equal facility from archaeology to mythology. *The Great Mother*, and *Art and the Creative Unconscious* are two of his greatest works.

In the first one of these books, he examines the beliefs and myths about motherhood all over the world and, as a result, delves into the mystery of creation. In the second, he examines the workings of the inner, dark recesses of the human mind and shows how splendid and amazing art has developed from this pregnant darkness. The inspiration that impels both of these books is the same, and the method of investigation is also the same. To investigate the creative darkness before generation and to investigate the direct and indirect symbols that humans have created for this purpose was what Neumann had in mind. With many convincing examples, this amazing thinker has shown that a cave is a symbolic perception by humans of the mother's womb. The entrance to the cave is the mouth of that womb, the mouth of the container. In the light of Eric Neumannn's pioneering thought, it becomes clear that the extraordinary origin of all of human ingenuity and arts is the creative and mysterious darkness situated within the complexity of the human mind.

The Creative Darkness that Generates Light

Eric Neumannn revealed the comprehensive symbolism dealing with the association of motherhood with caves. In doing so, he examined the inner darkness of the creative mind, a precursor to light–inspiration. One of the greatest of Marāṭhī poets, B.B. Borkar, also hints at this creative darkness in his 'Tamaḥstotra'.[26] Discerning readers have experienced the impact of this amazing poem:

> *Om namaḥ śribhagavān tamā* |
> *prakaśajanakā puruśottamā* ||
>
> (I bow to you, God Darkness! You the creator of light and the supreme being!)

Borkar invokes the creative darkness with these adjectives and then says:

> *bāpā tujhiyā oṭi-poṭī* |
> *tārāmaṇḍaḷe asankhya koṭī*
> *jyotiṣkamaḷe aticokhaṭī* |
> *gomaṭī lāvaṇyabhāṇḍare* ||

(Oh God Darkness, I bow to you. You are the supreme being, the creator of light. Oh father! Hidden within yourself are crores of stars, lustrous and pure plants and flowers and scores of excellent, graceful and comely things.)

In this devotional fervour, Borkar explains the origin of human creativity. Eric Neumann explained the mystery of creativity through his reasoned argument and thinking. Borkar tackles the mystery through his poetry.

Naturally, this creative darkness is quite different from the destructive darkness that extinguishes human endeavours and aspirations. When such destructive darkness engulfs all of the creative and wholesome impulses within our minds, we have to invoke Ānandanāyakī, who restores the purity in our life. This is because she is not only the genetrix but also the one who gives us inspiration and shows us direction. One has to light lamps during the generative and creative darkness of the night in order to welcome the morning light. Similarly, during the darkness of the destructive night, in order to invoke the Śakti that will show us the morning, we need to light the lamps to welcome her. We need to invoke her with ardent devotion similar to that expressed, in Marāṭhī, by the poet Maṅgeś Pādgāvkar:

sakhi tū gāyatrī mantra prāṇāntuna gāve |
bhagavatī uṣepari tū ghanatamī phulāve ||

(Oh my love! You should chant the Gāyatrī Mantra in your breath. Oh Goddess! like Uṣā, the morning goddess who opens up through the clouds, you should flower.)

Endnotes

1 Translator's note: For details of the worship of a cave in the form of a vagina by early man, see Footnote 42 in the Chapter, 'Introduction to Ḍhere's *Lajjāgaurī*' by the translator.

2 Translator's note: *The Ānandanāyakī* is a small booklet of 104 pages and contains six chapters. In the introduction, Ḍhere remarks that due to his failing health and other major difficulties, he has been unable to conduct an extensive tour of South India and complete the research required for an exhaustive book on the goddess *Ānandanāyakī*. In the end, he says he has had to be satisfied with this small booklet. Chapters 1 to 3 are a background to his pilgrimage to the *Ānandanāyakī*. Chapter five is an interview Ḍhere gave to a newspaper journalist on his journey from *Lajjāgaurī* to The

Ānandanāyakī, whereas chapter six is his proposed research project on this theme. Chapter four is the only chapter that discusses the topic concerned and hence I have chosen to translate only that chapter.

3 Translator's note: Jñānadeva or Jñāneśvar (1275–1296 C.E.) was one of the foremost of Marāṭhī saints. He wrote his famous commentary on the *Bhagvadgītā*, called the *Jñāneśvarī*. Here, Ḍhere is alluding to the pilgrimage places that Jñaneśvara visited.

4 Translator's note: Throughout his book '*Lajjāgaurī*', Ḍhere used 'miles' in quoting distances. In Ānandanāyakī, he has used kilometres. I have kept things as they are in this translation.

5 Translator's note: A *dīpamāḷa* is often a part of a temple complex. It is a circular stone or brick structure which is normally very tall and narrows toward the top. All around this structure are places to mount small oil lamps with wicks right up to the top. On special days of religious celebration, these lamps are lit at night, providing a spectacular show.

6 Translator's note: Tripurī or Tripurārī Pūrṇimā (Kārtika Pūrṇimā) is a Hindu festival celebrated on the full moon day of the month of Kārtika (November–December).

7 Translator's note: It is not clear what Ḍhere means here. They could perhaps be Śivaliṅgas which have other faces on them, such as that of Brahmā.

8 Translator's note: *candrakoṭisuśītala* | *śūla kheṭa asi kapāla* | *hastapallavī śobhāḷa* | *pītāmbaradhara je* || (In Marāṭhī).

9 Translator's note: Ḍhere has stated more than once that he feels uncomfortable examining the womb of the mother. He asks her for forgiveness for doing so and says that he is her child and it is with a sense of great apprehension that he wishes to examine the mystery that surrounds her image. That is why he says he is always abashed when researching *Lajjāgaurī* images.

10 Saṃskṛt to Marāṭhī translation by Ḍhere. Marāṭhī to English translation by Jayant Bāpaṭ.

11 Translator's note: Kusumāgraj (V. V. Shirwādkar, 1912 –1999), was an eminent Marāṭhī poet, playwright, novelist and short story writer. He won many prestigious awards, including the 'Padmabhūṣaṇ'.

12 Translator's note: *Vaḍ* is the Indian name for the *Ficus religiosa* tree.

13 Translator's note: A *māntrik* is a Śāman who acts as a medium between god and devotees.

14 Translator's note: The word *saubhāgya* is used specifically to describe a woman's state of being happily married. In the past, only a married woman whose husband was still alive was allowed to put the vermillion mark on her forehead and take part in rituals reserved only for married women. She was called a *saubhāgyavatī* (lit: one who possesses *saubhāgya*).

15 Translator's note: An *Ārati* is a devotional song sung to address the deity at certain specific times during the day and on special occasions, usually done with the waving of candles or lamps.

16 Translator's note: *Dāśarathī Rāma* is the son of the king Daśaratha and the hero of the epic *Rāmāyaṇa*. Bhārgavarāma is Paraśurāma, the son of the Brāhmin sage Jamadagni and his wife Reṇukā.

17 Translator's note: Families who hold traditional rights to the main worship at a *kṣetra* place are called Kṣetropādhyāya. Only if they are absent, other Brāhmins can perform the daily worship of the deities at such places.

18 Translator's note: *Yeḷkoṭ, yeḷkoṭ* is the popular chant for the god Mailāra (Malhāra) alias Khaṇḍobā. *yeḷkoṭ* is a word in the Kannaḍā language and means 'seven forts' (of the deity Khaṇḍobā).

19 Translator's note: A Vāghyā is a male offered in the service of the god Khaṇḍobā for life. His religious duty to the god is to dress in the guise of a tiger and dance in front of him during processions, covered in turmeric (*bhaṇḍārā*).

20 Translator's note: Neither the inscription nor Ḍhere explain who the deity Nemeśvaradeva was.

21 Translator's note: It is considered highly auspicious to give donations during the time of eclipses.

22 Translator's note: *Lit.* the lustrous womb goddess who resides in the cave.

23 In Marāṭhī.

24 Translator's note: Since Vedic times, darkness has always been associated with inauspicious things such as ignorance, sin, evil spirits and even death, in Indian thought. Light on the other hand is associated with godliness, knowledge, rebirth and even *Brahman*, the ultimate 'it'. Thus, a prayer in the *Bṛhadāraṇyaka Upaniṣad* seeks divine help to go from darkness to light (*tamaso mā jyotirgamaya*). *Pūjā* rituals contain a prayer to light equating it with *Brahman*. The Hindu idea of reincarnation is based upon the cycle of birth, death and regeneration. This is what Ḍhere is hinting at here. The night before the start of Dīpāvalī is a totally dark, moonless night. The first day of Dīpāvalī is the first day of the month when the moon appears in the sky. The totally dark night before the first day of the month thus bears the foetus of light that will be born the next day.

25 Saṃskṛt to Marāṭhī translation by Ḍhere. Marāṭhī to English translation by Jayant Bāpaṭ.

26 Translator's note: *Tamaḥstotra* literally means 'an ode to darkness'.

Glossary

Abhiṣeka
Hindus believe that when invoked, a deity visits their home in human form. The metal or clay image of the deity is thus treated in the same way as an important guest who is visiting the home. Of the many rituals that are performed, one involves bathing the image with warm water (occasionally milk) while chanting the mantras appropriate for the particular deity. This procedure is called an Abhiṣeka. The water used is then sprinkled all over the house to sanctify and purify it.

Ādimailāra
The original mailāra. The name mailāra is derived from 'mallāri', meaning the destroyer of the demon Malla. Śiva, in his form as Khaṇḍobā, killed this demon. Khaṇḍobā's main temple is at Jejurī near Puṇe in Mahārāṣṭra.

Ādi-Śaṅkarācārya
See Śaṅkarācārya

Aditi
A goddess from the *Ṛgveda*. She is considered to be the mother of the gods and the universe, a personification of the infinite.

Airāvata
The elephant of the God Indra.

Ārdrā Śrī
Ārdrā (*Skt.* Wet) an adjective applied to the Goddess Lakṣmī in the hymn *Śrisūkta*, denotes the menstruation phase of the goddess. In this hymn, Lakṣmī is equated with Pṛthivī, the earth. Until she menstruates, she will not be able to create new life through her union with the sky, her male counterpart.

Āṣāḍha
Aṣāḍha is the fourth month in the Hindu (lunar) calendar which begins on the 22nd of June. The monsoon season starts in India in this month.

Aṣṭādaśapīṭha
A list of eighteen important seats of Śakti (Goddess) thought to have been written by the Ādi-Śaṅkarācārya. There are 108 main seats of the Goddess and these eighteen are part of the bigger list.

Aśvin
The seventh month in the Hindu calendar.

Asyavāmīya Sūkta
Composed by the seer Dīrghatamas Aucathya, the Asyavāmīya Sūkta is one of the most enigmatic and complex *suktas* (hymn) from the *Ṛgveda* (1.164.1-52). It deals with the creation and evolution of the universe.

Ausā
The favourite disciple of Cakradharasvāmī, the great preceptor of the Mahānubhāv sect founded by Govindaprabhu. Cakradharasvāmī spread the teachings of the sect all over Mahārāṣṭra. Ausā originally belonged to the Nāth sect, but after meeting Cakradharasvāmī, converted to the Mahānubhāv sect.

Avatāra
Loosely translated as 'incarnation' of a deity on earth. Viṣṇu, the maintainer of the world according to Hindu thought, is thought to have visited the earth in nine Avatāras; the tenth one, Kalki, is still to come. Other gods and goddesses also take Avatāras on earth in order to destroy evil.

Badāmī
Known formerly as Vātāpi, Badamī is an ancient town in Karnāṭaka State. It is well known for its rock cut temples. It was the capital of the Cālukyas between 540 and 757 CE. The museum here houses a life size image of the *Lajjāgaurī.*

Banaśaṅkarī
(*Lit.* goddess of the forest.) Also known as Śakaṃbharī, Banaṣankarī is thought to be an incarnation of Pārvatī, Śiva's consort. She is the goddess of vegetation who protects and nourishes people during the times of difficulty.

Baubo
A Greek goddess who was said to be sexually liberated. She has a peculiar iconography. Her head is placed directly onto her legs and, lacking a torso, the chin and vagina merge into one another.

Becārā Devī
Becārā (*Skt. Bahucārā*) is a Hindu goddess of chastity and fertility. She is the patroness of the Hijrā (*Hijḍā*) community and has her temple in the town of Becarājī in the Mahisānā district of Gujarāt state. She is also thought to be a tāntric deity situated on the Śrī Cakra.

Bhādrapada
This is the sixth month of the Hindu calendar which falls between August-September in the Gregorian calendar. The popular festival of Gaṇeś-Caturthī falls during this month.

Bhairava
This is a fierce form of Śiva. Also called the Kālabhairava, it is a tantric deity worshipped by left-handed tantrics during their Cakrapūjā.

Bharāḍī
Bards belonging to the Nāth sect. They are also known as Bharaṭaka. Originally belonging to the Pāśupata sect of Śaivism, the Bharāḍīs accepted the Nāth sect and became its followers. Bhairava is their chosen deity of worship.

Bhāskarācārya
Also known as Bhāsurānanda, this 18th century scholar was a well-known left-handed tāntric who wrote a commentary called *Saubhāgyabhāskara* on the *Lalitāsahasranāma*

(*Lit.* the 1000 names of Goddess Lalitā). He knew about the seat of Goddess *Lajjāgaurī* at Ālampūr.

Bhūdevī

(*Skt.* Earth-Goddess.) In Hindu thought, the earth (Bhūdevī) has always been considered to be the mother of everything that there was, there is and there will be. She is the one who produces and sustains everything living and non-living.

Bṛhadāraṇyaka Upaniṣad

This is one the principal Upaniṣads in the canon of the main Upaniṣads. Its authorship is attributed to the seer Yājñyavalkya, and it is the concluding section of the *Śatapatha Brāhmaṇa* of the Śukla Yajurveda. It is a highly philosophical work which deals with the concepts of *ātman, brahman*, *satya* and *ahiṃsā*. Commentaries written by the Ādi-Śaṅkarācārya and Madhvācārya are well-known. Oft-quoted aphorisms such as '*asato mā sadgamaya*' (take me from untruth to truth) and '*pūrṇamadaḥ pūrṇamidam …*' (this brahman is totality in itself) come from this Upaniṣad.

Bṛhaddharmottara Purāṇa

One of the minor Śaivite Purāṇas.

Bṛhannīla Tantra

A tantric work that discusses, amongst other things, the importance of the seats of the goddess (Pīṭhas) in the Indian subcontinent.

Caitra

The first month of the Hindu calendar.

Cakrapūjā

Cakrapūjā is a left-handed tantric ritual which celebrates sexual union. Left-handed Tantra views sexual union as a spiritual action that provokes a deeper and more intense experience beyond physical sensation. The ritual allows a yogi to gain control over sexuality and use this energy as a way to connect with the universal energy of love and joy. The procedure involves couples sitting naked in physical union in a circle. In the middle sits the yogi as Bhairava in congress with the Bhairavi, his sexual partner. Mantras invoking the goddess and her Bhairava are then chanted. The ritual is thought to remove barriers between physical and spiritual experience that hold the yogi back from reaching enlightenment.

Caṇḍīkavaca

This is a hymn in praise of Caṇḍī, the ferocious form of the goddess. Called the armour of the Goddess (kavacam), it is supposed to protect the devotee during crisis.

Carpaṭpajarikā Stotram

This popular hymn is so called because it elaborates a person's journeys through hundreds of cycles of life. The oft-quoted verse in this hymn is, 'one gets born again, just to be able to die again and once again to stay as an embryo in the mother's womb, to be born again' ('*punarapi jananam, punarapi maraṇam punarapi janani jaṭhare śayanam*'). It is thought to have been composed by the Ādi-Śaṅkarācārya.

Caturvarga Cintāmanī

This ancient work was written by Hemādrī, a minister of the Yādava kings, around 1270 CE. It deals with aspects of the Hindu code of conduct including religious observances, pilgrimage, *dāna* (donation to charities) and *Mokṣa.*

Cauṣaṣta Yoginīs

(*Lit.* 64 Yoginīs) Also called 'matṛkās, the Yoginīs are subordinate goddesses who vary between 7 and 64 in number. They have the ability to fly, to become larger or smaller, and to control the minds of people. The yoginī cult is thought to have originated in village Hinduism. Yoginīs are often worshipped before undertaking important rites of passage such as a wedding, and on important occasions such as blessing a new home. Yoginīs are sculpted with heads of animals and birds, and are feared as a rule. They are also associated with tantric worship. Their temples are normally circular. Ranipur-Jaharial and Hirapur in Orissa are two good examples.

Cowrie Shell

Because of its resemblance, the cowrie shell has always been considered a symbol of the human vagina. It is also considered auspicious and is used in many folk rituals.

Crore

Also called a Koṭī, a crore is an Indian term used to denote 10 million.

Ḍagobā

A Ḍagobā is another name for a Buddhist *stūpa.* It is a round, cone-shaped monument that houses Buddha's relics.

Ḍāṅk

In Mahārāṣṭrian folk culture, the potters have an important role to play after a death occurs. With the help of an instrument called 'Ḍāṅk', they sing and tell stories about the dead. This ritual chanting after death is itself called 'Ḍāṅk.'

Darśana

Darśana is perceiving and beholding an object of worship in one's mind. Most of the time this is an image of a god, but it can also be a revered person or object.

Dattātreya

A god who is considered to be the synthesis of the three gods: Brahmā, Viṣṇu and Śiva, the Hindu trinity. He is typically shown with three heads and six hands. In the Nāth tradition, Dattātreya is revered as the Ādi-Guru. An annual festival celebrating his birth is observed all over India in the month of Mārgaśīrṣa (November/December). Dattātreya is also a very important god in Yogasādhanā.

Devadāsī

Devadāsīs were women dedicated to temple gods in large temples, mostly in South India. The dedication ceremony was similar to a marriage ceremony. They remained at the temple for the rest of their lives. Devadāsīs looked after the temple, danced in front of the deity and also performed some rituals. They learned classical dancing and music. Unfortunately, they were often degraded to being temple prostitutes and bore children to the temple priests and temple officials. The practice was outlawed by the British.

Devībhāgvata
One of the minor Purāṇas (*upa-purāṇa*). It has 12 chapters (*Skandhas*) and 180,000 hymns (*Ślokas*). The main purpose of Devī Bhāgvata is to sing praises of the primordial Śakti in the form of Goddess Durgā. It stresses that everything living and non-living including gods and goddesses has been created by her. In the ninth Skanda, it describes how Viṣṇu, in his boar form, saved the earth by taking her out of the bottom of the netherworld (*Naraka*) and had intercourse with her for one divine year.

Ḍhago-Megho Sampradāya (Sect)
This tantric sect, also known as Mātaṅgīpaṭṭa, was established by the four sons of a Brāhmin called Kṛṣṇambhaṭa. The latter married a woman from an untouchable caste, the Mahārs, in Mahārāṣṭra. That is probably why the followers of this sect were mostly Mahārs. Mātaṅgī, also known as Reṇukā, Mesko and Māyārāṇī, was the presiding deity of this sect and the followers were given tantric initiation for this goddess. The sect also worshipped water and mother earth. The followers were also known as Gopāḷa, Kāyāpākhī and Dhūta.

Ekavīrā
This goddess, thought to be an *avatāra* of goddess Reṇukā, is the main deity for the Kolī fisher community and the C.K.P. (Cāndrasenīya Kāyastha Prabhu) community in Mahārāṣṭra. Her temple is situated on Kārlā hill, near the town of Lonāvaḷā. The temple is directly in front of the important Buddhist monuments on the hill.

Ellammā (Yallammā/Yellammā/Yelluāī)
A goddess, considered to be the same as Reṇukā, whose main shrine is at Soundatti in Karnāṭaka. She is invoked both as Ādiśaktī and as a spouse deity, married to Jamadagni, who is an avatāra of Śiva. Her devotees revere her as the mother of the universe.

Fālguna (Phalguna)
The last month of the Hindu calendar. The festival of Hoḷī is celebrated on the full moon day of this month.

Gajalakṣmī
In her most popular representation, goddess Lakṣmī is shown seated on a lotus with two elephants showering her with water. This posture of the goddess signifies abundance, plenitude, good luck and prosperity.

Garbha
Garbha is a child in its mother's womb.

Ghaṭa
(*Skt.*) A pot.

Ghaṭasthāpanā
Ghatasthāpanā, also known as Kalaśathāpanā, is performed on the first day of Vijayā Daśamī or Dussera. A pot brimming with water is an auspicious symbol in Hinduism and *sthāpanā* means 'to establish'. Combining both words, the literal meaning is to establish a pot full of water in a consecrated place.

Gopāḷa
See Ḍhago-Megho Sampradāya (Sect).

Gotra
In Hindu society, the term *gotra* means a 'clan'. It broadly refers to people who are descendants of seers in an unbroken male line from a common male ancestor. According to the *Baudhāyana Dharmasūtra*, the Gotra system started with eight seers. The reason for the creation of the system was to prevent a man and a woman from the same clan marrying each other. At present, there are over 200 Gotras. Only the Brāhmins seem to have adhered to the Gotra system.

Guṇa
The word *Guṇa* means virtue, merit or excellence. It is a concept described by all schools of Hindu philosophy. Three *Guṇas* have been described: *sattva* (goodness, harmony and wholesomeness), *rajas* (passion, creativity) and *tamas* (anger, darkness, destructive behaviour). All Guṇas are present in every individual in varying degrees.

Hara
One of the names for the god Śiva.

Hari
One of the names for the god Viṣṇu.

Hijaḍā (*Hijrā*/*Hijḍā*)
Indian name for eunuchs, transgender people and intersex people. They are officially recognised as such in South Asia.

Irraṇṇā
A Kannaḍa name for Śiva.

Jain Religion (Jainism)
One of the three ancient religions in India, the other two being Hinduism and Buddhism. It is generally believed that Jainism originated somewhere between the 7th to 5th centuries B.C.E. Their religious leaders were called *Tīrthaṅkara* (*Skt.* Ford maker), and the Jains believe that there were 24 of them. The twenty-third was Pārśvanāth (around 7th century B.C.E.) and the last one was Vardhamāna Mahāvīra (599-527 B.C.E.). Jains believe in the abandonment of worldly pleasures, asceticism and eventually reaching freedom from re-birth through renunciation. There are two sects within Jain monks: the Digambaras (going about naked with sky as the only clothing) and Śvetāmbaras (who always wear white cloth).

Jejurī
A town in the Puṇe district of Mahārāṣṭra. It is famous for the shrine of the folk-god Khaṇḍobā.

Jñānadeva (Jñāneśvar)
A 13th century Marāṭhī saint poet. In his short life of only 21 years, he authored an important work, a commentary on the Bhagvadgītā, called the 'Jñāneśvarī' which is religiously read and chanted by Mahārāṣṭrians all over the world.

Jogulāmbā
A famous goddess, considered to be the fifth seat of Śakti in the well-known list of 18 seats. Her temple is in the small town of Ālampūr in the state of Telangaṇa. The goddess has a fierce aspect. She is shown sitting on a corpse with a scorpion, a lizard and a frog on her head. Also, she is naked with her tongue protruding. In Telugu language, she is called '*Yogula Ammā*' which translates as 'the mother of the yogis'.

Jyeṣṭha
The third month of the Hindu calendar.

Kali Yuga
Saṃskṛt scriptures have described four stages of the world before total annihilation and subsequent regeneration take place. Each of these stages is called a '*Yuga*.' The first three were the *satya*, *tretā* and *dvāpara* yugas. Our current stage in this cycle is *Kali Yuga*. This is the stage of degeneration and moral corruption.

Kalpakāmbā
The presiding goddess of the modern day Mylāpore, a suburb of Cennāī. Her other name is *Kalpakavallī*.

Kāmākhyā Temple
A famous temple in Assām, one of the seats of Śakti (Śaktipīṭha), which houses a symbolic image of the vagina of Sati, Śiva's wife. The temple celebrates the goddess' menstruation with great pomp and ceremony each year.

Kamalaśīrṣā
A female with her head replaced by a lotus. An adjective used to describe the *Lajjāgaurī* image.

Kāpālika Śaiva
A monastic order within Śaivism. The Kāpālikas smeared their bodies with ashes and used an empty human skull as a begging bowl. They were also known to practise left-handed tantrism, and worshipped the fierce Bhairava form of Śiva.

Karma
An important concept in Hinduism which states that the sum of one's actions during the present birth and all of the previous births decides the future of the individual. Every deed of a person, good or bad, generates Karma. By righteous behaviour, one can extinguish one's Karma. The total loss of Karma leads to *mokṣa* (salvation) for an individual. The concept of Karma is tied to the concept of reincarnation. One has to take many births on this earth to work through one's Karma so as to eventually extinguish it and reach mokṣa.

Kārtika
The eighth month in the Hindu calendar.

Kārtikeya
Śiva and Pārvatī's second son and the brother of Gaṇeśa. He is also known as Murugan, Skanda, Subramahṇya and Kumara. Kārtikeya is an ancient god, traceable to Vedic times. He is often described in the form of a serpent.

Kaula
Pertaining to Kula or Kaulācāra, meaning a self-contained unit of people who practise sexual tantrism with the aim of obtaining bliss. This tradition is a part of Śāktism or tantric Śaivism which makes use of the pañca-makāras.

Kedāra
Kedāra or Kedāranāth is one of the most important shrines of Śiva, situated in the Himalayas. It is part of the twelve sacred Jyotirliṅgas.

Khaṇḍobā
A popular folk deity (*kṣetrapāla*) of Mahārāṣṭra. The most important shrine of Khaṇḍobā is at Jejurī in Mahārāṣṭra. This folk god has now coalesced with Śiva.

Koṭṭāvāī-Koṭṭavī
Also known as *Koṭarā*, *Koṭṭamahikā*, *Koṭṭakiriyā*. An ancient mother-goddess in South India. Originally she was a naked demoness, who was later worshipped in the form of Durgā.

Kṛtyaratnākara
An important work on religious observances in Hindu religion by Caṇḍeśvara. It discusses Dharma, *vratas*, astrological calculations, etc.

Kṣetrapāla
Also known as a *kṣetrapati*, the *kṣetrapāla* was a guardian deity in Hinduism, Jainism and Buddhism. Originally a deity of farmland, the *kṣetrapāla* was worshipped for obtaining abundant crops and for the wellbeing of farmers and farm animals.

Kula
See Kaula.

Kumbha
A pot. Also known as a *Kalaśa*.

Kumbhakāra
A potter.

Kuṇḍalinī
Also known as serpent power, the Kuṇḍalinī is thought to be a manifestation of Śakti which normally resides in a coiled form at the base of the spine near the *Mūlādhāracakra* in every person. She is the latent spiritual power which can be awakened by Yogic techniques. Through Yoga, it is possible to raise the Kuṇḍalinī from the *Mūlādhāracakra* to the top of the head where the *Sahasrāracakra* exists. This leads to a state of liberation and spiritual bliss (Kaivalya).

Lakh
One hundred thousand.

Līḷācaritra
The *Līḷācaritra*, written by Mhaiṃbhaṭ, is a biography of Cakradhara Svāmī, the preceptor of the Mahānubhāva sect. It is one of the earliest books in the Marāṭhī

language and describes the many miracles (*Līḷā* in Marāṭhī, *Līlā* in *Skt.*) performed by Cakradhara Svāmī.

Liṅga
Also referred to as *śivaliṅga*, a *liṅga* is an abstract aniconic symbol of Lord Śiva. It is how Śiva is worshipped in all Śaivite temples.

Macchanda
Another name for Macchindranātha, a yogi, who was the founder of the Nāth sect and of Haṭha Yoga. He is revered by both Hindus and Buddhists.

Māgha
This is the eleventh month in the Hindu calendar.

Mahānubhāva Sect
Also known as Jai Kṛṣṇa Paṅtha, the Mahānubhāva refers to a Hindu sect in India, started by Govinda Prabhu around 1100 CE. It was propagated in Mahārāṣṭra by Cakradhara Svamī. A Vaiṣṇavite sect, the Mahānubhāvas preached that Kṛṣṇa was the only god and that devotion to him was paramount. The sect admitted people of all castes and women.

Mahār
The Dalits. A formerly untouchable caste in Mahārāṣṭra. They are also known as Mātaṅga.

Mahikāvatī
The town of Keḷve-Māhīm near Mumbai. The presiding goddess of this town is also known as Mahikāvatī. Legend has it that king Bimb established his kingdom here and erected the Mahikāvatī temple.

Māhūr
A town in the Nandeḍ district of Mahārāṣṭra. It is famous for two reasons. First, it is considered to be the birthplace of the god Dattatreya. Second, it is well-known for the temple of Goddess Reṇukā who is the clan goddess of many Brāhmin families.

Maithuna
Sexual intercourse.

Maṇḍodarī
The wife of Rāvaṇa, the almighty king of Śrī Laṅkā. She is known as one of the five great women, the *pañcakanyās*, in Hindu mythology.

Māṅg
The Dalits. Formerly an untouchable caste in Mahāraṣṭra.

Maṇṇumailār
The god Mailāra, made out of Mṛttikā, the earth. This refers to the snake, especially the cobra, who occupies ants' nests and is worshipped by women all over India.

Mārg
A path.

Mārgaśīrṣa
The ninth month in the Hindu calendar.

Mātaṅg
A ropemaker caste in Mahārāṣṭra.

Mātaṅgī
The goddess of the Mahārs and many other communities. The Bhakti saints made many derogatory references to her and persuaded people not to worship her. She is also a tantric goddess who is said to govern speech, music and the arts.

Matsyapurāṇa
This is one of the 18 main (*mahā*) Purāṇas, which is mainly a Vaiṣṇavite text. It is named after the fish incarnation of Viṣṇu and contains 291 chapters (*Adhyāyas*) with 14,000 verses. In chapter 53, this Purāṇa discusses the contents of all of the main eighteen Purāṇas. Its contents include a large variety of topics such as the genealogies of kings, specifications for the iconography of deities, description of various *vratas*, etc. It was most probably composed between 200-400 CE.

Mesko
Same as Mātaṅgī.

Mhaskobā
A folk god in Mahārāṣṭra, considered to be an *avatāra* of Śiva. He also appears in a snake form. Mhaskobā is the main deity of the Dhangar (sheep herder) community. His temple is at the village of Vīr, near Puṇe.

Mleñccha
A derogatory term used to describe a foreigner.

Mūlamṛttikā
The soil inside an ant's nest where a male cobra resides. This soil is thought to be impregnated by the potent seed of the cobra, which is consumed by women desirous of having children.

Muni
A sage, a seer.

Nāgakāṣṭha
A staff of wood with bends, somewhat resembling a serpent. Such a staff is very important in the worship of the Goddess Mātaṅgī.

Nāgārjunakoṇḍā
An historic town in Āndhra Prades. It takes its name from Nāgārjuna, a second or third century master of *Mahāyāna Buddhism*. Before a dam was built at this site, the place was one of India's richest Buddhist sites. Many Buddhist relics submerged under the dam have now been placed in a museum at the town.

Nāth Sampradāya
The Nāth Sampradāya (sect) is a religious sect founded by Gorakhanath in the 11th century. In its teachings and practices, it combines the teachings of Buddhism,

Śaivism and Haṭhayoga. Nāth Siddhas have been known for their tantric and esoteric practices and magic.

Nīlamata Purāṇa

A Saṃskṛt work composed by a seer called Nīlamunī. The work describes religious rituals and celebrations particularly for the Brāhmins from Kāśmīr. It was written sometime after the 6th century CE.

Nirṛti

A Vedic goddess. She is mentioned in the *Atharvaveda* (6.29) and in the Maitrāyaṇī Saṃhitā as an inauspicious goddess. The *Śatapatha Brāhmaṇa* (7.2.1.11) describes her as associated with both birth and death.

Nirvāṇa

The Buddhist equivalent of *mokṣa* or salvation. It is the ultimate spiritual goal for every Buddhist and means elimination of desire, greed and ignorance. It also means liberation from the cycles of rebirth.

Padma

A lotus flower.

Padmā

Another name for goddess Lakṣmī. One whose seat is a Padma.

Padmapurāṇa

One of the Vaiṣṇavite Purāṇas, which belongs to the list of the 18 Mahāpurāṇas. This work has five parts (*Khaṇḍa*): *Sṛṣṭikhaṇḍa*, *Bhūmikhaṇḍa*, *Svargakhaṇḍa*, *Pātalakhaṇḍa* and *Uttarakhaṇḍa*. Each one of these parts has several chapters (*adhyāyas*). Reading of this Purāṇa is claimed to remove all of the sins of the reader.

Padmāvatī

The goddess who is the wife of the folk god Vyaṅkaṭeśa, also known as Bālājī, whose main temple is at Thirupati in Āndhra Pradeś. Legend has it that Padmāvatī and her husband had a disagreement and, as a result, she left him. Her own temple is at the bottom of the hill whereas Bālājī's temple is on top.

Parā Śakti

Parā Śakti is considered to be the supreme Śakti or *Ādi-Śakti* in Śaktism. She is the original creator, protector, and destroyer of the entire universe.

Paraśurāma

See Paraśurāmabhūmī.

Paraśurāmabhūmī

(*Lit.* Land of Paraśurāma.) The Koṅkaṇ area of the state of Mahārāṣṭra is considered to be land created by Paraśurāma, who was the son of the sage Jamadagni and his wife Reṇukā. Legend has it that he, with the heat of his penance, created a strip of land on the western coast of Mahārāṣṭra by ordering the sea to recede. This is the area of Mahārāṣṭra occupied by Koṅkaṇtha Brāhmins, who claim their lineage from Paraśurāma.

Parjanyadeva
The rain-god. His other name is Pāṇadeva. He is worshipped by the untouchable castes in Mahārāṣṭra, the Mahār and Māṅgs. The other deity they worship is the mother earth, *Dharaṇī*.

Pauṣa
The tenth month of the Hindu calendar.

Peśwā/Peśwās
The word Peśwā in Persian means 'a ruler'. The Peśwās were the chief ministers of the Marāṭha kindom in Mahārāṣṭra. While initially they were the ministers under the kings Śivājī, Saṃbhājī and Rājārām, they subsequently became de facto rulers. The most powerful Peśwā was Bajirao 1. During his time, the Marāṭha empire reached its zenith and ruled major parts of India.

Pūjā
Worship according to Hindu custom. There are two kinds of Pūjās. A short daily Pūjā consists of offering invocation, sandalwood paste, flowers, waving incense and a lamp. It ends with offering of some kind of food called *prasāda*. An elaborate Pūjā performed on special occasions is called a 'sixteen-part (Ṣoḍaśopacārī) Pūjā. This involves treating the god like a guest and performing every ritual of welcoming him/her. A priest chants the appropriate mantras in Saṃskṛt.

Pūrṇimā (Paurṇimā)
The full moon night which occurs once a month.

Rājnī
A queen.

Rajomahimā
(*Lit.* importance of the menstrual fluid.) Because it is intimately connected with the process of creation, menstrual fluid has a special importance in tāntrism. For the left-handed tāntrics, worship of the menstruating vagina is highly important. At the Kāmākhyā temple in Assām, where – according to the legend – the vagina of Sati fell, menstruation of the goddess is celebrated in the month of June. Devotees are given a small piece of red cloth so that they can keep it in their sanctum at home. This cloth is supposed to be impregnated with the goddess' menstrual fluid and is worshipped by the devotees.

Rakhamāī
One of the most important folk gods both in Mahārāṣṭra and Karnāṭaka is the god Viṭṭhal at Paṇḍharpūr. According to Ḍhere, Viṭṭhal, also known as Viṭhobā, is a synthesis of Viṣṇu (Kṛṣṇa) and Śiva. Kṛṣṇa's lawful wife is Rukmiṇī. Mahārāṣṭrians therefore consider Rukmiṇī, known colloquially as Rakhamāī or Rakhamābāī as the wife of Viṭṭhal. He is often addressed as Rukmiṇīpati or the lord and master of Rukmiṇī. Rakhamāī has a separate temple in the Paṇḍharpūr temple complex.

Rānḍāv Punav
In Marāṭhī, a Rānḍ means a prostitute. Because a prostitute never becomes a widow, she is supposed to be an auspicious symbol for a newly married woman. There

used to be a custom in some parts of western India to invite a prostitute to put fresh green bangles around the wrists of a newly married woman. By tradition, a married woman always wore green bangles. If her husband died, she had to break these bangles, signifying widowhood. This is the significance of Rāṇḍav Punav where a Jogtiṇ breaks her bangles for a period of four months and then puts them on again afterwards on a full moon night called the '*aheva punav*' (*ahev* is forever married).

Ratikalāmūrtī
The naked image (of a goddess) who is ready for coition.

Rāvaḷ
See Mātaṅgīpaṭṭa. Kṛṣṇambhaṭa, who was a devotee of goddess Mātaṅgī, had five sons: Datto, Dhago, Megho, Cāṅgo and Guṇḍo. All of these five sons became accomplished tāntrikas. They used to call themselves 'Rāvaḷ.' It is unclear why they chose to do so. Maybe, they wanted to be identified as 'Yogis'. There is a community called '*Yogi Rāvaḷ*' in India.

Reṇukā
The famous goddess at Māhūr in Mahārāṣṭra, who is the clan deity of many families. According to Ḍhere, she is the same as *Mesko*, *Māyārāṇī* and *Mātaṅgī*.

Reṇukāmāhātmya
Claiming to be a part of the *Sahyādrīkhaṇḍa* of the *Skandapurāṇa*, the *Reṇukāmāhātmya* tells us about the importance of the shrine of goddess Reṇukā at Māhūr. It says that Reṇukā is none other than the goddess Aditi of the Vedas, who will take birth on the earth as goddess Ekavīrā.

Reṇukāsahasranāma
A list of the one thousand names of Goddess Reṇukā. Such lists are available for the majority of the Hindu gods, to be used by the devotees for the purpose of the daily chanting of these names.

Ṛgveda
The oldest known Vedic text and an important scripture in Hinduism. Its first collection (*Saṃhitā*) was composed around 1500 to 1200 B.C.E.. Apart from the main Saṃhita, it also has *upaniṣads*, *āraṇyakas* and *brāhmaṇas* as addenda. The core *saṃhita* is a collection of 10 books (*maṇḍalas*) with 1028 hymns. Ten families of Ṛṣis have composed over 95 percent of the hymns in this work. The hymns were composed and preserved through oral tradition. Many of the hymns are in praise of the Vedic gods.

Rudra
One who cries (howls). An epithet for Śiva.

Sādhaka
A person who performs a goal-directed religious or spiritual practice.

Śāhū Mahārāj
Śāhū Mahārāj (1874-1922) of the Bhosale dynasty was the ruler of the princely state of Kolhāpūr. He was a social reformer and instituted many significant reforms during his rule. Primary education irrespective of caste or creed was one of his

major reforms. He became the leader of the non-Brāhmin movement and united the Marāṭhas under his banner.

Śakambharī
See Banaśaṅkarī.

Śakti
Śakti is the primordial feminine energy that is creative and sustaining as well as destructive. She is the creatrix, the great divine mother. Hinduism believes that each god has his Śakti and, without her, he is powerless and incomplete. Śakti, also called Mahāmāyā, is worshipped as the supreme being, the brahman, by the Śāktas, who are Śakti worshippers.

Śaktipīṭha/s
The important seats of Śakti in India. Legend has it that when Sati, Śiva's wife, committed suicide by throwing herself in her father's fire sacrifice (Yajña), Śiva was beside himself with grief and roamed around the world with her body on his shoulders. The world came to standstill. Viṣṇu therefore cut her body in many parts. Wherever they fell, the places became important shrines for the goddess. The number of Śaktipīṭhas varies from 18 to 108.

Saṃhitā
The word literally means 'a collection'. When used in conjunction with the Vedas, it means the oldest layer of text, mantras, hymns and prayers within.

Saṃpradāya
A sect.

Saṅkalpa
A resolution or oath taken by an individual to commit himself to perform a ritual.

Śaṅkarācārya
The Ādi-Śaṅkarācārya was an eighth century philosopher, Śiva worshipper and theologian. He revived the doctrine of *Advaita Vedānta* and established four *maṭhas* (seats) in four corners of India. He also founded the *Daśanāmī* monastic order.

Śaṅkha
A *śaṅkha* (conch shell) is very important in Hinduism as a sacred emblem of God Viṣṇu. It is still used as a trumpet in Hindu rituals to drive away evil spirits. During the worship regimen, it is offered prayers as well.

Sānterī
A goddess in South Koṅkaṇ and Goa. The popular goddess Śāntādurgā in Goa is thought to be a Brāhminised version of Sānterī, who was a folk deity (*Grāmadevatā*). Sānterī has some temples in this region as well, where she is worshipped in the form of an ant's nest. She is known to be a 'hot goddess' who is a giver of boons to her devotees.

Ṣaṭ
The number six in Saṃskṛt language. It is normally written as Ṣaṣ. It becomes ṣaḍ or ṣaṭ in composition.

Śatapatha Brāhmaṇa

The Brāhmaṇas are commentaries on Vedas. The *Śatapatha Brāhmaṇa* is a very detailed commentary on the *Śukla Yajurveda*. It contains information about constructing complex fire altars (*Vedi*), sacrificial rituals and mythology. It is thought to be significant in the development of *Vaiṣṇavism*. *Madhyandina* and *Kaṇva* are the two recensions of this Brāhmaṇa.

Saundattī

A town in the Beḷgāv district of Karnāṭaka. It is famous for the temple of Yellammā.

Skandapurāṇa

This is one of the eighteen main Purāṇas (*Mahāpurāṇa*) and is also the largest. It contains 81,000 verses and takes its name from Skanda, Śiva and Pārvatī's son.

Śrāvaṇa

The fifth month in the Hindu calendar.

Śrī Śailam

A town in the Kurnūl district of Āndhra Pradeś, famous for its Mallikārjuna temple, one of the twelve Jyotirliṅgas in India. It is a holy pilgrimage site for Śiva and Śakti worshippers.

Śrīsūkta

This is a devotional hymn in the 10th Maṇḍala of the *Ṛgveda*, addressed to Goddess Śrī, the goddess of wealth and prosperity. It is most probably a later addition to the *Ṛgveda* and differs in different recensions of the book. It is regularly chanted at important Vaiṣṇavite shrines such as Thirupati and is also a part of the daily prayers for many Hindus. The hymn describes the goddess as glorious, ornamented, royal, lustrous as gold, and radiant as fire, moon and the sun. In chanting, the *Lakṣmī Sūkta* is added at the end of the *Śrisūkta*.

Sthalamāhātmya

(Also called *Sthalapurāṇa*.) Important religious places (*Skt. Sthalas*) almost always have myths about the relevant gods associated with them. These are often described in detail in prose or verse form by a learned devotee. Such a compilation or commentary is called a 'māhātmya'(greatness) and is used in daily chanting by devotees. The *Reṇukāmāhātmya* is a good example of such a Purāṇa that describes the importance of Māhūr, the place well-known for the temple of Goddess Reṇukā.

Subrahmaṇya

See Kārtikeya.

Taraṅga

A Taraṅga is a painted and decorated piece of wood about two metres long, kept in the sanctum of temples in the region of Goa and southern Konkaṇ. Fitted on one end is a silver or copper mask, representing a male or female head. In some cases, in place of the mask, the palm of a hand made out of metal is found. They are often covered with a saree or dhoti as well. These Taraṅgas are considered to be gods and goddesses themselves and are worshipped on special occasions. They are paraded in front in religious processions.

Ter

A small town in the Osmābād district of Mahārāṣṭra. The town had several mounds. When excavated, a large number of coins and very small images of *Lajjāgaurī* made out of fired clay were discovered. These are now displayed in the Government Museum at Ter. Because of the sheer number of these images, it is thought that Ter may have been a factory where such images were mass produced.

Ucchāral

A festival that celebrates the menstruation of the earth-mother in the state of Keraḷa. It is celebrated in the months of January and February after all of the crop has been cultivated. For four days, all of the grain storage facilities are closed. Grain is not sold in shops either. Farming implements are not touched. After this period, shops re-open and the farms are ceremoniously burned so they are ready for sowing in the next season.

Unnayana

'Unnayana' means elevation. Hinduism has two main strands: the elite Brāhminic Hinduism and village Hinduism of the masses. Ever so often, a popular folk ritual or folklore is appropriated by Brāhmins and converted into a Brāhminic ritual in Saṃskṛt language. This then requires the services of a Brāhmin priest. In a similar fashion, many folk gods have coalesced with Brāhminic gods. Thus, the *kṣetrapāla* gods Jotibā and Khaṅḍobā are now considered as the avatāras of Śiva.

Uttānā Mahi

(*Lit.* the mother earth with elevated vagina.) Stella Kramrisch described the *Lajjāgaurī* image found at Mahākūṭa as Vedic Aditi, the mother of the world in the state of delivery. Agreeing with her, Ḍhere extended this argument to show that Aditi was in fact the mother earth. Hence the term, Uttānā Mahī.

Uttānā Yonī

(*Skt.* Elevated vagina.) The *Śatapatha Brāhmaṇa* (3.2.1.29) states that 'a woman who has elevated her vagina at the time of intercourse is the only one who can conceive'. Ḍhere believes that this description fits the image of the *Lajjāgaurī* appositely.

Vāḍī Ratnāgirī

The hill near the city of Kolhāpūr in Mahārāṣṭra state, which is famous for the shrine of the folk god, Jotibā.

Vaiśākha

The second month in the Hindu calendar.

Vājasaneyī Saṃhitā

One of the Saṃhitās of the Śukla Yajurveda. This Saṃhitā contains 40 Adhyāyās and 1975 mantras. The *Bhāgvatpurāṇa* says that this Saṃhitā was given by the Sun, who took the form of a horse and gave it to the seer Yājñavalkya. Since Vajī means a horse, the name of the Saṃhitā became Vājasaneyī Saṃhitā.

Vāyupurāṇa

One of the eighteen main Purāṇas (*mahāpurāṇa*) in Hinduism. Because of its mention in the *Mahābhārata*, it is thought to be one of the oldest Hindu scriptures. A very wide range of subjects are covered, including lineages of sages, mythologies of both Śiva and Viṣṇu, Yoga, Yugas etc.

Viṣṇudharmottarapurāṇa
One of the minor purāṇas (upapurāṇa), which is divided into three parts (Khaṇḍas). It is a Vaiṣṇavite work that describes the observances of the pañcarātra sect of Vaiṣṇavism. It is thought to have been composed around the 5th century CE, somewhere around Panjāb or Kaśmīr.

Viṣrunkhalā Devī
The goddess who is free of shackles. Goddess without fetters.

Vṛṣabha
This word has two meanings. Applied to various gods, it means 'eminent', 'chief', 'most excellent', 'benefactor' etc. The other meaning of it is 'a bull'.

Vyāghreśvarī
A small town near Hospeṭ in Karnāṭaka. This is one of the places where an image of the Lajjāgaurī was found.

Yallammā
See Ellammā.

Yoginī
The term Yoginī has several meanings in the Hindu, Buddhist and Jain traditions. The term can simply mean a female practitioner of Yoga. In medieval mythology, Yoginīs are mentioned as those with magical powers, their number varying from 7 to 64. Yoginīs have also been mentioned in tāntric practice. They are also called Mātṛkās.

Yonīpūjā
The worship of the *Yoni*(vagina) which is a part of left-handed tantrism. According to the Yonītantra, male ascetics who worship the Yonī equate the female organ with a Vedic sacrificial altar. As a part of the worship, female bodily fluids are consumed by the male. He is ultimately required to offer his semen into this altar. The worshipper then becomes Śiva and both participants acquire siddhis by doing so.

Yuga
In Hindu cosmology, a Yuga is an age for humankind. The Purāṇas mention four Yugas: *Kṛta*, *Treta*, *Dvāpara* and *Kali*. The *Kṛta* consisted of 4800 divine years, *Tretā*, 3600 divine years, *Dvāpara*, 2400 divine years, and the current *Kali* Yuga is supposed to last 1200 divine years. The sum of all of these, called a *Mahāyuga*, makes 12,000 divine years. One divine year consists of 360 human years.

Yugalā Devī
Also known as Joguḷāmbā, Goddess Yugalā is the presiding deity of the town of Alampūr in Āndhra Pradeś. She is one of the eighteen goddesses mentioned in the *Śaktipīṭha* list attributed to the Ādi-Śaṅkarācārya. She is the consort of the Śiva, known here as Brahmeśvara.

Reference Material

(By Dr R.C. Ḍhere)

(Note by the translator: Many of the references quoted by Dr Ḍhere are not complete; details of publishers etc. are often missing. However, it is now very difficult to obtain these, in view of the fact that many of the Saṃskṛt *pothis* and old Marāṭhī books quoted here are out of print. For his English references, details of the year and place of publication given by him do not, at times, match with the translator's literature searches. I have therefore decided to quote Dr Ḍhere's references as they stand).

[Note by Dr Ḍhere:] The following list is by no means comprehensive. Some of the material listed here has not been directly used, but simply referred to. Exact references to scriptural and other material such as the Vedas, Upaniṣads, Rāmāyaṇa, Mahābharata, Smṛtīs, Purāṇas, hymns in the praise of gods (*stotras*) and ancient Marāṭhī literature have not been included here. This is because their details have been included in the citations themselves. The order followed here is: Name of the book, details of the author, editor or publisher, the place where published and the date).

Saṃskṛt Literature

1. *Skandapurāntargataṃ Saṅhyādrikhaṇḍam,* Ed. J. Garsan dā Kunhā, Mumbaī, 1877.
2. *Śrīkālikākhaṇḍa* (Sārtha: Lit. with Marāthī translation), Ed. Vāsudevaśāstrī Jośī, Pusad, 1974.
3. *Śākambharimāhātmyam* (with Kannada translation), Publisher: Mallār Banambhaṭ Pujār. Badāmī, 1937.
4. *Kṛṣiparāśaraḥ*, Ed. Girijāprasanna Majumdār, Sureścandra Banerjī. Calcuttā, 1960.
5. *Śrīgarbhakulārṇavāntargataṃ bhagamālinīrajasvalāstotram* (handwritten manuscript).
6. Śrīkedāraliṅgamānasapūjāstotraṃ (Sārtha: Lit. with Marāthī translation).
7. Sakhārāmaśāstrī Bāpuśāstrī Bhāgvat. Sātārā. Śaka 1857.
8. *Saundaryalaharī*, Ed. H.B. Bhiḍe, Ahmedābād, 1969, and Ed. N.N. Svāmī Dhanapati. Mysore, 1946.

Marāṭhī Literature

1. *Līḷācaritra (Pūrvārdha)*, Volumes 1 and 2. Ed. S.G. Tulpuḷe, Nāgpūr-Puṇe, 1966.
2. *Sthānapothī*, Ed. V.B. Kolate, Malkāpūr.
3. *Śekh Mahammadabābā Śrīgondekar yāncā Kavitāsangraha*. Ed. B.C. Bendre, Mumbaī, 1961.
4. *Śrīkedarapadaratnamālā*., Ganeś Tatyāśāstrī Sāgāvkar. Kolhāpūr, 1896.
5. *Kumbhār Jñātibandhavānce ḍānkecī Kathā*, G.V. Majgāvkar. Kolhāpūr, 1934.
6. *Ek Hotā Rājā*, Ed. Sarojini Babar. Mumbaī, 1964.
7. *Lokakathākuñja*, Mahādevaśāstrī Jośī. Puṇe, 1962
8. *Reṇukāmāhātmya* (in Ovī form), Publisher: S.A. Sāvant, Beḷgāv.
9. *Śrīcchatrapatī Śāhūmahārāj Yancī Rojniśī*, Eds. G.C. Vāḍ and D.B. Pārasnis, Sātārā.
10. *Savāī Mādhavarāv Peśve Yāñcī Rojniśī*, Eds. G.C. Vāḍ and K.B. Marāṭhe, Mumbaī 1911.
11. *Śrīkedāravijay* Publisher: S.A. Sāvant, Beḷgāv, 1965.
12. *Bharatkhaṇḍācā Arvācīn Kośa*, Raghunāth Bhāskar Goḍbole, Puṇe, 1881.
13. *Mumbaī Ilākhyātīl Jātī*, G.M. Kālelkar, Baḍode, 1928.
14. *Bhāratīya Saṃskṛtī Kośa*, Volumes 4 and 7, Ed. Mahādevaśāstrī Jośī, Puṇe, 1967, 1972.
15. *Ādiśaktīce Viśvarūpa (Devikośa)*, Vol. 3, P.K. Prabhudesāī. Puṇe, 1968.
16. *Kannaḍ-Marāṭhī Śabdakośa*, Puṇḍalīkjī Kātagaḍe. Mumbaī, 1969.
17. *Reṇukā (Yallammā) Māhātmya*, Siddhāntī Śivabasavaśāstrī Pañcavaṇṇigī Bṛahanmaṭh, Pūvallī, Hūlī (Dist. Belgāv), 1965.
18. *Śrīmhaskobāce Caritra*, Vīr, 1889.
19. *Maṭhagāvcā Śilālekha*, B.A. Bāmbarḍekar, Mumbaī, 1925.
20. *Śrīravaḷnāth āṇi Konkaṇātīl Devaskī*, P.R. Behre, Borivlī, 1955.
21. *Tīrthayatrāprabandha*, Ganeśaśāstrī Lele Tryambakkar. Puṇe, 1964 (Second Edition).
22. *Yāṭrākalpalatā*, Gaurīśankaraśāstrī Anantaśāstrī, Puṇe, 1884.
23. *Badlāpūr*, N.G. Cāpekar, Puṇe, Śaka 1855.
24. *Nāgabhūmī Kāśmīr*, N.G. Tavkar, Mumbaī, 1974.
25. *Prācīn Draviḍa*, L.G. Ghaṇekar, Baḍode, 1933.
26. *Lokasāhityācī Rūparekhā*, Durgā Bhāgwat, Mumbaī, 1956.
27. *Lokasāhityāce Antaḥpravāha*, Prabhākar Mānḍe, Puṇe, 1975.
28. *Hindudharmāce Svarūp*, Vol. 2Bābā Padmanjī, Mumbaī, 1884.
29. *Marāṭhe āṇi Tyāñcī Bhāṣā*, Bhaskarrāv Jādhav, Kolhāpūr, 1932.
30. *Mahānubhāv Saṃśodhana*, Vol. 1, V.B. Kolte, Malkāpūr, 1962.
31. *Mahānubhāva: Ek Āhvān*, Puruṣottam Nāgpure, Amarāvatī, 1973.
32. *Śrījyotibā*, M.G. Guḷavaṇī, Kolhāpūr, 1968.
33. *Vākāṭak Nṛpatī āṇi Tyāñcā Kāḷa*, V.V. Miraśī, Nāgpūr, 1957.
34. *Tukārām Mahārāj Yāñcī Guruparamparā*, V.C. Bendre, Mumbaī, 1960.
35. *Khaṇḍobā*, R.C. Ḍhere, Puṇe, 1961.
36. *Marāṭhī Lokasaṃskṛtīce Upāsaka*, R.C. Ḍhere, Puṇe, 1964.
37. *Śrīnāmdeva, Ek Vijayayātrā*, R.C. Ḍhere, and A.P. Kamat, Puṇe, 1970.
38. *Cakrapāṇī*, R.C. Ḍhere, Puṇe, 1977.

Hindi Literature

1. *Kāmarūp Kāmākhyā*, Dharaṇīkānt Dev Śarmā, Kāmākhyā, 1953.
2. *Bhāratīya Sanskṛtīme Aryetarānśa*, Śivaśekhar Miśra, Lakhanau, 1952.
3. *Bhāratīya Āryabhāṣā aur Hindi*, Sunitikumār Cāturjī, Delhi, 1957.
4. *Harṣacarit: Ek Sānskṛtik Adhyayana*, Vāsudevaśaraṇ Aggrawal, Paṭnā, 1953.
5. *Prācīn Bhāratīya Lokadharma*, Vāsudevaśaraṇ Aggrawal, Ahmedābād, 1964.
6. *Āndhrakā Sāmājik Itihās*, Suravaram Pratāp Reddy, New Delhi, 1959.
7. *Jain Āgama Sāhityame Bhāratīya Samāj*, Jagadīscandra Jain, Vārāṇasī, 1965.

English References

1. *The Great Mother*, Erich Neumann. London 1955.
2. *Myths, Dreams and Mysteries*, Mircea Eliade. London, 1957.
3. *The Mothers* (Abridged), R. Briffault. London, 1959.
4. *The Tree of Life*, E.O. James. Leiden, 1966.
5. *Mohenjodāro and the Indus Civilization*, John Marshall. London, 1931.
6. *Sources of Karnāṭaka History*, Vol. 1, S. Srikānta Sāstri. Mysore, 1940.
7. *Archaeology of Gujarāt including Kathiawar*, H.D. Sāṅkaliā. Bombay 1941.
8. *From History to Prehistory at Nevāse*, S.B. Dev, Poona, 1960.
9. *Reports of the Excavation at Ter*, B.N. Cāpekar, Poona, 1969.
10. *Excavations at Bhokardan*, S.B. Dev and R.S. Gupte. Nagpur, 1974.
11. *Māhurjhari Excavation*, S.B. Dev. Nagpur, 1973.
12. *Writings and Speeches of the Late Hon. R.B. Viṣvanāth Nārāyaṇ Maṇḍalīk*, Ed. By N.V. Maṇḍalīk. Bombay, 1896.
13. *The Village Gods of South India*, H. Whitehead. Calcutta, 1921.
14. *Dravidian Gods in Modern Hinduism*, W.T. Elmore. Madras, 1925.
15. *Dravidian India*, Vol. 1, T.R. Seśa Iyengār. Maḍrās, 1925.
16. *The Mahār Folk*, A. Robertson. Calcuttā, 1938.
17. *Myths and Symbols in Indian Art and Civilization*, H. Zimmer. New York, 1947.
18. *The Śakta Pīṭhas*, D.C. Sarkār (Reprint from the Royal Asiatic Society of Bengal, Vol. XIV, No. 1, 1948).
19. *Aspects of Early Viṣṇuism*, J. Gonda. Utrecht, 1954.
20. *The Cultural Heritage of India*, Vol IV, Ed. By Haridās Bhattācārya, Calcutta, 1956.
21. *Indian History Congress: Proceedings of the Twenty-first Session*, Trivanḍrum, 1968.
22. *Lokāyata*, Debiprasād Caṭṭopadhyāya. New Delhi, 1959.
23. *Myth and Reality*, D.D. Kosāmbī. Bombay, 1962.
24. *Vision in Long Darkness*, V.S. Agrawāl. Vārāṇasī, 1963.
25. *Kalidās' Vision of Kumārasaṃbhava*, Sūryakānta. Delhi, 1963.
26. *The Elephant and the Lotus*, V.S. Naravaṇe. Bombay, 1965.
27. *Pūrṇa Kalaśa or the Vase of Plenty*, P.K. Agrawāl. Vārāṇasī, 1965.
28. *Śiva Mahādeva*, V.S. Agrawal. Vārāṇasī, 1966.
29. *Śakti Cult and Tārā*, Ed. By D.C. Sarkār. Calcutta, 1967.
30. *Tantra Art-Tantra Āsana*, Ajit Mūkerjī. New Delh – New York – Paris, 1966–1967.
31. *Epic Mythology*, E.W. Hopkins. Vārāṇasī – Delhi, 1968.

32. *Indian Puberty Rites*, N.N. Bhaṭṭācārya. Calcutta, 1968.
33. *Burial Practices in Ancient India*, Purushottam Singh. Vārāṇasī, 1970.
34. *Indian Mother Goddess*, N.N. Bhaṭṭacārya. Calcutta, 1971.
35. *Studies in Religious Life of Ancient and Medieval India*, D.C. Sarkār. Delhi, 1971.
36. *The Sangam Age*, K.A. Nilakānta Sāstrī. Madrās, 1972.
37. *The Nīlamata Purāṇa*, Vol II (Text and English Translation), Ved Kumārī. Srinagar, 1973.
38. *Kārtikeya: The Divine Child*, Ratnā Navaratnam. Bombay, 1973.
39. *A Social History of the Tamils*, Vol. 1, K.K. Pillay. Madrās, 1975.
40. *The Peacock*, P. Thamkappan Nair. Calcuttā, 1977.
41. *Vedic Themes*, G.K. Bhaṭ. Delhi, 1978.
42. *History of Keralā*, Part1, Padmanābha Menon.
43. *History of Dharmaśāstra*, Vol V, Part 1, P.V. Kāṇe. Poonā, 1958.
44. *Indian Serpent Lore*, J. Ph. Vogel. Vārāṇasī-Delhi, 1972.
45. *Studies in Goddess Cults in Northern India* (Unpublished Thesis), J.N. Tiwārī. 1971.
46. *A Guide to Badāmī*, A.M. Aṇṇigeri. Dhārwār, 1966.
47. *Temples and Legends of Āndhra Prades*́, N. Ramesan. Bombay, 1962.
48. *Select Kākatiya Temples*, M. Rama Rāv. Tirupati, 1966.
49. *Folklore of Āssām*, Jogeś Dās. New Delhi, 1972.
50. *Kāmākhyā: Town of Āssām*, Mohan Sarmā. New Delhi, 1973.
51. *Mother Goddess Kāmākhyā*, Bani Kānt Kākatī. Guahātī, 1948.
52. *Lord Ayyappan*, Pyyppan. Bombay, 1962.
53. *Lord Śaṇmukha and His Worship*, Swāmī Śivānanda. Sivānandanagar, 1970.
54. *Nāgarāja Temple*, S. Padmanabhan. Rāmeśvarapuram, 1969.
55. *Malinithan-Heritage of Aruṇācala*, L.N. Cakravarty.
56. *A Guide to State Museum, Dubelā*, Nowgong (BKD), Vindhya Pradeś, S.K. Dikśit. Nowgong (BKD), 1957.
57. *A Kannadā English Dictionary*, Rev. Kittel. Mangalore, 1894.
58. *A Student's Saṃskṛt-English Dictionary*, V.S. Āpte. Delhi, 1963.
59. *Gazetteer of India*: Mysore State-Bijāpūr District, 1966.

Journals and Periodicals

1. *Bhāratīya Itihās Saṃśodhan Maṇḍaḷ Quarterly* 19.2, October 1938.
2. *Bhāratīya Itihās Saṃśodhan Maṇḍaḷ Conference Proceedings*, Śaka 1839.
3. *Bhāratīya Itihās Saṃśodhan Maṇḍaḷ Annual Issue*, Śaka 1835.
4. *Śaradāśram Annual*, Yavatmāḷ, Śaka 1855.
5. *Mahārāṣtra Sāhitya Patrikā*, Year 4, Issues 1 and 2. March-June 1931.
6. *Marāṭhī Saṃśodhan Patrikā*, 15.1 October 1967.
7. *Navabhārat*, February 1974, April 1976.
8. *Vidarbha Saṃśodhan Maṇḍaḷ Annual*, 1958 and 1971.
9. *Lokaprabhā Weekly*, Mumbaī, 6th of March 1977.
10. *Prabuddha Karnāṭaka* (in Kannaḍā): The Mouthpiece of the University of Mysore, 25.2, No. 96, Dīpāvalī 1943.
11. *Kalyāṇ* (in Hindi), Issue on Tīrthas, 31.1, January 1957.
12. *Samanvaya* (in Hindi), Published by Kendrīya Hindi Saṃsthan, Agra. 14.14, 1972–1973.

13. *Sammelan Patrikā* (in Hindi): Published by Hindi Sāhitya Sammelan, Prayāg. 62.1, Pauśa-Fālgun, Saka 1897.
14. *Journal of the Royal Anthropological Institute of Great Britain and Ireland*, Vol. XIV, 1934.
15. *Man*, Vol. XXXV, 1935, No. 70.
16. *Indian Culture* (Calcutta), Vol. VIII, No. 1 (July–September), July 1941.
17. *Journal of Oriental Research*, Vol. XIV (Madras).
18. *Quarterly Journal of the Mythic Society*, Vol. XLIX, No. 1, April 1958.
19. *Journal of Indian History*, Vol. XLII, Part 1, April 1962.
20. *Artibus Asiae*, Vol. XIX, XXXIII.
21. *Bhavan's Journal*, XVIII, 23, 11th June 1972.

Previously Published Articles that are Included in the Book *Lajjāgaurī*

1. *Śaktipīṭhancā Śodha* (Booklet), Moghe Prakaśan, Kolhāpūr-Puṇe, 25th October 1973. [Two articles: '*Lajjāgaurī*' and 'Joguḷāmbā'].
2. *Subrahmaṇya: Ek Ākalana*, Ānandavan Quarterly, Puṇe, 2.1, January – February – March 1974. [Article on Subrahmaṇya].
3. *Hī Laṅkecī Pārvatī Āhe Tarī Koṇ?* 'Kesarī', 8th of June 1975; 'Laukik āṇi Alaukik', Indrāyaṇī Sāhitya, Puṇe, 14th January 1976. [Part of the article on *Lajjāgaurī*].
4. *Bāśingāce Rahasya*, 'Kesari', 13 July 1975; 'Laukik āṇi Alaukik' [Part of the article 'Aditicī Rūpe'].
5. *Mātaṅgīpaṭṭa*, 'Pratisṭhān', September-October 1975; Booklet, Akhil Bhāratīya Mahānubhāv Pariṣad, Aurangābād, February 1976. [Two articles: 'Mātaṅgī' and 'Mātaṅgīpaṭṭa'].
6. *Tryambakamaṭhikā*, 'Navabhārat', November-December 1975 (Special issue on Jñaneśvar). 'Cakrapāṇī', Viśvakarmā Sāhityālaya, Puṇe, 14 January 1977 [Part of the chapter 'Aditicī Rūpe'].
7. *Jotibā: Śodh āṇi Bodh*, 'Navabhārat', January 1976 [The chapter on Jotibā].
8. *Jotibā: Śodh āṇi Bodh*, 'Navabhārat', January and February 1976. [Supplement 1] [Discussion with Mr. Tikekar].
9. *Śrīkalpakāṃbecī Kāhāṇī*, 'Navabhārat', April 1976. [Part of the article 'Kumbhapratīk'].
10. *Punarapi Jananī Jaṭhare Śayanaṃ*, 'Navabhārat', June 1976. [The entire article 'Kumbhapratīk'].
11. *Ambuvācī*, 'Navabhārat', August 1976 [The entire article 'Ambuvācī'].
12. *Sṛṣṭīce Māher*, Santakṛpā, November-December (Dīpāvalī), 1976. [The entire article 'Sṛṣṭīce Māher'].

Index

About the Author

Dr Rāmacandra Cintāmaṇ Ḍhere

(1930–2016)

Known popularly as Aṇṇā, Ḍhere was a prolific writer on many aspects of religion in India and on Indian folk culture, especially that of Mahārāṣṭra. He was second to none in the study of ancient Marāṭhī and Saṃskṛt literature and was responsible for bringing to light many rare and lost manuscripts. Ḍhere produced over a hundred books on the religion of the masses. Often working with dense and obscure subject matter, such was Ḍhere's poetic style of writing that it attracted not only the literati but the average reader as well. Unfortunately, he wrote mainly in Marāṭhī, and occasionally in Hindi. For the first time, this translation makes Ḍhere's enlightened study of the mother goddess available to English readers, in a substantial contribution to the field.

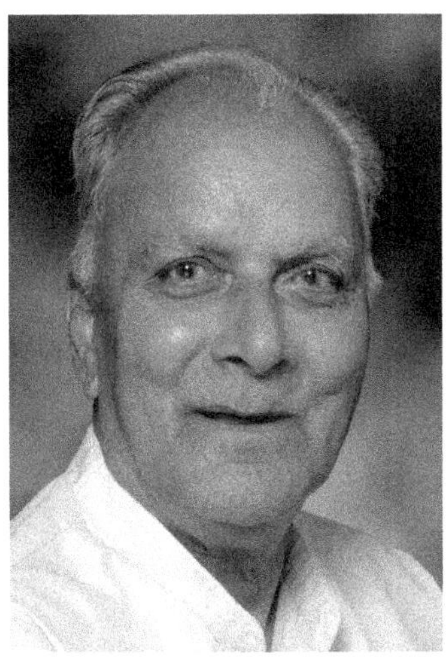

R.C. Ḍhere
© Milind Ḍhere

About the Translator

Dr Jayant Bhālcandra Bāpaṭ

Jayant Bhālcandra Bāpaṭ holds doctorates in Organic Chemistry and Indology, and is an adjunct research fellow at the Monash Asia Institute at Monash University. His research interests include Hinduism, goddess cults, the Fisher community of Mumbai, and Jainism, and he has published widely in these areas. He is co-editor with Ian Mabbett of *The Iconic Female: Goddesses of India, Nepal and Tibet* (Monash University Press, 2008) and *Conceiving the Goddess: Transformation and Appropriation in Indic Religions* (Monash University Publishing, 2016), and a co-author of *The Indian Diaspora: Hindus and Sikhs in Australia* (DK Printworld, 2015). For his work in education and for the Indian community, Jayant was awarded the Medal of the Order of Australia (OAM) in 2011.